Anne-Pia Godske Rasmussen

Quilt & Sew Country Style

Photography
Hanne Stroyer

SEARCH PRESS

First published in Great Britain in 2012 by Search Press Limited, Wellwood, North Farm Road, Tunbridge Wells, Kent, TN2 3DR

The original Danish edition was published as:
Liv i kludene – sy, quilt og appliker
by Klematis, 1998

This edition is published by arrangement with Claudia Böhme Rights & Literary Agency, Hannover, Germany (www.agency-boehme.com)

Text, models and illustrations
© Anne-Pia Godske Rasmussen
Photographs © Hanne Stroyer
Copyright © 1998 Forlaget Klematis A/S, Denmark
www.klematis.dk
1st edition.

English translation by David Young (translator) and Ana Madel Morfe (proofreader) at Cicero Translations.

English edition typeset by GreenGate Publishing Services

Publisher's note: Anne-Pia is Danish and some of her designs therefore include Danish words. These can be replaced easily with whichever words you choose. We hope that this will not affect your enjoyment of the book.

ISBN 978 1 84448 801 8

Printed in China

ANNE-PIA GODSKE RASMUSSEN HAS PREVIOUSLY HAD THE FOLLOWING BOOKS PUBLISHED:

Sy tøj til babydukker, 1999
Mere liv i kludene — sy, quilt og appliker, 2000
Tøj og tilbehør til babydukker, 2001
Tag tråden op, 2002
Træd nålen, 2003
Følg tråden – sy, quilt & appliker, 2005
Sødt og blødt – sy til de mindste, 2007
Hånd i hanke – sy og quilt, 2008

PUBLISHED BY SEARCH PRESS:

Flower Power Patchwork, 2011
Noah's Ark, 2012

Contents

Foreword

Armed with this book, you now have a way to create new, fun projects from the old fabrics hiding in your remnants basket and transform them into all kinds of decorations to personalise your home. You can also use some of the many fabrics found in patchwork shops, or combine fabrics from different sources.

The cute characters and accessories in this book are made to the same small scale, so the ones you make should all get along well together. The characters shown have been made from fabrics in slightly muted colours for a snug, shabby-chic look. To enhance the antique look, you can stain the fabrics with tea as explained on page 4. Of course, you can also make them in bright, fresh colours if you prefer.

Buttons, twine, long limbs and randomly placed stitches help give the models personality. And by moving the various parts around, it is not difficult to create your own look.

I hope the sewing machine will be put to good use and I wish you many happy hours enjoying this book.

Anne-Pia Godske Rasmussen

Equipment and materials

This section briefly describes the materials and techniques used in this book.

Scissors and rotary cutter

A good pair of scissors is essential when cutting, but a rotary cutter with a cutting mat and ruler is an extra help if pieces of fabric are to be cut straight. These items can be purchased from hobby, quilting and sewing shops.

Fabrics

All woven fabrics can be used, but heavy or loosely woven fabrics do not lend themselves well to smaller items. To prevent fraying, the edges of any loosely woven fabrics for the larger items should zigzagged beside openings and across seam allowances that are to be pressed open.

Aging fabrics with tea Cotton fabrics can be mellowed and 'aged' by staining them with tea. Use 4–6 tea bags, 2–3 tablespoons of salt and 1.5–2 litres (2½–3½ pints) of boiling water for four or five small pieces of fabric. The tea bags should be left to brew for 4 to 5 minutes, while the fabric is soaked in water. Take the tea bags out and immerse the fabric in the 'tea', where it should stay for about 24 hours. Move the fabric around now and then. Rinse the fabric in clean water, with a little vinegar, if desired, in the final rinse water.

Pencils

For drawing on pale fabrics, use a soft 1B or 2B pencil. For dark fabrics, use a light-coloured fabric pencil.

Needles and thread

For machine sewing, choose a standard needle (no. 70 or 80) and a stitch length of 2.5–3 (except for quilting, when a length of 3–3.5 should be used). Sew with a synthetic thread in a colour to match the fabric.

When sewing by hand, use a no. 9 or 10 needle; a cotton thread is recommended because it is strong and tends not to get tangled. Topstitches (see page 6) should be sewn with quilting thread, 2–3 strands of DMC embroidery cotton or another embroidery thread, usually in a colour that contrasts with the fabric. If a quilt is to be assembled with knots as explained on page 9, pearl thread, thin twine or cotton thread can be used.

Filling, wadding (batting) and interfacing

Synthetic fibrefill toy stuffing or tufts of wadding are practical fillings for small items that may need washing.

Quilted items are interlined with wadding (batting), which is available in various lofts. For small items, a thin quality is best. Fusible wadding, which has an adhesive side consisting of small 'dots' of glue, can be ironed on so it will not slip as you sew.

Vilene interfacing is used for simple appliqué (see page 7). It is used as a backing fabric for the appliqué shape and is not fused in place, therefore the non-fusible version can be used.

Buttons

For many of the models in this book, buttons, both recycled and new, are used for decoration. The buttons should be sewn on extra tightly if the final model will be kept within reach of young children.

Flowerpots or plinths

Some objects, such as the flowers and birds pictured on page 15, have stems or legs and require the support of a flower stick to stand up correctly. This stick can either be 'planted' in a flowerpot or stuck into a wooden plinth. These items are not suitable for young children.

If you use a flowerpot, fill it almost to the top with Oasis floral foam and secure the foam to the bottom of the pot with double-sided tape. The foam can be covered with moss, if desired.

A wooden plinth can be either a square block or a piece of round pole or dowel, into which you drill a suitable hole. The stick should be glued in place in the hole and the plinth and stick can be painted, if desired (see the photograph on page 55).

Techniques

Here you will find an explanation of the techniques used to produce the models in the book.

Templates

When the patterns are to be transferred to fabric, it is much easier if you have cardboard templates to draw around:

1 Photocopy or draw the parts of your pattern on to paper, including all the markings.
2 Glue the paper on to thin cardboard, e.g. the back of a writing pad.
3 Cut out the template along the drawn line.

Patterns

If desired, patterns for clothes can be drawn on pattern paper, along with all markings. CB stands for 'centre back', and CF for 'centre front'.

For some of the models, enlarging the pattern on a photocopier is recommended. This is the case with the rabbits, teddy bears and cats, on pages 20, 32 and 38 respectively.

When cutting measurements are provided, a seam allowance of 7–8mm (a generous ¼in) is always included, equivalent to the width of a presser foot.

Stitching the pieces

The following method is used for many of the projects in this book and the intention here is to sew before cutting.

1 Iron the fabric and fold it right sides together.
2 Draw around the template on the wrong side of the folded fabric with a pencil.
3 Mark any openings, as shown in figure 1 and sew the piece as instructed, except across the opening.

4 Fasten by sewing back and forth on each side of the opening, as shown in figure 2.
5 Cut out the shape with a 3mm (⅛in) seam allowance – except by the opening where it should be 5–8mm (about ¼in), depending on the size of the model.
6 Cut small slits in the inward curves and small triangular notches in outward curves and at corners, as shown in figure 3, so that the fabric will not pucker when turned right side out.
7 Fold the seam allowance at the opening and press it with your fingers, so that there is a visible fold.
8 Turn the fabric right side out. For nice, crisp, fully extended tips and corners, use a thin tapered flower stick or a needle to push the fabric out, being careful not to pierce the fabric. A flower stick is also good for stuffing the filling into the fabric.
9 Stuff with the filling and sew up the opening with small slipstitches (see overleaf).

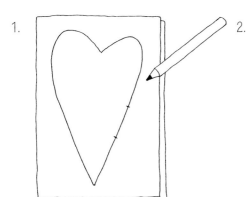

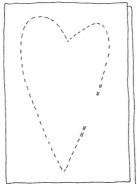

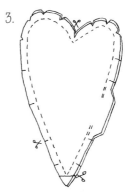

Topstitches

Running stitch

This stitch can be used for quilting. It is sewn with uniform spaces, and several stitches can be worked on the needle at a time.

Slipstitch

This is used for appliqué and joining openings. The stitches are sewn so that they become almost invisible, as shown in the illustration.

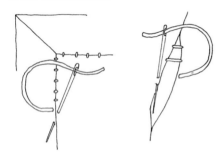

French knots

These are often used for eyes. The needle is pushed up through the fabric from the wrong side and the thread wrapped once or twice around the needle as illustrated. The needle is then pushed down again, right beside the up stitch. The more times the thread is wrapped around the needle, the larger the knot.

Satin stitch

This can be used for sewing noses and snouts. The stitches are sewn as short or long parallel stitches, where the new stitch lies adjacent to the previous one.

Buttonhole stitching

Used for such tasks as attaching appliqué shapes. Stitches are worked from the left and the needle is inserted from behind a little way from the edge. Then the needle is inserted into the loop and the thread pulled into place without being too tight.

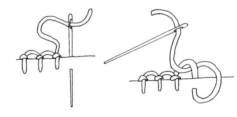

Blanket stitch

This slightly easier version of buttonhole stitch is sewn in a similar way but with the edge downwards.

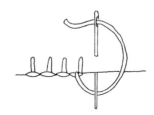

Overcast stitch and cross stitch

Both these stitches are used for decoration in this book. Overcast stitches can be sewn from both right and left. If you sew back again, the stitches become cross stitches.

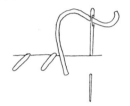

Chain stitch

Used for sewing hair in place and also for decoration. The thread is sewn as a loop, the needle being inserted close to the start of the stitch and then brought through again a short distance away. The thread is tightened lightly, keeping the working thread under the point of the needle. Continue as shown in the illustration, keeping your stitches even and being careful not to pull them too tight.

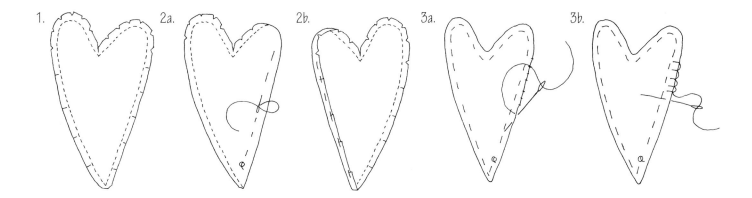

Appliqué

There are several ways to appliqué and here the traditional method is explained first. Although it is somewhat time-consuming, it does give the best result. Next, an easy appliqué method is explained.

Traditional appliqué

1 Draw around the template on the wrong side of the fabric and cut out the shape with a 5mm (scant ¼in) seam allowance.
2 Place the template in the middle of the fabric and score with a sharp needle all the way around the edge of the template and/or press the seam allowance over the template with the tip of your iron.
3 Cut slits in the inward curves of the seam allowance and small triangular notches in the outward curves and at corners, as shown in figure 1.
4 If desired, tack the seam allowance in place so that it lies neatly on the back; see figures 2a and 2b.
5 Position the motif on the background and tack it in place with large stitches or hold it in place with pins.
6 Appliqué the motif in place with slipstitches or with buttonhole or blanket stitches, as shown in figures 3a and 3b.

Easy appliqué

This appliqué method is easier and faster than the one just explained. Thin interfacing is used to draw on but it must not be ironed in place.

1 Draw around the template on to the front of a piece of interfacing.
2 Place the interfacing with the back against the right side of the fabric and sew all the way around along the drawn line.
3 Secure the stitching by reversing the machine to sew back over the first and last stitches.
4 Cut out the shape with a 3–4mm (⅛in) seam allowance and cut notches in the curves.
5 Cut a slit in the middle of the interfacing, as shown in figure 4.
6 Turn the fabric out through the slit.
7 Press the motif with your fingers and, if desired, iron lightly so the interfacing just becomes invisible on the front.
8 Stitch the motif on to the background as explained for the traditional method in step 6.

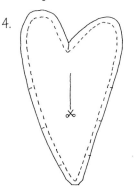

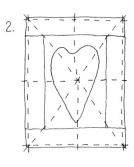

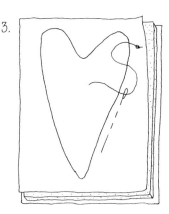

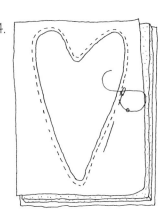

Assembling a quilt

When the front of the quilt is finished, it should be assembled with wadding and the backing fabric.

1 Iron the backing fabric and lay it on a table, right side down.
2 Place the wadding on top so it follows a straight edge of the backing fabric.
3 Now place the sewn piece on top, right side up, so it follows the straight edge and grain of the backing fabric. If it is smoothed and pulled too much, creases can be formed in the finished quilt.
4 Hold all three layers together with pins, as shown in figure 1, starting at the centre and working outwards.
5 Cut all the layers to size (usually the size of the top piece).
6 Replace the pins with small safety pins or tack, as shown in figure 2 – safety pins can be hard to get past if the quilting is being done on a sewing machine.

7 Now the quilt is ready for quilting and then binding, as described below.

Quilting

The quilting holds the front wadding and backing fabric together, and can be used to accentuate the shapes and lines. It can be done by hand or machine, but a golden rule says that a quilt that is sewn by hand should also be quilted by hand.

The layers can also be tied together as explained opposite.

Quilting by hand

When quilting by hand, use cotton thread or possibly a special quilting thread. Synthetic thread is not as good because it becomes easily knotted.

If the quilting is not going to follow a motif, the line to be sewn along can be marked with the point of a needle or drawn faintly with a fabric pencil.

1 Begin by tying a knot in the thread and pushing the needle through the front and down into the wadding a little away from the quilting line.
2 Push the needle tip out again next to the quilting line, as shown in figure 3.
3 Gently but firmly pull the knot through the front and down into the wadding and now quilt around the motif with short, regular running stitches. It is important to stitch all the way through all layers so the quilting also appears regular on the back.
4 When there is 5–10cm (2–4in) of thread left, make a small knot in the thread, as shown in figure 4.
5 Pull the knot through the front fabric so that it lodges in the wadding as the last stitch is sewn.
6 Continue with a new thread.

Quilting by machine

When quilting by machine, it will look nicer if the stitch length is set to 3–3.5.

1 First test the stitch on some scrap fabric and wadding to see if the stitch length is appropriate.
2 Then sew at a steady pace without pulling on the fabric.
3 Begin and end with 5cm (2in) thread ends.
4 Finally, pull the thread ends through to the back and fasten them in the wadding as explained for quilting by hand.

Quilting with knots and buttons

This method simply involves tying the layers together, just as was done in the past with mattresses. It can be used throughout a quilt or just in certain areas, as on the heart quilt pictured on page 37. You can use pearl cotton (maybe doubled), thin twine or cotton yarn.

1 Mark the tying points on the quilt and sew straight up and down through all the layers – if necessary, sew an extra time so there will be a stitch on the right side.
2 If desired, sew through a button and tie the ends in a reef knot.

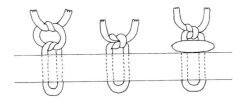

3 Cut the ends off about 1cm (⅜in) from the knot.

Hanging sleeve

1 Cut a strip of fabric to the dimensions given for your project.
2 Fold under 2cm (¾in) at each end of the strip and sew the hems in place.
3 Fold the strip lengthwise, wrong sides together, as shown in figure 1.
4 Pin the hanging sleeve on the back of the quilt, so the raw edge follows the top of the quilt and the strip is centred, as shown in figure 2.
5 Tack the sleeve in place, if desired, or just use pins.
6 Sew the sleeve on at the same time as the edge binding, as explained overleaf. When the edge binding is sewn in place, push the hanging sleeve upwards towards the top of the quilt, so there is room to slide a strip of wood into the casing.
7 Sew the bottom edge of the sleeve to the back of the quilt with slipstitches, as shown in figure 3.

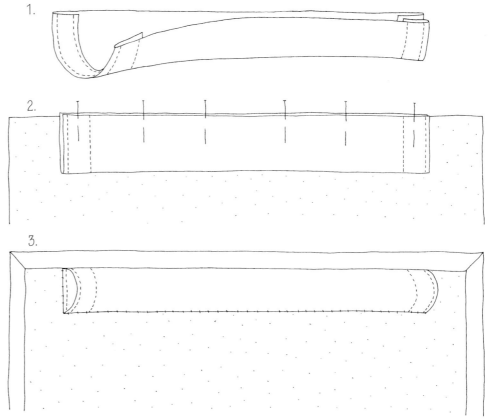

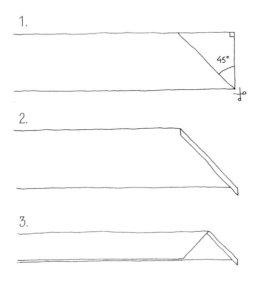

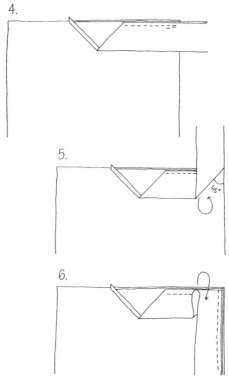

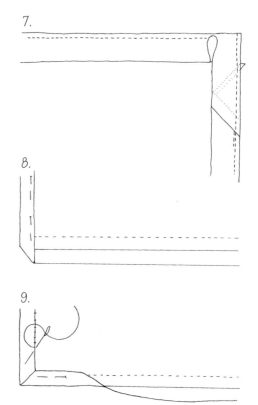

Edging with double binding

The strips of edge binding can be cut at a 45° angle or along the straight grain of the fabric. The fabric should not be too thick because the strip must be folded in half.

If the quilt is to have a hanging sleeve (see previous page), tack it in place before adding the binding.

1 For an edge that is to be 1cm (⅜in) wide, cut a 7cm (2¾in) strip. The length should be the circumference of the quilt plus 15cm (6in). If it is a large quilt, it may be necessary to piece several strips together.

2 Cut one end of the strip diagonally, as shown in figure 1.

3 Fold a 1cm (⅜in) seam allowance along the oblique end towards the wrong side, as shown in figure 2.

4 Fold the strip in half lengthwise, wrong sides together, and press, as shown in figure 3.

5 Position the strip on the quilt, right sides together, along one edge and starting about 5cm (2in) from one corner (see figure 4).

6 Sew the strip in place, taking a presser foot's seam allowance, but stop a presser foot's width from the corner and sew 2 or 3 stitches back.

7 Pull the work free of the presser foot and rotate the piece a quarter turn anticlockwise.

8 Fold the strip at a 45° angle up over the edge that has just been sewn (see figure 5).

9 Hold the diagonal fold and fold the strip down so that it follows the side you are about to sew (see figure 6).

10 Begin sewing right out from the edge, as shown in figure 6.

11 Continue sewing the other edges and corners in the same way.

12 When the starting point is reached, cut off the strip obliquely, so it overlaps the beginning of the binding strip by 1–1.5cm (⅜–¾in).

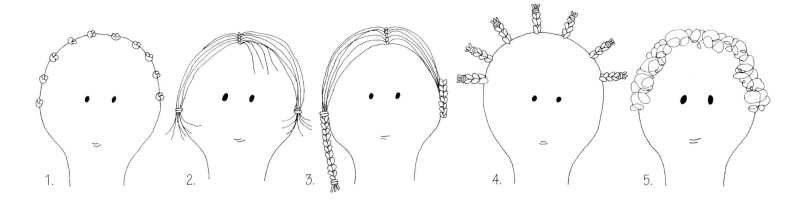

1.   2.   3.   4.   5.

13 Fasten by sewing 1.5cm (¾in) over and along the already sewn seam, as shown in figure 7.
14 Fold the binding over to the back and let it just cover the seam stitching (see figure 8).
15 Pin the edge in place and slipstitch by hand, as shown in figure 9.

Faces

Facial features should be faintly marked with a pen or by scoring with a needle before sewing. The eyes are usually French knots or beads. Nose/snout and mouth are sewn as explained in the instructions for each project. Blush can be applied with a crayon.

Hair

Hair is required for several of the dolls in the book (see, for example the photograph on page 57). For the hair you can use embroidery thread, cotton yarn, twine (unravelled, if necessary), torn-off strips of fabric or cotton fabric cut into narrow strips.

French knot

Fasten the yarn or thread on one side and then stitch French knots along the edge (see page 6). You can sew just a few or several knots (see figure 1).

Pageboy style

Lay strands of 'hair' across the head and attach them to the middle of the head with small chain stitches, but pull a few strands forward over the forehead and cut them off short. The hair should be attached at the sides, just below eye level, and then trimmed to length (see figure 2).

Plaits

Measure the 'hair' so that it reaches the waist and sew it to the head as for the pageboy style but then plait it and finish off with a bow. If desired, the plaits may be rolled up as buns on either side of the head and sewn in place against the head with thread in the same colour as the hair (see figure 3).

Small spiky plaits

These are made by sewing relatively thin yarn directly on to the seam. When the 'hair' is plaited, each plait is tied at the ends so it does not unwind. Finally, the ends should be cut off so the plaits are of equal length (see figure 4).

Tousled hair

Experiment with the hair, laying it on at angles and stitching it down as for the pageboy style. Have fun messing it up deliberately, perhaps making loops and stitching them down too. Alternatively, tear strips of fabric along the grain by making a small snip with scissors and then ripping the fabric apart. Spread out the strips on top of the seam and sew in place at three or four points with thread in a matching colour (see figure 5).

11

Hearts

This popular motif is used throughout this book, sometimes stuffed and sometimes as a flat appliqué (see page 73). To make a stuffed heart, follow the instructions below.

Fabric requirements
- Small fabric remnants

Other materials
- Filling, buttons and thread

1 Fold the fabric right sides together and draw your chosen heart template on top.
2 Sew around the heart, leaving an opening to turn through as indicated on the pattern.
3 Cut out the heart, leaving a small seam allowance. Turn right side out and stuff with filling (or leave unstuffed for a flat heart).
4 With the seam allowance neatly tucked inside, sew up the opening.
5 Press lightly with a hot iron and a damp ironing cloth.
6 Decorate you heart with hand stitches and add buttons, as shown in the drawings.

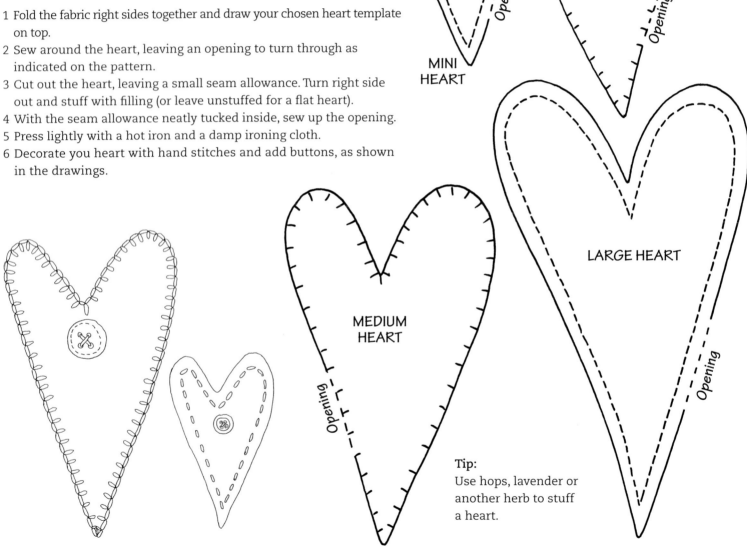

MINI HEART

SMALL HEART

MEDIUM HEART

LARGE HEART

Opening

Tip:
Use hops, lavender or another herb to stuff a heart.

Heart Quilt

This quilt measures 30 × 35cm (12 × 13¾in) and is shown in on page 37.

Fabric requirements

- Remnants for the hearts and centre panel
- 5.5 × 95cm (2¼ × 37½in) strip for the inner border
- 6 × 120cm (2½ × 47¼in) strip for the outer border
- Backing fabric: 33 × 38cm (13 × 15in)
- Binding: 7 × 145cm (3 × 57in) strip
- Thin wadding (batting): 33 × 38cm (13 × 15in)

Other materials

- Five buttons, threads and twine

1 Sew the centre panel together from four fabric pieces, each 11 × 13.5cm (4¼ × 5¼in). The panels can be in different colours or tones.
2 Trim the piece at an angle but with right-angled corners, so it measures 17 × 22 (6¾ × 8¾in). In figure 1, the outer edge represents the joined fabric and the inner edge shows how you could trim it.
3 Cut the 5.5cm (2¼in) strip into lengths to fit the sides of the panel and stitch them in place. Cut and attach the remainder to the top and bottom edges.
4 Trim the panel at an angle again with right-angled corners, as shown in figure 2. It should now measure 22.5 × 27.5cm (9 × 10¾in).
5 Now cut and stitch the 6cm (2½in) strip to the panel in the same way (see figure 3).

6 Cut and appliqué four medium-sized hearts on to the panels, using different stitches and fabrics for variety (see the photograph on page 37).
7 Assemble the quilt with wadding and backing fabric as explained on page 8.
8 Quilt the layers together around the hearts and in the inner frame, as shown in figure 4.
9 Make two or three mini hearts as explained on page 12 and decorate with buttonhole stitches or similar.

10 Sew or tie the small hearts and the buttons in place, fixed through all the layers.
11 Trim the quilt to measure about 30 × 35cm (12 × 13¾in) and bind the edges as explained on page 10.
12 Sew or tie a button in place on each of the top corners and wrap two twine loops around them to hang the quilt by.

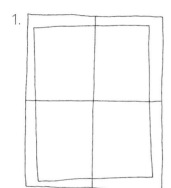

1.

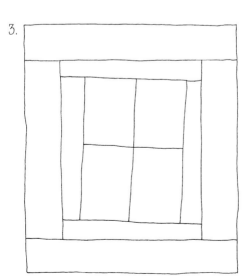

2.

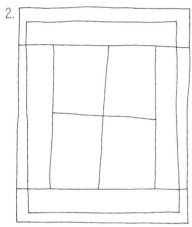

3.

4.

Flowers

These cheerful flowers go well with the songbirds on page 53. You can also make them in Christmas colours (see the photograph on page 71).

Fabric requirements
- Variety of fabric remnants

Other materials
- Filling, buttons, flower sticks, small flowerpots or plinths (see page 4)

1 Fold the fabric right sides together and draw your chosen templates on top.
2 Sew around each shape, leaving a gap to turn through.
3 Cut out each shape, leaving a small seam allowance. Turn it right side out and stuff with filling. The flower centres are filled only slightly and the leaves are filled only at the tips. Close up the openings with slipstitch but leave space for the stem at the opening on the flower head. On the tulip, the large top opening should be folded to the inside, and the stuffed petals sewn in by hand. Before the last petal is sewn in, stuff the 'cup' with filling.
4 Press the shapes with a hot iron and a damp ironing cloth.
5 Decorate the flowers with hand stitches (see the photographs opposite and on page 51).

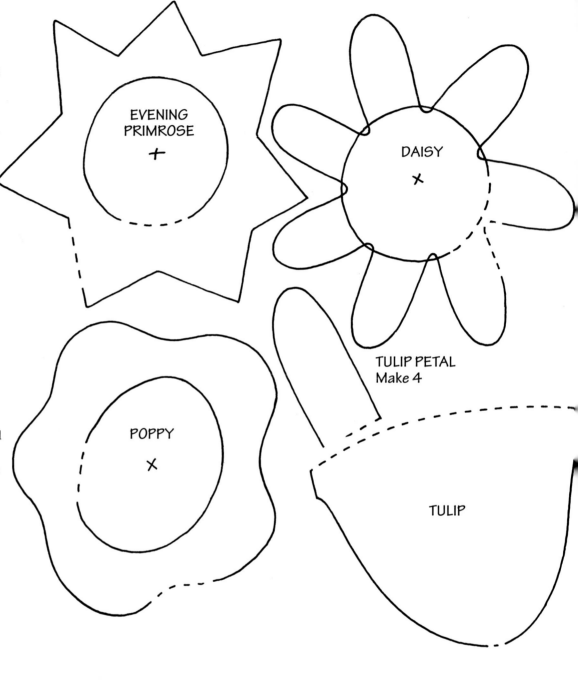

EVENING PRIMROSE

DAISY

POPPY

TULIP PETAL
Make 4

TULIP

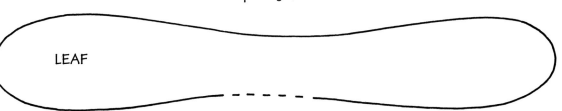

- - - - - Opening

LEAF

6 Sew the flower centres on to your flowers with buttons.

7 Insert a flower stick in the flower as the stem and sew it in place with a couple of stitches.

8 Tie the leaf around the stem and plant the flower in a flowerpot or fix it firmly to a wooden plinth (see page 4).

Flowers and songbirds (see page 53). The poppies are shown in the photograph on page 51.

Stars

Stars are used throughout this book, both stuffed and as appliqué motifs. These stuffed stars are shown on page 77.

Fabric requirements
- Variety of fabric remnants

Other materials
- Filling, buttons and threads to tie them on with

1 Fold the fabric right sides together and draw the template on top. For each star you need two triangles of equal size.
2 Stitch around the shape, leaving openings as indicated on the pattern – you need one opening on one of the triangles and three on the other.
3 Cut out the triangles, leaving a small seam allowance, then turn them right side out and stuff the triangle that has one opening. With the seam allowances inside, slipstitch the opening on this triangle closed.
4 Press lightly with a hot iron and a damp ironing cloth.
5 Place the finished triangle into the triangle with the three openings and pull it into position so the points stick out.
6 Stuff filling in the empty points of the star and press lightly again.
7 Secure the triangles, experimenting with different stitches, and attach a button to the centre as shown on page 77.

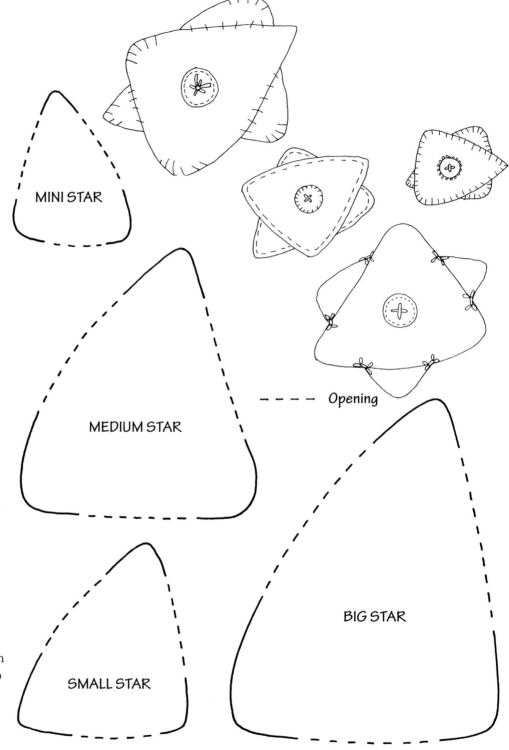

MINI STAR

MEDIUM STAR

SMALL STAR

BIG STAR

– – – – – Opening

Apples

Whole and partial apples, both large and small, make a quirky autumnal display (see the photograph on page 19). You can add even more different sizes, either by scaling the patterns on a photocopier or by positioning the sewing machine needle to the right.

Take seam allowances of at least 4mm (⅛in) and finger press these to the wrong side at the openings before turning the shapes right side out.

Fabric requirements
• Various fabric remnants

Other materials
• Filling, hand-sewing thread and buttons (optional)

Whole apple
1 Cut five outer sections (see the templates on page 18). The dots on

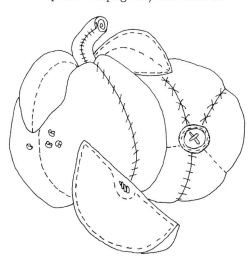

the pattern should be transferred to the wrong side of the fabric, and this is easier to do if holes are cut in the template at the dot markings. No seam allowance is required.

2 Place the pieces right sides together in pairs and sew them together from dot to dot.

3 Place the last section right sides together with one of the stitched pairs and sew it on.

4 Pin the two parts right sides together, matching the edges.

5 Mark an opening in one seam.

6 Sew the pieces together, but begin 2–3mm (⅛in) from the dot markings at one end to leave space for the leaves and stalk. Do not stitch across the opening.

7 Turn and stuff the apple firmly with filling and slipstitch up the opening.

8 Thread a darning needle with a strong doubled thread and push it through from the stalk opening to the bottom. Use this thread to sew on a button or about ten short 2mm (⅛in) wide strips of fabric as sepals.

9 Make a medium and small leaf for the small apple or a large and medium leaf for the large apple as explained on page 5. Turn the leaves right side out and stuff them. Add character with different hand stitches.

10 Cut a 4 × 4cm (1½ × 1½in) square of fabric to make a stalk for the small apple, and for the large apple cut a 4 × 7cm (1½ × 2¾in) rectangle.

11 Roll up the stalk fabric, right side out, turn in the raw edges at the ends, and secure with small, invisible stitches. Fold the long raw edge under and sew it along the length of the stalk, tightening the thread a little, so the stalk takes shape.

12 Position the leaves and stalk in the gap at the top of the apple and sew them in place with small stitches.

Half apple
For a half apple, use three outer sections (see the templates on page 18) and two cross-sections and sew them together using the photograph on page 19 as your guide. Be careful not to overstuff the apple. Decorate with hand stitches.

Three-quarter apple
For a three-quarter apple cut four outer sections and two cross-sections. Assemble as for the half apple.

Quarter apple
Cut one outer section and two cross-sections. Assemble the pieces and decorate with hand stitches.

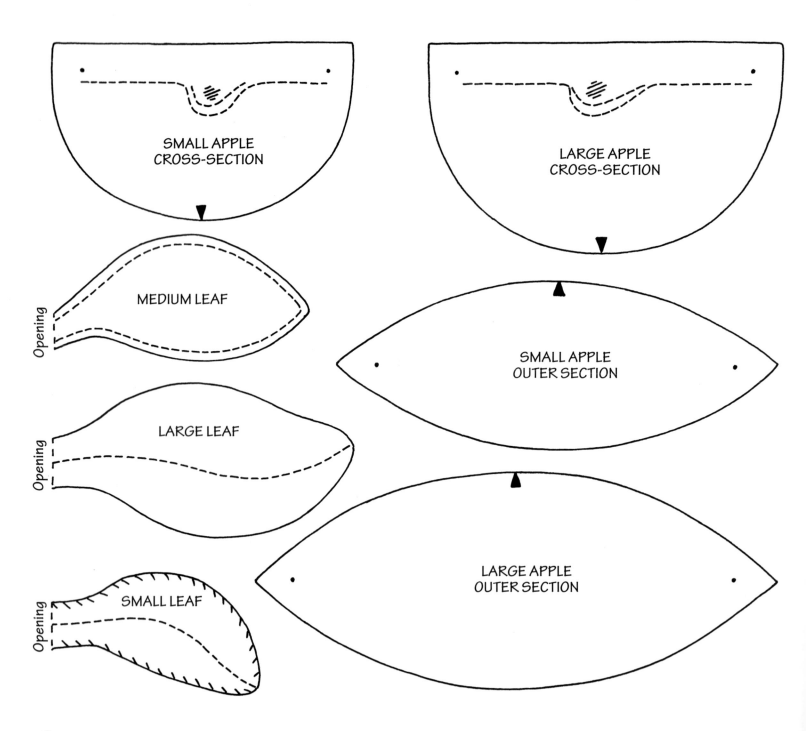

SMALL APPLE
CROSS-SECTION

LARGE APPLE
CROSS-SECTION

MEDIUM LEAF

Opening

SMALL APPLE
OUTER SECTION

LARGE LEAF

Opening

SMALL LEAF

Opening

LARGE APPLE
OUTER SECTION

These apples and apple segments make excellent projects for experimenting with your quilting skills (see page 17).

Rabbit Family

This family comprises two parent rabbits and their two children (see the photograph on page 23). For the large (parent) rabbits, use a photocopier to enlarge the pattern for the small rabbits by 135%. The fabric requirements for the clothing are provided with the instructions for each garment.

The large rabbit is 42cm (16½in) tall and the small one is 30cm (12in) tall.

Fabric requirements
• Small rabbit: 23 × 80cm (9 × 31½in)
• Large rabbit: 30 × 100cm (12 × 39½in)

Other materials
• Stuffing and embroidery threads for the features

1 Fold the fabric right sides together, pin the layers and draw the parts on top, as shown in figure 1. Draw two ears, two arms, two legs and a body.
2 Sew each shape, leaving openings as indicated on the patterns. On the body, sew from the bottom corners up to the two triangles. Strengthen the neck by sewing a second time on each side, as shown in figure 1.
3 Cut out all the parts with a 3–4mm (⅛in) seam allowance but at the openings cut along the drawn line, and for the part of the head that hasn't been sewn, cut a seam allowance of 1cm (⅜in).

4 Cut slits for ears in the middle of the head at the top.
5 Turn out the ears, finger press them and fold them approximately in half at the opening.
6 Place an ear into each of the ear slits, with right sides matching, 5–10mm (¼ –½in) from the bottom of the slit, as shown in figure 2.
7 Sew the ear slits together from the wrong side like a dart that is 4–5mm (¼in) at the end (see figure 3).
8 Push the ears down into the body and sew the rounded top of the head.
9 Trim the seam allowance and cut small slits in the curves on the neck.

1.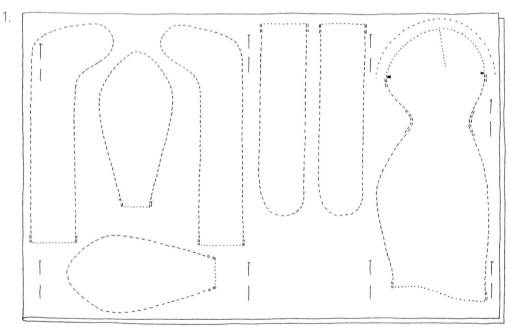

2.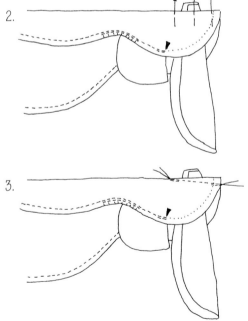

3.

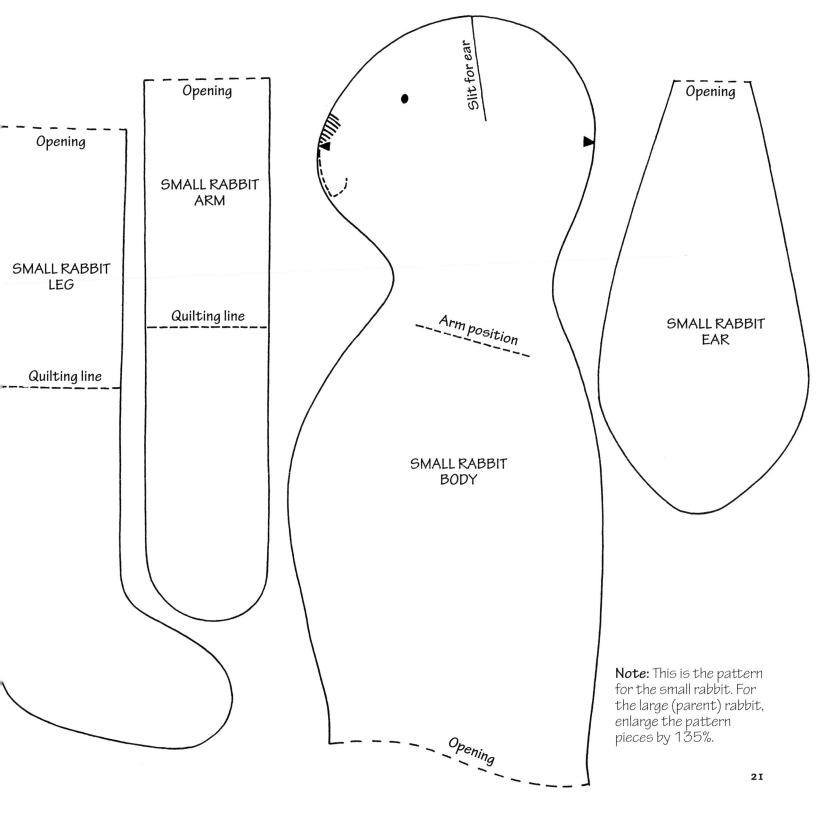

Opening

SMALL RABBIT
LEG

Quilting line

Opening

SMALL RABBIT
ARM

Quilting line

Slit for ear

SMALL RABBIT
BODY

Arm position

Opening

Opening

SMALL RABBIT
EAR

Note: This is the pattern
for the small rabbit. For
the large (parent) rabbit,
enlarge the pattern
pieces by 135%.

10 Fold and finger press a small seam allowance at the bottom over to the wrong side and then turn the body right side out.
11 Turn the arms and legs out and fill them up to the quilting line. Stuff well.
12 Sew running stitches over the elbow and knee joints (at the quilting line). If sewing by machine, it is a good idea to use the zip foot. Note that the knees should be sewn across the sewn seams, so the feet will be pointing forward (see figure 5).
13 Stuff a little filling in the arms and legs above the stitched quilting line.
14 Sew the legs to the front of the body, right sides together, on each side of the mid-seam.
15 Stuff the head, neck and body well so the head cannot nod.

16 Fold the folded seam allowance at the back of the body forward so it just covers the stitches where the legs have been sewn in place. Pin the back of the body in place and sew up by hand, as shown in figure 4.
17 Tuck in the seam allowances at the top of the arms, position them on the body at the marked line and sew them in place with slipstitches.
18 Mark the eyes, nose and mouth as shown on the pattern. The eyes should be sewn as French knots with all six strands of embroidery cotton.
19 Work the nose and mouth in satin stitch using all six strands of embroidery cotton, as shown in figure 5.

Dress

The dress pattern is on page 26. This is for the small size. For the large size, use a photocopier to enlarge the pattern by 135%. The bodice of the dress has a 'built-in' front and neck facing, which provides a neat finish.

Apron

Fabric requirements

• Small apron: 13 × 21cm (5 × 8¼in) plus a strip 5 × 60cm (2 × 23½in) for the waistband/tie
• Large apron: 17 × 25cm (6¾ × 10in) plus a strip 5 × 65cm (2 × 26in) for the waistband/tie

1 Zigzag the side and bottom edges of the apron rectangle.
2 Fold and sew a 3mm (⅛in) hem along the zigzagged edges.
3 Sew gathering threads (running stitch) from one side to the other, 3mm (⅛in) and 15mm (½in) from the top edge but do not finish these threads off.
4 Mark the centre; pull up the threads to gather the edge and distribute the pleats evenly, so the edge measures 12cm (4¾in) on the small apron or 14cm (5½in) on the large one.
5 Fold and press a 1cm (⅜in) hem to the wrong side along all edges of the waistband/tie.
6 Mark the centre of the long edges.
7 Fold the tie in half with wrong sides facing, enclosing the gathered edge of the apron rectangle and matching the centre marks. Topstitch the tie in place from one end to the other.
8 Remove any visible gathering thread.

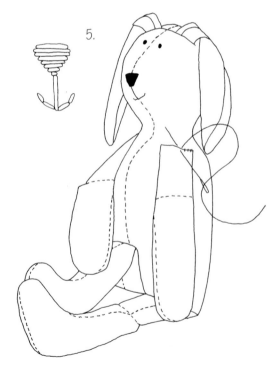

4.

5.

Instructions for making this fine family of rabbits and all their clothing begin on page 20.

Fabric requirements

- Small dress bodice, 14 × 90cm (5½ × 35½in); skirt, 16 × 60cm (6¼ × 23½in)
- Large dress bodice, 18 × 120cm (7 × 47¼in); skirt, 21 × 70cm (8¼ × 27½in)

Other materials

- Two small buttons, fine elastic

Bodice

1. Fold the fabric for the bodice right sides together and draw the front and back pieces on the fabric, as shown in figure 1. The back piece must be placed on the fold.
2. Mark a 1cm (⅜in) seam allowance next to the edges marked with a broken line in figure 1.
3. Cut out the parts – you do not need a seam allowance on the sections where one isn't shown in the diagram so cut along the drawn line on these edges.
4. Zigzag the edges of each piece, as shown in figure 2.
5. Place the front pieces right sides together with the back piece and fold the front facing down, out of the way, while sewing from sleeve hem to neck opening on both sleeves, as shown in figure 3.
6. Place the two facing sections right sides together and sew them together along the short seam, which will be at the centre-back (CB) neck, as shown in figure 4.

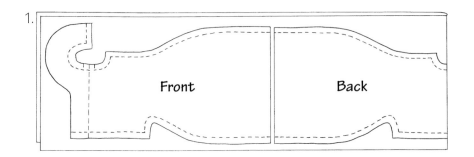

1.

Front   Back

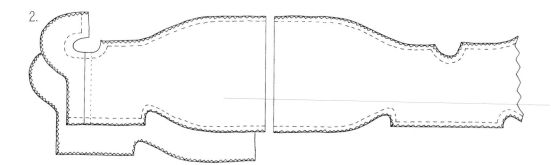

2.

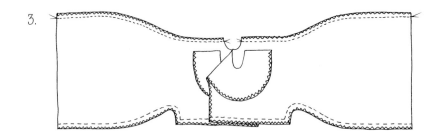

3.

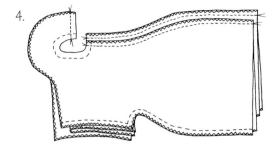

4.

5.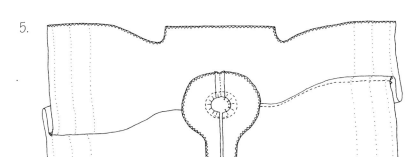

6.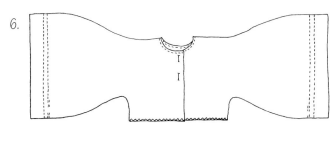

7 Finger press the seam allowances open.

8 Arrange the facing so that the stitched CB edge of the facing is right sides together with the centre of the back piece, and match the curve of the facing to the neck curve of the dress, as shown in figure 5. Stitch this curved neck seam.

9 Cut small slits into the seam allowances of this edge for ease, turn the facing over to the wrong side, iron and topstitch the seam just inside the neck edge.

10 Fold and press the drawstring hem at the edges of the sleeves; unfold.

11 On each side, sew the underarm and side seam. Cut small slits in the inward curves for ease.

12 Refold and sew the hem at the sleeve edges, leaving an opening so you can pull the elastic through the drawstring hem (see figure 6).

13 Mark and sew two buttonholes on the centre-front line and sew two corresponding buttons to the opposite front.

Skirt

1 Zigzag the raw edges of the skirt fabric all round.

2 Fold and press a 3mm (⅛in) hem at the bottom of the skirt; unfold.

3 Fold the fabric right sides together, so the longest side is halved and sew the side seam, as shown in figure 7.

4 Press the seam allowances open.

5 Refold and stitch the hem at the bottom.

6 Fold the skirt so the seam is at CB and mark the sides and CF with pins.

7 Sew two rows of gathering threads (running stitch) around the top edge, 1.5cm (½in) apart.

Assembly

1 Put the bodice into the skirt, right sides together, matching the CFs and CBs (see figure 8).

2 Pull the gathering threads to match the skirt to the bodice and distribute the pleats evenly.

3 Sew the skirt and bodice together, taking a 1cm (⅜in) seam allowance. Remove the gathering threads (see figure 9).

4 Turn the finished dress right side out.

7.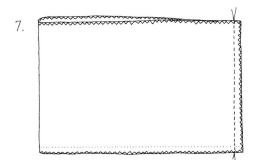

8.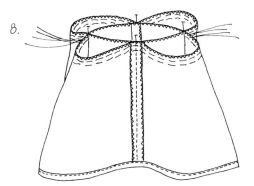

9.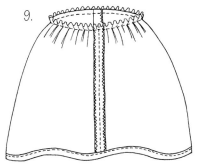

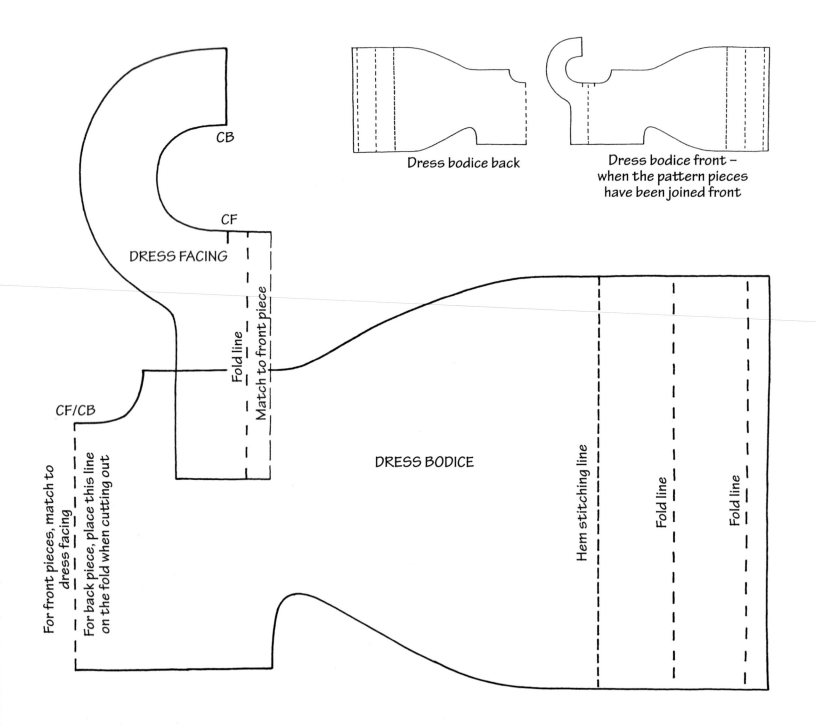

CB

CF

DRESS FACING

Fold line

Match to front piece

CF/CB

DRESS BODICE

For front pieces, match to dress facing

For back piece, place this line on the fold when cutting out

Hem stitching line

Fold line

Fold line

Dress bodice back

Dress bodice front – when the pattern pieces have been joined front

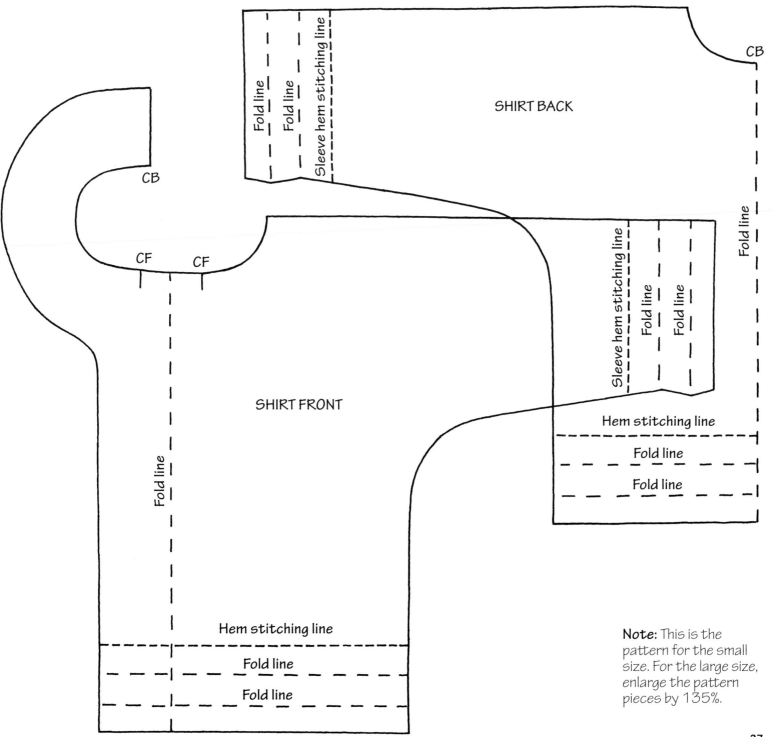

SHIRT BACK

Fold line
Fold line
Sleeve hem stitching line
CB
CB
Fold line

Sleeve hem stitching line
Fold line
Fold line
Fold line

Hem stitching line
Fold line
Fold line

CF   CF

SHIRT FRONT

Fold line

Hem stitching line
Fold line
Fold line

Note: This is the pattern for the small size. For the large size, enlarge the pattern pieces by 135%.

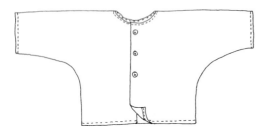

Shirt

The shirt pattern is on page 27. This is for the small size. For the large size, use a photocopier to enlarge the pattern by 135%.

Fabric requirements
- Small shirt: 19 × 72cm (7½ × 28½in)
- Large shirt: 25 × 95cm (10 × 37½in)

Other materials
- Two small buttons

1 Follow the instructions for the dress bodice (see page 24) but omit the elastic in the sleeves and add a small hem allowance to the bottom of the shirt. On the small shirt, it is better to sew the sleeve hem before the underarm seam.
2 Fold and sew the hem at the bottom of the shirt.

Large rabbit's headband

Fabric requirements
- A strip 6 × 75cm (2½ × 29½in)

1 Fold the fabric strip right sides together, lengthways.

2 Sew the long edge seam, leaving a 4cm (1½in) opening in the middle of the band.
3 Sew the ends so they are slanted.
4 Trim the seam allowances neatly, cutting off the corners at the ends for ease. Turn the band right side out and press.
5 Sew up the opening by hand.

Pantalettes

Use the pattern given opposite. This is for the small size. For the large size, use a photocopier to enlarge the pattern by 135%.

Fabric requirements
- Small pantalettes: loosely woven fabric 25 × 44cm (10 × 17¼in)
- Large pantalettes: loosely woven fabric 34 × 60cm (13½ × 23¾in)

Other materials
- Fine elastic

1 Fold the two short sides of the fabric right sides together into the centre.
2 Make a template from the pattern and place it on the fabric fold, as shown in figure 1. Cut two trouser legs, adding a 1cm (⅜in) seam allowance at the curved CF/CB edges and inside legs (the edges facing inwards on the folded fabric).
3 Fold the hems at the top and bottom over to the wrong side as marked on the pattern, press and then unfold.

4 Place the trouser legs right sides together, as shown in figure 2 and sew the two curved CF and CB seams.
5 Zigzag the seam allowances together, as shown.
6 Place the two stitched seams over each other, with right sides facing, and sew the inside leg seams from one hem edge to the other (see figure 3).

1.
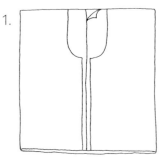

2.
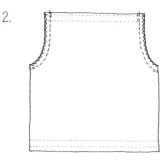

3.
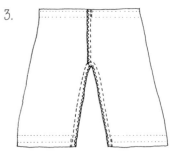

7 Fold the waist and bottom hems to the wrong side and sew just inside the inner folded edge, leaving openings on the waist edge at CB and on the bottom hems at the inside-leg seam.

8 Sew at least one presser foot's width from the first stitching to form drawstring hems for elastic (see figure 4).

9 Thread the elastic through the drawstring hems, tighten and tie so it fits the rabbit.

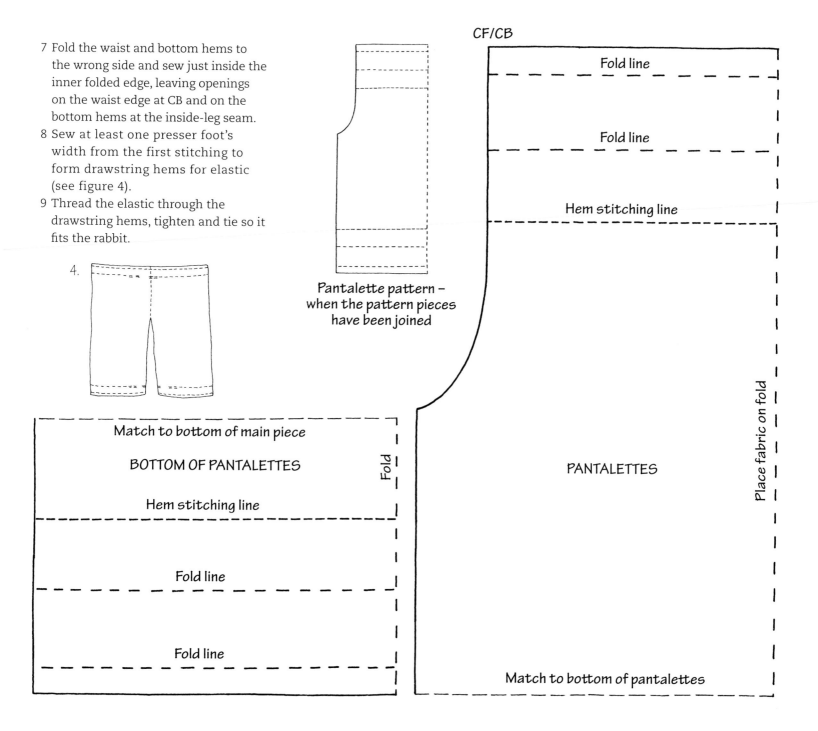

4.

Pantalette pattern – when the pattern pieces have been joined

CF/CB

Fold line

Fold line

Hem stitching line

Place fabric on fold

PANTALETTES

Match to bottom of pantalettes

Match to bottom of main piece

BOTTOM OF PANTALETTES

Hem stitching line

Fold

Fold line

Fold line

Dungarees

The pattern for the small size is opposite. For the large size, use a photocopier to enlarge it by 135%.

Fabric requirements
- Small dungarees: 28 × 50cm (11 × 20in)
- Large dungarees: 34 × 66cm (13½ × 26in)

Other materials
- Two small buttons

1. Fold the fabric right sides together so the longest side is halved and draw the pattern pieces, as shown in figure 1. The strip for the shoulder strap of the small dungarees should be 5 × 34cm (2 × 13½in) and for the large dungarees it should be 5.5 × 38cm (2¼ × 15in). All the parts except the main piece are cut on the fold.

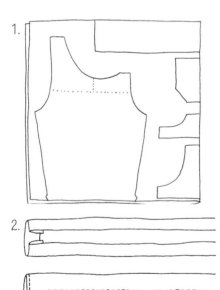

2. Cut out the pieces, adding a 1cm (⅜in) seam allowance all round, except at the lower edges of the trouser legs and at the bottom of the facings.
3. Fold and press a 1cm (⅜in) seam allowance to the wrong side all round the fabric strip for the shoulder straps (see figure 2).
4. Fold the strip in half lengthways with wrong sides together and topstitch across the ends and along the long edge. Cut the strip into two shoulder straps of equal length.
5. Zigzag the sides and the bottom edge of the facings.
6. Sew the facings together at the short side edges and press the seam allowances open.
7. Fold and press the hems at the bottom of the trouser legs and then unfold.
8. Zigzag the dungarees along the curved CF and CB seams and along the inside-leg seams.
9. Match the two main pieces, right sides together, and sew the curved CF seam, pulling out a little in the curve. Press the seam allowances open.
10. Fold and press a 1cm (⅜in) seam allowance all around the pocket on the wrong side.
11. Topstitch along the top edge of the pocket.
12. Place the pocket over the CF seam on the dungarees, as marked on the pattern, and topstitch it in place around the sides and bottom edge.
13. Sew the curved CB seam with right sides together and then press the seam allowance open.
14. With right sides facing, position the two shoulder straps on the back of the trousers so they cross each other in the middle, as shown in figure 3.
15. Place the facing on the dungarees, right sides together, matching CF to CF and CB to CB.
16. Sew all around (see figure 4).
17. Cut small slits in the seam allowances at curves and trim off the seam allowances at the corners.
18. Turn the facing over to the wrong side.
19. Press and topstitch 4–6mm (a scant ¼in) from the edge.
20. Mark and sew the buttonholes on the bib.
21. On the small dungarees only, fold the trouser hems to the wrong side and sew in place.
22. Place CF over CB and sew the inside-leg seam from hem edge to hem edge, as shown in figure 5.
23. On the large dungarees only, fold and sew the trouser hems.
24. Turn the dungarees right side out and sew buttons on the shoulder straps to correspond with the buttonholes.

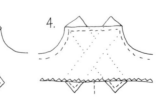

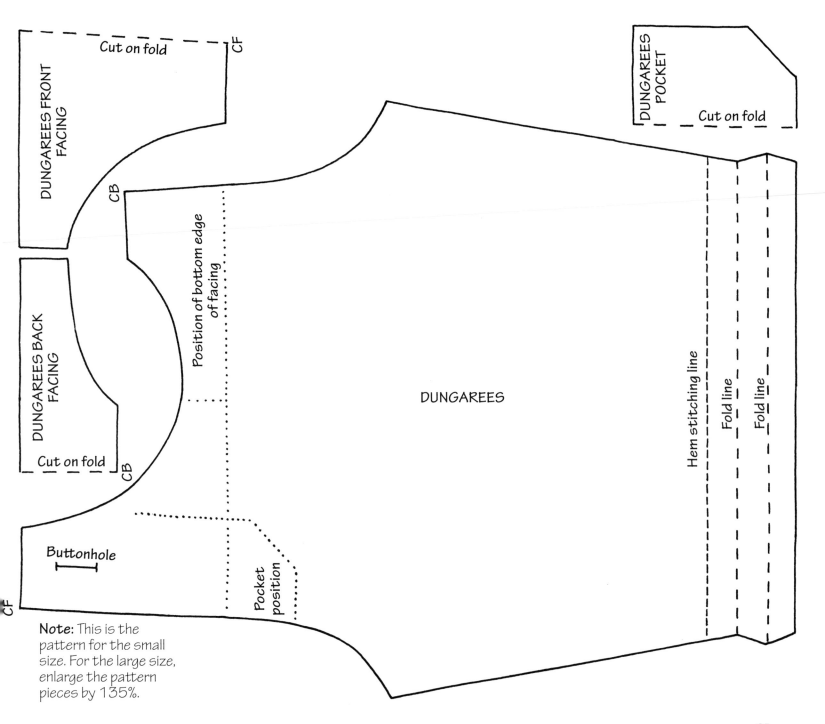

DUNGAREES FRONT FACING

Cut on fold

CF

DUNGAREES BACK FACING

Cut on fold

CB

CB

Position of bottom edge of facing

DUNGAREES

Buttonhole

Pocket position

CF

Hem stitching line

Fold line

Fold line

DUNGAREES POCKET

Cut on fold

Note: This is the pattern for the small size. For the large size, enlarge the pattern pieces by 135%.

Teddy-bear Family

There are two parent teddies and two children (see page 37). For the large bears, use a photocopier to enlarge the pattern (opposite) by 150%. The large bear is 30cm (12in) tall and the small one is 20cm (8in) tall.

Fabric requirements
- Small teddy: 21 × 52cm (8¼ × 20½in)
- Large teddy: 30 × 75cm (12 × 29½in)

Other materials
- Filling, four buttons for arms and legs and possibly two for eyes, embroidery cotton for face, a long doll-maker's needle and strong thread or twine

1 Fold the fabric right sides together, as shown in figure 1 and pin the layers together. The fabric is folded in this way because the back piece should only be cut from one layer of fabric.
2 Draw two ears, two arms, two legs and a front body on the doubled fabric; draw the back body on the single layer.

3 Sew around the shapes but only sew the front body along the front edge from triangle to triangle.
4 Cut out all the parts, adding a small seam allowance, but at the side of the front body and the back piece, cut with a more generous 1cm (⅜in) seam allowance.
5 Cut small slits in the seam allowances at inward curves and turn the arms, legs and ears right side out.
6 Pin the front body pieces and the back piece right sides together so the triangular markings match at the top and bottom (see figure 2).
7 Stuff a little filling in the ears and place the ears between the front and back body pieces at the positions marked on the pattern.
8 Sew the body seams, leaving an opening for turning.
9 Cut small slits in the seam allowance at the neck curves and at the ears and turn the body right side out.
10 Fill all the parts and stuff well. Sew up the openings by hand.

11 If needed for strength, tie a matching thread around the neck (see figure 3).
12 Mark the eyes, nose and mouth as shown on the template. The eyes can be sewn as French knots with six strands of embroidery cotton or you can use small buttons. Work the nose and mouth in satin stitch using six strands of embroidery cotton.

Attaching the limbs

1 Attach the arms and legs as explained here, matching the crosses on the pattern. Insert the needle through a button and an arm or a leg, pass it through the body and then through the other arm/leg and a button, as shown in figure 4.
2 Tighten the thread and sew through the opposite hole in the button, back through the body and opposite arm and through the opposite hole in the button.
3 Tighten the thread, tie a neat knot and trim the thread ends.
4 Repeat, starting from the opposite side.

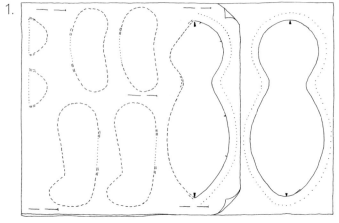

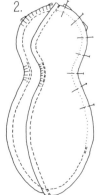

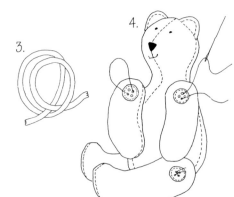

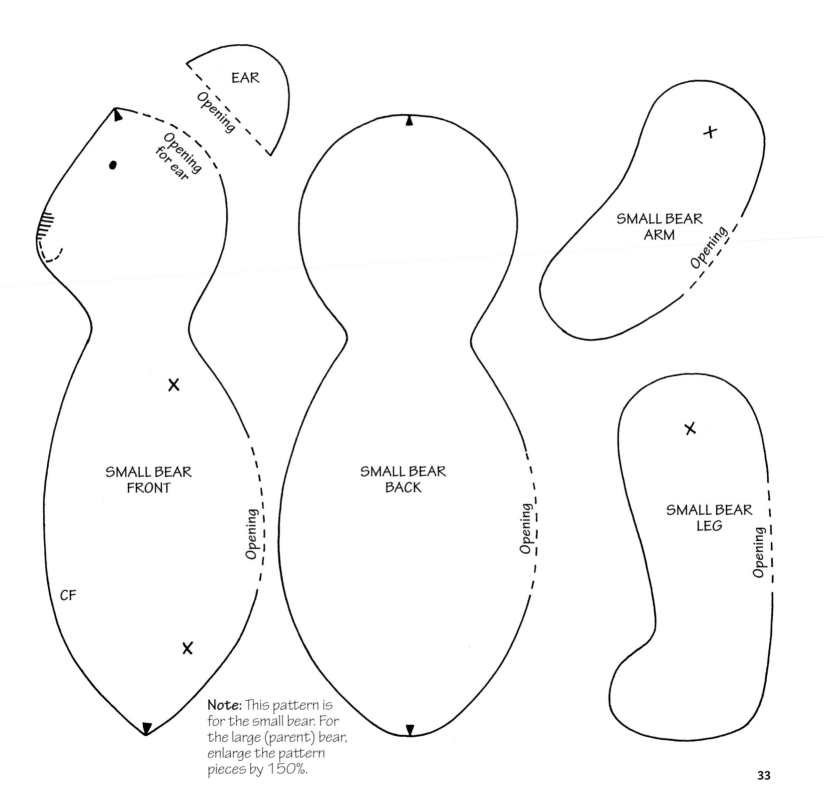

EAR

Opening

Opening for ear

SMALL BEAR
FRONT

CF

Opening

SMALL BEAR
BACK

Opening

SMALL BEAR
ARM

Opening

SMALL BEAR
LEG

Opening

Note: This pattern is for the small bear. For the large (parent) bear, enlarge the pattern pieces by 150%.

Bear's pinafore

The pinafore is easy to make from rectangular off-cuts of fabric. Use the same fabric for the skirt and shoulder straps or, if you wish, cut the bib section from a coordinating fabric (see the photograph on page 37).

Fabric requirements for small pinafore
- Skirt: 9.5 × 36cm (3¾ × 14¼in)
- Shoulder straps: 3 × 25cm (1¼ × 10in)
- Bib: 4.5 × 6cm (1¾ × 2½in)

Fabric requirements for large pinafore
- Skirt: 16 × 45cm (6¼ × 17¾in)
- Shoulder straps: 4 × 28cm (1½ × 11in)
- Bib: 5 × 6cm (2 × 2½in)

Other materials
- Fine elastic and a pair of buttons for the front (optional)

Skirt

1 Zigzag the short sides of the skirt and the top edge.
2 Fold and press a 1cm (⅜in) hem to the wrong side along the top edge.
3 Fold and press a 3mm (⅛in) double hem along the bottom edge.
4 Unfold the hems at top and bottom, fold the fabric in half with right sides facing, matching the short side edges, and sew the side seam.
5 Press the seam allowances open.
6 Refold the bottom hem and sew it by hand or machine.

Bib

1 Fold the strip for the shoulder straps as described on page 30 and cut it into two pieces of equal length.
2 Fold the bib piece lengthways, so the small one measures 3 × 4.5cm (1¼ × 1¾in) and the large one measures 3 × 5cm (1¼ × 2in). Sew two lines of topstitching a little way from the fold.
3 Place the bib piece between the shoulder straps, as shown in figure 1, with the folded edge of the bib facing upwards.
4 Sew the bib and the shoulder straps together.
5 Zigzag along the bottom edge of the bib.

Assembly

1 Rearrange the skirt so the seam is at centre back (CB). Pin the bib right sides together with the skirt, matching the waist edges, with the bib centred at the front (see figure 2).
2 Stitch the bib in place along the pressed line of the hem.
3 Fold the waist hem over to the wrong side and sew it in place just inside the zigzag edge so a casing is formed, leaving a small opening at CB so you can thread the elastic through.
4 Thread the elastic through the casing, cut to fit and tie the ends together.
5 Turn the pinafore right side out.
6 Sew the shoulder straps to the back of the skirt. If desired, add a crossover, as shown in figure 3.
7 As a finishing touch, sew on buttons over the shoulder straps (optional).

Hair bow

The small girl bear has a hair bow. Make this in the same way as the bow tie (see page 36) from a 3.5 × 8cm (1½ × 3¼in) fabric remnant. Embellish with a button, if desired.

1.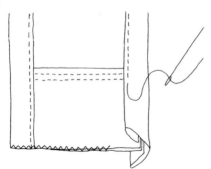

2.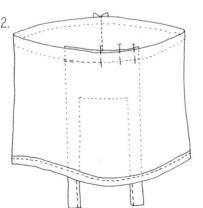

3.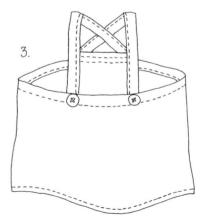

Trousers

The pattern for the small size trousers is given below. For the large size, use a photocopier to enlarge it by 150%.

Fabric requirements

- Small trousers: 16 × 46cm (6¼ × 18in) plus a 3 × 24cm (1¼ × 9½in) strip for the braces
- Large trousers: 17 × 75cm (6¾ × 29½in)

Other materials

- Small trousers: fine elastic and four buttons
- Large trousers: two buttons (optional)

1 Fold the fabric right sides together and cut four trouser legs. Do not add a seam allowance at the top and bottom but everywhere else add a 1cm (⅜in) seam allowance.

2 Zigzag around the edges to prevent fraying except at the lower edges of the legs.

3 Fold and press hems at top and bottom as marked on the pattern.

4 Unfold the hems and place the parts together in pairs, right sides facing.

5 Sew the outside leg seams, as shown in figure 1 and press the seam allowances open.

6 Place the two open trouser legs right sides together and sew the curved CF and CB seams, as shown in figure 2.

7 Cut two or three slits in the seam allowances at the deepest part of the curves, as shown in figure 2, and press the seam allowances open.

8 If sewing by machine, it is easiest to sew the bottom hem now, otherwise it can wait.

9 With right sides facing, match the CF and CB seams and then sew the inside-leg seams, as shown in figure 3.

10 Refold and sew the bottom hems if you haven't already done so.

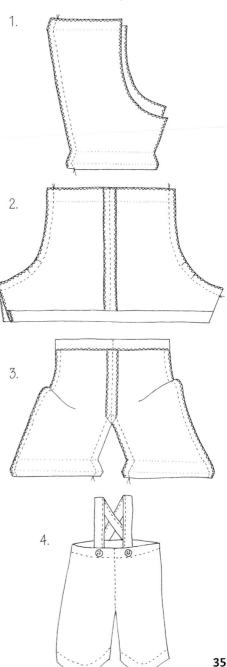

TEDDY BEAR TROUSERS

Fold line · Fold line · Sewing line · Sewing line · Fold line

CF CB

1. 2. 3. 4.

35

5.

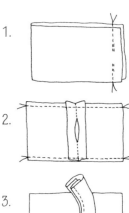

1.

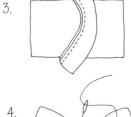

2.

3.

4.

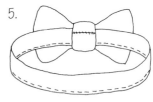

5.

and then 5mm (¼in) further down, as shown in figure 5. Alternatively, topstitch first, then make the pleats and secure with buttons. If desired, you can make buttonholes to make it easier to fit the trousers on the bear.

Completing the small trousers

1 Fold and press a 1cm (⅜in) seam allowance to the wrong side all round the strip for the braces. Fold the strip in half lengthways with right sides together and sew the ends and along the long edge (see figure 2 on page 30). Cut the strip into two pieces of equal length.
2 Refold the top hem of the trousers over to the wrong side and sew it in place along the stitching line so a casing is formed, leaving a small opening at CB so you can thread the elastic through. Thread the elastic through the casing and tie the ends together.
3 Sew the shoulder straps in place with buttons on top at the front and rear, as shown in figure 4.

Completing the large trousers

1 Refold the top hem to the wrong side and pin or tack it in place.
2 Instead of elastic, the waistband is shaped with two pairs of pleats. On the front these point outwards and on the back they point inwards, as shown in figure 5. Fit the pleats to your bear, then hold them in place with pins while you sew just inside the top edge

Bow tie/hair bow

Materials
• Small fabric remnant

1 Fold a small strip of fabric in half, right sides together, and sew the ends together, leaving an opening (see figure 1).
2 Rearrange the fabric so that the seam is at CB (see figure 2).
3 Sew the seams on the two long edges, turn right side out through the opening and stuff a little filling in the ends.
4 Fold a small strip of fabric so that the raw edges are hidden (figure 3). Stitch, if desired, but this isn't essential.
5 Wrap the strip around the centre of the other piece, as shown in figure 4 and stitch in place.
6 Cut a fabric strip to fit around the neck of your bear, fold in half lengthways and sew the long edges together, as shown in figure 5.
7 Slide the bow on to the band, place the band around the bear's neck and sew the ends of the band together. Hide the seam under the knot in the bow. Another option is to sew press fasteners on to the ends of the band so that it is removable.

The bear family in their Sunday best (see page 32). Instructions for the quilt are on page 13.

Cats

These cute cats come in two sizes. The large cat is 23cm (9in) tall and the small one is 16cm (6¼in) tall. The pattern is for the small size; for the large size, use a photocopier to enlarge this pattern by 145%.

Fabric requirements
- Small cat: 18 × 40cm (7 × 15¾in)
- Large cat: 26 × 56cm (10¼ × 22in)

Other materials
- Filling, two buttons, yarn or some bristles from a broom for whiskers and embroidery cotton

1 Fold the fabric right sides together so the longest side is halved and draw two front legs, a tail and a body.
2 Pin the layers together and then sew all round the legs and tail, leaving openings as indicated on the pattern pieces. Stitch the cat body without stitching around the right-angled notches at the bottom of each side.
3 Cut out the pieces, leaving a small seam allowance but with a larger 1cm (⅜in) seam allowance at the bottom of the body piece and across the opening for the tail.
4 Turn the tail right side out and stuff it firmly at the tip and loosely towards the opening.
5 Position the tail inside the cat body (which is still wrong sides out) with the end matching the tail opening in the body, as shown in figure 1. Stitch it in place.
6 Press the seam allowances open at the bottom of the cat.
7 Place one side seam over the bottom seam and sew a seam across, taking a seam allowance the width of the presser foot, as shown in figure 2. Repeat with the other side seam.
8 Turn the body and legs right side out and stuff with filling. Fill the body firmly and make the bottom as even as possible. Stuff the paws firmly at the bottom but stuff the legs loosely from the middle.
9 Sew up the openings.

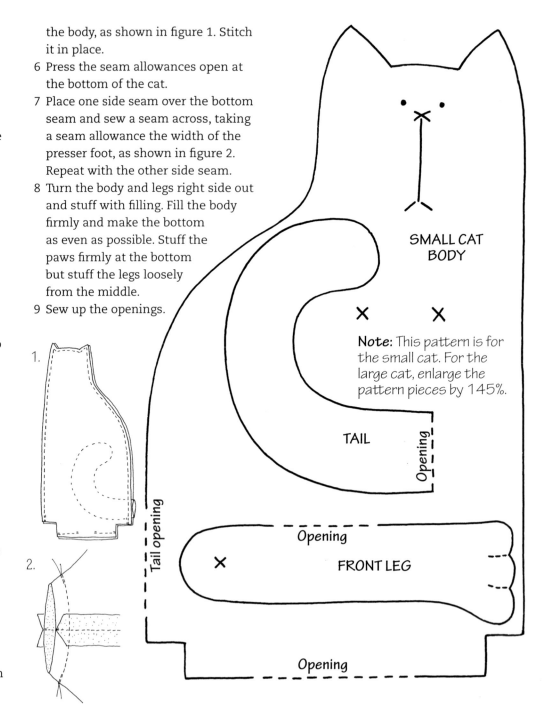

SMALL CAT BODY

TAIL

Opening

Note: This pattern is for the small cat. For the large cat, enlarge the pattern pieces by 145%.

Tail opening

FRONT LEG

Opening

Opening

1.

2.

10 Stitch between the toes, pulling the stitches tight to gather the fabric in.

11 Sew the legs in place with buttons over them, positioning them on the body to match up the crosses, and tie reef knots in the thread ends.

12 Sew the eyes as French knots using six strands of embroidery cotton.

13 The whiskers are made from broom bristles or unravelled yarn. Stitch these down by working the nose over them with two or three cross stitches worked on top of each other. From the nose, sew one long stitch and two short ones for the mouth.

14 Decorate, if desired, with a padded heart (see page 12) and bow (page 36).

These cats are simple to make and lots of fun – everyone will want one.

Angel Cats

There are two cats here, one sitting and one standing. Give them wings if you like, and let them take flight. The patterns are on page 42.

Fabric requirements

- Fabric for cats: 16 × 30cm (6¼ × 12in)
- Fabric for wings: 5 × 22cm (2 × 8¾in)
- Thin fusible wadding (batting): 5 × 11cm (2 × 4¼in)

Other materials

- Filling, buttons, yarn or broom bristles for whiskers and embroidery cotton for the faces

1 Fold both pieces of fabric in half, right sides together, so the longest side is halved.
2 Iron the wadding to the wrong side of the wing fabric.
3 Draw the body, head, tail, the legs for the sitting cat and the wings (optional) on the appropriate folded fabric.
4 Pin the layers then sew around each shape, leaving openings as indicated on the pattern.
5 Cut out the shapes, adding a small seam allowance, turn them right side out and stuff all parts except the wings.

6 Sew up all the openings.
7 Press all the parts with a hot iron and a damp ironing cloth.
8 Quilt with running stitches as marked on the patterns – the wings should also be quilted around the edge.
9 Add the eyes with French knots, using three strands of embroidery cotton.
10 Place the whiskers on the face and secure with a cross stitch. Work a second cross stitch directly over the first for added strength. From there, sew one long stitch and two short ones for the mouth.
11 Attach the tail and the legs of the sitting cat to the body with buttons over them, positioning them so that the crosses on the patterns match up.
12 Sew the head in place on the body. It can be angled in many ways, as shown in the photographs opposite and on page 43.
13 Attach the wings to the back of the cat with slipstitches. For the standing cat, these should be folded first (see the photograph on page 43).
14 Finally, make mini-hearts (see page 12) if desired, to decorate your cat.

With or without wings, these cats are great fun. Once you get started it is hard to stop making them – there are more shown on page 43.

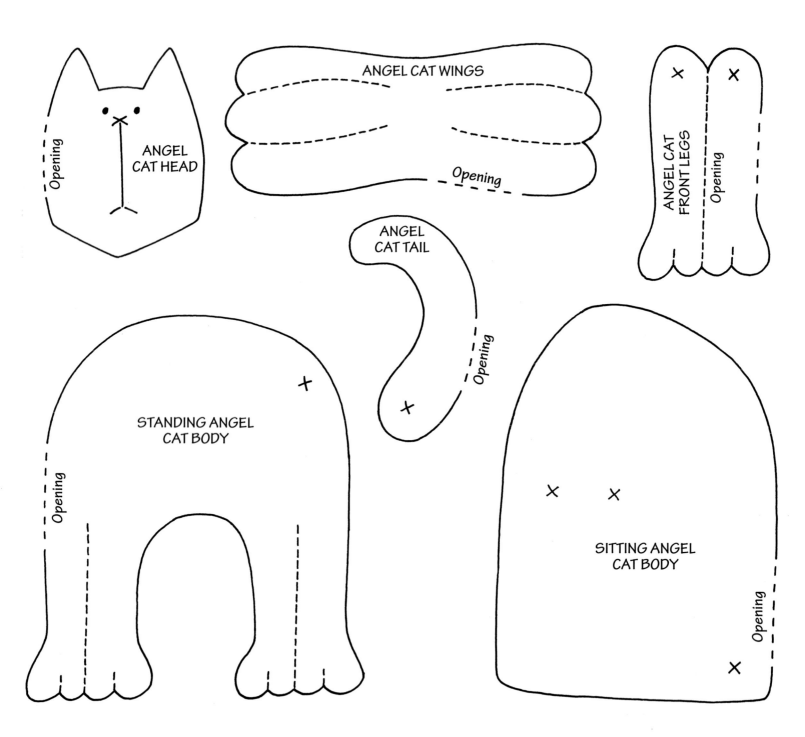

These angel cats can be propped up, but look especially good hung on a wall.

Pumpkins

The pumpkins are shown on page 47.

Fabric requirements
- Small single-coloured pumpkin: 14 × 28cm (5½ × 11in) plus 10 × 15cm (4 × 6in) of fabric for the stalk
- Large single-coloured pumpkin: 20 × 40cm (8 × 16in) plus 14 × 18cm (5½ × 7in) of fabric for the stalk
- For multi-coloured pumpkins, use a variety of remnants

Other materials
- Filling, a doll-maker's needle, one button, a pair of compasses

Single-colour pumpkin

1 Fold the fabric right sides together and draw a circle on top. For a small pumpkin the circle should have a radius of 6.5cm (2½in), so set your compasses to this width. For a large pumpkin, the radius should be 9.5cm (3¾in).
2 Pin the layers and sew along the drawn line, leaving an opening of about 3.5cm (1½in) for turning.
3 Sew a second time just inside the first line of stitching.
4 Cut out the circle, adding a 3–4mm (⅛in) seam allowance but leaving a little more – 5mm (about ¼in) – by the opening.
5 Turn, stuff with filling and sew up the opening by hand. The pumpkin should be well stuffed, but not too firm or you won't be able to shape it.
6 Fold about 2m (2yd) of matching strong thread in half and thread on a doll-maker's needle. The thread will be used to lace the pumpkin.
7 Insert the needle right through the pumpkin. If the centre is chosen as the insertion point, the shape will be symmetrical, but the pumpkin can also be made asymmetrical by inserting the needle a little off-centre.
8 Wrap the doubled thread around the pumpkin and insert the needle back through the starting hole.
9 Tighten the thread well, so it 'disappears' into the pumpkin and gives it shape.
10 Repeat so there are six 'segments'.
11 Make a stalk (see below), pin it to the top of the pumpkin and then sew it in place with small slipstitches. Attach a button to the bottom of the pumpkin to hide the join.

Pumpkin stalk

1 Draw the template (opposite) on the wrong side of your stalk fabric and mark where the fold lines should be.
2 Cut out the piece. No seam allowance should be added.
3 Fold and finger press along all the broken lines, as shown in figure 1 on the following page.
4 Fold the seam allowance at the top and bottom over to the wrong side and then work running stitches just inside the finger-pressed folds along the lines marked with an asterisk (see figures 2 and 3).
5 Fold the seam allowances on the sides to the wrong side and match the folds together, right side out.
6 Sew the stalk together with running stitches – start at the bottom and do not fasten off the thread when you reach the top of the stalk (see figure 4).
7 Stuff the stalk with filling.
8 Gently pull the thread to bend the stalk slightly. Once the shape is to your liking, fasten the thread and sew the top together with a couple of stitches.

Multi-coloured pumpkin

This pumpkin is slightly more advanced.

1 Cut six pumpkin sections (see template opposite). The dots on the pattern should be transferred to the wrong side of the fabric, and this is easier to do if holes are cut in the template at the dot markings. No seam allowance is required.
2 Place the pieces in pairs, right sides together, and sew them together from dot to dot.
3 Pin the three joined pairs right sides together with edges matching.
4 Mark an opening in one seam of about 3.5cm (1½in).
5 Sew the pieces together, leaving the opening.
6 Turn right side out, stuff with filling and sew up the opening by hand. Stuff the pumpkin well, but not so firmly that it can't be pulled into shape.
7 Follow steps 6–10 for the single-colour pumpkin, letting the lacing thread follow the seams.
8 Make a stalk, pin it to the top of the pumpkin and then sew it in place with small slipstitches. Attach a button to the bottom of the pumpkin to hide the join.

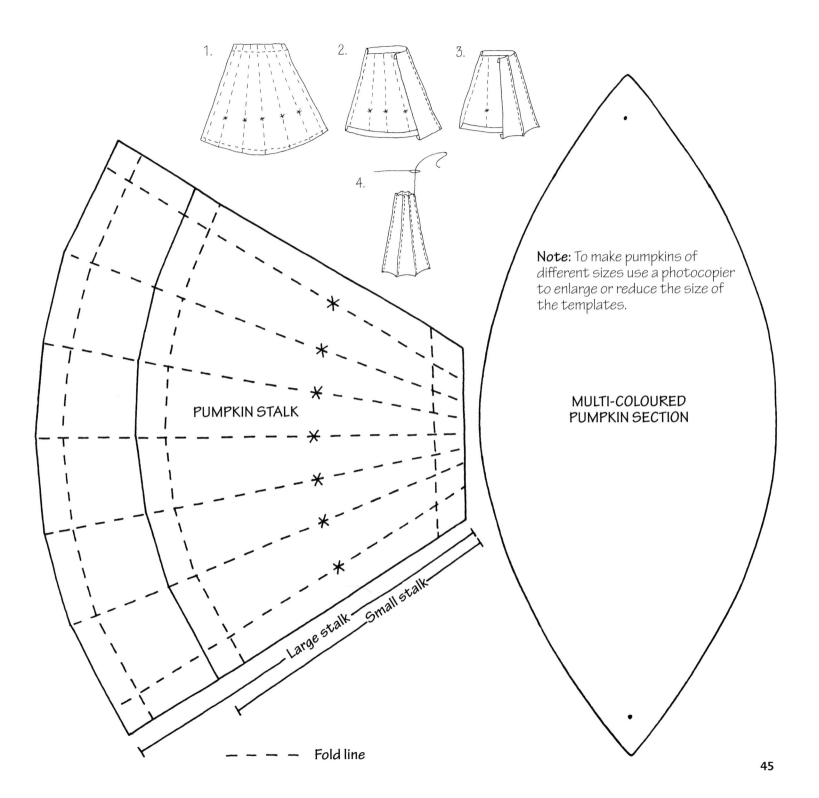

1.

2.

3.

4.

PUMPKIN STALK

Large stalk Small stalk

— — — — — Fold line

Note: To make pumpkins of different sizes use a photocopier to enlarge or reduce the size of the templates.

MULTI-COLOURED PUMPKIN SECTION

Pumpkin Quilt

Finished dimensions: 34.5 × 34.5cm
(13½ × 13½in)

Fabric requirements

- Remnants for centre panel and pumpkins
- Various fabric strips for borders: a total of 5 × 230cm (2 × 90½in)
- Thin wadding (batting): 35 × 35cm (13¾ × 13¾in)
- Backing fabric: 35 × 35cm (13¾ × 13¾in)
- Hanging sleeve: 9 × 33cm (3½ 13in)
- Edge binding: 7 × 150cm (2¾ × 59in)

Other materials

- Wooden batten for hanging: 2.5 × 33cm (1 × 13in)

1 Piece together the centre panel from remnants. It should measure 22 × 22cm (8¾ × 8¾in). Copy the divisions shown in figure 2 or divide it up to suit your own taste.

2 Sew two borders around the centre panel using 5cm (2in) strips.

3 Make templates of the pumpkin parts by enlarging the pattern in figure 1 by 200% on a photocopier.

4 Put a small mark on the front of all the templates to ensure that they will be facing the right way when you cut them out.

5 Cut out the parts for the pumpkins and appliqué them on the centre

panel. The edges with a broken line are slipped under the neighbouring section, and therefore the seam allowance should not be folded under (see figure 1).

6 Assemble the quilt with the wadding and backing fabric as explained on page 8.

7 Quilt the layers together, using stitching to echo the shapes of the pieces (see figure 2).

8 Trim the quilt and attach the hanging sleeve and edge binding as explained on pages 9 and 10.

9 Pass the wooden strip through the hanging sleeve.

1.

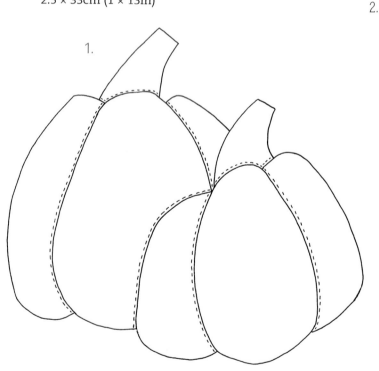

2.

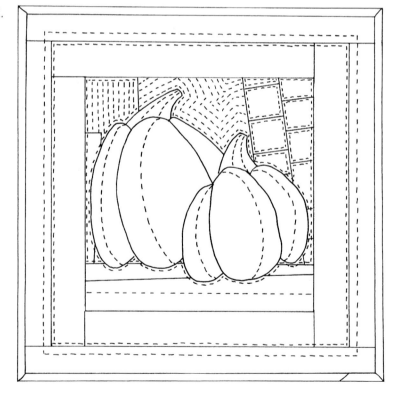

The pumpkin quilt (page 46) and stuffed pumpkins (page 44) are easy to make and lots of fun.

Long-legged Hens

These well-fed hens can be made from four or five different fabrics. Use the hen pattern on this page and the legs (with a rounded top) from page 52.

Fabric requirements
- Fabric for the body: 20 × 28cm (8 × 11in)
- Fabric for the legs: 29 × 30cm (11½ × 12in)
- Remnants for wings, comb and beak

Other materials
- Filling, four buttons and two small beads for eyes (optional)

1 Fold the fabrics right sides together and trace on a body, two legs (see page 52), two wings, a beak and a comb.
2 Sew round each shape, leaving gaps as indicated on the patterns.
3 Cut out the pieces, leaving a small seam allowance, but on the comb allow a wider seam allowance – 1cm (⅜in) – next to the opening.
4 Turn all the parts right side out and stuff the comb, wings and legs with filling. The legs should be empty in the middle, as the knee will be tied with a knot.
5 Sew up the openings on the wings and legs.
6 Quilt the comb and wings, as shown in the pattern.
7 Position the comb in the upper opening on the body and slipstitch it in place.
8 Stuff the body with filling.
9 Press all the parts lightly with a hot iron and a damp ironing cloth.
10 Play with the positioning of beak, wings and legs (see the photograph opposite).

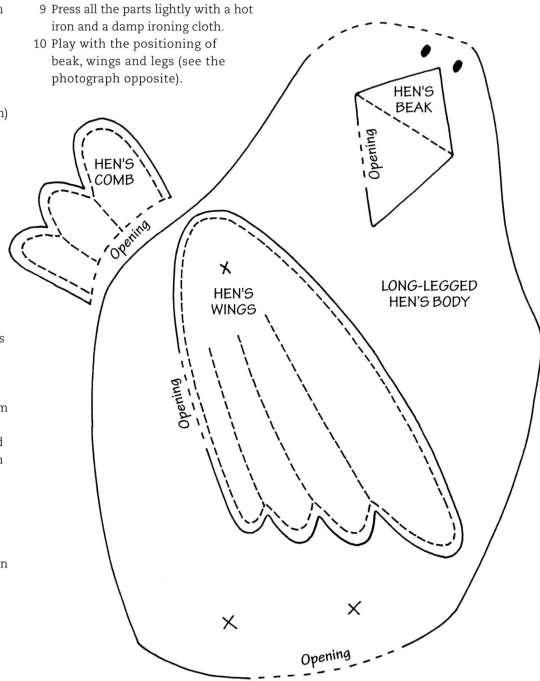

HEN'S BEAK

Opening

HEN'S COMB

Opening

HEN'S WINGS

Opening

LONG-LEGGED HEN'S BODY

Opening

11 Sew the beak in place with running stitches along the marked broken line.
12 Sew the wings and legs in place on the body with the buttons over them, matching the crosses on the patterns.
13 Add small beads for eyes or work French knots, if preferred.
14 If one of the hens is going to be a rooster, the mini heart from page 12 can be sewn under the beak as a wattle (see the photograph opposite).

The tip of the heart is hidden under the beak. A mini heart can also be stitched to the chest.
15 If desired, sew a cord to the back of the neck to hang your bird up.

These long-legged hens love to lounge about together (see opposite).

Three French Hens

These chic hens are cousins to the long-legged hens (page 48) and are made in basically the same way but their legs are inserted into the body so that they can sit more elegantly.

The pattern is on page 52.

Fabric requirements
- For the body: 22.5 × 30cm (9 × 12in)
- For the legs: 29 × 30cm (11½ × 12in)
- Remnants for wings, comb and beak

Other materials
- Filling, two buttons and two small beads for eyes (optional)

1 First cut the body pieces. Lay out the body fabric, right side up. Place the front pattern right side down on top and the back pattern wrong side down. Cut out the pieces, adding a 1cm (⅜in) seam allowance all round. Fold the fabrics for the other parts right sides together and cut two legs, one wing, a comb and beak through both layers.

2 Pin the body pieces right sides together around the shoulders and head only, as shown in figure 1.

3 Place the bottom edges over each other and hold in place with pins, as shown in figure 2. The extra length on the back is to provide a pleat, as shown in figure 3.

4 Put a pin on each side 1cm (⅜in) above the bottom edge and smooth the pleat up the back, as shown in figures 4 and 5.

5 Sew the pieces together along the drawn line from bottom edge to bottom edge, as shown in figure 6, leaving an opening at the top for the comb.

6 Make the other body parts as explained for the long-legged hen, steps 2–7 (page 48), but do not turn the body out yet.

7 Position the legs' right sides together with the bottom edge of the front body piece and sew them in place.

8 Sew the bottom seam of the body, with right sides facing, leaving an opening of 3–4cm (1¼–1½in) in the centre for turning.

9 Turn the body right side out and stuff it well for a smooth, rounded shape.

10 Finally, sew up the opening with slipstitches. Cut a mini heart to stitch on the chest (see page 12).

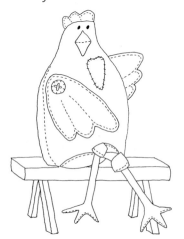

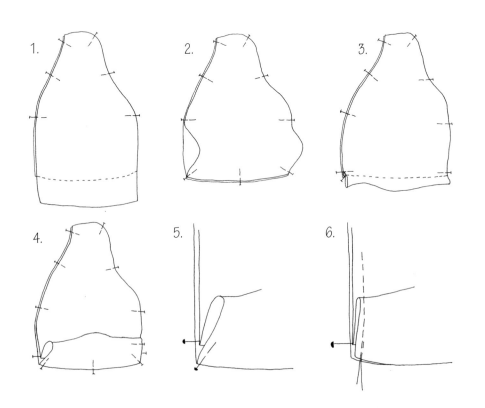

1. 2. 3.

4. 5. 6.

The three French hens relaxing among the flowers (see page 14).

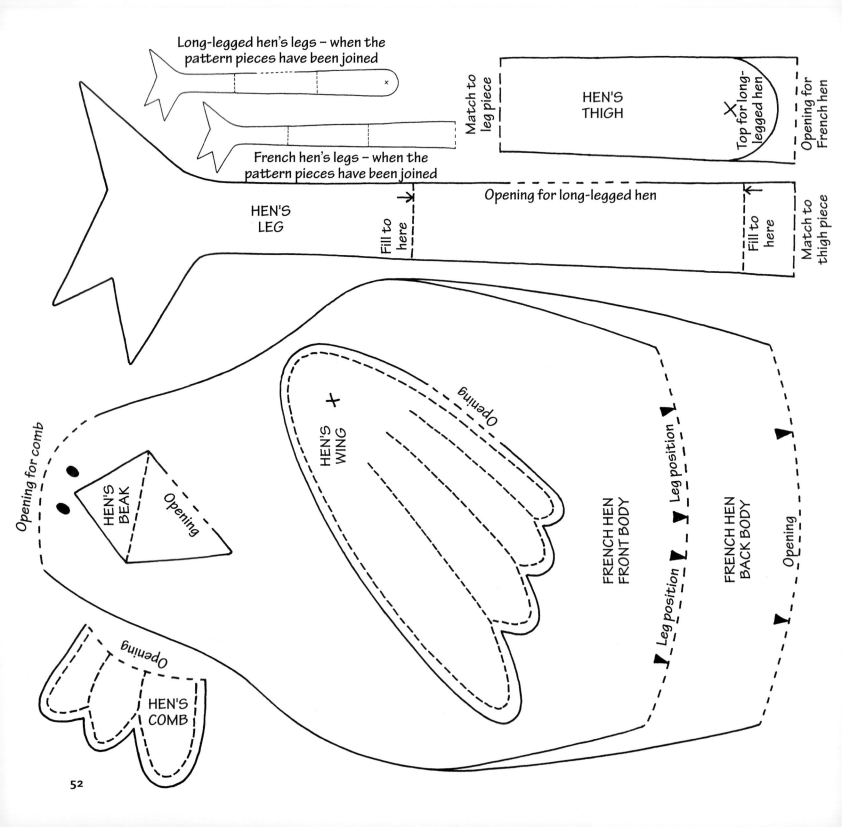

Long-legged hen's legs – when the pattern pieces have been joined

French hen's legs – when the pattern pieces have been joined

Match to leg piece

HEN'S THIGH

Top for long-legged hen

Opening for French hen

HEN'S LEG

Opening for long-legged hen

Fill to here

Fill to here

Match to thigh piece

Opening for comb

HEN'S BEAK

Opening

HEN'S WING

Opening

FRENCH HEN FRONT BODY

Leg position

Leg position

FRENCH HEN BACK BODY

Leg position

Opening

Opening

HEN'S COMB

52

Songbirds

There are two types of songbird, long-legged and short-legged. The short-legged birds have fabric legs supported by a garden stick, while the long-legged birds stand tall on two garden sticks. You can use just one stick (see page 15), or omit the legs and hang your bird from a cord. The birds come in two sizes and the patterns are on page 54.

Fabric requirements
- Coordinating fabric remnants – three or four per bird

Other materials
- Filling, two buttons for the wings, two small buttons or beads for eyes (optional), thin flower sticks and a small flowerpot or plinth (see page 4)

Short-legged songbird

1 Fold the fabrics' right sides together and trace on one beak, two or three tail feathers, two wings, one body and one foot, noting that the body and beak should be cut on the fold. The same tail feather and beak patterns are used for both the large and small birds.

2 Sew around each shape, leaving openings as indicated on the patterns, and on the body part do not sew where the beak and tail feathers should be placed. Note that the placement of the opening (at the bottom) determines whether the bird will be looking up, down or straight ahead.

3 Cut out the parts, adding a 1cm (⅜in) seam allowance for the body and 3mm (⅛in) seam allowance elsewhere.

4 Turn the beak, tail feathers, wings and foot (not the body) right side out and lightly stuff them with filling.

5 Press all the parts lightly with a hot iron, using a damp ironing cloth to protect the fabric.

6 Sew up the openings on the wings by hand and stitch all round.

7 Stitch around each of the tail feathers and between the legs.

8 Position the beak and tail feathers in the body, with the raw edges aligned and stitch them in place.

9 Trim the seam allowances on the body and turn it right side out.

10 Stuff the body well and press again with the iron.

11 Position the foot and sew up the opening by hand.

12 Gently manoeuvre a short length of flower stick into the foot seam or sew it in place on the back.

13 Position the wings and sew them in place on the body with the buttons over. You can tie the buttons on if you like, for a more decorative look.

14 Attach buttons or beads for the eyes, or work French knots.

15 Place your finished bird in a flowerpot or on a plinth (see page 4).

Long-legged songbird

1 Cut out and sew the pieces for the long-legged songbird as for the short-legged songbird, omitting the foot piece and following steps 1–10 above.

2 Close the leg opening by placing one triangle mark over the other triangle mark to make a pleat. It will look as though the bird is wearing trousers. Before sewing up the gap completely, put a flower stick in each end of the pleat and stuff in a little extra filling.

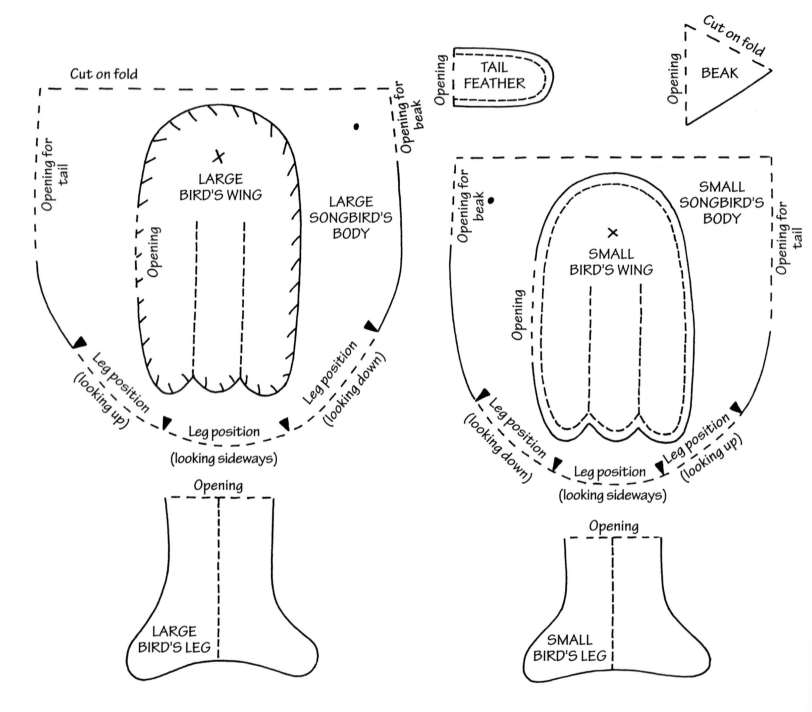

The instructions for making these sociable long- and short-legged songbirds are on page 53.

Lavender Ladies

Could there be anything nicer than these whimsical dolls that smell of glorious lavender? Try filling them with other herbs, such as rosemary or hops, or just with wadding to use for decoration.

The pattern is on page 58.

Fabric requirements

- Skin-coloured fabric for face and hands: 6 × 28cm (2½ × 11in)
- Patterned fabric for the dress and sleeves: 16 × 28cm (6¼ × 11in)
- Skin-coloured fabric for the legs: 4 × 14cm (1½ × 5½in)
- Single-colour fabric for the shoes: 4 × 14cm (1½ × 5½in)
- Remnant for the hanging strap: 2.5 × 9cm (1 × 3½in)
- Patterned fabric for the apron (optional): 9 × 11cm (3½ × 4½in)

Other materials

- Filling, buttons (optional), yarn or similar for the hair, embroidery cotton for the features, red crayon to colour the cheeks and dried lavender flowers (optional)

1 Sew the appropriate skin-coloured strip right sides together with the dress and shoe strips, taking a presser foot's seam allowance, as shown in figure 1.
2 Iron the seam allowance away from the skin-coloured fabric and fold each joined fabric so that the longest side is halved, as shown in figure 2. Pin the layers.
3 Trace on the body, two arms and two legs, as shown in figure 2.
4 Sew round the shapes then cut them out, leaving a small seam allowance.
5 Turn the pieces right side out and stuff with filling. When the head and upper body are filled, place the dried lavender in the rest of the body and, if desired, stuff a little filling in afterwards.
6 Turn in the seam allowance on the body at the opening and press all the parts lightly with a hot iron and a damp ironing cloth.
7 Position the legs in the body opening and sew it up by hand. As shown in the photograph, the feet can turn in several ways.
8 Sew up the openings on the arms and sew them to the body. If you wish, attach buttons over the top.
9 Sew the eyes as French knots with three strands of embroidery cotton. Sew two or three straight stitches for the mouth and colour the cheeks with a red crayon.
10 Sew the hair as explained on page 11.
11 If desired, make the heart from a fabric remnant and sew it in place on the hands (see the instructions on page 5).

Making the hanging strap

1 Fold the strip for the hanging strap, as shown in figure 3. Press and sew the strap together.
2 Slit a stitch at the CB of the doll's neck and manoeuvre the strap in place (see the illustration on page 58).
3 Stitch the strap to the neck.

1.

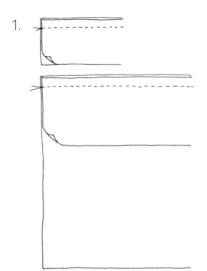

2.

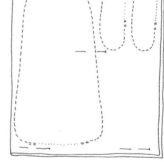

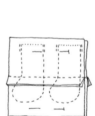

3.

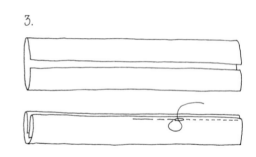

Making the apron

1 Fold and press a very narrow double hem along the sides and the bottom edge of the apron fabric.
2 Sew the hems with running stitches.
3 Fold and press a 4mm (⅛in) hem at the top and sew with running stitches. Do not fasten off.
4 Pull up the thread to gather the apron to 4.5cm (1¾in) and fasten off.
5 Sew the apron in place on the dress at each side.

These lavender ladies have lavender in their skirts so they smell as good as they look.

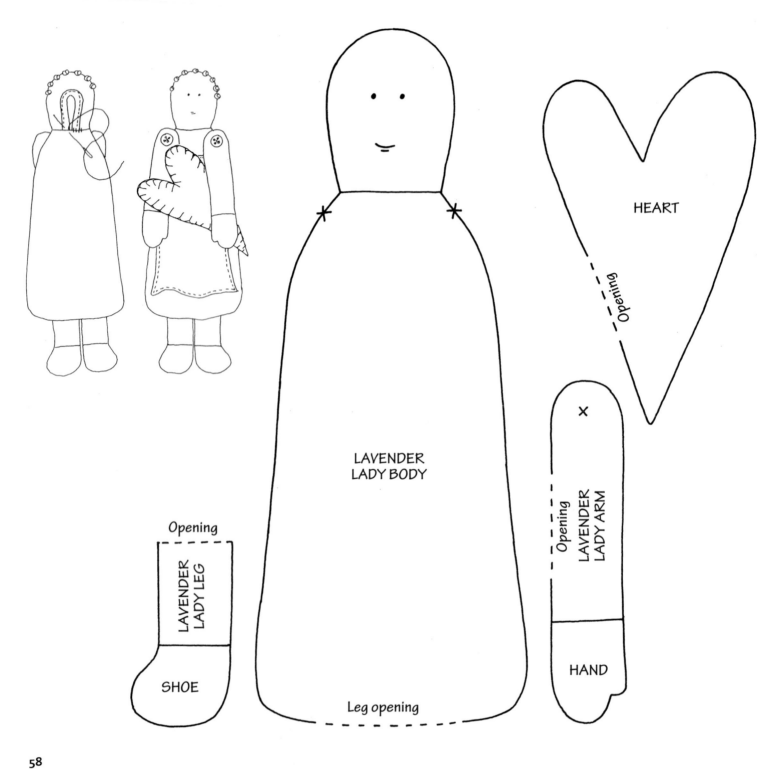

HEART

Opening

LAVENDER
LADY BODY

LAVENDER
LADY ARM

Opening

Opening

LAVENDER LADY LEG

SHOE

HAND

Leg opening

Fir Trees

These trees make great Christmas decorations.

Fabric requirements
- Fabric remnants in various shades of green or in Christmas fabrics.

Other materials
- Filling, a button or two (optional), a thin flower stick and a small flowerpot or plinth (see page 4)

1 Choose two or three different fabrics. Fold each one in half with right sides facing and trace on a triangular tree shape.
2 Sew around the triangles – the bottom edge of the upper triangles should be open for almost the entire width while the lowest triangle should only have a small opening for the trunk (see figure 1).
3 Cut out the triangles, leaving a small seam allowance. Turn them right side out and stuff them lightly with filling.

4 Assemble the tree, as shown in figure 2 and pin the layers. Sew the triangles together with decorative hand stitches.
5 Sew or tie on one or two buttons at the top.
6 Press the tree carefully with a hot iron and a damp ironing cloth.
7 Saw or cut the flower stick so it is 5–6cm (2–2¼in) long for the trunk.
8 Insert the trunk up into the tree and sew up the opening completely (see figure 3).
9 Plant the tree in a flowerpot or fix it firmly to a plinth (see page 4).

Alternatively, if the tree is going to be held rather than planted, you can make a fabric trunk. Cut a 3 × 5cm (1¼ × 2in) piece of fabric, roll it up, fold in the raw edges and then sew then edges down with small invisible stitches. Attach this to the bottom triangle instead of using the flower stick (see the photograph on page 63).

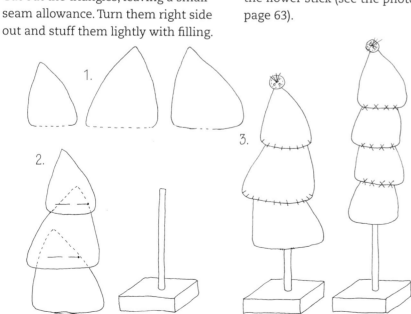

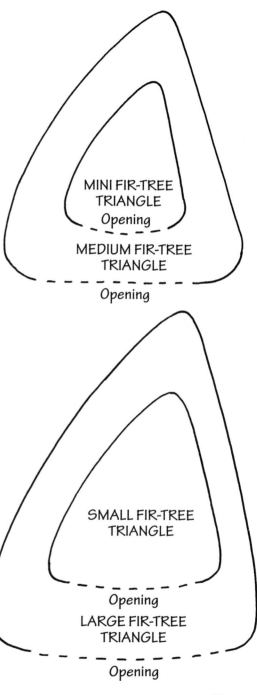

MINI FIR-TREE TRIANGLE
Opening

MEDIUM FIR-TREE TRIANGLE
Opening

SMALL FIR-TREE TRIANGLE

Opening

LARGE FIR-TREE TRIANGLE

Opening

Snowman Family

Fabric requirements
- Child snowman: 18 × 40cm (7 × 16in)
- Adult snowman: 23 × 52cm (9 × 20½in)
- Felt for hat: 10 × 28cm (4 × 11in)
- Remnants of fabric and/or felt for the nose, apron, earmuffs and bow

Other materials
- Filling, thin cardboard, buttons, raffia for hair and broom bristles, red crayon, embroidery thread for the features and a thin flower stick for the broomstick

1 Fold the fabric right sides together so the longest side is halved and trace on two arms, a body and the circular bottom piece. Pin the layers.
2 Sew around the arms and body, leaving a gap as indicated on each pattern, then cut out these stitched pieces, adding a small seam allowance.
3 Turn the arms and body right side out, stuff the arms lightly with filling and sew up the openings.
4 Cut out the bottom piece along the drawn line.
5 Using strong thread, work running stitch 5mm (a scant ¼in) from the edge of the fabric circle. Do not finish off the thread.
6 Draw a circle on cardboard using the inner circle on the base template and cut out.
7 Place the cardboard circle in the middle of the fabric circle and pull up the tacking thread to draw the edges of the fabric smoothly over the cardboard. Fasten the thread.

Assembling the body
1 Mark the facial expression and neckline with a pencil.
2 Using strong white thread, work running stitch along the neckline and 5mm (a scant ¼in) from the bottom of the body piece. Do not fasten off either thread.
3 Stuff the head and upper body well with filling and pull up the thread around the neck, so that the neck disappears into the body. If desired, stuff a little extra filling in before knotting the thread and cutting off the ends.
4 Finish stuffing the body and pull the lower tacking thread together so the gathered edge can be hidden by the bottom piece. Knot the gathering thread securely and trim off the end.
5 Position the bottom piece on the snowman and sew it in place with small slipstitches.
6 Position the arms on the body and sew them in place. If you wish, put buttons on top (see page 32).

Adding the facial features
1 Sew the eyes and mouth as French knots with 3–6 strands of embroidery cotton.
2 Colour the cheeks lightly with a red crayon.

3 **For the round nose,** cut the circle from red fabric. Work running stitch just inside the edge all round then place a small ball of filling in the middle of the fabric and pull up the thread. Knot securely. Sew on the nose so the raw edge is hidden.

Alternatively, for the carrot nose, cut the nose from orange felt or fabric. If using fabric, fold in the narrow seam allowance, as shown in figures 1 and 2. If using felt, don't include the seam allowance. Sew the nose together as a cone, as shown in figure 3 and stuff lightly with filling. Sew on the nose, slipping a small seam allowance underneath as you do so.

Finishing the snowman
1 Sew buttons on the front, if desired, as marked on the pattern. If you wish, tie them on, cutting off the thread ends about 1cm (⅜in) above the buttons.
2 Wrap the raffia 5 to 7 times around a couple of your fingers for the hair. Sew the hair in place on top of the snowman's head, just above the seam, so it sticks out backwards and forwards or to each side. Cut the loops.
3 Make and attach clothing and accessories following the instructions below.

1.
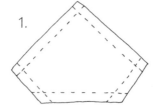

2.
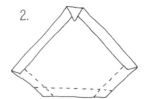

3.
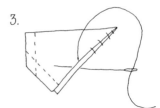

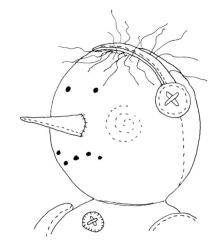

Hat for the large snowman

1 Using the pattern on page 62, cut out the outer hat circle from felt for the crown.
2 Work running stitch all round, about 1cm (⅜in) from the edge; do not fasten off.
3 Dampen the felt well, pull it down over an empty kitchen-roll tube, and pull the tacking thread tight, as shown in figure 1. Knot off the thread securely. Pull the bottom edge out horizontally and leave the crown to dry on the tube.
4 Fold the remaining felt in half and draw the full hat pattern on top. Sew 3mm (⅛in) inside the large circle through both layers and cut out along the drawn line. Now cut out the centre hole.
5 Carefully turn the hat brim right side out through the hole and press with a hot iron and a damp ironing cloth.
6 Place the brim on the table and gently position the flattened seam allowance of the crown between the upper and lower brims.
7 Sew together with running stitches through all the layers, as shown in figure 2.
8 Put the hat on the snowman's head and hold it in place with a couple of stitches on each side.

Broomstick

1 Saw or cut the flower stick so it is around 14cm (5½in) long.
2 Wrap raffia around three fingers to obtain an adequate skein of broom bristle.

3 Hold one end of the skein together with string and cut the loops at the other end.
4 Position the raffia on the broomstick and bind tightly with raffia or twine, as shown in the photograph on page 63.
5 Trim the ends of the binding twine and the broom bristles.
6 Sew the broom in place on the snowman's body.

Snow-woman's outfit

1 Cut and make the hair bow as explained on page 36.
2 Cut a 9 × 13cm (3½ × 5in) rectangle of fabric for the apron and sew a rolled hem (as small as you can make it) along the sides and the bottom edge.
3 Fold 5mm (¼in) over to the wrong side at the top and work a line of running stitches 3mm (⅛in) from the edge. Pull up the thread to gather in the apron to 6cm (2½in) and fasten the thread.
4 Sew the apron to the body with a couple of stitches on each side and tie around the snow woman with raffia or twine.

Earmuffs

1 Cut a 2 × 6.5cm (¾ × 2½in) strip of fabric for the headband. Fold and stitch it in the same way as the hanging strap for the lavender ladies (page 56).

2 Position the headband over the head seam and hide the ends with a button on each side.

Hearts

Make hearts to decorate your snowman following the instructions on page 12. A fir tree can also be sewn as explained on page 59.

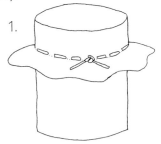

1.

2.

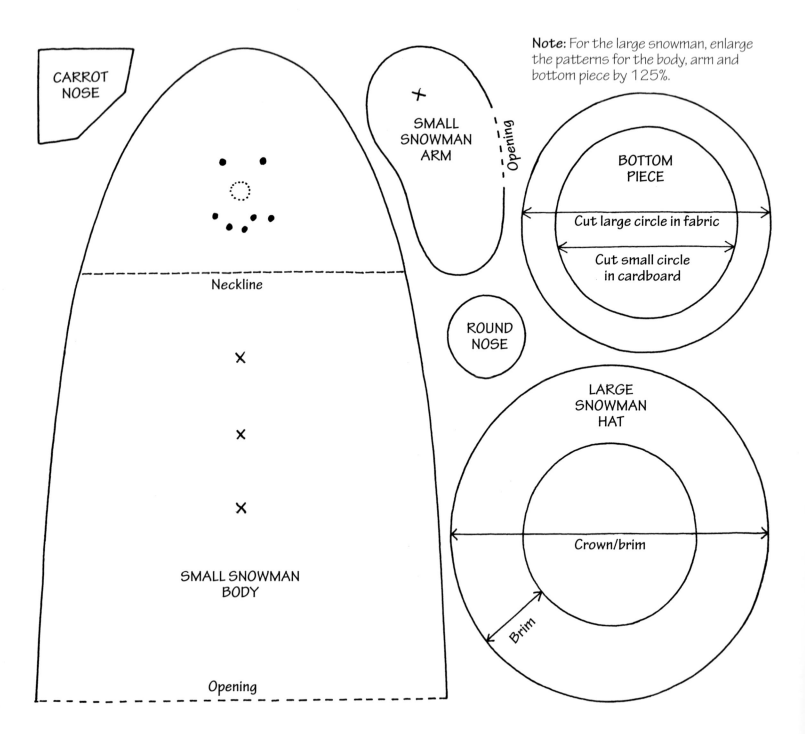

CARROT NOSE

SMALL SNOWMAN ARM

Opening

Note: For the large snowman, enlarge the patterns for the body, arm and bottom piece by 125%.

BOTTOM PIECE

Cut large circle in fabric

Cut small circle in cardboard

Neckline

ROUND NOSE

SMALL SNOWMAN BODY

LARGE SNOWMAN HAT

Crown/brim

Brim

Opening

Even if it doesn't snow outside, this snowman family brings Christmas cheer indoors. Instructions for making the trees are on page 59.

Father Christmas and his Wife

The smaller figures, shown on page 67, are 30cm (12in) tall while the larger couple (see page 71) are 47cm (18½in) tall.

Fabric requirements for both figures

- Skin-coloured fabric for the bodies: 18 × 27cm/27 × 36cm (7 × 10¾/10¾ × 14¼in)
- Skin-coloured fabric for the arms: 3.5 × 34cm/4.5 × 56cm (1½ × 13½in/1¾ × 22in)
- Skin-coloured fabric for the legs: 9 × 21cm/13.5 × 27cm (3½ × 8¼in/5½ × 10¾in)
- Red fabric for the arms: 12 × 34cm/18 × 56cm (4¾ × 13½in/7 × 22in)
- Red fabric for his coat: 17.5 × 20cm/26.5 × 29cm (7 × 8in/10½ × 11½in)
- Red fabric for her dress: 19 × 21cm/ 28 × 32.5cm (7½ × 8 ¼in/11 × 12¾in)
- Red fabric for the hats: 19 × 23cm/30 × 32cm (7½ × 9in/12 × 12¾in)
- Checked/striped fabric for his legs: 3.5 × 21cm/4.5 × 27cm (1½ × 8¼in/1¾ × 10¾in)
- Checked/striped fabric for her legs: 6.5 × 21cm/9.5 × 27cm (2½ × 8¼in/3¾ × 10¾in)
- Brown fabric for his boots: 8.5 × 21cm/9.5 × 27cm (3½ × 8¼in/3¾ × 10¾in)
- Brown fabric for her shoes: 3.5 × 21cm/4.5 × 27cm (1½ × 8¼in/1¾ × 10¾in)

- Green fabric for his trousers: 12.5 × 16cm/19.5 × 25cm (5 × 6¼in/7¾ × 10in)
- Salmon-coloured fabric for her pantalettes: 15 × 16cm/24 × 25cm (6 × 6¼in/9½ × 10in)
- White fabric for his beard: 8.5 × 14cm/13 × 19cm (3½ × 5½in/5 × 7½in)
- Apron fabric: 11 × 15cm/15 × 25cm (4¼ × 6in/6 × 10in) and 2.5 × 40cm/3 × 55cm (1 × 16in/1¼ × 21¾in)
- Sack fabric: 6 × 34cm/8.5 × 50cm (2½ × 13½in/3½ × 19¾in)
- Additional fabric scraps for pockets and edgings

Other materials

- Four buttons, fine ribbon or cord, red crayon, embroidery cotton and small bells for decoration

Making the bodies

1 Sew the strips for the arms and hands right sides together, taking a presser foot's seam allowance. Repeat for the legs/socks/shoes.

2 Iron the seam allowances away from the skin-coloured fabric and fold the joined fabrics right sides together, so the longest side is halved.

3 Trace on two bodies, four legs and four arms, as shown in the illustrations below.

4 Sew around the shapes, leaving gaps as indicated on the patterns.

5 Cut out the pieces, leaving a small seam allowance then turn them rights sides out and firmly stuff with filling so the parts are not floppy.

6 Tuck in the seam allowance at the bottom of the body.

7 Press all the parts lightly with a hot iron and a damp ironing cloth.

8 Position the legs in the body and sew in place by hand. If necessary, stuff a little more filling in before the last stitches are made. Leave the arms for now.

9 If the couple are going to be hung up, fold and sew a narrow hanging strap (see page 56) in the position marked on the pattern. If they are going to stand, they must be supported by a stick. Sew a support flap on their backs – the flap should be open at the bottom so the stick can be inserted.

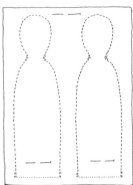
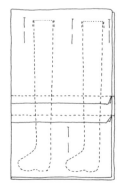
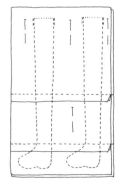
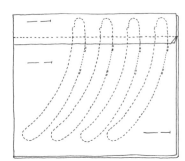

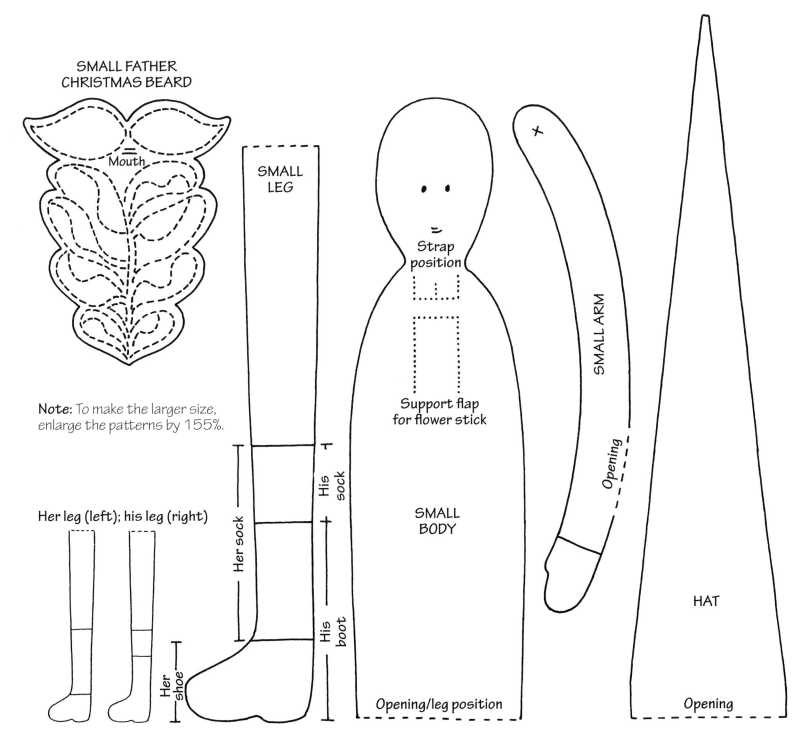

SMALL FATHER CHRISTMAS BEARD

Mouth

Note: To make the larger size, enlarge the patterns by 155%.

Her leg (left); his leg (right)

Her shoe

SMALL LEG

Her sock

His sock

His boot

SMALL BODY

Strap position

Support flap for flower stick

Opening/leg position

SMALL ARM

Opening

HAT

Opening

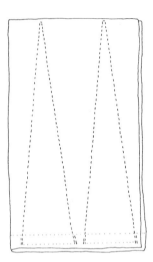

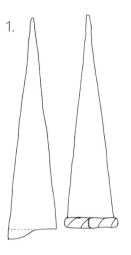

1.

Hats

The pattern is on the previous page.

1 Fold and press a 7–8mm (generous ¼in) hem along the bottom (long) edge of the hat fabric; unfold.
2 Fold the fabric so that the longest side is halved and trace on both hat patterns as in the illustration above.
3 Sew around the two hats and cut them out, leaving a small seam allowance on the angled edges (see the illustration above).
4 Turn the hats right side out, pulling out the tip carefully with a needle.
5 Refold the bottom hem to the wrong side.
6 Cut a fabric remnant for each edging, 4 × 9cm (1½ × 3½in) for the small figures or 5 × 13cm (2 × 5in) for the larger ones.
7 Roll up the fabric lengthways and fold under the raw edges. Stitch the roll then join the ends into a ring.

8 Sew the rolled edging to the hat with overcast stitches, as shown in figure 1, while folding small tucks on the hat so the width of the hat fits the edging.
9 Work a line of running stitches up one of the side seams of each hat and pull it a little, so the hat curves round. Fasten the thread.
10 If desired, decorate the end of each hat with a small bell. Bells can also be sewn on the legs of the boots.
11 Only sew the hat on the figure after the dress/coat has been put on. Then it can be slipstitched in place with the side seams at the sides of the head.

Trousers and pantalettes

The pattern is on page 69. Note that her pantalettes are longer than his trousers.

1 Fold and press a narrow hem at the bottom of the fabrics for the trousers or pantalettes and tack in place. Repeat to fold and press a slightly wider seam allowance at the top edge. Unfold the top hem.
2 Fold the pieces right sides together and sew the seam, as shown in figure 2.
3 Press the seam allowances open and place the seam at CB, as shown in figure 3.
4 Trace on the trouser/pantalette pattern and sew the inside-leg seam, as shown in figure 4.
5 Cut out the piece, adding a 3mm (⅛in) seam allowance on the inside-leg seam.
6 Turn the piece right side out and sew the hem at the bottom with running stitches.
7 Fold the top hem down and fit the trousers/pantalettes on the figure. Fold small pleats at CF and CB to fit and sew the trousers/pantalettes in place with running stitches.

2.
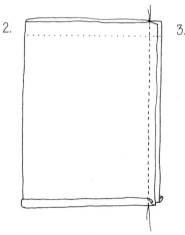

3.
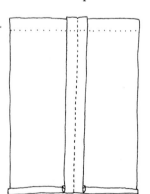

4.
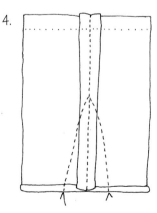

Father Christmas and his wife in the smaller size. To make the fir trees, see page 64. Instructions for making the heart are on page 12.

Dress

For the pattern, see page 69.

1 Roll a narrow double hem at the bottom of the fabric for the dress. Press the hem and tack it in place.
2 Fold and press a hem at the top edge; unfold the hem.
3 Fold the fabric right sides together and trace the dress pattern on top.
4 Sew the side seams and cut out the dress, adding a 3mm (⅛in) seam allowance.
5 Turn the dress right side out and sew the hem at the bottom with running stitches.
6 Fold the top hem back over to the wrong side and sew running stitches 3mm (⅛in) from the edge, starting and finishing at CB and leaving the thread ends hanging; see the illustration opposite.
7 Fit the dress on the body (the top of the dress goes round the neck), pull up the thread ends and distribute the gathers evenly. Knot off the thread.

8 Finally, sew the arms on the body as explained for the teddy bear on page 32.

Coat

The coat is made in basically the same way as the dress, except that it has a vertical tuck at the front, which is a fake opening. The pattern is on the next page.

1 Roll and press a hem on the coat fabric as explained for the dress. Divide the fabric into two pieces: for the small coat, the two pieces should be 9.5 × 17.5cm (3¾ × 7in) and 10.5 × 17.5cm (4¼ × 7in), and for the large coat, the pieces should be 13.5 × 26.5cm (5¼ × 10½in) and 15.5 × 26.5 (6¼ × 10½in).
2 Fold the larger piece wrong sides together so the short side is halved. On the small coat, sew 4mm (⅛in) from the fold and on the large coat sew 1cm (⅜in) from the fold (see figure 1).
3 Place the fabric right side up and press so that the seam is at CF (see figure 2).
4 For the small coat pockets, use a checked fabric remnant 4 × 8cm (1½ × 3in) and a plain fabric remnant 5.5 × 8cm (2¼ × 3in). For the large coat pockets, the two pieces should

be 5.5 × 11cm (2¼ × 4¼in) and 8.5 × 11cm (3¼ × 4¼in).
5 Pin the two pocket pieces right sides together and then sew them together.
6 Iron the seam allowances open. Find the centre and fold the sides in to the centre with right sides facing, as shown in figures 3 and 4.
7 Press the pocket piece with an iron and draw the two pockets on top, using the pattern opposite.
8 Sew the pockets, as shown in figure 4. Cut them out, leaving a small seam allowance, then turn right side out and press.
9 Position the pockets on the coat as marked and sew them in place along the sides and bottom edge with running stitches.
10 Place the front and back pieces of the coat right sides together, draw the pattern on top and sew as explained for the dress (see figure 5). Fit to the body with the top gathered around the neck.
11 Finally, sew the arms on the body as explained for the teddy bear on page 32.

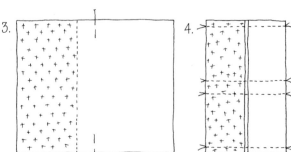

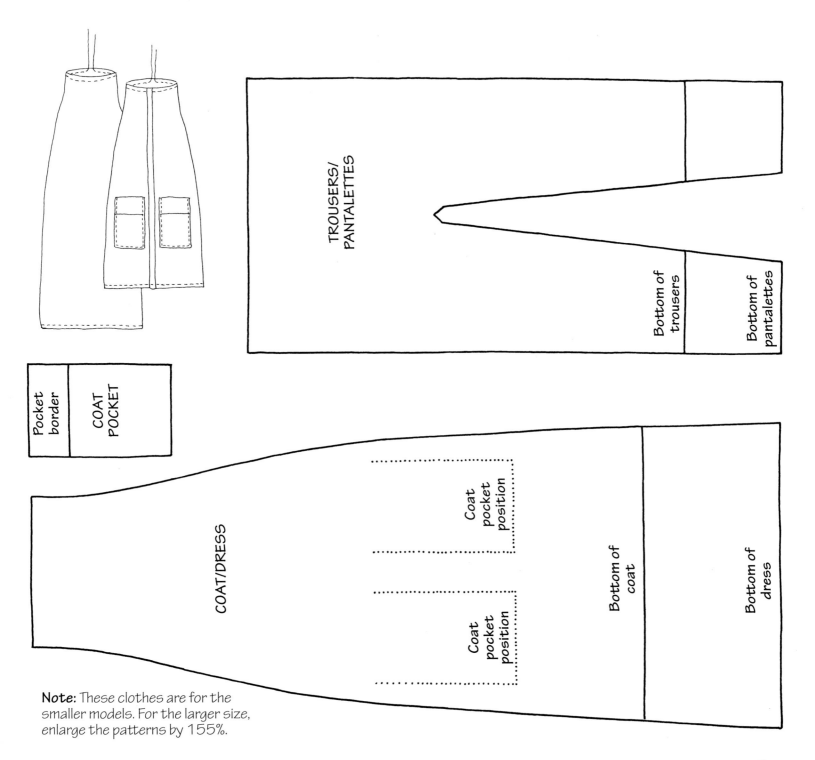

TROUSERS/PANTALETTES

Bottom of trousers

Bottom of pantalettes

Pocket border

COAT POCKET

COAT/DRESS

Coat pocket position

Coat pocket position

Bottom of coat

Bottom of dress

Note: These clothes are for the smaller models. For the larger size, enlarge the patterns by 155%.

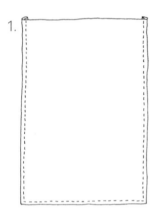

1.

2.

Apron

1 Roll a narrow double hem along the sides and the bottom edge of the apron piece and press in place.

2 Sew the hems with running stitches, as shown in figure 1.

3 Fold small pleats or gathers at the top, so the small apron is 3.5cm (1½in) wide and the large one is 4.5cm (1¾in) wide.

4 Fold the sides and ends of the waistband tie 5mm (¼in) over to the wrong side.

5 Fold the waistband tie in half with wrong sides together lengthways and press it.

6 Centre the ribbon tie over the apron top, enclosing the raw edge of the apron.

7 Sew the strip together with running stitches from one end to the other, enclosing the apron in the seam (see figure 2).

Santa's sack

1 Roll a narrow double hem at each short end of the bag fabric, press and unfold.

2 Fold the fabric right sides together, matching the short edges, and sew the side seam. Turn the sack right side out.

3 Refold the hems at the top and sew in place with running stitches.

4 Stuff a little filling in the bag or find some tiny toy items to fit inside. Tie up the sack with fine ribbon or cord and perhaps trim the ends with tiny bells.

5 If desired, sew the sack in place on Santa's hand with tiny, invisible stitches.

Santa's beard

For the pattern, see page 65.

1 Fold the fabric right sides together and draw the beard pattern on top. Pin the layers.

2 Sew all round the beard (without leaving a gap for turning) and cut it out with a small seam allowance.

3 Carefully cut a 2cm (¾in) long slit in the middle of the back of the beard to turn it through.

4 Turn the beard right side out, stuff it lightly and sew up the opening.

5 Press the beard with a hot iron and a damp ironing cloth.

6 Quilt the beard as marked on the pattern. It is important that the moustache is shown clearly.

7 Sew the beard in place on Santa's face with two stitches to mark the mouth.

Faces

1 Stitch the woman's mouth with two straight stitches using embroidery cotton.

2 Sew the eyes as French knots using 3–6 strands of embroidery cotton.

3 Colour the cheeks with a red crayon.

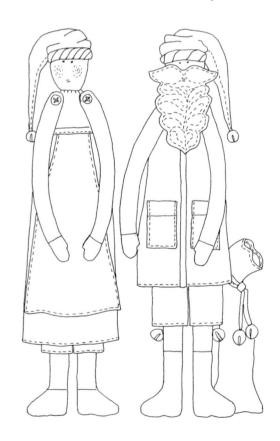

The large size Santa and his wife (see page 64). To make the flowers, see page 14 and for the fir trees see page 59. Instructions for making the hearts are on page 12.

Christmas Elves

These elves go well with Santa and the snowmen but they would also make good companions for the lavender ladies (page 56) or the cats on page 38. Make them with one-piece limbs, as shown in the photograph on page 75 or with two-piece limbs (see the photo opposite). The table below shows the fabric requirements. Each strip should be cut 16cm (6½in) long and the width shown in the table. In addition, 14 × 18cm (5½ × 7in) of red or green fabric is required for a cap and you'll need buttons for the limbs and yarn for hair. For the faces you will need some embroidery cotton, a red crayon and a black waterproof pen or fine fabric marker. The pattern is on page 74.

1 Sew the strips for the head and body together with right sides facing, taking a presser foot's seam allowance. Repeat with the fabrics for the hands and arms and then with the fabrics for the legs and feet.

2 Iron the seam allowance away from the skin-coloured fabric and fold each joined fabric right sides together, so the longest side is halved.

3 Fold and press a 7–8mm (generous ¼in) hem on one short end (the bottom end) of the hat fabric and then unfold it. Fold the hat fabric in half with right sides facing.

4 Now draw the appropriate patterns on the folded fabrics, as shown in the illustrations, right. Pin the layers.

5 Sew around each shape, leaving openings as indicated on the pattern pieces. Cut out the pieces, leaving a small seam allowance and turn right side out. Stuff all the parts except the hat with filling and close up the openings with small hand stitches.

6 Press all the parts lightly with a hot iron and a damp ironing cloth.

7 Stitch the joints of the one-piece arms and legs with running stitches as shown on the patterns. Alternatively, assemble the two-piece arms and legs with buttons or a couple of stitches.

8 Sew the arms and legs in place with buttons so they can be moved (see page 32).

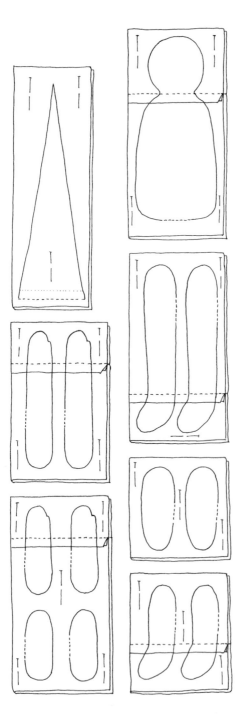

Type of fabric	Head/body	Two-piece arms	One-piece arms	Two-piece legs	One-piece legs
Skin-coloured fabric	6cm (2½in)	4cm (1½in)	4cm (1½in)		
Blouse fabric	12cm (4¾in)				
Sleeve fabric		13cm (5¼in)	10cm (4in)		
Shoe fabric				4.5cm (1¾in)	4.5cm (1¾in)
Sock fabric				6.5cm (2¾in)	
Trouser fabric				8cm (3¼in)	12cm (4¾in)

9 Add the hair as explained on page 11.

10 Refold the hem on the hat, pulling it down over the head, preferably a little crooked, and sew it in place with small, invisible slipstitches.

11 If desired, tie a knot at the tip of the hat.

12 Work a line of running stitch through one of the side seams of the hat and pull up the thread so the hat curls over. Fasten off the thread securely.

13 Work French knots for the eyes, using three strands of embroidery cotton. Mark the mouth with one or two straight stitches, and redden the cheeks with a crayon. Freckles can be added with a waterproof pen.

14 Follow the instructions to make heart decorations, if desired. These or other items can be stitched on to the elves' hands.

These elves have two-piece articulated arms. The elves shown on page 75 have simple one-piece limbs.

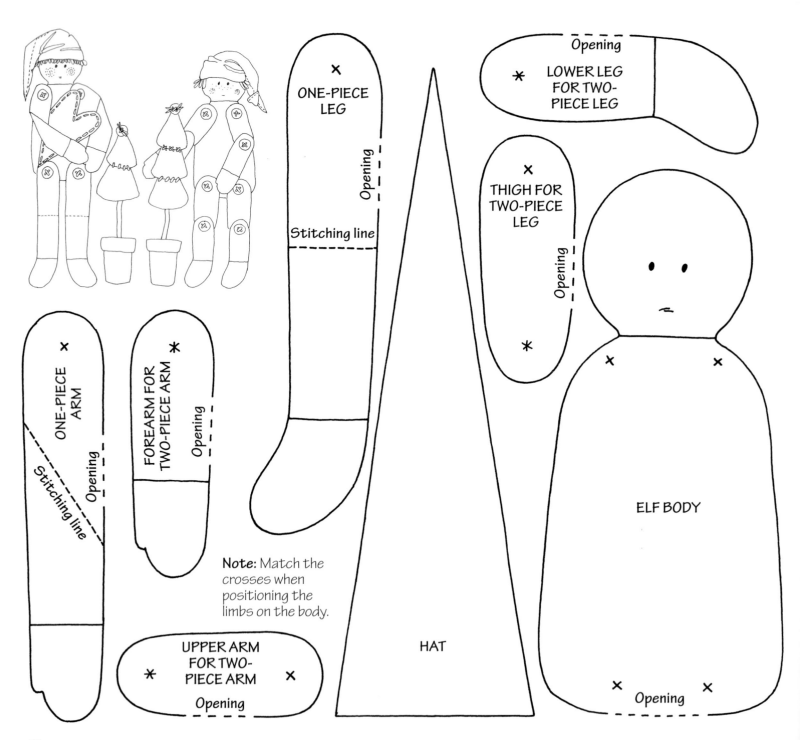

ONE-PIECE LEG

Opening

Stitching line

Opening

LOWER LEG FOR TWO-PIECE LEG

THIGH FOR TWO-PIECE LEG

Opening

ELF BODY

ONE-PIECE ARM

Stitching line

Opening

FOREARM FOR TWO-PIECE ARM

Opening

Note: Match the crosses when positioning the limbs on the body.

UPPER ARM FOR TWO-PIECE ARM

Opening

HAT

Opening

74

These elves, and the variation shown on page 73, are surprisingly easy to make. For the best results, take time over the hair and features to give each elf his personality.

Angels

These magical angels can be made with long legs, knotted at the knee, as shown opposite, or with short legs, as for the angels on the star garland (see the photo on page 79). The pattern is on page 78.

Fabric requirements
- Skin-coloured fabric for face and hands: 7 × 28cm (2¾ × 11in)
- Patterned fabric for the dress and sleeves: 16 × 28cm (6½ × 11in)
- Skin-coloured fabric for short legs: 11 × 14cm (4½ × 5½in)
- Skin-coloured fabric for long legs: 14 × 18cm (5½ × 7in)
- Fabric for wings: 6 × 30cm (2½ × 12in)
- Wadding (batting) for wings: 6 × 15cm (2½ × 6in)

Other materials
- Filling, two buttons, yarn or similar for hair, embroidery cotton and a red crayon for the features and a plinth (optional – see page 4)

1 Place the face/hands fabric right sides together with the dress fabric, matching one of the long edges and sew together, as shown in figure 1.
2 Iron the seam allowance away from the skin-coloured fabric and fold the fabric right sides together, as shown in figure 2. Pin the layers.
3 Fold the fabric for the legs right sides together. Repeat with the wing fabric. Iron wadding on to the wrong side of the wing fabric.
4 Draw a head/dress, two arms, two legs and the wings on the appropriate folded fabric.
5 Sew around each shape, leaving openings as indicated on the patterns, then cut out the pieces, adding a small seam allowance all round.
6 Turn the pieces right side out. Stuff the body, the arms and the short legs or just the lower half of the long legs. Knot the long legs at the knees and then stuff the rest of the legs.
7 Press all the parts lightly with a hot iron and a damp ironing cloth.
8 Close up the openings on the arms with slipstitch.
9 Mark the fingers and toes with running stitches and topstitch the wings.
10 Attach the arms, using buttons so that they can move (see page 32). Slip the top of the legs in the dress opening and sew in place with slipstitches. Attach the wings to the back.
11 Sew the eyes as French knots, using three strands of embroidery cotton. The nose is a long and a short stitch and the mouth one or two straight stitches, but work the face as you wish to give the angel character.
12 Sew the hair as explained on page 11.
13 If desired, make a heart (page 12) or star (page 16) to sew on the angel's hands.
14 Sew a suspension thread to the back of the angel so it is balanced. Alternatively, the angel could stand on a plinth (see page 4) with the aid of a flower stick (see photograph). The stick should be sewn in place behind the legs and at the top of the back.

1.

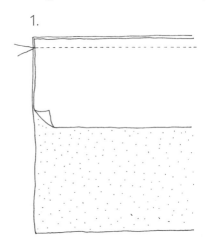

2.

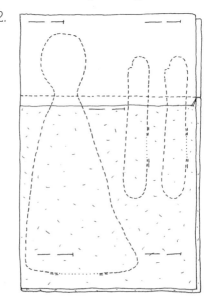

3.

4.

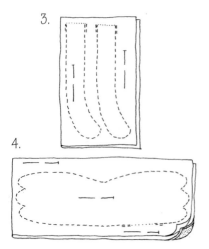

These angels walk among the stars (see page 16).

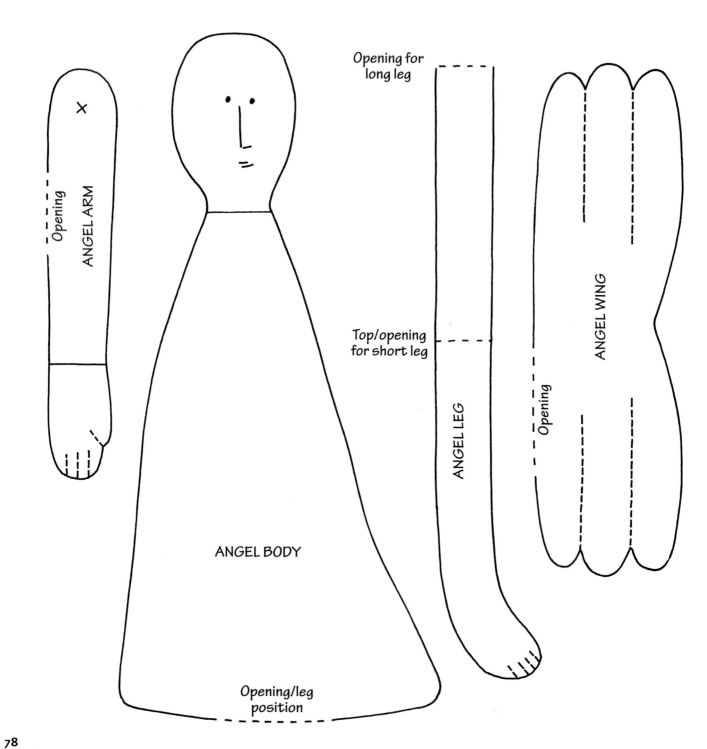

ANGEL ARM

Opening

ANGEL BODY

Opening for
long leg

Top/opening
for short leg

ANGEL LEG

Opening/leg
position

Opening

ANGEL WING

The short-legged angels look lovely suspended from the star garland (see page 80).

Star Garland

You can have lots of fun customizing this garland with tiny scraps of your favourite fabrics. It is pictured on page 79 with the angels dangling beneath it, but the songbirds (page 53) would also work well.

Fabric requirements
- Two pieces 29 × 103cm (11½ × 40½in)
- Thin wadding (batting): 29 × 103cm (11½ × 40½in)
- Remnants for stars and angels

Other materials
- Filling, buttons, nylon cord and a 1.5 × 46cm (5/8 × 18in) wooden batten for hanging

1 Draw a 52 × 30cm (20½ × 12in) grid of 2 × 2cm (¾ × ¾in) squares and draw the garland on the grid, as shown in figure 1 to make a half template.
2 Place one piece of fabric right side down and transfer the garland on to the wrong side.
3 Lay out the wadding and place the two fabric rectangles right sides together on top so that the garland pattern is uppermost. Pin the layers (see figure 2).

4 Sew along the drawn line through all the layers, leaving an opening at the bottom for turning.
5 Cut out, adding a 5mm (¼in) seam allowance, trimming this down to half that at the tips.
6 Cut small slits into the seam allowance at the top curve for ease and snip the seam allowance right up to the stitching at the V at each end.

7 Turn the garland right side out so the wadding is inside and then carefully pull the points out with a needle.
8 Finger press the seams and sew up the opening by hand.
9 Press the garland with a hot iron and a damp ironing cloth.
10 Quilt 5mm (¼in) from the edge all round with running stitch.

1 square = 2 × 2cm (¾ × ¾in)

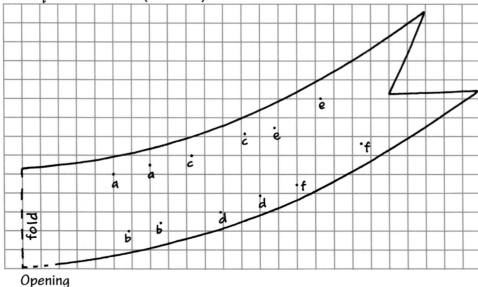

Opening

1.

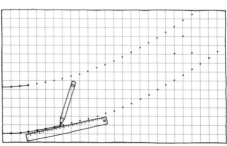

2.

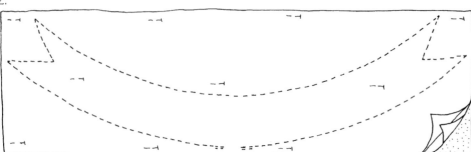

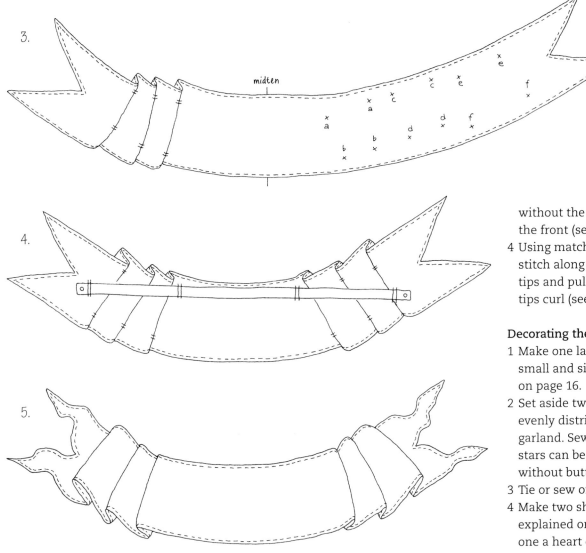

3.

midten

4.

5.

Pleating the garland

1 Mark the points a–f on the back of the garland on both sides (see figure 3).

2 When a is sewn to a, b to b, etc., there will be three pleats on the front of the garland on both sides. Sew two

or three stitches at each spot to hold the pleats. The stitches must not be visible on the front.

3 Drill holes through the wooden batten a little from each end. Position the batten on the back and sew it in place

without the stitches being visible on the front (see figure 4).

4 Using matching thread, work running stitch along the back of the garland tips and pull up the thread so that the tips curl (see figure 5).

Decorating the garland

1 Make one large, two medium, six small and six mini-stars as explained on page 16.

2 Set aside two or three stars and evenly distribute the rest on the garland. Sew them in place. The stars can be tied or sewn on, with or without buttons.

3 Tie or sew on extra buttons, if desired.

4 Make two short-legged angels as explained on page 76 and give each one a heart or a star to hold (see pages 12 and 16).

5 Attach a hanging thread to each angel and to the stars you set aside previously, and attach the threads to the back of the garland.

6 Tie nylon cord through the holes on the batten for hanging.

Angel Quilt

This charming quilt measures 50 × 58cm (19¾ × 23in) and would look lovely hanging in the same room as the star garland.

Fabric requirements
- Remnants for the sky, stars and angel
- Border around the sky: 55 × 55cm (21¾ × 21¾in)
- Thin wadding (batting): 55 × 65cm (21¾ × 25½in)
- Backing fabric: 55 × 65cm (21¾ × 25½in)
- Fabric for the hanging sleeve: 9 × 50cm (3½ × 19¾in)
- Edge binding: 7 × 230cm (2¾ × 90½in), joining strips as necessary to obtain the length

Other materials
- 2.5 × 48cm (1 × 19in) wooden batten for hanging, buttons (optional) and embroidery cottons for the face and hair

1 It may be helpful to draw a full-size paper pattern. If you want, use figure 1 as a general guide. Draw assembly guide marks and possibly the grain direction on all parts. Alternatively, allow the size and shape of the remnants to determine the design of the sky, but do not use too many small pieces because it makes the quilting more difficult.

2 Cut out the different parts, adding a uniform seam allowance.

3 Sew the pieces for the sky together into strips and then join the strips.

4 Sew the border around the sky, making sure that the corners form right angles (trim if necessary after joining).

5 Cut stars to the patterns on page 16 and appliqué them in place. In the example, one large, two medium, three small and one mini star are used. The large star is placed slightly above the centre, as shown in figure 2.

6 Cut the parts of the angel to the pattern on page 78. Note that two half wing pieces are required, with a seam allowance around all the edges. The legs should be short.

7 Sew the head and dress fabrics together and also the hand and arm fabrics before cutting, as explained on page 76.

8 Appliqué the angel in place, as shown in figure 2.

9 Sew the angel's face and hair and mark any fingers and toes using embroidery cotton.

10 Assemble the quilt with the wadding and backing fabric, following the instructions on page 8.

11 Quilt the layers together; for example, as shown in figure 2. The transverse lines are the rays from the large star.

12 Trim the quilt, attach the hanging sleeve and add the binding as explained on pages 9 and 10.

13 Sew or tie on buttons for added decoration as desired.

14 Drill holes through the wooden batten a little from each end and

1.

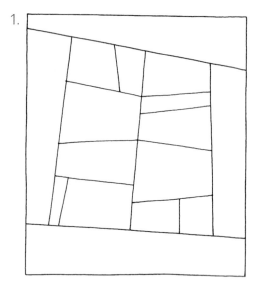

2.

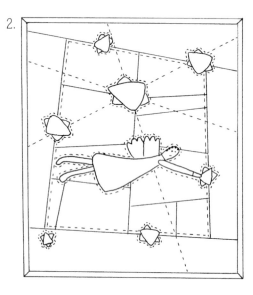

pass the strip through the hanging sleeve. Hang the quilt by threading a hanging cord through the holes in the batten and securing it.

The angel quilt is an excellent project for using up any remnants you have accumulated making the projects in this book.

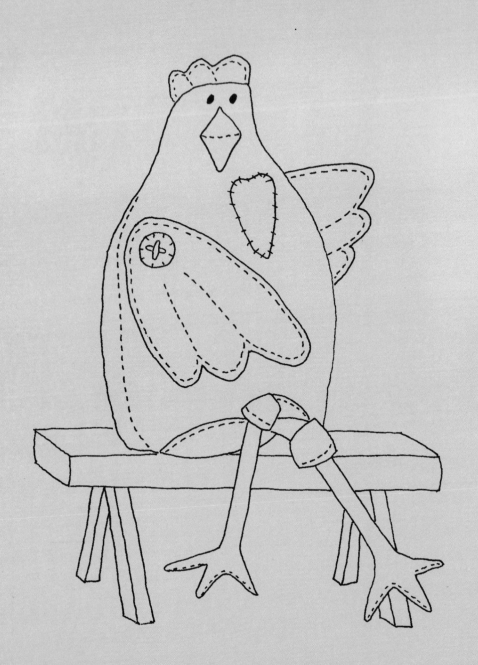

One

Hannah stopped her car where she always did on her way up to the farm. Just here the Polden Hills, ancient, tree-covered outcrops of stone that even over aeons of time the rivers hadn't been able to wash away, lifted themselves out of Sedgemoor's flatness. The landscape was familiar to her, though much of it now lay under water. It was beautiful at any time in her view, but most itself like this at flood-time, silvered and mysterious under a sky that promised more rain before evening came. Her brother's fields, submerged like the rest, were only marked out by the bare willows fringing them; darker lines drawn on the shining surface of the water.

Joshua wouldn't mind as long as the floods didn't last too long. 'Thick' water, he and the other farmers called them, unlike rain, which was thin. The river silt left behind when they went down would mean rich pastures in the spring, but the floods brought him another pleasure, too. He never went to the Friends' meeting house now, hadn't done since Sarah died in childbirth more than twenty years ago; but old Quaker attitudes survived. The experts – scientific know-alls, he called them – reckoned they'd got nature well in hand with their drains and pumping stations. But every now and again the Creator showed them who was still in charge.

The dairy herd was penned in the yard when she drove in, with Joshua in the middle of the beasts, doling out feed. Only a slight lift of his hand said that he'd seen her but it was all she expected. The Venns didn't run to gestures of affection. She couldn't remember that he'd ever given her a kiss, or wept – even on the night Sarah died.

'Go on inside,' he called out to her. 'I'll be finished soon. You could put the kettle on.'

She waved back, then let herself in. The kitchen seemed already dark on an overcast February afternoon and she switched on more lights than Joshua would think necessary. The paraffin lamps remembered from childhood had long gone, but otherwise the room looked much the same; still, something was missing. Her mother's old preserving pan gleamed with polish on the dresser, but it was empty now – no pots of herbs or hyacinths filling it with scent and colour. Only men lived in the house now and to a woman it showed. The tea was waiting to be poured when Joshua kicked off his boots in the back porch and walked in. He nodded his thanks for the mug she pushed across the table, and sat down with a small sigh of relief. Sixty-five wasn't old by today's standards, but Hannah thought years had to be reckoned by the effort that had gone into them, and Joshua's had been full of hard work and very little joy. He'd been in charge of Rushey Farm since the night his elder brother, Gideon, had drowned in a much worse flood than the present one. Since then the years had given him a grizzled, dour authority; no one questioned that he was a man to be reckoned with on Sedgemoor, but she doubted if any of his scattered neighbours sought him out unless they needed him.

'Rufus not here today?' she asked.

'Gone to look at a sick cow of Randall's – it's cheaper than calling in the expert, and probably better, too.' Joshua spooned sugar into his tea and found something else to say. 'Just goes to show – a vet's book-learning and degrees and such are well enough, but it's experience and instinct that count when an animal needs help.'

It was an argument she'd heard before but it led Hannah to suddenly put into words a question she'd carefully skirted until now, almost certain that her brother would resent it.

'Is Rufus a fixture now, Josh? Have you said that you expect to have him stay and carry on after you?' No reply came from across the table, and she ploughed on, determined to be given an answer. 'It's time you thought about the future, and if he's not told, he might start his wanderings again.'

Joshua leaned over and deliberately refilled his mug from the brown earthenware teapot on the table. 'I dare say he'll

2

stay if I ask him, and I dare say I *will* ask one of these days.' A faint glimmer of a smile unexpectedly lightened his frown. 'Is that what brought you up from Cossenford – to fuss over a man you've got a kindness for?'

Hannah shook her head. 'No, though I do love Rufus – have done ever since I tried to pen a small boy in a classroom when he wanted to be outdoors, looking for otters' holts or watching for the lapwings and curlews to arrive.' She was silent for a moment, wondering how to tackle what *had* brought her there. 'There's something else I want to talk to you about. You remember the old Baptist chapel and graveyard we've been waiting years for them to sell off? Well, they've made up their minds at last.'

'So why don't you look pleased?' Joshua wanted to know. 'Must be ten years at least you've been dreaming of turning it into a museum for Cossenford.'

'Dreaming's a good word. There was a Town Council meeting last night and what do you think we heard? A developer is putting in a bid. He wants to raze the building to the ground and use the entire site for a small new estate in the heart of the town – 'executive' homes, they're called, which means expensive houses for rich incomers who'll like the idea of living in a beautiful old town but despise the people who belong there.'

Joshua wasn't a museum-minded man, and only the Levels were his own concern, but he knew that Cossenford's preservation had become a sort of sacred duty for his sister. He even recognized its value himself in a world that increasingly rubbished quality. What Hannah wanted to protect *was* precious – a perfect example of age-old town planning: church, manor house, market cross and attendant cottages, all harmonious, all hewn out of the blue-grey lias stone of which the Poldens themselves were formed.

'It's not to say the developer will win,' he finally suggested. 'Council might turn it down.'

'And the moon might be made of green cheese. You know what will happen as well as I do, Josh. He'll buy his way in – promise a new playground for the school or a clutch of computers for old ladies like me to sit and gawp at in the library!'

3

She seemed so likely to be right that he found nothing to say and she spoke again herself. 'But I haven't told you the worst bit. I know who the developer is – Max Hasler. What chance shall we have against *him*?'

Her brother's sudden frown confirmed that he was angry now himself, as she'd known he would be. 'Then you'll have no chance at all!' Aware of having shouted at her, he tried to speak more quietly. 'He's got money to burn and expensive lawyers waiting at his beck and call. What's more, winning will be all the sweeter if he knows he's got a Venn against him.'

Hannah considered for a moment what she was going to say next. It would make his anger worse, but it was the real reason for her visit. 'I went to Bath this morning, to call on our sister-in-law.'

'That's *not* what she is!' Joshua was shouting again. 'The woman married James Westover, remember, and even gave *his* name to Gideon's daughter.'

The wounds were unhealed, Hannah knew. After twenty-five years he still hadn't forgiven Elizabeth for running away from the farm and taking the child with her. Gideon had been found drowned a month later and, though accidental death, not suicide, had been the official verdict, it was Elizabeth that Joshua had continued to blame.

'I had a reason to go,' Hannah insisted quietly. 'Months ago I saw the name of Jane Westover mentioned in a news-paper report; she was a lawyer involved in some big case or other. I needed to be sure she was *our* Jane; that's what I went to ask Elizabeth.'

'I suppose you'll tell me next you were greeted with open arms!'

'She was . . .' Hannah hesitated over a word. 'Pleasant enough; not friendly, but then I hadn't expected that.' Honesty obliged her to add something else. 'She's still beautiful, even now. Life on the moors was never what she was cut out for, but we always knew that, of course.'

Joshua shrugged the comment aside, not even noticing how generous it was coming from a woman who'd never been anything but very plain herself. What did it matter now whose

4

mistake the marriage had been, Elizabeth or Gideon's. 'And *is* Jane a London lawyer?'

'Yes. Very clever and successful, apparently. So I've written to her, Josh. Elizabeth gave me the address. We can't afford the sort of advice Max Hasler can buy, but Jane's still Gideon's daughter, still family – even if my letter has to remind her of the fact.'

Joshua surveyed his sister across the table and slowly shook his head. 'She won't come, if that's what you've written to ask her. You could've saved yourself the price of a stamp; she'll not even trouble herself to reply.'

'Maybe not,' Hannah said briefly. 'In that case *you*'ll have to help me think what else to do. But now I'd best get home; we'll have night come in half an hour and I don't like driving in the dark.'

She stood up to leave but lingered for a moment, looking round the room. There was nothing wrong with the way it was kept; Josh wouldn't have lived messily even if the wife of one of the farm men hadn't cleaned and polished for him. Even so, she knew what was amiss: there'd been no love shown it since Sarah died. The sure, small signs of affection that a man or a home needed didn't come from hired help. That was sad enough, but a worse grief was Joshua himself, who no longer realized the extent of his isolation. Not counting the human contacts that running the farm obliged him to make, the sum total of his emotional credit with the rest of the human race was a tepid affection for herself and the grudging friend-ship that Rufus and his young son, Tom, had slowly won from him.

'I hope you're wrong about Jane,' she suggested, at last walking to the door.

He shook his head. 'I hope I'm right. No point in stirring up old things that are best forgotten. If she came at all it would only be to laugh about us afterwards with her smart London friends.'

He waited for as long as it took Hannah to turn the car outside, then he firmly closed the house door. Gideon's daughter, fleetingly remembered as the small, silent child who hadn't seemed to belong even when she lived there, could be

5

returned now to the shadowy corner of his mind where memories were hidden.

But Hannah drove home still thinking about the past. She pictured the letter she'd written arriving at a house that imagination painted for her as tall and narrow – a terraced, red-brick villa like the ones she saw in the expensive magazines in the dentist's waiting room. But the truth, she slowly acknowledged to herself, was that it didn't really matter what Jane Westover's home looked like. Joshua was right. The girl they hadn't been allowed to watch grow into a young woman wouldn't come, not even to laugh at her unknown country-bumpkin relatives. She'd simply want nothing to do with them at all.

Two

Jane's house wasn't terraced, tall or narrow; far removed from her aunt's imagining, it squatly filled the end of a quiet mews off Sloane Square. The ground floor was little more than a garage – precious as rubies in the centre of London – and a green front door but, up above, whitewashed walls and flowering window boxes gave the small house a pleasant country air.

Luck had led her to it at just the right time, but she claimed the rest of the credit for herself. Her home had been bought with the slog of dedicated hard work ever since she came to London. It had also cost her the lover she had wanted very much to keep. But Mark Rubens had refused to play second fiddle to a job that all but consumed her and she'd chosen to let him go in the end. A junior partnership in the City's most prestigious firm of corporate lawyers couldn't be turned down even if she still ached sometimes at night for what she'd lost. There was always the next day's challenge to convince her that she'd made the right choice after all.

The letter from Cossenford arrived while she was in the thick of a company takeover more complicated than most. It lay on the doormat when she got back one evening – the stamped, handwritten envelope nowadays a quaint novelty in itself; but the note inside was even more of a surprise. The neat, precise signature at the bottom of the page seemed to fit the schoolteacher she dimly remembered Hannah Venn to have been, but memory could supply no picture of what this unknown aunt had looked like.

It was too late to think of food, but she poured wine instead and was trying to conjure up the past when the downstairs doorbell rang. Her neighbour was there, holding a small parcel.

'Sorry to bring you down, ducks,' said Amanda Crichton, 'but the postman couldn't get this through your letter box.' Her friendly gaze inspected Jane's face. 'You look knackered – bad day?'

'Not bad, just busy. Come in and share my wine; it's no pleasure drinking alone.'

Upstairs, while Jane fetched another glass, Amanda stooped to pick up the letter that had fallen on the floor.

'My God – handwritten! I thought no one did that any more.'

'My aunt in Somerset does; no truck with email technology for her!'

Amanda grinned, then looked a question. 'I didn't know you had country relatives – you don't mention anyone except your mother, and her not very often.'

'I don't suppose they mention me! Aunt Hannah has just remembered my existence after twenty-five years.' It would have been easy to stop there, but Jane suddenly found herself talking of a past that she'd long since given up thinking about.

'I was trying to remember her when you rang. I was five when my mother finally decided to walk out of the family home, with me in tow, and I can just recollect being pleased to go. My father was a shadowy figure I scarcely knew, but even now I can recall the bleak winter landscape around the farm and my grandfather, Amos Venn, hunched in his chair like an Old Testament prophet.'

'Sounds grim,' Amanda conceded. 'What happened next?'

'We went to live on the other side of the hills, in Glastonbury. My father died soon afterwards but even that I can't remember minding very much. All went well for a while but then my mother married again, an American I never learned to like, and we moved to his house in Bath. He made so little fuss about financing me through school and Cambridge that afterwards I realized the dislike was mutual. Anything was better than having me under his feet in Bath.'

Amanda smiled, but decided that her own growing up – painful though it had seemed at the time – had been a good deal easier than her neighbour's. 'So you struck Somerset off

your visiting list and headed for the Great Wen. Funny – you're so smart and streetwise that I always reckoned you'd been born and bred here.' Then another thought occurred to her. 'Why the letter from distant parts now, or shouldn't I ask?'

Jane gave a little shrug. 'Aunt Hannah seems to be sufficiently in touch with the real world to know that I'm a lawyer. She has some acute local problem that I'm expected to deal with – an argument over a boundary fence, probably, or a neighbour's dog that won't stop barking! One day when I have the energy to do it I'll write and explain that even Somerset has lawyers up to the job of sorting out such things.'

There was silence in the room for a moment while Amanda tossed off the last of her wine. 'It's time I went – you look ready to drop.' On the point of recommending that Jane should forget her aunt and do something about getting back the nice man who seemed to have disappeared, she remembered just in time that very smart lawyers only expected to *give* advice. 'Need you work quite so hard?' she asked instead. 'I doubt if the Old Testament prophet is watching you now from up above.'

'I'm afraid he probably is,' Jane answered with faint smile. 'In life he was a Quaker, and his philosophy was simple: no frills, no frivolity, and everyone's nose very seldom lifted from the grindstone! To answer your question, I'll take a break when the present negotiations are sewn up, but thanks for coming round; I was in need of company.'

It wasn't, Amanda knew, the sort of admission the woman in front of her was inclined to make, self-containment being almost an article of faith with her. They'd been neighbours for two years, and helped each other when help was needed, but Jane Westover had never invited intimacy before. More tactful than to comment on the fact, Amanda stood up to leave.

'I'll call again then, with or without parcel! Good luck with the present battle, Jane.'

Then she clumped down the staircase and silence descended once more. Half-tempted to throw Hannah Venn's letter in the wastepaper basket, Jane put it on her desk instead and switched off the lamps. She would take herself to bed, and pretend that

loneliness hadn't invaded the house again with Amanda's departure. It was only born of her own tiredness; she'd be her usual calm, efficient self in the morning.

The day dawned grudgingly and her bedroom was still dark when the alarm clock pinged. She hated February mornings like this one, so unendingly grey and overcast that even a lunatic optimist might give up hope of seeing another spring. Remembering that she'd gone supperless to bed, she made toast for once as well as black coffee, then forgot to eat it while she thought about the day ahead. Unless something totally unforeseeable arose – the odds-on chance that could always trip them up – today should see the end of months of delicately orchestrated bargaining. *Her* clients would get what they wanted, the other side would not, but in an imperfect world someone had to lose. There'd be a very fat fee for the firm and a sizeable bonus again for herself, but the real reward lay in pitting her own skill and knowledge against what the opposition could offer. She usually felt sorry when a difficult negotiation was close to being completed, but the tingle of regret was missing this morning; she just wanted the battle safely won and over.

Sleety rain was falling when she walked out into the street, and the Underground would be jammed with damp-smelling, surly people. Damn the expense – she'd wave down the first empty cab she saw and take an extravagant ride to the City instead. Then, halfway there, something very strange happened: for a split second her mind went completely blank. She couldn't even remember why she was there, sitting in a taxi in the Strand! But at least she knew that it was where she was, and even as she registered that small relief, the moment's darkness had gone. She'd simply imagined it; nothing was wrong. All the same, her hands were still cold when she fumbled for money to pay the fare, and she didn't even notice the driver's saucy comment about a sleepless night. But she did hear him mutter as he drove away about bleeding stuck-up City women who were too high and mighty to share a joke.

Inside the building, waiting for the lift, a male colleague

10

she didn't like came to stand beside her, and unpleasantly seemed to echo the cabbie's view.

'Good morning, Jane. No friendly smile for a fellow toiler in the vineyard? Or don't I rate high enough for that?' It was said lightly, but with his usual edge of malice underneath, and she knew why: exactly a year older than herself, he'd expected to get the promotion that had gone to her instead.

'Sorry, Dominic,' she apologized briefly. 'I was deep in thought – busy day ahead.'

'Of course, and we look forward to another star performance from Ms Jane Westover; how very fortunate we are!'

She thanked him with a smile for the compliment he hadn't meant, then walked into the lift that had arrived. But the small incident underlined what she already knew: she was resented by her colleagues. Some, like Dominic, reckoned that she worked unnecessarily hard; the more junior ones complained that she asked too much of them. The result was that she could call none of them a friend.

The day hadn't begun well, one way or another, and she had to stifle a small prickle of fear that it was how it might continue. A trained legal mind ought to be able to ignore the whispers of tribal superstition – disagreeable things didn't necessarily go in threes. Nor did it worry her to be without friends or the web of relationships that most people wove around themselves. She was used to managing on her own.

Six hours later anxiety, admitted or not, was at an end. The takeover contract was safely signed and sealed. For the first time in weeks she could go home with the evening still in front of her, slowly unwind, and for once even sleep the night through.

Content, but suddenly disinclined to join in the celebrations, she left the boardroom and went back to her own office. After hours of concentrated discussion it was blessedly quiet, and she was glad to lean her head against the cool surface of her desk. It was the last thing she remembered doing before darkness closed in.

She awoke bathed in sweat that turned to clammy coldness on her skin. The bed she was lying in was not her own, and the white counterpane that covered her and the equipment

poised above her head spoke of hospital things. *Why* she was there was anxiety enough; even worse was the certainty that she had no memory of being brought there. A red call button beside her bed was obviously meant to be pressed, but before she could stretch out her hand the door opened and a large nurse walked in.

'That's good – you're awake again,' she said in a soft West Indian accent. 'What about a nice cup of tea?'

'Talk first, please,' Jane insisted hoarsely. 'It sounds silly, but I don't know why I'm here.' Her voice shook, and a warm black hand at once reached out to cover her own, offering comfort.

'You're in St Martha's, but nothing terrible's happened – just a little blackout, that's all. When Doctor comes round I expect he'll say you can go home soon.' A smile lit her dark face, giving it a fleeting gentle beauty, and Jane wanted her to stay, but the woman went away in search of tea.

Alone again, panic closed in. Why couldn't she remember the 'little blackout', or even one damn thing that had happened after walking back to her own room? The watch still on her wrist showed her the time: more than twelve hours of her life had passed without her knowing anything about them.

The promised tea was brought, then breakfast which she couldn't eat, and finally a tired-faced man in a white coat appeared. He was brusque and to the point. Her collapse had been, in technical terms, a transient ischaemic attack – a mini stroke in layman's language; a common enough occurrence nowadays even in people of her age if they ignored the fact that their bodies needed regular amounts of sensible food, sleep and relaxation in the fresh air. He supposed, rather wearily, that she'd been going short of all those things.

'It's not easy to regulate workloads,' she said defensively, and saw him give a faint smile at last. He knew all about that, of course; he was probably guilty himself of exactly the behaviour he condemned in her. 'Will . . . will it happen again?' She couldn't utter the shattering word *stroke* – it was too terrible in its connotation with the helpless humiliation of the old – but he saw the fear in her face and suddenly became human.

'At your age there's no reason why it should. Just take this

12

as a warning. Give yourself a good long holiday – I'll write a note for your employer, insisting on it – and afterwards for God's sake treat your body and mind with more care.' He was silent for a moment, studying her white face. 'You young women are worse than men – does it mean so much to you to fight your way up the ladder ahead of them?'

The question was irritating enough to sting her into recovering some of her normal poise. 'And that's *exactly* the sort of Victorian attitude that makes the fight necessary: we're supposed to be content to assist our male colleagues. Why shouldn't mine assist me if I can do the job better than they can?'

He held up his hands in a little gesture of defeat. 'I'll have to duck a promising argument, I'm afraid – I've got a round to finish.' But at the door he turned to look at her. 'I'll tell you what really worries me about women like you – success *can't* be good for you because it never seems to make you happy.'

He'd gone before she could frame a reply. What she should have shouted after him, of course, was that she had exactly the life she would have chosen, thanks to efforts that were entirely her own. It was the shock of her collapse, as well as tiredness and relief from strain, that caused her to want to turn her face to the wall and weep instead of arguing with him.

By lunchtime she'd been allowed to telephone her boss and agree that she'd return to the office only to discuss what should happen next. Then she was officially discharged and conveyed home in a taxi with a box of sleeping pills that she knew she wouldn't take, and the advice not to try to recover the memory of the hours she'd lost, because it wouldn't return. Instead, she must think positively about the future.

Obedient to the doctor's warning about sensible living, she scrambled eggs and even managed to eat them, but for the moment optimism and even hope were beyond her. She couldn't even see a future at all. In the driven world she worked in, the race was to the swift; physical handicap was difficult enough, but what place could there be for someone whose mind and memory might go dark again in the middle of a vital

negotiation? She wept herself into a sleep troubled by frightening dreams, then woke to find the room dark and the telephone ringing. The caller was someone she hadn't expected to hear from again, and all he said was that he was on his way to see her. There was just time to wash the tear stains off her face and brush her hair before Mark Rubens was at the door. Outwardly composed again, she poured the whisky that he preferred and soda water for herself.

'I was worried about you,' he said at once, reminding her that directness had been the first thing she'd found attractive in him. 'Anna told me what happened yesterday – I'm sorry, Jane.'

'Very little happened,' she said sharply. 'I had a brief blackout – "transient" is the charming medical word for it. Nothing for my colleagues to get dramatic about.'

She wanted to add that, without trying very hard, Anna Soames could dramatize the day's forecast of a shower of rain, but she bit the words back unsaid. Anna was the junior *she* liked least, but what Mark or any other impressionable male probably took into account were her stunning looks and blue-chip family connections in the City.

'You were taken to hospital,' Mark pointed out with his usual persistence, like a terrier at a rabbit hole. 'It was dramatic enough for that.' He seemed to be studying the golden liquid in his glass but she knew that he understood exactly all the distress she was trying to hide. They'd known each other too well for concealment.

'I lost my memory for a few hours,' she said at last. 'It's intact before and afterwards. The doctor called it a mini stroke common in people who drive themselves too hard. I was sent home with a warning to live more sensibly and enough pills to put a horse to sleep. End of story!'

'Not quite,' Mark answered quietly. 'What happens next?'

Jane gave a little shrug. 'I go to see Piers Clifford tomorrow, to clear up some loose ends. Then I'm ordered to take a long holiday.' She stared at him for a moment, thinking how quickly his face had become unfamiliar. Already the knowledge of him that she'd possessed probably belonged to someone else. The thought was hateful enough to prod her into speaking

14

again. 'It had nothing to do with our break-up. What happened was my fault – you don't have to feel to blame.'

But she could see that he found it hard to believe. Perhaps he even *wanted* to feel responsible, they'd been lovers as well as friends, and that must count for something.

'All right,' he admitted with a wry smile. 'I won't feel guilty if you insist.'

Concern for her had brought him there, but now she wanted him to leave. It hurt too much to see him spreadeagled untidily in his armchair, as he always had been at the start of an evening together.

'Thanks for coming, and thank dear Anna, too. I suppose she suggested that I was probably in a sorry mess but, as you can see, I'm not!'

It sounded bitchier than she meant it to, but to have him frown at her was more bearable than seeing pity in his face.

'You're never in a mess,' he agreed with a faint trace of bitterness in his voice. 'Jane Westover is always in control; the elegant, clever mistress of events who can manage very well without the rest of us. No wonder you turned me down when I asked you to marry me.'

'You gave me a choice: I could either have the junior partnership or you. It seemed then – still does – a very unfair ultimatum. I don't remember putting any restrictions on *you*.'

'I know how it seemed to you – it was very clearly explained to me at the time. You should take silk, Jane; you'd make an excellent advocate.' He stood up to go, then nearly destroyed her by unexpectedly leaning forward to kiss her on the mouth. 'Do what the man said,' he suggested gently. 'Take care of yourself.' Then he walked out of the room and a moment later she heard the slam of the door downstairs. At the window she watched him turn his car, very neatly as he always did, and drive away.

This time yesterday she'd been in St Martha's, unaware that between one heartbeat and the next her life, so carefully plotted until then, and so intensely worked for, had been unravelled. Whatever Piers Clifford might be going to pretend tomorrow, she knew that everything had changed. Mark had known it too, but he'd been merciful enough not to point out that she'd have done better to choose him after all.

15

Three

It was hard to walk into the office building the following morning. Beneath the token words of sympathy she sensed curiosity, even a certain malicious glee, and it was hard not to shout aloud at every inquisitive face that she was neither dead nor daft.

Her meeting with the chairman was both easier and more difficult than she expected. Feeling tense and slightly sick as she walked into Piers Clifford's room, it came as a surprise to be ushered to one of the armchairs facing the huge windows with their panoramic, bird's-eye view of London. There was coffee on a low table between the chairs to indicate that this was going to be one of the great man's more genial interviews.

'Now, Jane,' he began pleasantly, 'tell me how you are. I've read the doctor's note, of course.'

'Apart from a small hole in my memory, I'm perfectly all right,' she answered, as calmly as she could. 'I don't think I need be considered unfit for work.'

Clifford pointed at the note lying on his knees. 'That's not what *this* suggests. I'm instructed – the good doctor doesn't mince his words – to give you extended leave of absence, so that's what I propose to do. You can come back in six months' time, ready for the fray again. No special bonuses, I'm afraid – that wouldn't be fair to the others – but your basic salary should allow you to live comfortably.'

'Of course it will,' she agreed at once. 'But six months! Must I really stay away as long as that?'

The wistful question made him smile but he was perceptive and fully aware of the anxiety that prompted it. He was informed of more than she realized, and knew that to the

16

rest of the staff she was an unpopular, clever loner intent on carving out a career for herself. But for the moment he could see that she was shaken, and trying hard to conceal the fact.

'You'll need three months to unwind,' he insisted. 'Then use the next three months to just enjoy yourself.'

'My enjoyment is in working here,' she pointed out, forgetting that the only argument he relished was debate about a point of law.

'Then start enjoying something else – study Russian, cruise the Greek islands, even rent a cottage in the country if you must.'

He offered the final suggestion as a desperate last resort, and her taut face suddenly relaxed into a smile. He registered the alteration with a small shock of surprise. Her usual effect, he'd have said, was to merge into the background. Above-average ability distinguished her, of course, but otherwise she made no demands on anyone's attention. There was nothing wrong with her looks: fine, clear skin, dark hair beautifully cut, excellent figure beneath the City woman's uniform of tailored suit and crisp white shirt. Nothing marked her out, but this, he now realized, was what she'd deliberately intended.

'I suppose I'll find something to do,' she finally agreed, aware that it was time to leave. She stood up to go but suddenly added something else. 'Thank you for not writing me off as too much of a risk in future. I was terribly afraid you would.'

Again she surprised him, being more direct than most of the women he knew, which made him answer honestly as well. 'You're too good to lose – that's why I'm behaving so nicely!' It was said with a wry smile as he got up to shake hands with her, but he grew serious again. 'The truth is that we've worked you too hard, absorbed too much of your life, I'm afraid. *Au revoir*, Jane; we'll see you back here at the beginning of September.'

Dismissed, she went back to her own room, collected papers and files, and then went to see the senior partner who led her team. Two hours later she was on her way home, free for the

17

first time in her life to do exactly as she pleased. It should have felt exhilarating – *would* do, she told herself desperately, as soon as she got used to it. But she'd too suddenly become what she now was: an observer, isolated from all the busy people milling around her. Unlike them she had nothing she need do, nowhere she must go.

It had begun to rain again and she spent the rest of the afternoon by the window in the sitting room, watching raindrops chase each other down the glass. Still hunched in her chair, even when darkness seeped into the room, she pretended that she was occupied with some serious inner discussion. Clifford had suggested studying Russian, but why not Arabic or Chinese? Why not all three, when she had so many empty days and weeks to fill? There were enough Greek islands to keep a conscientious tourist busy, of course – she could see them in her mind's eye, lying like a gorgeous necklace on the blue waters of the Aegean – but Mykonos and Delos weren't places to visit alone. No, she wouldn't go to Greece.

Cramped from sitting still for so long, she had to haul herself out of her chair when someone rang the doorbell downstairs. Her heart leapt at the thought that Mark might have decided to check up on her again, and she was suddenly so sure of finding him on the doorstep that it was a bitter disappointment to find her neighbour there instead.

'You don't have to ask me in,' Amanda said, reading her expression correctly. 'I just wanted to be sure you were all right. Mrs Drew-Brown, dear soul, who has nothing better to do than monitor our every movement, happened to mention that two days running you'd come home in a taxi at lunchtime.'

Jane pulled a rueful grimace. 'Who says you can live and die alone in London with no one being any the wiser! Come on in if you want to – it seems a pity to spit in our well-meaning neighbour's eye.'

Upstairs, she switched on lamps, then turned to look at her visitor. 'If you haven't eaten yet I can offer you soup and bread and cheese.'

'Accepted with pleasure,' Amanda answered promptly.

'My dear sweet man is out this evening, covering a film premiere in Leicester Square. He pretends that a critic's life is a hard way to earn a crust, but I tell him he should try working in the A & E department at St Thomas' instead.' She sat down at the kitchen table with a little sigh of relief and smiled over the glass of wine Jane had poured for her. 'It's good for the blood, they say – and who cares if it isn't, say I!' Then the smile faded from her tired face. 'I'm only chattering in case you think I'm waiting to hear what's wrong. You don't have to talk – we can ignore our watchdog's report.'

'We'll eat first,' Jane suggested. 'Then I'll talk.'

She laid the table and put soup on to heat. The simple food put fresh heart into them both and then, with their glasses refilled, she began to tell her tale. The visit to St Martha's could be briefly described because she remembered that a nurse would be familiar with what had happened to her.

'The doctor didn't quite call me a fool,' she finished up, 'but his message was clear enough – I'd brought the trouble on myself.'

'What happens next?' Amanda asked, just as Mark Rubens had done.

'All the holidays I've not taken for several years have been handed to me like an obligatory dose of medicine – kindly swallow six months' leave at once!' She stared at Amanda across the table. 'Go on – say I'm an ungrateful cow for sounding so resentful about it. The truth is that I feel completely lost. No one should have nothing to do, except perhaps a hermit content to sit on the top of a mountain, contemplating God.'

'You're a bit frightened as well, I expect,' Amanda observed bluntly. 'I hope the doctor insisted that you needn't sit in fear and dread of another T.I.A. – provided you stop pushing yourself to the limit. And the chances of being overtaken by someone else at Clifford's while you're away are surely just as unlikely. So why not relax and enjoy yourself?'

'Piers Clifford's words, almost exactly,' Jane conceded. 'As a matter of fact I *was* considering options when you arrived. No conclusions reached as yet, though.'

19

Then there was silence in the room. She sipped her wine, and resisted a strange desire to weep, while Amanda studied her across the table. It wasn't hard to understand what ailed Jane Westover: a clever, successful and very self-reliant woman had suddenly had her feet knocked from under her. What she needed was the very thing she hadn't had – some loving by people she cared about.

'You must get out of London for a bit,' Amanda decided at last. 'I think Grandfather Amos must be tapping on my shoulder, because I've just remembered your aunt's letter. Jane, why not go and see what *her* problem is?'

'I promised myself I'd never go back,' Jane said slowly. 'Granted my mother abandoned her husband, but they weren't happy together. What she did was probably a blow to Venn family pride, but they were very cruel to her after my father died.' She fell silent for a moment, drawn back to remembering the past.

'It's hard to describe how different our life was there – the farm itself, half submerged in water for weeks during the winter, and at all times remote and isolated beyond anything you can imagine sitting here in the middle of London. After that there was Glastonbury, in its own way equally strange and haunting.'

Amanda looked doubtful. 'Pop-mad teenagers, middle-aged flower power hippies and squalid campsite living – that's what Glastonbury says to me, I'm afraid.'

'That's what it *is* for the week of the summer festival,' Jane agreed. 'But for someone like my father it was nothing short of a holy place, steeped in magic and the legends of the once and future king, who was only sleeping until England should need him again.'

'Dear God – you mean Arthur and Guinevere . . . Camelot and all that stuff?' Amanda asked incredulously.

'There's much more – the Christian bit as well,' Jane said, trying not to smile. 'Joseph of Arimathea with his Holy Thorn, and even Christ himself perhaps, still haunting the ruins of the abbey. There apparently wasn't a single myth about the place that my father, Gideon Venn, didn't believe.'

'I thought you said he was a farmer – a salt of the earth,

feet firmly planted in the soil sort of man,' Amanda argued.

'So he was, outwardly, but according to my mother he was hopelessly unsuccessful, both as a farmer and a husband – a throwback to some long-dead Venn who'd also been a dreamer of dreams and a seer of visions! It must have been a relief to Amos when his younger son, Joshua, had to take over, but that didn't stop the family claiming that my mother had driven Gideon to suicide. She hadn't, of course – the verdict was accidental death by drowning.'

'Well, I can see why you aren't anxious to go back,' Amanda admitted. 'It sounds to me just like Cold Comfort Farm! Still, it would have to be a change from the gentle, sweetly undemanding life of a London corporate lawyer.' She smiled at the idea, then went on more thoughtfully. 'You've got a strange-sounding family, though. I can positively swear I don't know anyone else with kith and kin called Amos, Gideon and Joshua. Even Hannah Venn is a name to conjure with. Promise me you'll at least go and see *her*.'

'I'll think about it,' Jane agreed, 'but I shan't stay long, if I go at all.'

'That means you're hooked on the idea, and I can tell Mrs Drew-Brown that you're visiting your family's estate in the country. That will put our rating up a notch or two. She reckons that her end of the Mews, being nearer to Sloane Square, is nearer social heaven.'

'If I do go, will you let yourself in now and then, just to see if there's mail that looks as though it needs dealing with? I'll keep in touch to let you know where I am.'

Amanda cheerfully agreed, and went home a few minutes later with an unexpectedly warm hug from Jane, and a key to the front door in her pocket.

'You'll be all right,' she was able to predict with convincing firmness, but she walked back to her own home afterwards wondering whether that was true. At the moment Jane Westover put her in mind of a story she'd once read about a performing bear. Let off its chain at last, the poor animal had continued to dance all by itself, not knowing what else to do with the freedom it had suddenly been given.

Four

Two days later Jane locked up the house and set out, with a wave as she went past for Mrs Drew-Brown – invisible but no doubt watching. It was the first of March, she realized, trying to draw hope from the fact; not quite spring officially, but at least in the south-west the primroses would be out, and the blackthorn hedges would be foaming with blossom. The memory of them came back to her unexpectedly, one of many childhood images that she must have buried in some unvisited corner of her mind.

By now the strange landscape she was headed for should have emerged out of its winter floods, but first she'd decided to go to Bath. A visit there was long overdue, and she was curious to know how Aunt Hannah had got hold of her London address. There had been no contact between the Venns and her mother for years, as far as she knew, so surely there must have been something more compelling than a squabble with a neighbour to overcome a quarter of a century's hostility.

Long before she was threading her way through the outskirts of Bath the day's early brightness had gone. The grey drizzle that had set in was depressing, but she was in no hurry to leave the car when she reached her mother's house. Midway round the lovely curve of Royal Crescent, the house was worth looking at – a perfect example of Georgian domestic architecture. But what she was seeing in her mind's eye was the lonely child who'd lived there – herself, even at the age of ten aware that her mother's remarriage had changed everything.

A sibling, born a year later, had seemed a wondrous gift – an exquisite doll-like creature that was far better than any doll, because she was alive and real. But the happiness didn't last.

By the time Jill Westover was old enough to see her elder sister as a competitor for their parents' attention, there was only mutual dislike, for which Jane got all the blame. Now, even with James Westover dead at last, there was no pleasure in going back to see her mother. Jill was still the obstacle – sweetly inimical and determined to insist that, despite being given the name of Westover, her half-sister didn't really belong there.

At last she got out of the car and lifted the brass dolphin knocker on the front door. It was opened by her mother, who looked astonished and then faintly pleased.

'Jane, my dear – come in! Did we know you were coming down? I don't think so, but anyway it's a lovely surprise.' She led the way upstairs to the drawing room on the first floor, still talking over her shoulder. 'Naughty of you, though, not to telephone; I'm very often out.'

'If so, I was going to find a B & B,' Jane replied. 'I still can if this isn't a convenient call.'

'Don't be silly; of course you must stay here.' Elizabeth Westover's still-beautiful blue eyes examined her elder daughter's face for a moment. 'Darling, you don't look awfully well – I expect you've been working too hard.'

On the way down Jane had supposed that she would mention casually what had taken her to St. Martha's. It might even be possible to confess that the little episode had left her vulnerable and frightened. But with the perfect opening in front of her, she couldn't take it after all.

'It was a tiring drive this morning,' she suggested instead. 'Heavy traffic all the way and poor visibility. You look fine, though.'

She wanted to steer the conversation away from herself, but what she'd just said also had the merit of being true. Age seemed to make no impression on her mother's beauty. Flawless bone structure would probably have remained in any case, but Elizabeth had taken care of her looks as well – her hair and skin could have proudly belonged to a much younger woman.

She made up the fire, and then sat down facing her daughter. 'Now, what's brought you to Bath in this beastly

weather when you don't normally seem eager to come at all?' Then, before Jane could speak, she answered the question herself. 'It couldn't have anything to do with Hannah Venn, could it? Of all extraordinary things, I had a visit from her some weeks ago. We hadn't spoken to each other for years, and there she suddenly was on the doorstep, asking for your address.'

'She wrote,' Jane admitted with a faint smile. 'Just the sort of letter you'd expect from a retired schoolteacher! A local problem has cropped up which she thinks I might be able to handle. I happened to have some leave due, so I came; but probably curiosity more than anything else is taking me to Cossenford tomorrow.'

Elizabeth's skilfully darkened eyebrows drew together in a frown. 'You stay away forever, it seems, then come for one night. It's not very kind, you know.'

The reprimand was expected but not, Jane thought, sincere. It provoked her to answer by implication what her mother hadn't said. 'Jill's still living with you, I assume?'

'She's in Bristol, studying, of course, but comes home at weekends. The house seems dead without her.' There was no response to this, and Elizabeth was provoked in turn. 'They're *very* pleased with her at the Old Vic School. She's their star pupil – a natural actress in the making.'

Still Jane said nothing, which took considerable self-control, but even that was wrong – or perhaps her expression gave away her feelings too clearly.

'Can't you try to be more generous? You are sisters after all,' Elizabeth reminded her sharply. 'Her talents may be different from yours, but that's no reason to despise them.'

It was worse than irritating to still be the one always in the wrong, and anger welling up suddenly drove Jane to brutal frankness. 'We have *you* in common, nothing else. As far as my sister is concerned, I'm what I've always been – an interloper who doesn't belong here – and if I stay away it's because that's what Jill has always made clear.'

She waited for her mother to suggest that a B & B might be needed after all, but, struggling with herself, Elizabeth managed to speak quietly. 'The original mistake was mine; I

24

should have let you keep your father's name. You *are* a Venn; Jill's right about that. But she hasn't ever meant to hurt you – you've imagined ill feeling.'

Jane's mouth sketched a wry smile. 'Shall I remind you of the day I came proudly home from school with my drawing of Bath Abbey? It was good – even the art mistress said so – and I hoped you'd want to keep it, frame it maybe, but Jill made a grab at it and tore it into shreds. My stepfather laughed, which I might have expected, but all *you* said was "well, dear, now you must try again". Did I imagine any of that?'

A tinge of colour disturbed Elizabeth's delicate make-up. 'Perhaps not, but remember that Jill was a child at the time; how could she know that the drawing was precious to you?'

It was a pointless argument, Jane realized; truth, like beauty, was always in the eye of the beholder. She brushed the past away with a small, defeated gesture and chose to talk of something else. 'Tell me about Aunt Hannah – did you even recognize her?'

'Of course. Women with her sort of plainness change very little as they grow older; it's an advantage the poor things deserve, I think.'

Jane smiled wholeheartedly for the first time at a comment that was typical of a woman sure of her own beauty. 'All I remember of the farm is Grandfather Amos addressing me as "child" in a voice I mistook for thunder, and the river spreading like silver over the fields below the house. It was frightening, but beautiful at the same time.'

'What about your father – no memory of him?' Elizabeth asked, suddenly curious to know what she would say.

Jane shook her head. 'Only the vague recollection of a gentle, quiet man who smiled at me without seeming to know who I was.'

'That was Gideon,' her mother agreed drily. 'Very sweet, but lost in a world of his own most of the time. For him Arthur and his knights still inhabited the Isle of the Blessed at Avalon: I think he came to believe that he was one of them, searching for the Holy Grail.'

She inspected her daughter's face for a moment, trying to

identify a change in this girl she had never properly understood. 'Are *you* looking for something, too?' she suddenly asked. 'What is different about you – a new man, perhaps? No, I don't think so; you wouldn't have left him in London to come and waste your time with Hannah.'

'There's no man at all,' Jane admitted. 'I couldn't face being absorbed into a close-knit Jewish family instead of running my own life, so Mark and I agreed to part company.' Then, aware that she hadn't yet answered her mother's question, she tried again. 'I'm supposed to be taking a rest, but not liking the idea very much. It just feels strange to be at a loose end.'

Tactful for once, Elizabeth accepted the explanation. The split with the man called Mark had probably been more unsettling than she would want to admit. It was tempting to return to the subject, but her daughter's white, tired face didn't invite probing.

'If you've been told to rest, I assume you need it,' Elizabeth pointed out instead. 'The bed in your old room is made up; why not go and sleep until suppertime?'

Jane walked out of the room, not sorry for the respite from a conversation that was full of hidden pitfalls. She heard a telephone ringing somewhere in the house as she closed her bedroom door, then swallowed two pills to ward off a hovering headache, and lay down on the bed with a small sigh of relief.

An hour later, still in the clothes she'd set out in but showered and tidy again, she went downstairs. The sound of voices came from the kitchen at the back of the house but, feeling hungry for the first time in days, she was more aware of the good smell of food wafting along the hall. It suddenly seemed possible that she and her mother might enjoy spending an evening together.

The drawing-room door was ajar and, as she pushed it open and went in, a large young man turned to look at her. His smile faded with the surprise of being confronted by a total stranger.

'Not a burglar, I assume,' Jane suggested, the first to recover herself. 'No mask, or swag bag.'

'Charles Rutherford,' he said, coming towards her and beginning to smile again. 'I'm sorry – we've arrived rather unexpectedly, Jilly and I. Mrs Westover hasn't had time to mention that she already had a guest.'

'I'm not quite a—' Jane was trying to explain when her sister's unmistakeable laugh sounded outside the door, and a moment later she and Elizabeth walked in. Incapable of not taking charge of any scene, she at once linked arms with her mother and the young man, and stood smiling at her sister.

'Dear Jane – what a surprise! Mama's just been telling me that you were here. She expected *us* tomorrow, but I must have heard a little voice telling me to come this evening. Charlie, this is my sister, Jane, by the way. She normally hangs out in London, of course; we don't see her in the backwoods of the provinces very often.'

'Jane's a lawyer – very high-powered,' Elizabeth said hurriedly, 'so of course she lives in London.'

Aware of some prickle of tension in the air, Charles smiled as if he hadn't noticed it was there. 'Well, I'm just a student thesp like Jilly, and not at all high-powered, I'm afraid. One dry-up and three fluffed lines in today's rehearsal scarcely suggest a new Olivier in the making!'

'Size might help,' Jane suggested cheerfully, having to glance up at him. 'At least you *look* noble enough for Mark Antony or Henry V at Agincourt!'

'You probably aren't aware that his father can help even more,' Jill pointed out quickly. 'The rest of us try to ignore the fact, but it doesn't hurt to be the son of a famous theatre director.'

She smiled at him as she spoke, the confident, bewitching smile of a girl who knew that its effect would never fail her. She was the completely finished article, Jane had to admit – small but perfectly proportioned, seductively husky of voice, and with all her mother's delicate beauty to conceal the iron will inherited from James Westover. She might look harmless, but God help any other ambitious actress who got in her way.

At a sign from Elizabeth, Charlie had begun to pour sherry – a pre-dinner ritual that he seemed very familiar with. It suggested to Jane, watching the little scene, that her sister by

27

no means 'ignored' his theatrical connections; 'Jilly' would have picked him out from the rest of the student herd deliberately. A nice, well-mannered admirer wasn't to be sneezed at anyway in this day and age, but if he could be useful as well she would have made sure that no other aspiring actress ever got hold of him.

The thought – not only ungenerous but downright spiteful, her mother would certainly have said – brought her up short. She even resented the girl for coming home unexpectedly just when there'd been a chance to talk openly at last with her mother. What if simple green-eyed jealousy *had* always been at the root of the problem between them?

When Elizabeth left the room to attend to matters in the kitchen, Jane turned towards her sister; generosity's moment was at hand.

'Mama says you're doing very well at the Old Vic School – a star pupil, in fact. Congratulations, Jill.'

She was offered an ironical bow in return. 'How nice – a pat on the head from big sister! At almost twenty, you can call me a student, if you like, but *not* a pupil, please.' Then she turned to smile at Charles Rutherford. 'Jane really *is* one of those high-flying City women that you read about – so very clever, and weighed down with huge responsibilities. It makes what we do seem terribly frivolous and unworthwhile, don't you think?'

The question sounded innocently sincere. Charlie obviously thought it was because he took it at face value and shook his head. 'We're trying to do different things, that's all. Your sister doesn't despise us because we're entertainers instead of actuaries or brain surgeons – do you, Jane?'

His charming smile invited her to agree but it was Jill who got in first. 'Not just *entertainers*, Charlie – we're the stuff that dreams and celebrities are made of. I'm afraid that can't be said of City types forever cutting deals and fixing takeovers.'

'Quite true,' Jane agreed quietly, tired of a conversation that, pointless as it was, nevertheless had an edge to it. 'We corporate lawyers are a humdrum, boring lot, and some of us are probably dishonest, too, as you suggest.'

28

It was a relief to have Elizabeth reappear and shepherd them into the dining room. From then on Jane took little part in the conversation, knowing that if she seemed to be occupying her mother's attention or, worse, successfully amusing Charlie, Jill's adder tongue would flick out with a little sting not even noticeable to them. Generosity was slain before it even had a chance to raise its head, and all she wanted was for the evening to end. Come the morning she would drive away and probably never come back.

By the time she left after breakfast the next day only Elizabeth was up, a fact that seemed to need some excuse.

'They have to work so hard,' she explained, 'it's good for them to relax when they're here.' She waited for a reply that didn't come, and then made a small, helpless gesture. 'You think I favour Jill, take her side even when she's wrong. Remember if you can, Jane, that her father was very good to me – apart from you, everything I have came from him. I should love Jill for *his* sake even if she weren't the enchanting child she is.'

'Love her as much as you like,' Jane managed to say after a struggle with herself. 'But please stop calling her a child. That wouldn't be true even if she weren't already sleeping with Charles Rutherford, which I assume she is.' It was time to leave, before more came spilling out than she intended. But her mother's troubled face made her add something else more gently. 'I promise you there'll never be any need to worry about Jill – she's destined for success.'

'But do I have to worry about you?' Elizabeth asked unexpectedly. 'Have you really been unwell?'

Jane shook her head and achieved a reassuring smile. 'I had what is called a transient ischaemic attack – a temporary blip. I'm all right now, unless Aunt Hannah proves more than I can cope with!' Then she quickly kissed her mother's cheek and walked out to the car.

Relief washed over her on leaving the house that still seemed to belong to James Westover, but there was a core of sadness underneath as well. Whatever she'd hoped for from the visit hadn't happened; nothing had changed, and she could be sure now that it never would.

Five

From Bath the road she took climbed over the Mendips, slid down into the black-peat marshlands of the Brue Valley, and then rose again up the smaller, wooded slopes of the Polden Hills. Mindful of the doctor at St Martha's who'd instructed her to live sensibly, she stopped at a pub on the way to Cossenford and ate a sandwich. The truth was, though, as she very well knew, that she was dawdling, putting off the final debacle of a journey that she should never have started.

Cossenford, when she drove into it early in the afternoon, was unfamiliar. She had no recollection of going there in the years she'd lived not far away at Rushey Farm, and its beauty took her completely by surprise. There were probably the usual ugly additions to the fringes of the small town, but nothing could spoil the ancient heart of it.

Built of the local blue lias limestone, the buildings clustered round the central square made a perfect, harmonious group. The grey stone might have seemed depressingly cold, but, ornamented with white paintwork on doors and windows, and softened by the creepers that swarmed up every wall, the effect was peaceful and serenely sure of itself.

She got out of the car and walked towards the church. In front of it, on a wide pavement leading to the churchyard was Cossenford's memorial to its dead from two world wars. The stone figure of a soldier, helmeted and putteed, was dignified and very touching. The roll-call of names, listed alphabetically, almost ended with two Venns, William and Walter, both of them the brothers of her grandfather, Amos. Other families, it seemed, had suffered even more cruelly, with some of the distinctive Somerset names occurring again and again.

Across the neatly kept graveyard the door of the church,

set at the foot of the octagonal-shaped tower, stood open and Jane surprised herself by walking in. A practising Christian had to do more than make an occasional Christmas or Easter attendance. She'd paid these rare visits in the past in the subconscious hope of finding something – she didn't know quite what – but there had been no blinding light, and certainly no discovery of her own Holy Grail. Now, she tended to avoid the inside of churches; it was enough to stand outside and accept that other men's faith had been strong enough to raise these great monuments to the god they believed in.

The church was empty but it felt welcoming. A gleam of late-afternoon sunshine threw down shafts of colour from the stained glass behind the altar, and white chrysanthemums amassed on the font scented the dry air. Staring up at the wooden roof of the nave, intricately carved and presided over by an angel in the middle of every cross beam, she discovered that she wasn't alone after all. Someone invisible from where she stood was picking out a note on the organ. Then suddenly the patient repetitions ceased and the church was flooded instead with glorious music.

She sat with closed eyes for as long as it lasted, too transfixed by the sound to register the quality of the organist, only aware that a miserable day had been redeemed by these few minutes of pure joy. But now it was time to start thinking again. Bone-tired as she felt, the temptation was very great to simply head back to her own home.

'Are you tired, perhaps unwell . . . or just considering that not very beautiful window above the altar?'

The pleasant voice, with a faint foreign intonation, brought her wide awake. A man – the organist most probably – had come to stand beside her, but something half careless in the way he asked his question seemed to say that he wasn't much interested in how she was going to answer. She decided to ask a question of her own instead.

'Was it you just now, playing the Bach Chorale?'

He gave a little bow that confirmed her impression of his foreignness. 'It was I,' he agreed, with the care for grammar that again marked him out as . . . probably German, she decided. His hair was fair, but not Nordic-blond, and the fine

regularity of his features reminded her of other Germans she had met. The memory of the war memorial outside the church came into her mind but, whatever the Old Testament said, she refused to believe that the sins of the fathers should be visited on their children, and their children's children. This man, probably half a dozen years older than herself, belonged to a generation still unborn when Nazi Germany was setting fire to Europe.

'I was listening, not admiring the window – although I can't see anything wrong with it,' she said firmly.

'None of us is perfect,' he acknowledged, 'and at least you *did* enjoy the Chorale! That makes you a rare bird here. Andrew Lloyd Webber represents the high-water mark in Cossenford's musical tastes.'

At any other time she might have confessed to avoiding Lloyd Webber's musicals herself, but now she was perversely irritated into sticking up for them. 'He composes for today's theatre, not for the court of some eighteenth-century German princeling. Why sneer because he gives a lot of people pleasure?'

'Why indeed! I shall blame my sourness on the weeks of horrible weather we've been living through – isn't that what English people do?'

'We refer to it a good deal,' she had to admit, answering his sudden charming smile with a smile of her own. 'You aren't English, I take it.' It seemed an odd conversation to be having with a chance-met stranger, but her feeling was that he enjoyed offbeat encounters, and was practised in the art of promoting himself to maximum effect.

'I'm half-English, officially,' he explained, 'because I have an English mother, but three-quarters German by inclination! And now you'd like to ask what such a hybrid creature is doing in the rural depths of Somerset?' She nodded and his glimmering smile anticipated her reaction. 'I live here.'

'Why,' she couldn't help asking, 'if your German inclinations are so strong?'

'Well, it's a long family story that I won't bore you with. But a couple of years ago the Manor House here came on the market and I couldn't resist buying something so perfect. I

shan't stay forever, but at the moment I'm rather enjoying the life of an English country gentleman.'

'And acting as Cossenford's organist at the same time?'

'No, I'm not that; the man whose job it is never tunes the organ properly, and I doubt if *he* even hears what is wrong, much less the rest of the parishioners. But he allows me to play it and even to tinker with it when I can find someone to help me.'

Jane stood up quickly, suspecting that she was about to be enrolled as organ-tuning assistant. She intended to say goodbye and walk away but he retained his grip for a moment on the hand she held out. 'You don't live here, I think – I should have remembered seeing you around.'

She shook her head, surprised to realize how completely she'd been sidetracked from her purpose in being there. 'I was born not far away, but I live in London now. I'm here to visit an aunt. Perhaps you know her – Hannah Venn?'

A smile of pure amusement lit his face, making him seem younger and much less alien. 'Oh yes, I know Miss Venn. I'm even acquainted with her brother, Joshua. It's a small world down here, but I expect you've been away long enough to have forgotten that.'

It was all he seemed inclined to say. She could see that even a conventional hope of meeting her again in this small world wouldn't be forthcoming, because he didn't trouble himself with meaningless courtesies.

'Thank you again for the music,' she said briefly, and walked out of the church. But her hand retained the memory of his hand, and she would have liked to see him again, if only to make up her mind about him – he was a man who made an impression, but it was a toss-up whether like or dislike would win out in the end.

With no idea in which direction to go, she took the first turning out of the square and found herself in the very spot she was looking for: Silver Street. It seemed an apt name in this little citadel of blue-grey stone, which probably did look silvery under the shine of frequent rain. She drove along slowly, checking names, and found Maundy Cottage at the far end of the row. It was a charming small house, unexpectedly

so, because with vague memories of Rushey Farm in her mind, she'd anticipated bleakness here too, not a sparkling white front door and new spring greenery beginning to veil the stone walls. On the upper floor there was even a thatched roof, curved down over the dormer windows like bristly but engaging eyebrows. It made her smile to look at them.

It was a happy start to her visit, but when the door opened and Hannah Venn stood there looking at her, gaiety disappeared.

'You're Jane,' her aunt said grimly after a moment's inspection. 'You don't take after your mother, but you're not much of a Venn, either.'

'However I look, are you going to invite me in?' Jane enquired. 'I'm here because you asked me to come.' Even if she hadn't favoured directness as a general rule, it seemed necessary in dealing with this angular, intimidating woman.

Apparently not put out, Hannah responded in kind. 'I've got to get over the surprise of seeing you – you took your time about answering my letter.' Then she peered shortsightedly at the ground, looking for something. 'No luggage?'

'It's in the car. I'll find a B & B somewhere nearby presently.'

This, it seemed, *did* upset her aunt, who now almost hauled her across the doorstep. 'You'll stay here, I reckon, not in someone else's house. Leastways, I'll show you to the spare room and you'll have to say if it isn't grand enough. Your mother kept telling me how successful you are in London.'

'It's the sort of things mothers do say,' Jane pointed out. 'But your house is very charming, and I should like to stay here.' She waited, hoping that this change of tactic might take the wind out of her aunt's sails: it seemed downright silly to go on squaring up to each other like contending boxers.

Hannah stared at her for a moment, then gave a little sigh. 'That's what your father always did when I got cross with him. He used to say the soft answer turned away wrath; then he'd smile his sweet smile, and of course he was forgiven.'

'Were you often cross with him?' Jane enquired. 'I expect you realize that I scarcely remember him.'

Hannah's plain, square face looked suddenly sad as she was

asked to think about the past. 'Gideon was a year or two older than me, but he was a dreamer, always forgetting any task that had to be done. Father would shout at him but it made not a scrap of difference – he had other things to think about.'

Limping painfully, Jane noticed, her aunt led the way into a parlour on one side of the passage that ran through the middle of the house. It was as different as any room could be from her mother's elegant drawing room in Bath, but it wore its difference comfortably. The thick walls and wide stone hearth were just as the builder had left them a couple of hundred years ago. Plush armchairs had faded to a soft old-rose, and a sprinkling of watercolours and ornaments testified to Hannah's good taste in such things.

She noticed her niece's glance round the room and waited for this pale-faced, sophisticated stranger either to patronise her or to go to the trouble of finding something tactful to say.

What Jane actually said was, 'I think you must like living here. I know I should if it belonged to me.'

Nonplussed because it sounded sincere, Hannah still reckoned they had a long way to go before they trusted one another. 'Suits me very well,' she agreed briefly. 'I moved out of the farm when Joshua got married. It was time to leave then; I wasn't needed there any more. I was already teaching in Cossenford, so this is where I settled.' She threw a fresh log on the fire, gave it a decisive poke, and when it was burning nicely, turned round to stare at her niece again.

'We're kin, you and I, but we don't know each other. It seems all wrong.'

'And for that you blame my mother,' Jane said, putting into words what she knew Hannah had meant. 'It takes two to make an unhappy marriage – and she was also running away from the farm and the rest of your formidable family.'

For the first time a faint smile lifted the corners of Hannah's mouth. 'Spoken like a Venn!' she said, almost approvingly. 'No point in wrapping things up in fine linen.' Her lined face quickly frowned again. 'My father and Joshua convinced themselves that Gideon chose to do away with himself after Elizabeth took you away. I never did quite believe that – he drowned accidentally on a very wild night – but your mother

35

certainly broke his heart. I suppose you reckon she did well for herself marrying James Westover afterwards.'

'She did well for *me*,' Jane pointed out sharply. 'My stepfather's money allowed me to go to Cambridge; I'd never have got there otherwise.' Hannah would probably have liked to hear that James Westover had been only too pleased to keep his awkward stepdaughter away from Bath, but she couldn't bring herself to say it, or to talk about her hostile half-sister. It was a relief when Hannah suddenly abandoned the subject of the past.

'I expect you're used to fancy food late at night. I'm not. But you're welcome to share the shepherd's pie I've got in the oven.'

'It sounds good. I don't enjoy fancy food, and I'm quite used to getting home too late to eat at all,' Jane pointed out.

'So that's why you look all skin and bone, and tired to death as well! What's the point of living like that? My family worked hard enough on the farm – had to, so as not to go hungry, but it was *real* work, with more than just money to show for it at the end.'

'What I do is real enough,' Jane insisted, stung by the scorn in her aunt's voice. 'It earns me a large salary, but that isn't the attraction – I like pitting my skill against other people's. It's tiring, nerve-racking at times, but very exciting. I've been away from it for a few days and already I'm missing it.'

Hannah shook her head, not pretending to understand. 'Go and bring your suitcase in. The spare room's the door on the right at the top of the stairs. You can come down when you're ready; I don't like being helped.'

'Of course not,' Jane agreed calmly. 'You're more than twice my age, and probably in a good deal of pain from rheumatism or arthritis, but you aren't about to let me lift a saucepan.' Then, instead of arguing with her aunt – something she thought Hannah expected – she walked out of the room.

An hour later they were facing each other across the dining-room table, eating a simple but delicious supper. There had still been no mention of the pressing problem that Hannah had written about, and Jane had decided not to broach it

herself, but *some* conversation was needed, and she cast about for a subject that didn't bristle with family difficulties.

'When I drove into Cossenford I stopped first in the square,' she explained. 'The church was open, so I went in. Someone was playing the organ, and when I mentioned your name he said he knew you and Uncle Joshua.'

'You mean Andrew Yeo, I suppose; he tries, poor man, but he makes a better chemist than he does church organist,' Hannah said drily.

'This man wasn't the organist, and he played beautifully,' Jane insisted. 'He didn't tell me his name but he lives at the Manor House.'

She didn't think she imagined the chill that suddenly descended on the room. Her aunt's manner hadn't so far approached anything that could be described as cordial, but her first hostility had given way to a kind of acceptance. Now, even her thick grey eyebrows seemed stiff with disapproval. The conversation could have been steered on to an easier tack, but Jane refused to do it. She'd seen enough of Hannah Venn to know that the only way to deal with her was head-on, even at the cost of some bruising on both sides.

'You don't like the man I met,' she suggested. 'Why? Because he's half-German and there are two Venn names on the war memorial?'

'Two of our uncles – Walter was barely nineteen when he was killed – and our Aunt Emily's fiancé. Are you going to tell me we should love the Germans?'

'No, but why hate a man who wasn't even born when the Second World War started? I found him pleasant enough – in fact, very easy to talk to.'

There was no reply for so long that Jane thought she might have managed to silence her formidable aunt at last. But Hannah was only deciding what she would say.

'It's too long a story to start now, because I get tired and go to bed early. But I'll tell you this to be going on with. The man you met is Max Hasler, and by marriage – not blood, God be praised – the Venns are unfortunately related to him, in a very distant way. We never approved of his mother's family but it was easy to have nothing to do with them. With

her son it's different – he lives almost on my doorstep, and *he*'s the problem I wrote to you about.'

Hannah got up from the table, supporting herself against it with misshapen, arthritic hands that trembled slightly. 'If you like Max Hasler you're no use to me. Stay here if you want to, but I'll find someone else to help.'

She was maddeningly bigoted and ungracious, but Hannah Venn came from a long line of Levels people accustomed to hardship and not giving in; Jane recognized the fact and couldn't help but find something gallant in her stubbornness.

'I'll stay for a few days,' she promised gently, 'and we'll talk in the morning about whether I can help you or not.' A faint smile touched her mouth. 'Am I allowed to do the washing-up?'

'It can be your evening entertainment,' Hannah suggested with a perfectly straight face. 'I've never bothered with a tele-vision-set.' And with that she limped out of the room.

Jane stayed where she was, not inclined to make a dash for the kitchen sink. Her highly motivated life in London, and her little house there, had never seemed more precious than they did now. Every instinct she possessed warned her not to get embroiled with her father's family and a stormy past that seemed to involve the Venns even now in bitter vendettas. She was committed to staying for a day or two, but she would leave the first moment she could, and if the Fates were kind she need never come to Somerset again.

Six

A t least the following morning dawned fine. Jane went downstairs hoping to find the kitchen empty, but Hannah was already there, stirring a saucepan on the stove. Her greeting and a nod towards the door were unexpected.

'Go outside and sniff the air – spring's coming.'

Jane accepted the instruction – given regardless of the weather, she felt sure – but had to admit a moment later that Hannah's garden was worth visiting. Just as in Shakespeare's magic phrase, her daffodils *did* 'take the winds of March with beauty'. It was old-fashioned, of course; a muddle, in fact, compared with her own expensive, minimalist layout in London of pool, raked gravel, and artificially stunted trees in tubs. But the serenity and meditative calm she was supposed to have achieved in it had so far eluded her. Now, looking round the lovely confusion of Hannah's creating, she couldn't help wondering whether ignorance had led her to back the wrong horticultural horse after all.

She went indoors again to find her aunt pouring the contents of the saucepan into bowls – oh God, it looked like porridge, thick and rich with cream.

'You need fattening up,' Hannah said at once. 'If a cup of black coffee is your usual breakfast, you'll have to wait for it until you get back to London.'

Jane sat down at the table, strongly tempted to point out that a hostess's duty was to give her guests whatever *they* desired, not to push unwanted porridge down their throats. But her aunt's deadpan face prevented her. A suspicion was growing that Hannah was enjoying herself, and that it amused her to test the patience, or perhaps the humour, of a niece she'd had no chance of getting to know.

So Jane swallowed a spoonful of her aunt's concoction instead, pronounced it delicious, and tried not to smile at Hannah's baffled expression. Then she spoke again, seriously. 'Your garden is lovely, but isn't it more than you can manage now? I expect I'll be told that it grows without any help from you, but I think there's more to it than nature's bounty, or God's'

'Same thing,' said Hannah, quick to put a city-dwelling sophisticate in her place. But in a tactic Jane was beginning to recognize she suddenly climbed off her high horse and confessed to the truth. 'I can't do it now myself, but Rufus comes to give me a hand.'

If she wanted to be asked who Rufus was, she was disappointed. Jane reckoned it was time to talk about Hannah's 'problem'.

'Tell me first of all how the Venns and Max Hasler come to be related,' she suggested firmly.

'It's complicated, so pay attention, please.' The schoolroom phrase echoed in the room while Hannah decided where to start. 'You saw the name of William Venn, my father's eldest brother, on the war memorial. His childless widow, another Jane, was the daughter of a farmer across the hills in the Brue Valley. He died almost at the time William was killed, and Jane inherited his farm, but instead of staying at Rushey with us she quite soon married again.'

'That wasn't unreasonable,' Jane objected. 'Presumably she was still a young woman.'

'Well, losing her land was bad enough, but losing it to Horace Winters – a man my father couldn't stomach at any price – added insult to injury.' Hannah stared at her niece for a moment. 'It won't make much sense to you, but Levels people are different, even from the rest of Somerset; outsiders never know what to make of them at all.'

'I'm doing my best – go on with the story, please.'

'Well, Jane and Horace had two children, James and Mary. Mary disgraced herself in our view by marrying a German, and Max Hasler is their son.'

Jane was silent for a moment, thinking about the alien 'hybrid', as he'd called himself, that she'd met in the church.

'He owns the Manor House here,' she said at last. 'Was *his* father very rich? I've had the impression all these years that farming on the Levels was pretty well subsistence living, so it surely wasn't Mary's father who handed down a small fortune?'

'No, but Horace was doing nicely by the time he died, and his son, James – Mary's brother – *is* rich.'

'Are you going to tell me how? Did they come across a seam of gold in the Brue Valley?' Jane asked incredulously.

'Black gold! They dug up peat – tons of it – and still do.' Hannah poured herself more tea, took a reviving sip, and went on with the tale.

'There on one side of the hills was my father, working all hours to keep us fed, farming in the hard, traditional way he believed was right – dairying and fattening beef cattle. Meanwhile across the Poldens men like Horace and James Winters drained their fields, set about excavating the peat, and made themselves a fortune. It didn't matter to them that what they had left at the end was worthless land and a ruined habitat for all the creatures and plants that had always lived there.'

'So it wasn't just a matter of money,' Jane said slowly.

'No; of course money came into it, but it was a question of water more than anything else. That's what everything on the Levels comes down to. Traditional farmers *want* floods – the rivers bring down the silt that makes good hay crops and rich pasture. The Winters of this world want more and more of the meadows artificially drained, either so that they can dig out the peat or else pretend that what they've got is good arable land – it isn't!'

Jane thought her aunt had been right to say that it was complicated. There were more questions she must ask in time, but there was one that couldn't wait.

'What brought Max Hasler here? I'll swear he isn't a farmer.'

'Peat used to be dug out by hand – back-breaking, slow work – but Max's father, Ernst Hasler, has a factory in Germany making agricultural machinery. His equipment meant the difference between a modest living and wealth. Max is an engineer – he came with the machines.'

41

'But that isn't why *you* object to him,' Jane hazarded, wondering what the truth really was. Did her aunt's dislike of all things German extend to the music of J.S. Bach that Max Hasler liked to play? Was every fibre of her stubborn Levels being outraged by an incomer, and a half-foreign one at that, lording it over them at the Manor House?

'He's trying to buy the Baptist chapel and graveyard,' Hannah explained, with such unexpected and deadly seriousness that an answering smile was out of the question. Jane thought of suggesting that at least Max Hasler shared out his attentions among the Christian denominations, but in the end said nothing at all. Her aunt hadn't reached the end of the story.

'The chapel's been shut for years, but the elders couldn't decide whether to sell it or not. Now they have, and Max Hasler knows that.'

'He wants to build a factory in the middle of Cossenford? Dear aunt, stop worrying – he'd never get planning permission.'

'No, but he might get it to build expensive new houses for people who think they'd like a weekend home in the country,' Hannah answered tragically. 'We've been slowly raising money for years to convert the chapel into a local museum, and turn the graveyard into a public garden. The plans are all ready – drawn up free of charge for us by a retired architect.'

It *was* a real problem after all, Jane realized; complicated in itself, but made much worse by bitter family grudges and vendettas.

'Does he know what you want?' she asked at last.

'We told him at the last Town Council meeting. He said, very politely of course, that we were a little bunch of aged has-beens, worshipping the past and setting our poor old faces against progress and the march of time!'

Jane thought she could almost hear him saying it, his tone nicely pitched between amused pity for the Ancient of Days he was up against and a quiet determination to win in the end.

'We're going to fight, of course,' Hannah finished up, 'but he can afford fancy lawyers and we can't. That's why I wrote

to you. But if you don't want to help we'll manage on our own.'

Jane took a deep breath and said, 'Listen, please. Lawyers, fancy or otherwise, are competent at different things. I'm a corporate lawyer, and I've no idea of what's involved in fighting a case of this sort; all I'm certain of is that it could drag on for months. But I don't belong here – my life is in London, and I'd like to get back to it as soon as I can. I think you *should* find someone else to help you, but recognize before you start just what you've got to beat – and that includes a government policy that seems to think we need houses more than we need anything else.'

Hannah was silent for a moment and her expressionless face gave no clue to what she was thinking.

'Joshua was partly right,' she said at last. 'But he was wrong at least to reckon that you wouldn't come at all. I have the feeling that you're here for a reason of your own – perhaps because you needed a hiding place; that's what animals have the sense to look for when they've been hurt. If that *is* how things are, stay for as long as you want to – we needn't talk about Max Hasler again.' Something that might have been a smile touched her long mouth for a moment. 'You can tidy up here – I've got things to do in the town.'

A few moments later the front door closed behind her, and Jane was left alone. The Baptist chapel tussle was in itself enough to think about, but it seemed more important still to mull over what her aunt had just said. With almost nothing to go on, Hannah had sensed that some hurt had been sustained, and help was needed. Her kindness wasn't going to be repaid, but it would be offered anyway – that, it seemed, was the country way of doing things.

Immediately, though, there was the 'tidying up' to be tackled. The breakfast dishes were washed and draining in the rack when Jane turned back to the sink for a moment and then took a more careful look through the window. No, she hadn't imagined it – there *was* a large dog in the garden, being chased by a small boy.

She flung open the kitchen door, took a path that met the

one the invaders were on, and stopped abruptly as the dog caught sight of her. She was accustomed to the only animal to be seen in Hay's Mews – Mrs Drew-Brown's minuscule Yorkshire terrier – but now something the size of a mastiff seemed to be bearing down on her. But its large tail was wagging and when she put out her hand the creature licked it as if an old friend had suddenly been delightfully rediscovered.

'Your dog?' she enquired of the child who'd now caught them up.

'Of course he is.' The boy sounded surprised that she didn't know what everyone else knew. 'He's called Ben, in case you don't know that either.'

'Well now, let me tell *you* something,' said Jane. 'This is a private garden, and the pair of you are trespassing. You shouldn't be here – and how did you get in anyway?'

'Through the gate at the bottom – it's the way we always come.' On the point of assuring this strange female that Ben understood about keeping to the paths, he suddenly had to yell at the dog instead, and it emerged backwards from a battered clump of forsythia with a scattering of golden petals over its black coat.

'He's still only a puppy,' his owner said quickly. 'You can't expect him to learn everything at once.'

It took considerable aplomb, she thought, trying not to smile, to claim puppyhood for an animal that already stood three feet high. Nevertheless, this thin, red-headed child must be made to learn that Hannah's garden wasn't his personal playground.

About to launch into an improving homily, she saw the boy's face suddenly light up, and turned to see what he was looking at. A large, bearded man, with hair that had faded a little with age but must once have been the same fierce colour as the child's, was also approaching via the garden gate – Hannah's jobbing gardener, no doubt; at least the right man to repair whatever ravages Ben inflicted.

'Good morning,' she said coolly. 'If you're in the habit of bringing the dog to work, perhaps he should be kept on a lead in here.'

He gave no sign of having even heard this suggestion; instead he was inspecting her with all the care of a prospective buyer considering a horse's points.

'You'll be Hannah's niece, I expect. I met her just now in the square and she said you'd be here.'

He spoke, surprisingly, with the voice of an educated man, but the rising inflection that turned every statement into a question marked him as someone born and bred with the everyday speech of Somerset.

'I'm Jane Westover,' she agreed, 'and I suppose you're Rufus, the gardener my aunt mentioned.'

Before answering, he smiled at the child. 'That's me, and this is my son, Tom – Thomas when he's being chastised for something.'

Assuming his father's arrival absolved him from further social duties, Tom darted away with the Labrador at his heels.

'I'm afraid I thought he was trespassing,' Jane said stiffly.

'I expect he thought *you* were,' the man pointed out. 'You'd both better start again.'

The gardener had a strange manner, Jane thought – not quite impertinent, but surely not quite respectful enough either. Jane considered what to say next, and decided to offer a compliment.

'You've made the garden look beautiful. Have you been coming to Miss Venn for a long time?'

A smile lurked again in the reddish beard, but he answered solemnly. 'In one way and another, yes, I have! I was a very troublesome pupil, but I could never quite get the better of her – still can't, in fact. But Tom winds her round his little finger.'

Jane was tempted for a moment to ask what he thought of Hannah's battle with Max Hasler, but then she remembered what he seemed happy to forget – that he was there to be useful. His son's social sense had been inherited, it seemed, because he stood there entirely at his ease, untroubled by a ragged sweater and a tear in his jeans that would soon render them indecent.

'You'll want to get on,' she said pointedly, 'and I came outside without a coat.'

45

He nodded but still didn't move, and she had to walk away with the infuriating feeling that it was she who'd been dismissed. But back in the house again, she saw him through the kitchen window, industriously stacking logs under Hannah's lean-to.

Her aunt returned ten minutes later, weighed down with bags of shopping, and the sight of them made Jane's accumulated irritations overflow.

'You're a tiresome, stubborn woman, do you know that?' But it was the wrong tactic, because Hannah Venn merely looked pleased. 'For as long as I'm here, I'll do the shopping, or take you in my car.'

Hannah didn't even look up from unpacking the bags. 'I have a car, but walking's good for me. In any case, I'll be doing it when you're back in London, so what's wrong with doing it now?'

The question seemed unanswerable and Jane took another tack. 'Your gardener's here, but of course you know that – he said he'd met you in the square. You taught him as a child, apparently.'

'I tried,' Hannah agreed with a hint of regret, 'but he preferred to learn in his own way. Later on he went wild, too, in his own way, and Tom's the result of that, but he became a very good father all the same. It's just as well, because the girl he chose didn't stay long.'

Jane was still digesting this fresh piece of local history when her aunt spoke again. 'If you're that set on driving me somewhere, we'll go over to the farm. It's high time you met your uncle again.'

Ten minutes later they were on their way to the village of Little Ham and the farm called Rushey.

'Good name for it,' Hannah said. 'It's got its own little river running down to join the Parrett. You can almost step over the stream in summertime, but when the rains come it's a different story.'

'I can remember flooding everywhere in winter,' Jane said, carefully negotiating the traffic in Cossenford's narrow streets. 'As a very small child I must have thought we lived by the seaside, except that there wasn't any sand and the water looked

cold and muddy. No wonder people contracted rheumatism and TB.'

Hannah shrugged this off; problems came with any territory, she seemed to say, but those born to the Levels knew what to expect. It was only weaklings like Gideon's ill-chosen wife who'd ever run away. But, aware of the silence in the car, she spoke again. 'I doubt if you'll see Rufus again today – Saturday's his day off.'

'Why would I be likely to see him – does he work for Uncle Joshua as well?' Jane asked.

'Yes, but he and Tom live at Rushey Farm.' Hannah let this sink in before going on. 'By rights it ought to be yours, of course, when Joshua dies. After all, you're Gideon's child. But what would be the point? You keep telling me you belong in London.'

'I've only told you once,' Jane corrected her, 'but it remains true.'

'So it won't bother you if Rufus gets the farm?' Hannah suggested slyly.

'My uncle can do what he likes with it,' Jane snapped. 'Though it seems rather a pity that it can't stay inside the family.'

Hannah allowed another mile to go by before she delivered her final piece of information. 'You needn't worry about that. The man you keep calling my gardener only helps me for kindness' sake; I don't employ him. His name's Rufus Venn, and he's our very distant cousin.'

She glanced at the girl beside her but Jane was staring grimly ahead. There was no doubt about it now: Hannah *was* enjoying herself. Then she remembered something else – Rufus Venn smiling at the joke he'd shared with his son. They were probably still laughing to think that the smart visitor from London had made such a fool of herself.

Seven

Little Ham, the village nearest the farm, awoke no memories in Jane when they got to it. It consisted of no more than a small church, post office-cum-general store, a pub, and a straggle of houses and farms along the western slope of the Poldens.

'All farms twenty years ago,' said Hannah, pointing at what they were passing. 'Now look at them – half the barns have been made into 'character dwellings' – that's what the estate agent calls them.'

'Perhaps there were too many farms,' Jane suggested, and got from her aunt the disgusted sniff she expected. 'Well, if you don't want new houses built you'll have to put up with conversions like these.'

Silenced for a moment, Hannah returned to the fray. 'I suppose it's being a lawyer that makes you so argumentative. You always know best.'

'Oh, I'm famous for it in London,' Jane agreed gravely. But it was a mistake to have mentioned London. With all her heart and mind it was where she wanted – needed to be. But she left it too long to say that she'd changed her mind about going to the farm. Hannah pointed at a side lane, and automatically she turned the car into it.

Now, in some unexpected way, what they were driving through *was* suddenly familiar. She'd been along this puddled lane many times before. With sunlight gleaming on the water-laden land, she acknowledged reluctantly to herself that it was beautiful, with duck-egg blue sky, and willows drawing dark lines on the silver water with the delicacy of a Chinese painting.

Ahead of them a gate led to a garden that had once been

lovely – Joshua's young wife had probably seen to that. Now it was a tangle of overgrown shrubs, and crowding daffodils that had reverted to wildness.

'Go past the house and into the yard,' Hannah instructed. 'I doubt if the front door's been opened for years.'

The long, low house built of the now familiar stone was joined to the barn by a typical covered archway that led to a stockyard, with outbuildings grouped round it. Behind them the land sloped gently upwards, and the green hillside above was scattered with sheep and very young lambs.

Jane got out of the car, assailed again by memories, and by the strange certainty that this moment of return had always been lying in wait for her. Something had been left incomplete for too long, but it was to be finished at last, and probably by the man who was now walking towards her.

Hannah had said he'd changed, but Jane still knew who he was, and with the advantage of surprise on her side, she was able to speak first. 'You won't remember me. Aunt Hannah said you thought I wouldn't come, but I hope you don't mind now that I'm here.'

He took so long to answer that she half expected to be told to leave, but finally he spoke to Hannah instead. 'Take her into the house; I'll be there soon.'

Whatever he needed to do, though, seemed to be forgotten, because he stood watching her follow Hannah inside. She'd grown tall, of course, and what he considered citified. He knew nothing of women's clothes, but even he could see that she looked different from the wives and daughters of his neighbours – amply built women for the most part, even though they all worked hard. There was nothing of the countrywoman about Jane Westover, but the unsettling thing was that she had changed so *little*. He could still see in her the silent, watchful child of all those years ago, never laughing or crying easily as children were supposed to do but just looking at them with her brown-eyed, unnerving stare. He hadn't known how to deal with her then and feared that he wouldn't manage any better now. Feeling so unsure of himself made him irritable.

They weren't in the kitchen when he went in – Hannah, not like her usual self, was acting daft. Jane Westover would know straightaway that he never used the sitting room; even to him it had the comfortless, unfriendly air of a dentist's waiting room. Sarah had had plans to change it once his parents were dead but, as if knowing what she'd intended, Amos had outlived her in the end, and the room had stayed just as it had always been.

'We'll have our coffee in the kitchen,' he said, sounding ill-tempered, because a reminder of his lost wife could still make him angry. 'Warmer in there.'

They trooped silently back along the passage to the kitchen, where a Raeburn stove did indeed warm the air. But Jane couldn't help staring at the old Windsor chair, still in the corner where it had always been. She told herself that it was only her imagination painting a picture of the stiff, upright figure of Amos Venn. He wasn't really there.

If she hadn't understood before, she could see now the utter hopelessness of her parents' marriage – the beautiful Glastonbury maiden that Gideon had probably seen as Guinevere come to life and Elizabeth, who had fallen in love with a gentle, charming man and discovered too late that he was a changeling in the Venn family. Farm life itself might have been too much for her, but she'd had to take on Amos, Joshua and Hannah as well.

Jane's glance went from the severe, no-nonsense face of her aunt, bent over the coffee she was making, to the man sitting opposite her at the kitchen table – grizzled, thickset, and weathered by a lifetime spent mostly outdoors. Were the three of them going to sit there forever, drinking coffee but not speaking? Amanda's comment came back into her mind – oh God, it *was* like Cold Comfort Farm – and with the memory came a sudden, shocking desire to burst out laughing. She tried desperately to think of something sad, but the bubble of hysterical mirth was in her throat, and now gushing up into uncontrollable laughter. Hannah's stunned expression as she turned round only made things worse, and Joshua looked for a moment like a man turned to stone. Then he roused himself to shout at his sister.

'Didn't I tell you so? She only came to laugh at us.'

Unable to speak at all, Jane got up and ran headlong to the door. She reached the car, fumbled her way inside, and sat with her streaming face against the steering wheel. But they were no longer tears of laughter; she was suddenly weeping for all the sad, unrecoverable things – her parents' unhappiness, the wasted lives of the young men listed on the war memorial, and even the certainties she'd so recently lost herself – about self-sufficiency, and cleverness, and success. In this strange place, half land and half water, its shifting light and shadows suggested that nothing was fixed and dependable any more.

By the time Hannah came out to the car Jane was quiet again, with only tear stains on her face to mark the recent storm of weeping.

'I'm sorry, Aunt,' she said, unaware that she'd just used the word for the first time. 'Shall I go back inside and apologize?'

Hannah was silent for a moment. 'Better to leave Joshua alone, I think; he won't know what to say to you. I told him you'd been ill – you have, haven't you?'

'Not ill, exactly,' Jane said with difficulty. 'I had a little collapse, caused by too much strain and work. That's why I've been sent away for six months. But the truth is that I have no idea what to do with myself!' She tried to smile as she said it, but her voice trembled.

'You came back to Somerset,' Hannah pointed out with a gentleness she hadn't used before. 'Came back home, in other words.' But she saw the expression on her niece's white face and knew she'd made a mistake.

'I certainly went to visit my mother first,' Jane agreed with the calmness of despair. '*She* was rather glad to see me, but my half-sister wasn't – no change there! Jill has never wanted to share *her* mother, *her* home, or anything else she could lay claim to. I always pretended that it didn't matter, but that was a lie, of course.' She shook her head at Hannah's concerned face, and tried to sound ruefully amused.

'Don't worry – now I'll drive you home after a disastrous visit, which is only what I should have expected.'

They made the return journey in silence, Hannah thoughtful and Jane aware of feeling very tired. It had been an emotional

morning, admittedly, but she was also unsettled by an echo of what her aunt had said about searching for something. She'd set out from London with a half-baked, unformulated notion of needing a stopgap to fill the aching void in her life. It was simply to be something that would keep mind and body occupied until she could tell Piers Clifford that her six-month exile was over. Then, as if the hiatus had never happened, her everyday life would be resumed, with a new protective skin neatly grown over a hole that would have disappeared.

But the temporary objective wasn't turning out quite as planned. Her little voyage of discovery seemed to be all about herself at the moment, and she was nervously aware that the Jane Westover who returned to Clifford's might be quite different from the one who'd been sent away.

Back at Maundy Cottage, aunt and niece shared a lunch of soup and cheese. Then Hannah suggested that the afternoon nap she was in need of might do Jane good as well.

'Perhaps later, but I want a walk first,' Jane answered. 'I must take a look at Cossenford before I leave.'

She smiled cheerfully at her aunt, to insist that she'd recovered from an unsettling morning, but breathed a sigh of relief when she got outside the house. To someone accustomed to living alone, family life – even to the extent that the Venns practised it – was an effort. What she now needed was solitude to do some thinking. But something was becoming clear in her mind: when she returned to London she'd find a small house to buy, not too far away; somewhere to escape to at weekends, where she could make herself a garden just like Hannah's. She'd been a fool not to think of doing it long ago.

With no idea of the route she'd taken through the streets, she found herself passing a line of shabby railings. The gate was missing and the path that divided a patch of unkempt grass was cracked and broken. But what it led to was surely Hannah's Baptist chapel. In a town of beautiful buildings this wasn't one of them; at best it could be called quaint, with its tall lancet windows and, above the steeply pitched roof, a single bell that hadn't called anyone to prayer for many years.

52

She skirted the side of the building and wandered on into its neglected churchyard. There weren't even any fallen gravestones left, just an occasional suggestion of where a grave might once have been. Hannah was right: it would be far better to make out of this depressing emptiness something that Cossenford's people could enjoy.

She turned to leave, but halted as two men came round the side of the chapel. They parted company and one of them walked away. The other, Max Hasler, strolled towards her with the easy assurance that she thought probably never abandoned him. No uncertainties for Mr Hasler, no wrong choices made or wrong decisions taken.

'It isn't yours yet,' she felt impelled to point out, but his amused smile said that she'd merely managed to sound childish.

'So Hannah told you who I am – the wicked baron in the fairy tale!'

She knew he wasn't surprised that she'd reported their meeting in the church – of course not; he expected to be remembered and talked about.

'Aunt Hannah told me more than that,' she went on. 'I know about Jane Venn who, alas, became Jane Winters, and I know about her daughter, Mary, who became Ernst Hasler's wife.'

'My mother, in other words.' He saw Jane nod, then shiver because the morning's brightness had gone and a sharp March wind was now blowing through the desolate space. 'It's too cold to stay here. If you'll agree to hobnob with the enemy over a pot of tea, we can be indoors in a few minutes. You've walked in a circle almost to the back of my house.'

She fell into step beside him, fearing that Hannah would call it treachery. But why not parley with the man – perhaps even negotiate? It was what she was trained to do.

They came almost at once to a wrought-iron gate leading to an expanse of grass too wide to be called a lawn. It was scattered with trees, and surrounded by a high stone wall that would soon be hidden under a blanket of greenery.

'Not a garden at all by Hannah Venn's standards,' Max Hasler said as they walked towards the house, reading her

mind. 'But my Portuguese handyman knows as little about growing things as I do. An English wife would soon carve it up into herbaceous borders and beds, but I rather like it un-cluttered, as it is now.'

'Definitely no English wife then,' Jane agreed, resisting the temptation to suggest that an obedient German *Hausfrau* would obviously suit him much better. She was more inter-ested in the house. At some point in its long history there had been changes made – the lovely, curved windows that now overlooked the terrace and sweep of lawn hadn't been installed by the original builders. But nothing about the alteration looked out of place or inappropriate.

It was the same story inside, too. Wealth had gone hand in hand with good taste to leave an old house unspoiled but user-friendly. In the library, where she waited while he ordered tea from the handyman's wife, there were lavishly book-lined shelves, comfortable armchairs, and a welcoming fire burning in the hearth.

'I envy you this room,' she said honestly when he came back, and saw again the smile that made his face so attrac-tive.

'Very little of the credit is mine, I have to say. Even empty the house was beautiful – that's why I bought it.'

He waited for the handyman's buxom, smiling wife to set the tea tray on a low table by the fire. Then he wasted no more time. 'I suppose you made a point of going to look at the chapel.'

'No, I found it accidentally,' she was able to say. 'And my aunt knows that I'm not going to be involved in her battle with you – I shall probably leave for London tomorrow.'

'Then we needn't discuss it at all,' he said calmly. 'You can be the charming visitor who just happens to have dropped in.'

She accepted the cup of tea he offered but shook her head. 'Not quite, because the visitor *is* interested. Will you tell me why – knowing what my aunt and her friends have been working towards for years – you're so determined to give Cossenford what it doesn't want?'

'How am I expected to answer that?' he asked almost curtly.

'Do you want me to confess that I'm a businessman who seeks to turn a handsome profit no matter who else is disappointed?'

'Why not if it's the truth?' But she followed the question with another one. 'Is it the truth? Can it really be worthwhile to build two or three expensive houses on that quite restricted site?'

Max Hasler nodded as if something he was unsure of had just been settled. 'The vicar, Clive Weston, was right, it seems; he would insist that Hannah had called in reinforcements in the shape of a clever niece from London! The shape is charming, let me say, but you aren't fully informed. The church elders were wise in their day, and the fields beyond the grave-yard also belong to them. Can it be that the Cossenford Preservation Society doesn't know that?'

'It's immaterial – they haven't the money to buy land they've no use for,' Jane said bluntly. 'Couldn't you be satis-fied just to build on the extra fields, and leave them the chapel? Wouldn't you like to give something to Cossenford – let's say a generous gesture to reconcile it to what the war memorial stands for?' There was a silence in the room that she was the first to break, apologetically. 'I'm afraid that was unfair. What happened then has nothing to do with this present tussle. But your family *has* done very well out of the black soil of the Levels. Couldn't this be payback time?'

His mouth twisted in a wry smile. 'You apologize for one foul by landing another one – a very feminine tactic, I'll have you know!'

She was forced to smile back, knowing that however many ghosts of outraged Venns gibbered behind her back, it would be very easy to like Max Hasler.

'Listen, please,' he said quietly. 'Sooner or later there will be other empty buildings more suitable than the chapel that Hannah and her friends can afford. They must wait for one of those, not waste their meagre funds in fighting me. The development I plan will make me a profit, of course, and the houses can't help but look new to begin with, but they won't be ugly or shoddily built. Their buyers will be incomers, but Cossenford must take them in hand – use them, and relieve them of some of their money! What is wrong with that?'

'This argument is pointless because we shan't ever agree,' Jane said rather sadly. 'You judge everything in terms of business opportunities – what *you* see as progress. My aunt and her friends don't want Cossenford moved on, modernized, jazzed up by rich people who don't belong here. Tell me what is wrong with *that*, please, before I go back to Maundy Cottage.'

'Just one thing, I'm afraid. In this harsh day and age, what doesn't move forward dies!' He said it emphatically but with a trace of regret as well. Then his hands swept the subject aside. 'You're going back to London, and I don't even know your name. Shall I guess at something biblical – Ruth or Rebecca Venn?'

She tried to accept his change of tone as something pleasantly amusing but trivial. All the same, the atmosphere in the quiet, fire-lit room had suddenly become intimate. She was aware that the change had been made deliberately, but did her best to ignore it.

'You guessed wrong, I'm afraid. My parents made no effort to be original – I'm another Jane. And after my father's death my mother married again; I was given my stepfather's name of Westover.'

'Then I'm glad I met you, Jane Westover,' he said gravely. 'May I see you in London, take you out to dine, or to the opera? You look doubtful – would that be treading on another man's toes?'

'Not now, and in any case the other man hated opera!' Her transfiguring smile shone for a moment. 'Actually I was remembering Grandfather Amos just then. Even playhouses were reckoned places for the Devil's work – what would he have made of *Salome* or *Tristan und Isolde*, I wonder!'

'If a thunderbolt strikes Covent Garden we shall certainly find out. So, *auf wiedersehen*, Jane.'

She got up to leave, holding out her hand, but it was lifted to his lips in a gesture she tried to remember was merely automatic to a Continental. But safely away from the house a few moments later she knew that the little interlude, unimportant as it certainly was, had had the effect of making her feel alive again.

Eight

The following morning, Sunday, Hannah got ready to go to church. In a neat grey tweed suit, circa 1965, and sensible brogue shoes, she could have been any rural English spinster about to engage in a brisk weekly consultation with her Maker. But appearances were deceptive, Jane now knew, where her aunt was concerned. Her fortitude was considerable, and so was her intelligence. Several generations of Cossenford's children had been fortunate to have her in charge of their school.

'Quaker meeting house or parish church?' Jane had asked, after refusing an invitation to go with her.

'Parish church – I like the music, and on a good day we hear a sermon worth listening to. I also got tired of waiting for the spirit to move one of the Friends to say something sensible.'

With the sound of the bells now floating along Silver Street, Hannah limped on her way to join the faithful, leaving Jane to wonder whether she would find Max Hasler there, flinching from an organ that wasn't quite in tune.

She hadn't said what she was about to do herself in case Hannah again tried to dissuade her. But it was clear in her own mind that she must return to Rushey Farm. She couldn't go back to London without at least trying to make peace with Joshua Venn.

Her aunt had been right about a change in the season. Almost overnight the flood water lying in the fields seemed to be shrinking. Patches of brilliant green were starting to appear; spring was on the way and soon the landscape would take on a different kind of beauty.

She found the farm easily enough and, as Hannah had told her to before, drove under the archway into the yard. Cows

were penned at one end, pulling out feed heaped in the mangers, but there was no sign of human life. Then the still-ness was suddenly broken; the red-headed boy she remembered from Hannah's garden came running round the side of the barn with the black dog lolloping at his heels. It was Tom – or Thomas when in trouble – and the Labrador called Ben.

The child stopped short at the sight of her but the dog came prancing up, still enough of a puppy to assume that muddy paws and a wet kiss would always be welcome. She managed to fend him off, and smiled at Tom.

'Hello – I've come to see my uncle, Mr Joshua Venn. Do you know where I can find him?'

Tom shook his head. 'He was up and off early, to look at some new lambs. I expect my father will know where he's at.' He disappeared into the dimness of the barn and emerged a moment later with the large man she'd mistaken for Hannah's gardener.

'Good morning,' she said quickly. 'I'm looking for my uncle, but Tom says I've come at the wrong time.'

'He's a farmer, I'm afraid – not always available for morning calls.'

It was said pleasantly, but the colour mounted in her pale face. Rufus Venn seemed to make a habit of catching her on the wrong foot.

'What do you suggest?' she asked instead. 'Shall I wait or go away and come back?'

'I suggest a mug of coffee in the kitchen – it's long past breakfast, and Joshua won't be back for an hour or so.' Then he smiled at Tom. 'Show our guest indoors, please, and put the kettle on. Ben stays outside until you've cleaned him up.'

There was no argument, Jane noticed; whatever rules applied in this male household obviously seemed to work. Tom threw a stick for the dog to fetch, and let her into the kitchen before the dog could get back with it.

'Neat!' she admitted when they were inside.

He grinned, deciding that he quite liked a female visitor who could say what needed to be said in a few words. Annie, the cowman's wife who came to clean, never stopped talking. 'Yes, but he'll soon learn that it's a trick. I'll see to the kettle,

but I won't stay – Ben doesn't like being left outside on his own.'

She was tempted to suggest that thirty cows ought to be sufficient company for one young dog, but decided not to risk another faux pas – Tom would probably think she meant it.

'Go right ahead,' she said instead. 'I can take over kettle duty.'

His blinding smile this time seemed like a gift she hadn't deserved. He then opened the door, and boy and dog greeted each other as if they'd been parted for days.

She was still smiling when Rufus Venn walked into the kitchen, bootless but apparently unconcerned about a large hole in one sock.

'He was supposed to stay and entertain you,' he said of his son.

'We agreed that Ben's need was greater,' she answered coolly. 'How old is Tom – eleven?'

'Nine and a bit – he insists on that. I expect I did too at his age.'

She watched while mugs were filled and brought to the table. For so large and untidy-looking a man, Rufus Venn's movements were unexpectedly neat. With none of Max Hasler's studied savoir faire, he was nevertheless so irritatingly at ease that she found herself wanting to ruffle him.

'Isn't it lonely for Tom here?'

She was stared at across the table, and decided that it wouldn't be wise to provoke her host too far. Something about him – size and colouring perhaps – suggested a lion that shouldn't be poked too freely with a stick.

'There are other children around, and Tom goes to school,' he finally pointed out. 'If you're alluding to his motherless state, then perhaps he *is* lonely.'

Once again she'd made a mistake, and it seemed necessary to say so. 'You aren't Hannah's gardener, and you don't need me to tell you about your own son; I apologize for both errors.'

His smile accepted the apology but she thought he still looked at her with the impersonal curiosity of a laboratory worker inspecting a specimen under a microscope.

'Hannah's report was so impressive that we didn't expect

you to materialize. Joshua reckons that you earn in a week what we labour to make in a year. The money doesn't bother him, but the unfairness of it does.'

'I know – what I do isn't "real" work; my aunt has already pointed that out.' She put the subject aside with a small, impatient gesture. 'Let's talk about her instead of me. I suppose you know the problem with the Baptist chapel.' She saw him nod, and went on quickly. 'I've seen Max Hasler, and Hannah knows as much as I know, but she's still determined to go on fighting. If you can talk some sense into her, please do. She won't win – *can't* win against a wealthy, clever and experienced businessman. But she will exhaust herself and waste the money that's been scraped together so laboriously.'

'She might have a better chance of winning if you stayed to help her,' Rufus Venn suggested. 'The arguments aren't all on Hasler's side, added to which—'

'Added to which,' Jane interrupted sharply, 'the man is half-German and probably disliked as much for that as for the fact that he doesn't fit very easily into Cossenford society.'

'So *Cossenford* should change, you obviously think!'

She waited for him to add that Max Hasler's Continental charm had made a traitor in Hannah's camp, but he wasn't, it seemed, a man to labour a point that looked obvious. She found it a relief to hear a telephone ringing in the passage outside the kitchen that Rufus Venn had to go and answer. He returned a few moments later, looking preoccupied, she thought.

'That was Joshua. He won't be back for a while. A neighbouring farmer is in trouble – too small an acreage to survive in the killing times we're living through. The man's desperate for help.' Rufus stopped speaking, then ran a hand through his already wild red hair. 'I mentioned that you were here, but Joshua said not to wait.'

'Was that all he said?' Jane asked.

'Not quite.' Again Rufus hesitated before going on. 'He sees no point in your coming back, I'm afraid. I'm sorry if that's hurtful.'

She gave a little shrug, intended to look careless but not quite successful. 'It's largely my own fault – I made a stupid

mess of my first visit. But I'm damned by the past as well –
for being Elizabeth Westover's daughter.' She collected their
coffee mugs together, and then stood holding them. 'None of
that is very important, is it, when a man like your farmer
friend has the much more real problem of how to survive?'
She managed a faint smile. 'I should never have left London.
I'll go back where I belong. But perhaps you'll tell Uncle
Joshua for me that I wasn't laughing at *him* . . . It was just
that . . .' But what it had been she was at a loss to explain,
and she gave up in despair.

They walked in silence to where her car was parked, and
Rufus politely opened the door for her to get in.

'Go back to London,' he agreed gently. 'Somerset isn't the
place for you.'

Without conscious thought she started the engine, put the
car in gear, and drove off. His quiet verdict seemed to sum
up the futility of the past few days. It wasn't very important
– she'd said that herself a few minutes ago – but tears pricked
her eyelids all the same, and she had to blink them away in
order to keep driving.

Cars were still parked in the square outside the church when
she got back to Cossenford. As she drew up, the door opened
and those of the congregation most anxious to get home to
lunch began to file out. She opened the car door as Hannah
approached, and got the greeting she might have expected.

'Thank you, but I can still walk as far as Silver Street, you
know.'

'I didn't come to collect you,' Jane answered with equal
bluntness. 'But it might have looked churlish just to drive
past, don't you think?'

Her aunt considered this in silence until they stopped again
outside the cottage. 'You sound cross – no, tired of being here.
Are you?'

Asked by anyone else, the question might have sounded
wistful, but Hannah spurned that approach; a straight answer
was all she required.

'I'm not tired of you,' said Jane, glad to know that it was
true. 'Uncle Joshua wasn't in when I drove to the farm this

morning, but I shan't try again. I'll go back to London tomorrow instead.' She turned to smile wryly at her aunt. 'I asked Rufus Venn to talk to you about the chapel, but I doubt if he will. He thinks I'm in cahoots with Max Hasler just because I don't like prejudice – perhaps you do, too!'

'If I said that, I was wrong,' Hannah confessed at once. 'I shan't take your advice, because I'm a stubborn old fool who won't be told. But I'm very glad I wrote to you, and very glad you came.' Then, afraid of having sounded sentimental, she got out of the car and stomped towards the front door.

Jane followed her indoors, wondering who had so successfully stifled all show of affection in a woman who was deeply kind at heart – her tyrannical, God-fearing father, the brothers reared in his shadow, or some fool of a man who hadn't seen beyond her plain face and awkward, angular figure? For something easier to talk about at the lunch table she described the morning's meeting with Tom.

'He isn't the handsomest of small boys, but he's got a smile that stops you in your tracks,' she said with remembered pleasure. 'Explain to me how any sane woman would walk out on a son like that.'

'She walked out on Rufus,' Hannah corrected. 'But there was nothing to stop her – they weren't married.'

Jane thought of Rufus Venn; in his rough working clothes he was not anyone's idea of a successful ladies' man. 'I suppose she grew tired of his unconventional way of life and ran off with a rich merchant banker instead.'

Hannah gave her time-honoured little snort of disgust at a wrong answer. 'Once Tom was born it was Rufus who reckoned it was time to settle down, instead of wandering about Europe with a horse and caravan. Selina wouldn't have known what a merchant banker was. She was half gypsy and wild as they come – not beautiful exactly, but hard to forget. I don't think Rufus has ever forgotten her.'

'What happened?' Jane asked curiously. 'Does he know where she went?'

'She joined a travelling circus – she could ride any horse ever foaled. He said to me once that she'd find him again if she ever needed help. I think he's still waiting for that.'

62

Jane said nothing at all. If Selina had been a rare bird, in his own way Rufus Venn seemed to be just as remarkable.

'What about you? I don't know whether it's a good sign or bad, but you're not quite the nervy, tensed-up creature who first knocked at my door . . . Leastways, I don't think so,' Hannah suggested suddenly.

The comment was left hanging in the air while Jane decided what to do with it. 'I left London because I was desperate for something to do,' she finally explained. 'If that sounds mad to you it's because life here is so completely different. You walk outside your front door and know everyone you meet, as well as having blood relatives scattered all over Somerset. That's not how my life is in London.'

'Oh, I know how your life is,' Hannah said calmly. 'Every other television drama I'm told I've missed is about young women who look like you – clever, sophisticated, driven creatures who work too hard, drink too much, and still have enough energy left to fall into bed with any man they meet! What I haven't worked out is why all that effort seems to add up to so little. The poor things aren't ever happy.'

Jane winced from a too-exact echo of what the doctor at St Martha's had said, but tried to speak for England's working women. 'You're not being fair. You're home and dry now, in peaceful retirement, but you were like us once, out in midstream, struggling to keep afloat. How often did *you* stop and ask yourself whether you were happy?'

'I *was* happy,' Hannah said gently. 'I was . . .'

'I know, doing something *real*,' Jane finished for her. 'Aunt Hannah, you began this conversation by asking a question. The answer is that I haven't changed, and don't intend to. As soon as I can I shall go back to work because I enjoy what I've been trained to do.' She waited a moment for that to sink in, then smiled at her aunt. 'That's enough about me. What is the Cossenford Preservation Society going to do about the chapel?'

'Meet tomorrow night to plan its next move,' Hannah answered. 'We shall hold a public meeting, and then lodge an appeal against Max Hasler's proposals. That all takes time.

He's an impatient man; perhaps he'll decide to look elsewhere for his expensive development.'

Jane stared at her for a moment, torn between pride in her aunt's spirit and irritation at her blind stubbornness. 'You don't like his family and you distrust all his works, so I shall be wasting my breath to ask you to give him the benefit of some doubt at least. He does believe that you can't cocoon a place like Cossenford in the past and not see it die.'

'He believes what suits him,' Hannah answered steadily, not inclined to give him the benefit of anything at all.

Jane's shoulders lifted in a little shrug of despair. If Max Hasler was the irresistible force, here was the living, breathing, immovable object itself in the shape of her aunt. 'All right, but I'm going to say one more thing. If Max Hasler comes to London when I get back, I shall accept an invitation to go out with him.'

Hannah regarded her without a blink. 'I'm told that women do enjoy his company as a rule,' she agreed quietly. 'Now I'm going to have my afternoon nap.' She gave her niece a faint smile and walked out of the room, leaving Jane with the unusual feeling that in some unspecified duel between them her aunt had come out best.

She spent the afternoon in the garden, pulling out anything she was certain was a weed, for which Hannah thanked her gravely when she came downstairs again.

A reading of *Pride and Prejudice* on the radio allowed them to pass the evening in shared pleasure, and the following morning Jane got ready to leave. When the moment came to say goodbye she held Hannah's hands for a moment, looking at their telltale misshapen knuckles and joints.

'I know I'm not supposed to notice that you've got arthritis,' she said gently. 'But will you promise to let me know if you need help? I can't leave unless you do.'

Hannah nodded, for once not inclined to argue. Instead she repeated, but with a little vital change, the remark that had first greeted Jane at the door.

'You don't take after your mother, and you're not much of a Venn, but you do remind me of Gideon after all.' Then, contrary to her usual habit when saying goodbye, she stayed at the door, watching until Jane had driven out of sight.

Nine

Even with her rational mind insisting that nothing would have changed in the few days she'd been away, Jane was aware all the way home of some unaccountable anxiety. It proved baseless, of course. London was still itself – the hectic, multi-faced muddle of noise and ugliness and grace that she had driven away from. Safely back in Hay's Mews she found her little house just as she'd left it, and, most comforting of all, she was certain that she was still where she belonged, waiting to be back at Clifford's, immersed in the next fascinating battle of wits. Rural jibes about 'real' work had just been based on ignorance or envy. What did the Venns know of the delicate, high-tension web of international finance that kept the world afloat? The Somerset journey had been a mistake. That admitted, she'd forget about it now and think instead about what to do next.

Inside the house, she found that Amanda Crichton had been a thoughtful neighbour. The potted plants were freshly watered, and mail had been picked up and left on the kitchen table. But the cold dampness of the day outside had somehow seeped indoors, and the house felt strangely lonely.

She unpacked the food she'd stopped to shop for and filled jugs with the armful of jonquils she'd bought from the barrow boy in Sloane Square. That was better; it looked like home again. Even so, it was a relief to have Amanda knock at the door later that evening, friendly and cheerful as usual.

'I saw the light on, thought I'd make sure it was you and not a thief!'

Jane smiled but shook her head. 'No burglar – I think they manage without switching on the lights. Come in if you've

time.' Upstairs, she looked a question. 'Coffee or a glass of wine?'

'Wine, please – we keep going on caffeine all day long.'

'According to my Aunt Hannah we drink too much wine as well,' Jane said solemnly. 'Alcohol and sex are the ruin of today's working woman, but as a television buff I expect you knew that already.'

'It was a jolly visit by the sound of things, and my fault you went at all. Sorry, Jane – bad advice, I'm afraid.'

'Not really; in fact it was quite an education. I kept making mistakes – no bad thing for a streetwise Londoner who reckoned she knew all there was to know!'

'Definitely grim,' Amanda decided. 'Still, I can't help wondering how Aunt Hannah, poor old thing, knew anything about our sex lives.'

Jane smiled wholeheartedly for the first time. 'To start with, she's nobody's "poor old thing", despite painful arthritic joints. Beneath the plain and rather prim exterior of a retired school-teacher, she's sharp, honest, brave and kind.'

'All right – dear Aunt Hannah, then,' Amanda said obligingly. 'Did you meet anyone else?'

Jane ticked them off on her fingers. 'In Bath my beautiful mother and my lovely but rapacious half-sister. At Rushey Farm my crusty Uncle Joshua, whom I managed to deeply offend, an unknown distant cousin who put me in my place several times, his charming small son and an exuberant dog called Ben. And, last but not least, in Cossenford a dishy man called Max – half German, you see – who is wrestling with Aunt Hannah and the local Preservation Society over a disused Baptist chapel! I don't think I've missed anyone out,' she ended, thoughtfully.

'A few crowded days,' Amanda suggested. 'But they haven't done you any harm. You look better than when you went away. Are you going back?'

'There's no reason to. Aunt Hannah may need a lawyer, but not one like me. So, I shan't be going back to Somerset.'

Amanda looked at her curiously. 'Do I hear a faint note of regret?'

'Only because it's undeniably beautiful, and different.'

'And the dishy Max – no urge to see him again?'

Jane gave a little shrug. 'He's very good company but a seasoned ladies' man, not to be taken seriously if his conquests don't want to get hurt.' She smiled the thought aside and asked for local news instead, but when Amanda had gone home her mind still lingered on the past few days.

She reflected that Hannah would almost certainly lose out against Max Hasler, but since he'd been right to say that the chapel wasn't Cossenford's only hope of a museum, no unbearable heartache would be involved. Real dramas had been glimpsed though, like desperate farmers who couldn't survive, or the battle between traditional ways and the new methods that men like her uncle saw as the ruin of a precious landscape. Smaller in scale but most vivid of all, there was the tragedy of Tom Venn, growing up with the knowledge that his mother preferred riding circus horses to staying with him.

None of these things were her concern, she had to remind herself. Even Jill wasn't a problem she need do anything about; she wasn't tied to another single human being. Her being alone hadn't worried her in the past – in fact she'd rather taken pride in being self-sufficient. Now, just for the moment, it seemed something to regret because it was unnatural.

The next morning she woke up full of resolve. She cleaned the house, wrote a thank-you note to her aunt, wrote but tore up a note to Joshua Venn, and then spread out on the kitchen table a map of the Home Counties. There was no use looking for a cottage further afield than that; she'd never have the time to visit it. With West Sussex settled on in her mind, and half a dozen places circled on the map, she was ready to set out. But the telephone rang and she heard her mother's voice at the other end of the line.

'Jane, dear, I called you at Cossenford but Hannah said you'd gone back to London. Was it a *very* disastrous visit?'

The phrasing of the question seemed theatrical and she answered curtly. 'I don't think so – in fact I rather enjoyed Aunt Hannah's company. But I didn't go intending to stay long.'

'Well, I was a tiny bit concerned about the T.I.A. thing, and

you were not quite yourself, I thought, while you were here. You'd tell me, wouldn't you, if there was anything really wrong?'

Jane didn't respond to that, not knowing what the true answer would be. 'Nothing's wrong,' she said instead, sounding firm. 'Having just been ordered not to work for six months, I was disorientated when I arrived in Bath. I'm fine again now – full of plans, in fact – but thank you for ringing.'

Elizabeth spoke again, a little hesitantly. 'Darling, there's one more thing. I know you've got this stupid *idée fixe* about not getting on with Jill, but I'm going to ask a favour all the same. She's just finishing at Bristol, and she'll need to make some contacts in London – find herself an agent, that sort of thing. She's very prepared to rough it, but I want to be sure she's somewhere safe, and a good address to offer as her base also won't do any harm. Could you put her up now and again, when she needs to stay a night? Is it too much to ask?'

How could it be, Jane reflected grimly, when James Westover's home had become hers when she was a child, and his money had helped finance her through university? Elizabeth was careful not to remind her of these things, but then she didn't have to.

'I've a spare room Jill can use,' she finally agreed. 'But I hope the arrangement doesn't have to last too long. There'll be a few house rules, but I'll make them clear when she comes.'

It didn't sound gracious and she waited to be told so, but Elizabeth merely thanked her and rang off. The request had obviously been the real purpose of her call, and she'd been grateful not to get the refusal she'd expected. Aware of having been manipulated, and disliking the idea of her sister as an occasional lodger, Jane wished she'd had sufficient strength of mind to say no. But she remembered her glibly made suggestion to Max Hasler – perhaps this was her own payback time.

She was almost at the door when the telephone rang again – Jill, already primed by her mother, very quick off the mark maybe? It was tempting to ignore the call. She hesitated, went back, and snapped into the mouthpiece, 'Hello, Jane Westover here.'

'And sounding very cross, I'm afraid,' said the amused voice of Max Hasler. 'Is that how you feel, my dear Jane?'

'I *was.*' She smiled as she spoke, forgetting that he couldn't see her. 'A call just before yours left my feathers ruffled, but I'm all right now – unless you're about to tell me that Aunt Hannah and her friends have barricaded themselves inside the Baptist chapel!'

'I wouldn't know – I'm in London. Now, what would you say to *Madame Butterfly* this evening at Covent Garden – too popular? Not enough notice?' She didn't answer at once and he continued. 'Perhaps you aren't going to say anything at all.'

'Sorry,' she quickly apologized. 'Of course I'm going to accept; it's an invitation much too good to refuse. But I thought all the performances were sold out weeks ago.'

'They were for most people,' he agreed. 'It sounds very rude, I'm afraid, but may I ask you to meet me there? I've got two meetings scheduled for this afternoon.'

She promised to arrive no later than seven fifteen, and with another '*auf wiedersehen*', he rang off. Not one to dally on the telephone, Max Hasler, and he would take it for granted that she understood how a busy man had to behave.

With half the morning gone already, she abandoned her own plan for going house-hunting. Sussex must wait until she could make an early start the following day. But the delay seemed unimportant now, and a morning that had begun badly was suddenly bright with promise.

Max was already in the foyer that evening when she arrived, considerately positioned where she could spot him easily in the crowd. He made a distinctive figure anyway, she noticed – immaculately suited, and not bearing any sign of having spent an exhausting day. His smile approved her appearance, too, in a suit of bronze-coloured silk that made a perfect foil for her clear, pale skin and dark hair. She'd never claimed beauty for herself – that belonged in the family to her mother and Jill – but money spent on achieving a certain individual style hadn't been wasted. If she'd not been sure of it already, Max Hasler's glance now told her so.

The bell was already ringing for the audience to take its seats, and it wasn't until the final notes of the first act were lost in a silence that erupted into rapturous applause that she again became aware of the man sitting beside her.

'I've got some of the great recordings at home,' she murmured. 'Victoria de los Angeles, Renata Scotto, Mirella Freni . . . but a performance as perfect as this has to supplant any recording ever made.' He didn't answer for a moment, and she smiled at him a little ruefully. 'I hope you aren't here just to give me pleasure. If asked to make a guess, I'd have said that Puccini wasn't really your operatic cup of tea . . .'

'If asked to be truthful I should have to agree! But this performance *is* sublime, and *Butterfly* contains the best music Puccini ever wrote, so please don't imagine that I'm not enjoying myself. After this I may even have to listen to *La Bohème* again with an open mind!'

It was shared pleasure from then on, delight in what they were being offered heightened by shared awareness of each other. She knew that it was a special evening and said so honestly as they left the theatre.

'Not quite over yet,' Max pointed out with a smile. 'In Cossenford we should have no option but to retire to our beds, virtuous or otherwise. Here we can call in at the Savoy first for a light, delicious supper!'

She didn't argue, knowing that the laughing jibe about Cossenford was true. But it was also clear in her mind that without her visit to Hannah Venn, they wouldn't have met at all.

When they were seated at their supper table ten minutes later he spoke of Somerset again after glancing round the room at the other diners. They were mostly theatre-goers like themselves, and he indicated them with a smile of deliberate provocation.

'Something of a contrast to what we've just come from: the good life lived by successful Londoners compared with subsistence farming on the Levels, which is what men like your uncle engage in, I'm afraid.'

'I see the difference, of course, but Uncle Joshua and his

friends probably don't even *want* this kind of life. In any case, they don't all toil for nothing – your uncle's grown rich, I believe.'

'Dear Jane, you disapprove – I hear a minatory note in your voice!'

'It's Grandfather Amos talking, I expect. His spirit surfaces now and again, even though I was terrified of him as a child.' Her lovely smile faded too soon in the opinion of the man watching her. 'I don't know enough about it to argue with you, but at least I'm sure there's something we ought to know. It's a special landscape down there, in danger of destruction if men come in who see it only as a way of making money.'

His little shrug warned her that the subject didn't interest him very much. 'If you're talking about the commercial extraction of peat – the reason for the Winters' wealth – how far can you take the argument? It's a natural resource, like coal or oil. Should we have left those undisturbed too?' He could see that she was prepared to argue, and held up his hands in a laughing gesture of defeat. 'I should know better than to provoke a brilliant lawyer! We're here to enjoy ourselves, not dispute the problems of the world.' His eyes held her own for a moment. 'It *is* enjoyment, isn't it, Jane, or are you troubled by the thought of Hannah Venn? Don't worry about her. She can't know, and would never guess, that you are dining with the enemy!'

'She doesn't have to guess,' Jane answered calmly. 'I told her that if you came to London and invited me out, I wouldn't refuse.'

'Then I'm deeply sorry I missed the conversation,' Max said with smiling regret. 'The invincible Miss Venn put in her place for once.'

Jane shook her head. 'That isn't how it was – in fact she won the round hands down.'

His fingers touched hers for a moment where they rested on the table in a brief gesture that suggested admiration not put into words, and even tenderness. But he didn't seem to mind when she led the conversation back to music and, from that, to his other home in Germany. It gave him the opportunity

to mention that he was flying to Dusseldorf in the morning, summoned there by his mother who was once again concerned about Ernst Hasler.

'She has my two sisters living almost on the doorstep,' Max explained. 'And a host of friends. Still, nothing will do except that I must drop everything here and arrive home in time to see my father recovered from his latest ailment.'

'He might be more unwell than you think,' Jane suggested, faintly chilled by Max's attitude.

'I doubt it; my father has been made into a hypochondriac to be fussed over by a doting wife! My uncle over here *is* sick, and rightly concerned about the future. His daughter, my cousin Emily, is married to what we call a *Taugenichts* in German – good for nothing except spending what someone else has earned.'

'I think you value James Winters,' she said thoughtfully. 'The Venn family, of course, does not, but I'm sure you know the reasons for that. Hannah probably thanks God every day for the fact that the very distant connection between us comes merely through marriage – Jane Venn's to Horace Winters. Other people probably wouldn't even recall that it happened, but memories are long on the Levels, apparently.'

She glanced round the room at the emptying tables, then at the tired face of Max Hasler. 'It's been a wonderful evening, but you've been working all day, and have to travel tomorrow. I think it's time to leave, don't you? There's no need to return me to my own doorstep – I can take a taxi.'

'We shall both take the taxi,' he said definitely, and she knew better than to argue. But he was quiet on the short journey, giving her no clue to what he was thinking, or how he expected the night to end. She couldn't even be sure that she knew herself how she wanted it to end.

But outside her house the cabbie was told to wait, and she knew then that Max intended her to go to bed alone. He smiled at her upturned face, made mysterious with light and shadow from the street lamp outside Mrs Drew-Brown's windows. Did she also keep watch at night? Jane briefly wondered, before she felt Max's lips cover her own in a sweet, gentle

kiss. Then he lifted his head, but kept her looking up at him, with his fingers beneath her chin.

'Dear Jane, I should like more than anything to stay and make love to you. But I have a dawn start ahead of me, and my impression is that you think important things should be taken slowly. Am I right?'

She nodded, and his free hand gently traced the outline of her mouth. 'You might let me stay, because you're very kind, but you'd much rather I didn't ask yet.'

Again she nodded, and felt herself released. 'Safe journey,' she said huskily, then he made her a formal little bow and walked back to the waiting taxi.

A wonderful evening, she recalled that she'd said. It had been that certainly, whatever happened from now on. But it might also turn out to be the evening that changed the course of everything in the future. Already it was difficult to call Mark's thin, dark face to mind, and in order not to feel guilty about that she had to remind herself that Anna Soames would be making sure he wasn't lonely. But she finally fell asleep, strangely certain that Mark Rubens and Max Hasler were very different men. She'd loved one of them, or so she'd thought at the time, and now she was falling in love with the other. But the strange certainty she was left with was that they wouldn't like each other.

Ten

Once the livestock had been seen to, and Tom had been sent on his way to meet the school bus, Rufus could settle down to his own breakfast. It was usually a silent meal even when it was shared with Joshua, but this morning he had a worry on his mind.

'Hannah's not well,' he said to the man sitting opposite him at the kitchen table. Joshua went on eating buttered toast and reading the *Farmer's Weekly* propped up against the teapot. 'Hannah isn't well,' he repeated, louder this time.

'I heard you the first time, but I don't know what you think I can do about it.' Joshua sounded irritable, as he mostly was when confronted with a problem he couldn't solve. 'She's got rheumatism, like most people raised on the Levels, and she's getting on for seventy.'

'You could start by talking her out of this fight over the chapel. I promised Jane Westover I'd have a go at her myself, but she just smiled and told me very nicely to mind my own business.'

'Which is what she'll tell me, only not so nicely because she's my elder sister.' Joshua dislodged the paper for long enough to pour himself another cup of tea, and then rearranged it again.

'It was daft of her to think the girl would help just because she's Gideon's daughter. Jane Westover would have done better not to come at all – she went back to London soon enough, didn't she?'

'Perhaps because she thought she wasn't welcome. Hannah said you didn't even speak to her.'

Joshua's face flushed with anger. 'I wasn't ready, didn't expect her. Any road, it's done with now; she won't come back.' He waited to see if he would be argued with again but Rufus accepted this time that he was right.

74

'I'll talk to Hannah,' Joshua went on, 'but it won't do a mite of good. She's always been an unbiddable woman – it's why she never got a husband.'

Rufus didn't even comment on this, although his own opinion was that Hannah had *chosen* to remain single. If her mind had been set on a husband she'd have found one easily enough. 'She told me that Max Hasler hasn't been seen in Cossenford for a week or two,' he said instead, 'and I know from old Walter Chedzoy that he's not over at Talbot's with James Winters, either.'

'No need, is there? Winters must have all the machinery by now that he's ever like to use. By the way, the man's poorly, I'm told. Is that what Walter says?' He saw Rufus nod, and gave a little shrug. 'Well, he's got money enough to pay for doctors.' With that he marched out of the room, with no sympathy to waste on someone he deeply disliked, but no pretence either; in Joshua Venn, Rufus reflected, you got what you saw. If it wasn't always likeable, at least it was honest.

Left alone, Rufus cleared the table. Then he settled down in the office with the milk returns, one of the many tasks about a modern farm that Joshua refused to have anything to do with. But form-filling wasn't an engrossing job, and Rufus found his mind straying to Joshua's unwelcome niece.

Jane Westover was the exact opposite of his lost, lovely Selina – alarmingly elegant and self-assured – but he was surprised to find that he'd ended up not disliking her, perhaps had even felt sorry for her. The reason, he suspected, was that her sophistication was no more than skin-deep. She'd apologized for her mistakes like any embarrassed girl, and Joshua's refusal to see anything funny in the fiasco of her first visit had upset her. Most telling of all, she hadn't outgrown a weakness for the surface glamour of a man like Max Hasler. Selina, unschooled though she'd been, would have ignored anyone who didn't understand the things she knew were important – like where the elusive godwits and whimbrels rested on their long migration flights, or the mute swans hid their nests, or skeins of wild orchids drifted over the meadows in late spring.

As always when he thought of Selina, the ache of loss was still there, and the sadness of knowing that what had happened

had been his fault, not hers. He should have understood that she couldn't ever be tied down to one place. Because of Tom he'd tried to do that, but he'd destroyed their life together. He could never regret Tom, the joy of his life now, but the thought of his son brought him back to Jane Westover again – wasn't a motherless only child lonely? she'd asked, although not in so many words. Of course he was, but God knew there was nothing that could be done about that.

A clatter of crockery from the kitchen warned him that it was time to go outside. Annie Clark had arrived, and short of brutal rudeness there would be no way of stemming the flow of words if she was given the chance to get into her stride. He waved to her from the passage, whistled in passing to Ben, patiently waiting by the kitchen door, and crossed the yard to climb the hill beyond. From this vantage point he could look down over Joshua's land and estimate how much longer it would be before they could turn the cattle out. That was something to see, the moment when the cows felt new grass under their feet again. The last of the flood water had disappeared and, enriched by the river silt left behind, the meadows would provide the sort of pasturage that chemically fed grass could never compete with.

The morning was fine and, whatever their problems, Rufus didn't want to be anywhere else. He sincerely pitied men and women whose work locked them inside buildings all day. Farming was hard, and often profitless, but he didn't want to change places with them, even on days when a cow that had strayed into boggy ground had to be hauled out, or young lambs had been mauled by foxes that the fool townee politicians now said they mustn't hunt. Joshua was right: they had to stay and work this land with proper care and raise the creatures that lived off it as generations of men before them had done.

The end of the long working day was in sight, and with Tom's help he was bottle-feeding the lambs of a ewe that had died when Joshua came out to find him.

'Trouble,' he said briefly. 'Telephone call from the hospital. Hannah's there with a broken ankle. It's been plastered up but

76

they say she's to stay for a day or two, seeing that she lives alone. She reckons she's all right – doesn't need visiting; but all the same . . .'

'All the same we'll go now shall we, Tom? Tea when we get back.'

His son nodded, quite certain that Hannah would want to see them whether she said so or not.

Half an hour later they were directed to where Hannah lay propped up in bed. She glared at her visitors, but there was a faint quaver in her brusque greeting.

'I told them to say you weren't to come. Trust you not to listen.' But she couldn't hold out against Tom's smile. 'I won't pretend I'm not pleased to see you though.'

'What happened?' Rufus wanted to know. 'Did you fall at home, Hannah?'

'I did better than that – missed a broken step at the market house. Perhaps *now* they'll do something about getting them repaired.'

'Does it hurt?' Tom enquired anxiously.

'Not now,' she said, smiling at him. 'No need to look worried; I'm not dead yet.' Then she spoke to Rufus. 'They're very kind here, but I want to go home.' Her voice held almost its usual decided tone, but her fingers trembled and he knew that his dear Hannah was more shaken than she wanted them to see.

'I'll take you home the moment they say you can leave,' he said gently. 'Not before. Right now you need to rest, so we won't stay. But we'll call at the cottage on the way home, just to make sure everything's all right.' He bent down to kiss her cheek, something he didn't normally dare do. 'Joshua sent his love, by the way.'

It was so unlikely a message that it made her smile, and when they turned to wave to her from the doorway she waved back with some of her old vigour. On the drive home Tom was quieter than usual, and when they'd left Maundy Cottage securely locked and were back in the car again, he said what was troubling him.

'It's a nice little house . . . Aunt Hannah *will* be able to go home, won't she?'

'Of course, but she may need someone to look after her for a bit. I shall have to think about that.' Then he smiled at his son. 'No need to fret, Tom – bones mend, they just take a little bit longer at Hannah's age.'

But with a belated tea eaten, and Tom at last in bed, Rufus confronted the problem of what to do about his friend. They could bring her to the farm, but its stone-flagged floors and draughts couldn't compare in comfort with her own home. Hannah wanted to be back in Maundy Cottage, but she'd need a companion there. With great forethought, he reckoned, he'd brought back her address book in case she asked for it. He found Jane Westover's number recorded in Hannah's neat script and, after a few a moments' debate, finally dialled the number.

He wasn't expecting her to answer as promptly as she did, and stumbled over beginning the conversation. 'It's Venn here . . . Rufus Venn,' he said hesitantly.

'Oh, good evening.' But she sounded disappointed, and he wondered who she'd hoped was ringing instead.

'It's about Hannah,' he went on more firmly. 'She had a fall in Cossenford this morning, and broke an ankle. They're keeping her in hospital for a day or two, much against her will.'

'I'm sure! Poor Aunt Hannah . . . I'm so sorry. If you're able to go and see her, please give her my love.'

'She'll need a little more than that when she's sent home,' Rufus pointed out. 'I was hoping you can come and look after her for a week or two – if you're still on holiday, that is.'

'Well, yes . . . I am,' said Jane, now sounding flustered herself. 'But I'm sure my aunt has dozens of friends in Cossenford – wouldn't they want to help?'

'I'm sure they will,' he agreed, 'but Hannah needs someone with her, staying in the house.' There was silence at the other end of the line, and Rufus spoke again in a crisp voice she hadn't heard him use before. 'If you don't want to come, then don't. She doesn't know I'm ringing, so she won't be hurt.'

'I haven't said I'm not coming,' Jane snapped. 'But until a couple of weeks ago I hadn't seen Aunt Hannah for twenty-five years. I'm sure she'd agree that it doesn't entitle us to feel dependent on each other.'

'She probably would,' he agreed unexpectedly. 'The two of you are rather alike.' This brought the conversation to a halt again, and he registered with a twinge of amusement the fact that Jane Westover hadn't altogether liked the comparison.

'I'll drive down tomorrow,' Jane said, to bring the discussion to a close. 'If I turn out to be a rotten nurse-companion it will be entirely your fault.'

'You don't know how to get in,' he pointed out before she could ring off. 'The key is in the flowerpot by the front door.'

'Of course! Where else? We mustn't make things difficult for burglars.'

With that he heard the line go dead, but he didn't mind letting her have the last word – he *had* cornered her, probably unfairly. She could have said that Hannah Venn was scarcely someone she need feel responsible for.

The same thought was occurring to Jane, along with a concern that she *did* feel about Max Hasler. He'd rung from Germany to say that the family crisis was genuine this time – his father had had a mild heart attack, which meant a longer stay than he'd expected, but he was relying on the proverbial promise that absence would make her heart grow fonder. His voice had been tinged with amusement but she felt sure she wasn't mistaken in thinking that their relationship, although brief so far, was important. When he insisted on her being in London to welcome him back, he had meant it.

She'd made a promise that she must now break, and it seemed all too likely that Max had other woman friends available who were not handicapped by a relative who was doing her best to thwart his next business venture. But she could see no way of not helping Hannah, and Rufus Venn, damn him, had known that. All she could do was send a note to Max's London address in Dolphin Square, apologizing for her disappearance.

There was another letter to write as well – she preferred that to telephoning her mother – explaining that Jill must get the house key from her neighbour next door if she wanted to stay in London. Finally, she rang Amanda to tell her what had happened.

'I tempted providence too far,' she finished up. 'I should never have said I was done with Somerset!'

'Then Aunt Hannah's little accident is probably meant,' Amanda suggested. 'It's preordained – part of your life's pattern that says you have to go back to Cossenford.'

'*Nothing* is preordained, let me tell you. Hannah's fall is very badly timed from my point of view, but it is *not* an act of God, or fate, or any other agency you care to think of.'

'Have it your own way,' Amanda agreed obligingly. 'But there are "more things in Heaven and earth, Horatio . . ."'

'I know the quotation; you can spare me the rest of it! But there's one more thing, Amanda: my half-sister, Jill, might turn up, asking for the key. As far as I know she hasn't got friends in London, but please feel free to object if she should invite a horde of theatre class-mates to party with her in Hay's Mews.'

'I'll send Julian round to restore order,' Amanda promised.

'Well, be warned – he's very nice, and she's beautiful, like my mother, but she has the instincts of an alley cat.'

There was a little silence before Amanda answered. 'I think you're getting paranoid about your family. Go to Somerset and sort out Aunt Hannah – we'll look after things here. *Ciao, cara!*'

That was an end to their conversation but Jane went on thinking about it. She refused to accept Amanda's idea of life being pre-arranged – that was simply the way feckless people evaded responsibility for themselves, and she'd have no more truck with it than Grandfather Amos would have done. But there *was* one change to be faced: since the day of her collapse at Clifford's none of her old certainties had seemed quite so secure. She was only unsure for the moment because she was aimless, but it was a relief to have something she must do, even if it was only going back to Cossenford.

She set off early the following morning but still got caught in the convoys of heavy lorries pounding along the A303. There was nothing to enjoy on the journey – she couldn't even take her eyes off the lorry in front to stare at Stonehenge, lit by the morning sun, as she drove past. But once off the trunk road and with the car turned towards the Polden Hills, things

got better. The spring that Hannah had predicted was probably arriving with no more than its usual headlong rush, but for years she'd been too immersed in study and work to even notice it at all. Now, it was everywhere about her – in the fat clumps of primroses that speckled the verges of the lanes, and the clouds of blackthorn blossom still floating along the hedgerows, and in the mist of newly minted green that had begun to soften the starkly beautiful patterns of even the trees that were still winter-bare. It was nearly April, nearly Eastertide, and a line of Housman's came into her mind: "Fifty years is little room to see the cherry tree in bloom". At nearly thirty-one, perhaps it was time she started looking at things – another new idea to grapple with in this altered world she was now living in.

At Maundy Cottage she heaved her suitcase out of the boot of the car, half heard a noise behind her, and a moment later felt a cold wet nose pushed into her hand. She turned round to be greeted with an enthusiastic embrace from its owner. Behind him, laughing at the dog but instructing him to try to behave, was Tom Venn, who finally succeeded in calling Ben to heel.

'He's learning,' Tom said hopefully.

'But we can't expect him to learn everything at once!' she quoted from memory.

Pleased that she understood matters so well, Tom nodded and smiled his shy, sweet smile. 'We came to open up, in case you couldn't find the key. Ben and me are here to welcome you while Dad does some shopping – stuff like bread and milk, because there isn't any.'

'It's kind of you both,' she said solemnly. She tactfully resisted Tom's intention of struggling indoors with her heavy suitcase, and by the time Rufus Venn found them, they were out in Hannah's garden, collecting twigs that Tom said would be useful for the sitting-room fire that he proposed to light for her.

'You got here early,' Rufus said by way of greeting.

'I left London early,' she agreed. 'I wasn't expecting to have the shopping done for me, or find a welcome committee at the door!'

Rufus Venn smiled, aware that while she stared at him she was trying to decide why he looked different. 'Haircut,' he suggested helpfully. 'I have one every spring.'

It made a difference, she thought. With beard and thatch of wild auburn hair neatly trimmed, he looked quite respectable – even his jeans were washed and freshly patched. She resisted the temptation to suggest that he should clean himself up more often, and asked instead when Hannah was coming home.

'This afternoon, the doctor said, seeing that you'd be here. I got a ticking off from Hannah, of course, for ringing you. It was so like old times of thirty years ago that it quite perked her up; she'd been looking rather sad when we arrived.' He hesitated for a moment before going on in a different tone of voice. 'Thank you for coming down – it probably wasn't convenient at such short notice, or indeed at all.'

Jane gave a little shrug. 'Perhaps not convenient, but Hannah wasn't to know that when she fell. Do I fetch her?'

'No, I'll do that. If it's your car outside, mine has got more legroom.'

'It would need to have,' she agreed, looking him up and down, but he was smiling at his son and didn't even notice.

Between them they lit the fire, brought in logs to stack on the hearth, and looked relieved when she said that she could now manage on her own. There was work waiting at the farm, and the day would be interrupted again when it was time to fetch Hannah home.

'You're good friends to my aunt,' Jane felt obliged to say as they got ready to leave.

'People have the habit of helping each other here,' Rufus said briefly. 'But Hannah's special – I expect you noticed that.'

He didn't wait for an answer, and her last glimpse of them was of Tom in the seat beside his father, and Ben in the back of the car, lovingly licking each of them in turn.

Eleven

Left alone in Hannah's cottage, Jane decided that it perfectly reflected its owner. Like her, it was homely in the true sense of the word – nothing fancy, nothing that wasn't solid and good. There was pleasure to be found in polishing the old furniture until it shone, and then in gathering masses of late narcissus and tulips from the garden to bring their colour and scent into the house.

On the watch after lunch for a car to arrive, Jane didn't recognize the one that pulled up outside the cottage late in the afternoon. Instead of Rufus helping Hannah out, it was Joshua Venn who stood there, holding her crutches at the ready. In the countryman's off-duty uniform of tweed jacket and shabby corduroy trousers, he looked a less intimidating man than she remembered, but she saw his expression change at the sight of her at the front door. It was Hannah who eased the moment by being true to herself as usual.

'You shouldn't be here,' she snapped at Jane. 'Rufus had no business telling you I was in hospital.'

'If he hadn't you'd have been kept there still,' Jane pointed out calmly. 'Didn't you want to come home?'

Hannah turned to her brother. 'You can't get the better of this one in an argument.' But she said it with a touch of pride.

'Londoners are good at talking,' he pointed out with the air of a man who knew many of them and therefore could confidently give an opinion.

He stared at Jane for a moment, trying to find something that he could reasonably dislike. She wore trousers, but then so did most of the young women he was now acquainted with. She probably made up her face, but if so, it was in some skilful way that he failed to detect. The only sin he could put

83

his finger on was that she didn't look ordinary enough, which meant that he had to keep remembering how far she'd travelled from the rest of them.

Still, something Rufus had said stuck uncomfortably in his memory: Gideon's daughter had so far received no welcome from him, and it was something she was entitled to.

'It's good of you to help your aunt,' he managed to say. 'She's grateful, though she'll find it hard to say so. Rufus told me you'd come back to the farm, too, when I wasn't there.'

'I wanted to apologize,' Jane said simply. 'That's all.' His large calloused hand brushed the idea aside, and she abandoned it as well for fear of embarrassing him. 'There's some tea ready, if you're going to come in. I expect Aunt Hannah's dying for a cup!'

'She's dying to sit down, not stand here listening to you two chitter-chattering,' said Miss Venn acidly.

It made Jane smile and, watching her, Joshua was suddenly prompted to an admission he'd never expected to have to make. 'You should have been called Venn, not Westover. I'll not stay for tea – there's work waiting at home.' He patted Hannah's shoulder, not ungently, and then quickly made for the car – thankful, they both felt, to have done for the time being with female relatives who in the nature of things were bound to need attention and soft speeches.

Jane turned to her aunt. 'What do you feel like? Tea by the fire, or a lie down upstairs?'

'My own armchair and hearth, thank you; I'm not one for taking to my bed.' But when she'd struggled into the sitting room, Hannah lowered herself into the chair with a little sigh of relief. 'They were kind enough in the hospital; it's the other patients that take some getting used to. The woman in the next bed wanted to pray for me all night. I had to remind her in the end that Almighty God might need some rest, even if she didn't.'

Jane brought in a tray of tea and placed her aunt's cup and saucer where she could reach it easily.

Hannah watched her for a moment, then spoke in a different tone of voice. 'I hope Rufus didn't push you into coming

back. It's a comfort you're here – I won't deny that – but you ought to be enjoying your own life in London.'

'I don't have a life there at the moment,' Jane answered truthfully. 'The fact is that I'm in limbo until September – enforced rest from too much pressure at work! So why shouldn't I spend some time here with you?'

She smiled to show how little there was to draw her back to London – the longing to see Max again was private, not something that Hannah need know about. She reminded herself again that any sane woman of her advanced age would take their friendship lightly. It amounted to so little in terms of time spent together that it was scarcely a relationship at all. But the conviction persisted that they'd shared more than passing attraction, passing desire, that lovely evening at Covent Garden. She needed to see him again, though, before she could be sure that she was right.

Hannah's voice broke into her thoughts, uncannily speaking of the man she was caught in the act of remembering.

'Max Hasler hasn't been seen in Cossenford for several weeks. I suppose he's got a finger in all sorts of pies in other places as well.'

'His father has been ill – he had to go back to Germany,' Jane said briefly.

Hannah took another sip of tea, considering her next move. 'We've called a public meeting about the chapel. His lawyer knows, so I expect *he* does as well. That will bring him back, of course.'

Jane didn't reply, and her aunt soldiered on. 'We're preparing our case, if that's what it's called, but this –' she pointed to her plastered leg – 'couldn't have come at a worse time. We shall have to rely on the vicar, and Arthur Cranston, the librarian – broken reeds, both of them, when it comes to speaking in public.' She came wistfully to the crux of the matter at last. 'I suppose *you* wouldn't lead the charge for Cossenford? I know it's not the sort of thing you normally handle, but the other side will romp home if I can't stiffen up our team a bit.'

There was a long pause. 'Have you spoken to the lawyer?' Jane finally asked. 'Has he said Max will be at the meeting?'

Hannah consulted with herself again. Temptation was very strong . . . were there not times of extreme need when an untruth might just be permissible? 'After all, what is a lie? 'Tis but the truth in masquerade.' But that was the wicked Lord Byron speaking and she could place no trust in him. At last she answered, despite feeling almost sure that the truth would be her undoing.

'The man was definite – Max Hasler will be here.' She watched Jane's face and knew what she must say next. 'I'm sorry, I shouldn't have asked – you said at the beginning that we'd need a different kind of lawyer. Arthur will have to find one, that's all.' She managed a cheerful smile, unaware that it didn't match the disappointment in her eyes.

'I'm sorry,' Jane was forced to say. 'If you think I'm a disgrace to the Venns, I can't blame you. But quite apart from the legal aspect, I don't even know whose side I'm on! You're sure of being right about what Cossenford wants, but Max has an argument, too. His development would bring outside wealth into the town, which it probably needs, and if it stays wrapped up in its own past it will slowly die.' She saw the mulish expression on Hannah's face, and made one final effort. 'Why not ask Max to help you find another building that would be more suitable than the chapel? Wouldn't that be better than a public fight that can't help but divide opinions and split the town in half?

Hannah shook her head. 'You don't understand. We *have* to hold the meeting. In the jargon of the half-witted fools who now run our affairs, in order to find "a joined-up solution to a joined-up problem" and "speak with a collective voice", we *must* consult the people of Cossenford. Don't ask me what their language means – I doubt if they know themselves – but don't ask me to give up either, because I can't. People of my generation see things differently from yours. Whatever's old isn't necessarily ripe for the scrap heap; and I don't share Max Hasler's belief that what *he* calls progress is going to be of value to Cossenford. If you doubt me, kindly remember what we now have in place of the Book of Common Prayer – that was supposed to be progress too!'

Jane held up her hands in a little gesture of defeat. 'Then

I hope you win, Aunt Hannah. But be prepared to fight a man who believes that common sense and present-day realities are on *his* side, not yours.'

Hannah didn't answer for a moment, then she gave a sad, sweet smile. 'You seem to know him very well. It's difficult for you, having a foot in both camps.'

Jane shook her head. 'Strictly neutral, that's me. Now, let's talk of something else. Are you going to be able to manage the stairs, or shall I make up a bed for you down here?'

'I shall go upstairs as usual,' Hannah said with dignity. 'Well, not quite; a step at a time on my backside isn't how I normally reach my bed, but I expect to get there in the end.'

At that point she was interrupted by a knock at the front door, and Jane went to open it. Standing there was a tall, thin man who scarcely needed the dog collar he wore to tell her who he was.

He smiled shyly at her. 'You must be Joshua Venn's niece. I saw him just now and he said you were here to take care of Hannah. How very kind of you that is.'

'Will you come in?' Jane asked. 'I expect she'd love a visitor.'

'Well . . . I mustn't interrupt . . . But perhaps just a brief call – or would that tire her too much, I wonder?'

Seeing that a decision seemed beyond him, Jane firmly closed the front door and led him to the sitting room. Hannah was right: if the public debate depended on the vicar, the chapel was as good as lost already. But settled by the fire with his old friend, the Reverend Clive Weston – formally introduced by Hannah – relaxed and became an intelligent, articulate man. There would be nothing wrong with his ability to marshal an argument; the problem would be his extreme reluctance to step into the limelight as the counsel for the defence.

Jane foresaw that her next task would be to call at the library and run an eye over the other unpromising contender. If he could be coached to do what the vicar couldn't, between them they might make an adequate team.

The following morning, Hannah having decreed that on what was Palm Sunday *somebody* had to represent Maundy Cottage, Jane got ready to go to church. She could see that

that her rig – plaid skirt and crimson suede jacket – was being inspected.

'Sufficiently "neat but not gaudy" for Cossenford's Sabbath?' she enquired.

Unexpectedly, her aunt's severe face shone with amusement. 'You'll do,' she admitted, 'but I dare say there'll be one or two ladies with their minds not altogether on the sermon this morning. They'll ask how I am, and then want to know where your jacket came from.'

Jane blew her a smiling kiss and set out along Silver Street. The morning was chilly but fine, the church bells rang sweetly, and golden light lay over the old grey stone of the buildings around the square. She acknowledged their beauty, and the see-saw of doubt on which she seemed to be uncomfortably perched tipped again, this time in favour of the Cossenford Preservation Society.

Aware of footsteps behind her, she took no notice of them until she was overhauled and a familiar voice spoke in her ear. 'Are we allowed to walk together? Dear Jane, you're not forgiven for leaving me high and dry in London.'

She was swept by a wave of pleasure at the sight of him, and had no thought of concealing it. 'Max – how lovely to see you, but I imagined it was Germany you were still left in! Is your father mending?'

'Well enough, but my only half-joking suggestion that he should pack the rest of the family off to some distant spot and recuperate in peace by himself didn't go down very well. Of course, when I *am* serious my extraordinary relatives see only something that they can laugh at!'

'You confuse them deliberately,' Jane said. 'How can the poor things not get in a muddle?'

He smiled at her as if happy, she thought, to be back in Cossenford. 'You didn't answer my question – do we brave vulgar curiosity and go into church together, or slink in by separate doors?'

'Together,' she said firmly. 'We're neighbours, after all; not enemies.'

A minute or two later at the church door, she couldn't help noticing that even the vicar greeted them with an air of

surprise, but it was obvious that Max was enjoying the little stir their arrival was creating. She knew that Hannah would strongly disapprove, but she couldn't regret being with him, and even the visiting archdeacon's sermon went mostly over her head while she pondered what an unforeseeable thing happiness was.

Released into the bright morning again after the service, she waited for Max to suggest a stop at the Manor House, but when they reached his gateway he halted, smiling regretfully.

'Dear Jane, how stupidly our lives are arranged at the moment – you're tied to Cossenford, and I must dash back to London and Germany again. I only came down to visit my uncle yesterday evening – there are problems there to be dealt with as well.'

'Everyone seems to need you,' she pointed out rather sadly.

'Well, I need *you*. I even called at Hay's Mews on my way back from the airport, wanting lovely cool Jane after an over-dose of emotional Hasler relatives! It was a blow not to find you there.'

'You got the note I sent to Dolphin Square?' she asked anxiously.

'Yes, but I knew before I read it where you were. A girl was staying at your home – very pretty but rather disagree-able, I thought. She told me about your aunt's accident.'

'You must have seen Jill, my half-sister,' Jane explained. 'I didn't expect her in London quite so soon; she's just finished at drama school. I'm surprised you didn't like her – she usually makes a *very* favourable impression!'

'Not on me, *Liebchen*. Twenty years ago perhaps, but not now.'

Jane tried not to look pleased, and suddenly asked a question he didn't expect. 'Why did you go to church this morning – because it was Palm Sunday and that matters to you, or because you wanted to remind Cossenford that you're still here?'

His blue eyes held a sparkle of amusement. 'I had a bet with myself that you'd deputize for Hannah. I wanted to see you, but I didn't quite have the nerve to call at Maundy Cottage!'

89

Colour rose under her clear skin, but she managed to shake her head. 'Don't shake my confidence in you – nerve enough for anything would have been my guess.' Then she spoke of something else. 'Hannah expects you here for the public meeting in three weeks' time.'

'I wouldn't miss it for the world,' Max said, still with that glimmer of amusement on his face. But she gave him no answering smile, and he spoke again in a different tone of voice. 'There's no need to fret, you know, even if Hannah is relying on you to fight her corner. It makes no difference to us; in fact if you win I shall feel proud of you.'

That did make her smile, though rather tremulously. 'You're a very nice man, Max. Why doesn't the whole of Cossenford realize that?'

His reaction took her by surprise, until she remembered that it might be one of the serious moments that his family would probably fail to understand, and laugh at. 'Cossenford is probably right in whatever it realizes,' he said gravely. 'And you, my dear Jane, must remember who you are – a professional lawyer trained to expect very little goodness from human nature.'

Then he kissed the hands she held out to him, bowed his formal little bow, and stood away from her; it was time to say goodbye. She said it for him this time.

'*Auf wiedersehen*, Max.' She turned and quickly walked away. There was no reason, she told herself, for happiness to have suddenly disappeared. She might feel a little sad and incomplete because they seemed doomed to be in different places, but Max himself had said that she needn't fret. It would have been a comfort not to have the public meeting looming, but she could believe what he'd said, and shake off a silly premonition that events were taking charge of them.

Twelve

Back at Maundy Cottage Jane had first to report as much of the archdeacon's sermon as she could remember, then she telephoned Amanda Crichton, who confirmed that the next-door house key had indeed been asked for.

'No need to worry, though,' she added cheerfully. 'Peace reigns – no loud music, no orgies, nothing that even Sonia Drew-Brown could object to at all.'

'Has Jill said how long she'll be staying?' Jane asked next.

'She sounded vague – a few days, probably. She has some interviews lined up. I thought people in the theatre called them auditions.'

'Not any more – you're out of touch, I'm afraid.'

'Oh, I realize that whenever I catch sight of your lodger – so young, so maddeningly sprightly! Still, I have to say she seems quite sweet as well; not the vampire you led me to expect. Julian was impressed when she called round with a bunch of flowers – a thank you for the key-minding, she said.'

'Touching, I'm sure.' But it sounded too acid, and Jane quickly apologized. 'Sorry – I'm missing my home, my job, and my familiar haunts. Less than a hundred and fifty miles from London and this feels like the far side of the moon.'

'Aunt Hannah being difficult?' Amanda enquired sympathetically.

'Well, she's herself at all times – I suppose you might call that difficult, but the truth is that she's doing rather well. She never complains, and apart from a plastered leg she also has painful arthritis to contend with.'

'Tough country stock – not effete townees like us,' Amanda pointed out. 'But you could surely nip up for a breath of polluted London air if rustic life gets too hard to bear.'

'I might at that,' Jane agreed, smiling as she said goodbye, because even a telephone chat with Amanda linked her to the real world again.

Reality for the moment, though, was a Preservation Society committee meeting to be held in Hannah's sitting room so that she could take part.

'Join us if you want to,' Hannah said when the room had been arranged to her satisfaction. 'It might help you make up your mind.'

'It might also worry everyone else,' Jane suggested. 'I'd rather not leave it to one of the others to mention that I was seen walking into church with Max Hasler this morning.' Something in her aunt's expression made her go on. 'I had no idea he was here; in fact he only came down for one night to visit his uncle. But we *are* friends; I can't pretend otherwise.'

'There's no reason why you should,' her aunt said calmly. 'It's agreed that our fight with him doesn't involve you. But you could attend the meeting as a neutral observer – that might be very useful.'

It was typical of her, Jane realized – entirely sensible, and entirely without pettiness. 'All right, I will!' she agreed with a smile.

The committee members arrived punctually and, since the vicar came last, perhaps in ascending order of piety. They accepted Hannah's introduction of her niece quietly enough, leaving Jane to think that she'd underestimated either their natural good manners or their considerable respect for her aunt.

The evening's business was to discuss the public meeting – crucial, as the vicar reminded them, to a campaign that depended on a majority vote from the people of Cossenford. If more of them were content to see the proposed development go ahead than not, then no appeal could reasonably be brought against it.

Jane listened to the discussion, aware that Max wouldn't quite have things all his own way. These were, apart from Clive Weston and the librarian, retired citizens, but they weren't decrepit or uninformed, and they believed passionately that right was on their side.

When the meeting had broken up and the sitting room was restored to order again, Hannah seemed in no hurry to begin her slow journey upstairs. 'Well – what's the verdict?' she asked.

'More impressive than I expected,' Jane admitted. 'Especially if they can talk as well in public as they do in your sitting room.'

'That's the rub – they can't! Anything else?'

'It seems to me they all represent the same section of the community,' Jane suggested cautiously. 'What about the shop-keepers and pub-owners, the working parents with young children, even the single mothers – I suppose Cossenford has some?'

'Certainly – tell me where doesn't? But if they bother to come to the meeting they'll probably vote against us – especially the shopkeepers. I can't blame them for thinking they'd like some more rich incomers in the town, but they might remember that the people who can afford to buy Max Hasler's houses won't shop here; they'll bring down car-loads of exotic muck from Harrods.'

Jane grinned but went on, now professionally interested. 'Another thing: I heard what funds you've managed to build up – not a huge sum, even after years of effort. I'm afraid it won't come anywhere near to matching what a wealthy businessman can offer as a bid.'

'We never meant to try outbidding anyone. Until Max Hasler appeared on the scene we imagined the church authorities would feel obliged to *give* us a building they could no longer use. It still seems shocking to me that they should ever think of selling a church.'

'Then maybe your battle should be with them, instead of Max,' Jane pointed out.

Expecting Hannah to dismiss the idea, she was astonished to see her aunt's worn face light up. 'There you are – I knew you'd help, just by giving us an idea we'd never have thought of. I'll get on to Arthur about it in the morning.'

Jane got up and deposited a kiss on the lady's cheek, a gesture that surprised them both. 'All right, but you're tired out. Go to bed, please, and let Cossenford take care of itself for an hour or two.'

Hannah heaved herself as far as the hall, followed by Jane whose job it was to hold her crutches while she negotiated the stairs. There, she stopped for a moment, with something more still to say.

'I think I was born to spinsterhood, but I very much doubt if you were. Speaking personally I hope Max Hasler isn't the man you want, but if he *is*, then you ought to be free of Cossenford. That's not a way of saying I don't want you here – you know that isn't true.'

Jane's nod accepted the last part of what had been said; the rest of it was more difficult. 'What I wanted a month ago was just to be allowed to go back to work. The unexpected thing is that I've discovered how interesting life is, even away from Clifford & Partners! Max is part of the discovery, a happiness that I certainly didn't expect, but nothing is spoiled by my being here. So *now* will you please go to bed?'

'It's coming to something when I'm ordered about in my own home,' Hannah grumbled, but she couldn't get the old snap back in her voice, and made no more objection to struggling up the stairs.

The following morning, according to a routine inaugurated after a battle that she'd finally won, Jane carried her aunt's breakfast tray upstairs. On the bedside table, as always, was Hannah's much-thumbed Bible, and a strange-looking twig, alternately striped pale and dark, that Jane hadn't noticed before.

'It's part of my childhood,' Hannah explained, seeing her stare at it. 'We all had a stripped willow wand like that – "pretty sticks", we called them. They were to bring us luck, and keep us safe from harm. An old wives' tale, I suppose, but I wouldn't get rid of it even now.'

Jane pretended to look severe. 'Trying to shade the odds in your favour – the Bible *and* a pretty stick? You still got a broken ankle!'

'Doesn't count – that was sheer carelessness on my part.' Hannah put the thought aside and got down to the important business of the day. Jane's first task, it seemed, was to

deliver to Cossenford's outlying villages the bundles of leaflets that Arthur Cranston had brought with him the previous evening.

With Hannah safely installed in her armchair downstairs, telephone within reach and papers neatly spread around, Jane was free to start on the route mapped out for her. She enjoyed the trip: the morning was fine again, and every day seemed to add to the vivid spring greenness that flowed over the landscape, touching even the most ordinary bush in the hedgerows to astonishing beauty.

Her last port of call was the post office at Little Ham. Outside it was a combination she recognized – a small, red-headed boy and a large black dog. But Tom Venn looked worried, and Ben stood piteously holding one paw clear of the ground as if uncertain what move to make next.

Jane drew up beside them and wound down the window. 'Hello . . . Remember me? Hannah Venn's niece, Jane. Is something wrong?'

'Ben's limping badly – I shall have to carry him home.'

It was, she calculated, a good mile to Rushey Farm, and boy and dog were much the same size.

'Better let me drive you,' she suggested. 'Just let me deliver my leaflets first.'

A few minutes later they'd lifted the wounded hero into the car, and she took the now familiar lane up to the farm.

'He *would* chase a rabbit on the way down,' Tom explained, 'and he got stuck in the brambles. Dad says he's not very bright, and I'm afraid it's true.'

Remembering that it was a Monday morning, Jane asked the obvious question. 'By the way, shouldn't you be at school?'

'Easter holiday – just started,' said Tom with evident satisfaction. 'Two whole weeks off.'

Jane nodded, thinking that yesterday's Palm Sunday service should have been enough to remind her that Easter would be next. 'Perhaps we should have taken Ben to a vet,' she suggested next, and saw the astonishment in the child's face.

'We just need to find Dad, that's all.'

'Of course, stupid of me,' she agreed cravenly, and saw the beam of a smile light up his thin face. Not a pretty child,

Rufus Venn's son, but in the appealing stakes Jane thought he'd win hands down any time.

There was no one about as they drove under the archway and into the yard, but sounds of hammering came from the barn.

'The tractor's playing up again,' Tom predicted. 'Dad's better with animals than he is with machines – well, that's what he says, but I reckon he's good with most things.'

'You go and find him,' Jane suggested. 'I'll stay here with Ben.'

Deserted by his owner, Ben did his best to climb into her lap, but a moment later the car door opened, and the dog was disentangled from the gear lever and steering wheel. Rufus Venn nodded a greeting, holding Ben cradled in his arms.

'Thanks for bringing them home.'

He was a man of few words, she reflected. Dismissed, she was about to start the engine, but Tom seemed to have a more hospitable instinct than his father.

'Jane's coming in – she'll want to see that Ben's all right.'

An ironical cocked eyebrow made her decide to stay. 'Ben would expect it of me,' she insisted solemnly, glad to see that Rufus Venn didn't know whether to take her seriously or not.

They made a small procession into the house, to a room she hadn't seen before.

'Rushey's nerve centre,' he said with his usual brevity. 'Office, surgery, storeroom – whatever the occasion needs.'

Obviously familiar with the routine, Tom fetched the first-aid box from a cupboard while Rufus washed his hands at a little corner sink. Then he looked at Jane with a faint smile lurking in his beard. 'Tom's the surgeon's assistant; *you* get to hold the patient!'

She was told to sit down with Ben in her lap, paws in the air.

'Front right,' Tom explained. 'That's where he was going lame.'

'Not surprising – it's full of thorns. The silly daft dog must have landed in the middle of a patch of brambles.'

With Jane clutching the dog and Tom whispering to him that he must be very brave, Rufus gently prized the pads apart

and extracted the thorns. Ben gave a little whimper of protest, but more as a matter of form than anything else. It seemed to Jane that he understood the situation perfectly well – he was in the hands of someone whose job it was to heal his wounds.

'He'll do,' Rufus said, when antiseptic powder had been dusted on the pads and Ben was standing on all fours again. 'Keep him indoors, though, this morning.'

Tom accepted this and now turned his attention to their guest – how was *she* to be entertained? 'I could show Jane where the swans' nest is – it's still a bit squelchy, but . . .' He stopped short because his father was pointing to her beautiful suede loafers, and Tom smiled forgivingly. 'Another time – when you've remembered to bring your wellies.' Then he kissed Ben's head in passing as he made for the door – many things still to do, apparently, and too little time for doing them.

'You have a very nice son,' Jane said to break the silence that had fallen.

'I think so too. Most of the credit goes to his mother.'

It seemed doubtful, but Jane knew better than to argue the point; she had been snubbed once already on the subject of Tom. She was on the point of saying instead that it was time to go home when Rufus suddenly surprised her with a question.

'What sort of childhood did you have – happy?'

'No . . . lonely, I suppose,' she answered slowly. 'I wasn't too young not to sense my parents' unhappiness here. Then afterwards, when my mother remarried, I felt excluded from her new life. Some of it was my fault, I expect; still, it was a miserable time. I became a loner as a result.' Then Rufus saw her smile. 'But rather late in the day, Aunt Hannah and I are discovering each other – it's an unexpected pleasure!'

'What do you know about me from Hannah – if anything?' Rufus asked next, even more surprisingly.

'Not much,' she replied, aware that she must tread carefully. 'Only that you were a reluctant pupil and became an . . . an unconventional young man. And I know that Tom's mother didn't stay – that's all.'

'My life in a nutshell' Rufus agreed. 'Well, not quite. Until I was a bit older than Tom I had a lovely childhood, running

wild on the smallholding my parents had over on the other side of the hills. Then it all went wrong – my mother died of cancer, and my father committed suicide, unable to face life without her.'

'What happened to you?' Jane managed to ask, shocked by the bare outline of so much tragedy, and fearful of seeming to pry into what might be too painful to remember.

'I was sent to live with my grandparents in Cossenford, and became a complete mess – full of hate, mostly towards them, I'm afraid, and the life they led. My grandfather was a bank manager!'

'And that's when you met Aunt Hannah?'

The quiet question made him smile. 'Miss Venn, she was then, and my saviour she became. We've been friends ever since, and now she's Tom's friend as well.'

It was, Jane realized, the end of the conversation; his life with the girl who'd refused to stop wandering wasn't for raking over. But there was one more question she *could* ask. 'Where do we meet on the family tree?'

'Our great-grandfathers were brothers, according to Hannah, who knows about such things.' Then he brushed the past aside. 'She won't give up the fight against Max Hasler, but I expect you know that.'

'It's why I was at Little Ham this morning – delivering leaflets!' Jane's smile faded, leaving her face regretful, and the man watching her noted the change. In fact, she'd changed a great deal from the self-possessed, wary creature who'd judged him that first morning in Hannah's garden and found him wanting. His impression then had been that she didn't know what normal emotions were, but he'd been wrong to advise her afterwards to go back to London. Somerset might be the making of her.

'The public meeting is going ahead,' Jane said as she got up to leave. 'I don't suppose you or Uncle Joshua will be there.'

'You suppose wrong then. Dressed in our Sunday best, we shall represent Little Ham. Nothing would keep Joshua away if there's a chance of seeing Max Hasler bite the dust himself instead of trampling on some other poor sod.'

It was like the sting of cold water thrown in her face. The friendly understanding of a moment ago had suddenly vanished, and she was staring at Rufus Venn over a wall of suspicion and prejudice again. The sheer stupidity of it made her angry, but anger was better than wanting to weep for the grief of having to choose one side or the other.

'He's successful because he's very clever, as well as being hard-working,' she said fiercely. 'That seems to be too much for you to manage down here – the idea that success isn't necessarily something to be fought against as being inherently evil.'

But her anger was useless, she could see. Entrenched in opinions that common sense and tolerance could never change, this large stubborn man would take no more notice of what she said than one of his cattle outside would take heed of a sparrow landing on its head.

She walked to the door, but stopped there for one last parting shot. 'Don't encourage Uncle Joshua to think he's going to see Max humiliated. It won't happen.'

'Probably not,' Rufus agreed calmly, 'but we unsuccessful country bumpkins will go along anyway. Thank you again for bringing Tom and the dog home.'

He was a polite but inimical stranger, standing there, waiting for her to go. She gave a little shrug of despair and walked to her car, the end of yet another failed visit to her father's home.

Thirteen

Easter was only a day or two away. Conscious of the fact, Hannah left the vicar to his purely religious duties. Apart from the fact that the poor man was worked off his feet, priorities had to be observed. The week of Passiontide was no time to be planning municipal warfare.

Jane found herself taking Hannah's place, especially at the simple, moving services that led up to the great celebration of Easter itself. She went reluctantly at first, as an uncommitted bystander, but then recovered a forgotten ambition to spend Holy Week in Seville.

'Why don't I take you there next year?' she suggested to Hannah one evening, after describing what she could remember of the Spanish approach to Easter.

'I don't think so, but thank you all the same,' said Hannah politely. 'Good Friday is a tragic day, I grant you, but I couldn't be doing with all that weeping and wailing in the streets. Much better do it quietly, as we do here, following the cross round Market Square.'

It shouldn't have been funny but it was, and Jane's ill-timed sense of humour got the better of her again. Unable to keep her face straight, she expected to see her aunt looking outraged, but Hannah was beginning to smile too, and in a moment they were both helpless with laughter.

Wiping her eyes at last, Hannah came back to serious matters in Cossenford. 'You'll have to go instead of me on Saturday morning,' she said unsteadily. 'Nan Masterson isn't an admirer of mine so, Christian charity not being a virtue evident in all church flower-arrangers, she'll give you the most awkward window sill to decorate.'

Struggling not to start giggling again, Jane pointed out that

some experience in the art of arranging flowers might at least be helpful, if not obligatory.

'No,' Hannah contradicted placidly. 'Nan won't mind if you aren't very good – it's what she'll expect of the Venn family!'

The Venn family: Jane heard the phrase echo in her mind, aware that a watershed had just been crossed. Perhaps without even noticing it, Hannah had finally accepted her as one of them. The irony of it was that Jane herself knew who she still really was – neither Venn nor Westover; an outsider to both families, who'd return as soon as she could to her life in London with the relief of a creature restored to its true habitat.

Strangely following her train of thought, Hannah suddenly broached the subject herself. 'I know I've said this before, but I'll say it again: you mustn't feel bound to stay here, any more than there'll be anything to keep you away in future. I hope that's understood?'

Jane nodded and smiled at the simplicity in her aunt's approach to life that suited them both very well. 'I'm staying until the meeting's over and your leg is out of plaster – then I'll go home. But there's a small problem cropping up. I need some thinner clothes than the ones I brought – and there's another reason as well for a trip to London. My boss gives a party every year that I ought to go to – I don't want Clifford's to forget I exist!'

'Of course, go,' Hannah agreed, sounding unconcerned about it.

'It means staying a night in London. Who can we ask to sleep here so that you aren't alone?' She saw refusal in the glint in her aunt's eye and shook her head. 'I'm not going otherwise, so think of someone, please.'

Miss Venn twiddled her thumbs. 'A virtuous woman is above rubies, but so is a biddable one, according to my brother. You, I'm afraid, are no more biddable than I was – you won't get a husband that way.'

'I know, but then I don't know that I want one,' said Jane, pleased to be taking the wind out of Hannah's sails for once.

*   *   *

101

When Saturday morning came Jane raided the garden for an armful of flowers – white and gold tulips, and sprays of delicate spiraea blossom. Hannah touched them gently.

'Lovely Bridal Veil – it's out early this year. Nan Masterson will say it doesn't last, but then she always does!'

'Who *is* Nan Masterson, and why doesn't she like you?' Jane wanted to know.

'Wife of the chairman of the Town Council – very important, of course! John Masterson's a pleasant, well-meaning man, but we're not allowed to forget that in choosing an estate agent, Nan reckons she married beneath her. She'd like expensive new houses here – more of the sort of people she prefers to mix with.'

'So it comes back to the chapel again?'

'At the moment, yes; but I can't recall anything we've ever both agreed on. She's very efficient,' Hannah added fairly, 'and a good flower-arranger.'

'I foresee a jolly morning ahead – she'll have a lovely time sneering at my handiwork.'

'No, she'll think you're elegant and sophisticated – a credit to her usual scruffy team.'

Ten minutes later Jane was indeed greeted warmly and directed to a window in the chancel, where two other women were already at work. A container filled with damp oasis awaited decoration, and Mrs Masterson left her to it with only one quick glance at the flowers she'd brought.

'Hannah's spiraea again, I see – so pretty! We must hope it lasts until tomorrow.' And with that she sailed away.

'Cow!' said a voice beside Jane, only just out of range. 'Mrs M, I meant – not you.' The speaker was a fair-haired, twenty-something girl, with a gap-toothed, friendly smile, 'You're new, I think – welcome to the chain gang!'

'I'm standing in for my aunt, Hannah Venn,' Jane explained. 'Jane Westover by name.'

'Ellie – Ellie Chant, and that's my young man hiding behind the pillar.' She pointed to an infant sleeping soundly in a pushchair.

Jane looked at the flowers she still held, and then at Ellie. 'Help's needed, please – I haven't the faintest idea what to do!'

102

'Tall things at the back, shorter ones in front, greenery trailing along the window sill. You can't really go wrong unless you stick the flowers in upside down!'

'You're a great help,' Jane said, smiling at her, and then set to work. Half an hour later she stood back to take a look at the result – adequate but not as beautiful as the delicate cloud of white cherry blossom that Ellie had produced next door. 'What do you think – will it do?' she asked anxiously.

'Pretty good . . . just needs a bit more height.' Ellie pounced on a discarded eucalyptus frond in her basket. 'There, I think.' She tucked it at the back of Jane's arrangement, and suddenly it looked complete.

'What happens now? Do we stand to attention and await inspection?'

'No, we tidy up and creep out. At least, I do. Daniel will be waking up soon.'

She helped Jane to sweep her corner, then with a cheerful wave to Mrs Masterson, busy haranguing some other acolyte, they left the church together.

'It does look beautiful,' Ellie admitted. 'Let's hand it to the woman.'

'I'm going to Silver Street. If you're walking that way, why not come in and meet my aunt?' Jane suggested. 'She's house-bound at the moment with a broken ankle.'

'We're just round the corner. I rent a cottage from the council,' Ellie said. 'It's about as big as a squirrel's drey, but it does nicely for Dan and me.' She saw the query in Jane's face and answered it. 'No man! Perhaps I should have mentioned that before. Your aunt, like my parents, probably doesn't hold with single mothers.'

'I haven't asked her,' Jane admitted. 'But she loves children – she taught them at Cossenford School for years.'

That seemed to settle the matter and they turned in at the gate together. Ellie smiled up at the thatch-fringed dormer windows. 'Nice house . . . I've often thought so, walking past.'

Hannah looked surprised to see a stranger come into the sitting room with a child in her arms, but the meeting in church was explained and Jane retired to the kitchen to make coffee. By the time she returned with the tray, Hannah seemed to

know most of her guest's brief history, including the tale of the lover who'd disappeared even before Daniel was born.

'So how do you manage?' Hannah asked bluntly, never one to baulk at a straight question.

'I do care work for the council. It's not quite what I planned once upon a time, but I rather enjoy it now, and I only get sent to places where I can take Daniel.'

'Don't you ever get a chance to meet young people?' Jane asked with her aunt's directness.

'All the inmates of Wash Row are women like me,' Ellie explained wryly. 'They're nice enough, but they only want to talk about the last night's showing of their favourite soap!' She said it with a smile, but Jane glimpsed the loneliness of someone else who didn't belong.

Hannah was thinking more positively. 'There are good adult evening classes at the school, but I suppose Daniel is the problem.'

Ellie nodded. 'I'd have asked to join the church choir, because singing is what I was going to do once upon a time, but they practise in the evening as well.'

'Then you'd better bring Daniel here,' Hannah suggested briskly. 'If you can sing, Andrew needs you. We'll speak to him about it tomorrow.'

Daniel, wide awake now, indicated that he was due for some attention, and Ellie got up to leave. Jane offered to escort them both home, mainly with the intention of assuring the slightly bemused-looking girl that her aunt had been serious in her offer. 'She never says what she doesn't mean,' she said as they walked along.

'I haven't met anyone quite like her,' Ellie confessed.

Jane grinned at the girl by her side. 'Nor had I. Until a week or two ago I hadn't seen her for twenty-five years – or Cossenford at all, for that matter. It's been a steep learning curve!'

'But you're not here for good, I suppose. My guess is an exciting life in London!'

'Well, yes – when Aunt Hannah's recovered enough to leave; I'm a lawyer by training.'

'I planned to be a world-famous opera singer,' Ellie said

ruefully. 'Talk about pride coming before a fall! Instead of that, I wash the feet of old ladies who can't do it for themselves, and collect their pensions for them.' But at that moment Daniel laughed at her from the pushchair and Jane saw the change of expression on her face.

'Given the chance, would you go back to where you were?' She asked the question but she already knew the answer. 'No, of course you wouldn't, and you're thinking that only a fool of a childless woman would have bothered to ask!'

She wasn't mistaken – Ellie's glance *was* tinged with pity, even though on the face of it that was absurd. 'Daniel's worth whatever I gave up,' she agreed, 'and budding opera-stars are two a penny nowadays.'

'Andrew won't be able to believe his luck,' Jane said, smiling at her as they came to a halt in front of Ellie's buttercup-yellow front door. 'See you in church tomorrow.'

'Nice girl,' Hannah remarked when Jane got back to Maundy Cottage. 'We shall have to do something to help her. I'll talk to Andrew in the morning.'

'Which means you're planning to go to church?'

'With a little assistance from you,' Hannah admitted without a blush. 'I want to see "our" window sill!'

So, with the bells ringing out the joy of Christ's resurrection, a good percentage of Cossenford's population packed itself into the old grey church. Jane drove Hannah as far as the square, from where she could walk and then be lifted bodily up the steps – protesting, of course, but not entirely displeased to be causing so much 'fuss', as she phrased it.

It was a lovely service, with an air of celebration about it that Jane hadn't ever associated with an Anglican church before. When the great moment came ('Christ is risen, He is risen indeed') she felt the hair lift on the back of her head, knowing that something real and moving was happening. She'd joked with Ellie Chant about being on a learning curve, but it wasn't a joke at all, and the truth was that she had no idea where it was going to end.

After the service Hannah was besieged by friends, to whom Jane then had to be introduced. But they detached themselves

at last, taking Ellie and Andrew Yeo with them. The matter of her joining the choir had to be settled, and Hannah wasn't one to allow any grass to grow under her feet. Andrew, a confirmed bachelor, looked slightly surprised to find himself in Hannah's sitting room with a strange young woman and a chubby baby for company, but as well as being kind he was a devoted choir master, and he suspected Ellie Chant of being a Good Thing.

Sherry was poured and the conversation was going merrily when Tom Venn appeared at the garden door, closely followed by his father and Ben. The reason for the visit, he explained, was to bring Hannah his Easter present – a little wicker basket lined with a silvery cushion of pussy willow and filled with speckled brown eggs. She thanked him for the eggs and for what she knew mattered more – the presentation on which he'd expended so much loving care.

From then on the party became disorganized, thanks to Ben, but even merrier. Daniel was entranced by this exuberant black creature bigger than himself, who licked his bare toes so warmly. Rufus, rather to Jane's surprise, at once got on friendly terms with Ellie, and even spoke knowledgeably with her about music. It was plain, too, that he admired her for making so little fuss about raising Daniel on her own – in fact he admired her altogether, Jane thought.

She was busy pouring more wine when the telephone rang out in the hall, and Rufus went to answer it. He signalled her from the doorway, and murmured as she reached it: 'It's Max Hasler for you.'

There was no detectable expression in his face, nothing in his voice to say that he disapproved, but still she was quite certain that she'd been identified once and for all. She might have been driven to coming to look after Hannah, but her allegiance was to the wrong side. She was Max Hasler's creature – a townee like him, with skills and tastes and values that Cossenford and Little Ham knew and cared nothing about.

The assumption was maddening in its wilful certainty that only one side could be right – no shades of grey in Mr Rufus Venn's colour scheme; only black or white. Anger stiffened

her first words when she picked up the telephone, but the sound of Max's voice disarmed her immediately.

'My dear – for a dreadful moment I thought I'd rung Joshua's number by mistake! I've nothing vital to say; I just wanted to wish you a happy Easter Day, which we ought to be spending together.'

'Where *are* you spending it?' she asked, with the bloom of the day restored, just by hearing from him.

'Still in Dusseldorf, alas. I shall be back in London in a day or two, but with not much hope of getting down to Somerset. Can't you escape? I see Hannah as a malevolent spider keeping you trapped in her web!'

'No, don't say it,' she protested, laughing. 'There's nothing malevolent about her, and I'm frequently being told that she can manage on her own. I've promised to be here until after the public meeting, but I do have to come to London next Friday for the night.' She smiled at the thought that had just occurred to her. 'Will you be in London then? I need an escort to Piers Clifford's annual birthday bash at Claridge's!' There was a brief silence at the other end of the line. 'Piers is my boss,' she explained. 'A big name in the City.'

'Jane, dear, I know exactly who Piers Clifford is, and I shall make a point of being there. I forbid you to consider any other escort! Just give me my instructions.'

'Seven o'clock at Hay's Mews – black tie,' Jane informed him happily.

'Until then, then,' Max said, and rang off.

Jane replaced the receiver, accustomed now to his disinclination to linger over farewells, and went back to the sitting room.

'All well?' Hannah asked innocently.

Jane smiled at her and then, very sweetly, at Rufus Venn. 'All is *very* well; Max will be back in London on Friday to take me to Piers Clifford's party.'

Hannah nodded. 'You told me to think about that, and I have. I'm going to ask Ellie to stay overnight – Daniel will be here anyway while she's at choir practice. She'll probably want to refuse payment, but I'll buy something she needs for Daniel.'

Jane hesitated for a moment, looking across the room at Ellie, now deep in conversation with Andrew. 'Are you sure? She's very sweet, but you haven't known her long.'

'I'm quite sure,' Hannah said firmly, 'and so is Rufus. I consulted him.'

'Then who am I to disagree when you've arranged it so neatly!' She'd managed, she thought, to sound pleasantly amused. The fact that what she felt was sidelined and, once again, shoved outside the magic circle of Venn family life would soon be immaterial. She'd be back in London and safe in her own circle again, with Max.

Fourteen

It was all arranged very easily, the only problem being Hannah's suggestion that Ellie should be paid for the job, which Ellie refused. With her room made ready, and food laid in, Jane had only one more thing to do. She telephoned her mother with a question about Jill.

'She'll be back this evening,' was Elizabeth's answer. Then, with a note of slight embarrassment in her voice, she admitted that Jill had been in London longer than expected. 'I hope you don't mind, darling, but she's been having such a good time. Charlie's father has been introducing her to all sorts of useful people.' Then as an afterthought Elizabeth remembered what she ought to ask. 'How are things in Cossenford – is Hannah's ankle mending?'

'She's doing very well,' Jane said. 'I think she'd even have managed without me, but I'm glad I came. Why don't you drive over one day and have lunch with us?'

There was a moment's silence at her mother's end of the line. 'You mean you're going back again? Jane, dear, is it really necessary? It isn't as if you owed the Venns anything, after all.'

'That's true, but I'm not going back to settle a debt, only to finish what I started.'

'Well, you'll do whatever you make up your mind to,' Elizabeth agreed tartly. 'When have you done anything else?'

That was true too, of course, but Jane thought it wouldn't help to say so. Instead she insisted that Hannah would appreciate a visit – which probably wasn't true – and rang off. As usual a conversation with her mother hadn't been tension-free, but one good thing had come out of it: she knew she wouldn't have to share her house with Jill, even for one night.

*   *   *

She left Cossenford early on Friday morning, planning to be in London early enough to get her hair trimmed and to replenish whatever supplies Jill had used and probably not replaced. It felt strange to be back – strange and unexpectedly nerve-racking. Had it always been this noisy without her noticing it? Her house wasn't what she'd grown used to either – grey stone had become familiar now, with greenery everywhere and sweet country air.

Inside, at least, she found what she had expected: the care that Jill would have taken of it. Her sister knew precisely where she belonged, and it wasn't in the squalor of a student squat. But in the bedroom she had used there were still some of her things – perfume left behind, and make-up, and a copy of the bestseller she'd been reading. Whether Elizabeth knew it or not, she was obviously planning to return to London. Jane could see a problem looming when she returned home permanently herself. Share a house with Jill for any length of time she could not, even if James Westover himself should rise from the grave to accuse her of rank ingratitude.

That evening, anxiety led her to get ready much too soon, and she walked about like a nervous adolescent awaiting the arrival of her first date. The stay with Hannah had been recuperative – fresh air and wholesome food did wonders for skin and hair – and she had no doubts about her dress of delicate black chiffon draped into something beautiful. But formative years spent beside Elizabeth, and then Jill, had been painful, and she didn't need to be told that Max's standards would be of the highest when it came to the matter of how a woman looked.

His ring at the doorbell came as a relief, and the pleasure of seeing him again drove anxiety out of her mind. He looked splendid, of course – someone she could introduce to Piers Clifford, another exacting man, with justifiable pride. But Max also looked tired when he walked into her lamp-lit sitting room and, although he smiled his attractive smile, he made no attempt to touch her. They needed time, she thought, to recover ease with each other.

'There's no hurry to leave,' she suggested. 'A whisky before we go?'

'Please, Jane! It's been an exhausting afternoon.' He took a little sip from the glass she gave him and then repeated almost what her mother had said. 'Must you really go back to Cossenford – haven't you done enough for Hannah Venn?'

'I promised to stay until her leg comes out of plaster. It's only another week or two. Don't imagine that I'm behaving with saintly generosity of spirit – the truth is that I rather enjoy being there now.'

Max cocked a quizzical eyebrow, and she was provoked into persisting. 'I know you bought the Manor House because it's beautiful, but isn't there also something about the place itself? The more I see of the Levels, the more haunting and addictive they become.'

'Different, I grant you – addictive, definitely not,' Max said firmly. 'If I can't enjoy the civilized pleasures of city life, I want grand scenery. Somerset is not grand, my darling one – admit it!'

She enjoyed the endearment, but wouldn't entirely cave in. 'All right, but I still think it's beautiful.'

He downed the last of his whisky, then abandoned Cossenford as a topic of conversation. 'I take it that your half-sister has returned to wherever it is she belongs?'

'Bath,' Jane explained. 'She lives there with my mother. But she's left some of her things here, so I'm afraid she means to come back.'

'Sibling rivalry?' Max teased. 'Surely not.'

'Well, perhaps – in part at least. But we have a long history of not getting on, which I won't bore you with. In any case, it's time we left, I think.'

He stood up, holding out the elegant fringed shawl that she had been waiting to put on. His arms closed hard about her as he draped it expertly around her shoulders, and she was suddenly reassured. Whatever constraint they'd started off with was over now.

The evening was perfect from then on – beautifully arranged, as all the Clifford parties were, and with Piers himself the best of hosts. He was genuinely glad to see Jane, and lost no time in registering the quality of her escort. It pleased her very much to hear him suggest to Max that they

should meet again, and she was at pains to explain when Piers had turned away to speak to someone else that he was famous for being a difficult man to impress.

'I am aware, dear Jane,' Max pointed out with a smile. 'It's part of my job to know who is worth impressing and who I can safely ignore!' He said it lightly, but she understood that something serious was meant; Max Hasler was a clever, ambitious man whose intention was to see that the world became properly aware of him.

It was instructive to introduce him to Mark Rubens, who was, predictably, partnering Anna Soames. Mark was younger of course, perhaps by ten years, because he was the same age as Jane. She couldn't be anything but pleased to see him, but standing beside Max he looked more ordinary than she remembered. The two men exchanged comments that held no cordiality, and she clearly recalled a moment when she'd decided that they wouldn't like each other.

The superb dinner was followed by a toast to Piers, whose birthday the party celebrated, and a brief responding speech from him – erudite as usual, and sufficiently spiced with malice to be amusing but not uncomfortable.

'*Now* tell me that you're missing Cossenford!' Max murmured as their host sat down to warm applause. 'This is where you belong, sweetheart, not squelching along some waterlogged Somerset lane, or attending a riotous evening with the ladies of the local Women's Institute.'

She smiled but shook her head. 'I didn't say I planned to take root in Cossenford. But, apart from Hannah, there are other nice, interesting people who can't be dismissed as not worth knowing. I'm in very good odour with Andrew Yeo, by the way, because I introduced him to a girl who may very well transform his choir.'

'She can't, at least, make it any worse,' Max pointed out with his glinting smile. 'Now, let us forget Cossenford and enjoy what London has to offer.'

Jane smilingly agreed and forbore to remind him that he was the one who'd brought it into the conversation.

At the end of the party he returned her to Hay's Mews and

helped her out of the taxi. 'A nightcap, or are you leaving at dawn for some other capital city?' she asked.

He seemed to hesitate, unusually for a man who always knew clearly what he was going to do next. The invitation had been too obvious, she thought; Max liked subtlety almost before everything else – finesse, he would call it – and perhaps she only imagined that the tug of something more lasting than simple physical attraction pulled them together. But with a faint smile he nodded and then paid the waiting cabbie.

'I'm in London for a few days, so why not a nightcap?' he agreed as they walked to her front door, and she knew that a further decision had been taken: he would spend the night with her in Hay's Mews.

'It was a good party,' he said when they were in her sitting room with brandy poured. 'I saw you shine in your proper element – no wonder Piers Clifford wants you back.'

Jane smiled at him over her brandy glass. 'I have to admit that reading the *Financial Times* in Cossenford isn't quite the same thing as being in the thick of it in the City! I shall be happy when September comes.'

He watched her for a moment, vividly alive still with the excitement of the evening, and woken by it to an unusual kind of beauty. Then he put down his glass and smiled at her.

'Why are we behaving like nervous beginners, I wonder. I refuse to sit here talking high finance with you when what I need to do is take you to bed and make love to you. If that isn't what you want, I must leave.'

'Don't leave,' she answered. 'I want you to stay.'

The simple answer seemed to silence him for a moment. '"Oh, rare for Antony",' he quoted softly. 'No pretence, never any dishonesty. You're an unusual woman, Jane Westover.'

It wasn't, she supposed, the most lover-like declaration he could have made, but it was the one that pleased her most because she knew it to be a compliment that he'd meant.

It was easy after that to give herself to him with a joyous delight that made him realize how inadequately she must have been loved before. Now, he, the connoisseur, had things to learn from the beautiful generosity of her giving. They made love, then talked a little – idle, tender talk that led them back

to loving again. Jane wanted not to sleep; the night was too precious to waste. But tired and deeply content she did fall asleep in his arms at last.

She woke again only when the room was bright with early daylight. There was a moment of remembering, and of happiness because Max would still be there. But he wasn't beside her, and when she got up it was obvious that he'd already left the house. There was only a scribbled note left lying on her desk.

My dearest,
Thank you for everything about last night. Forgive me for not staying to watch you wake up, but I loathe having to walk out into the light of day wearing last night's evening clothes – so very obvious! Now I have to let you return to Somerset, but damn that inconvenient Puritan conscience of yours. You should be here with me; lovely beginnings are all very well, but they aren't enough. I'll telephone when I can.
Auf wiedersehen, mein Liebling,
Max

She read the note again to let it dispel her disappointment that he wasn't there, then smiled at what she should have expected. Of course he'd have hated to be seen in a dinner jacket at breakfast-time! Now she must do without him for a while, but that had been her own choice, after all – not something she could blame him for.

She brewed coffee, trying to think rationally about the future. He accepted the demands made on him by his family, but she doubted whether commitment to a woman was something he'd yet bargained for. She must let him discover for himself how precious it could be – how necessary it would become, in fact, when nothing else seemed more important than belonging to each other. They would find a way of living their complicated lives that miraculously combined freedom with complete trust.

But her own immediate hurdle was going to be Aunt Hannah and the Venns. Her bright bubble of happiness was

suddenly pricked by the thought of what lay ahead – the fractious public meeting, Hannah's chapel fight with Max, and the Venns' bitter conviction that they had cause to hate the family he sprang from. She wanted, more intensely than she'd have believed possible a few weeks ago, not to lose her rediscovered family, but she could see that she might have to.

She gave a little sigh, but put the problem aside as one she could do nothing about. It was time to set off for Cossenford, where Ellie Chant would be waiting to be relieved of nurse-maid duty.

In fact, unknown to Jane, Ellie had already been released because Tom Venn was in the garden at Maundy Cottage, carefully folding over the leaves of spent daffodils and narcissi and securing the bunches with elastic bands.

'Why do we do this, Hannah?' he wanted to know. 'I'm not sure they like it.'

'It doesn't hurt them, if that's what you're worried about,' she said firmly. 'They must die down naturally while the bulbs are storing up food for next spring, but this way they don't look too untidy while they're doing it.'

He didn't argue, because Hannah knew about these things, but his next job was more to his liking. She'd taught him to handle the tiny seedlings in the greenhouse, and his thin fingers were more skilful at repotting them now than her misshapen ones were. He was engrossed in the task when his father arrived, gave his shoulder an encouraging pat, and then moved on to where Hannah was sitting on a bench under the apple tree on the lawn.

'Tom's happy,' he said, smiling at her. 'What about you? How did last night go?'

'Enjoyably for all concerned. Daniel and I exchanged intelligent conversation until he finally fell asleep. Ellie came back looking as if she'd been to a party.'

Rufus inspected his friend's face. 'But something's bothering you, all the same.'

Hannah frowned over this. 'Andrew rang a little while ago. He may not be a great organist, but he knows about voices –

Ellie's, he says, is exceptional, even half-trained as it is. The inference is that we must do something about her.'

Rufus recognized the signs in his friend – she was now hell-bent on another crusade. Once a teacher, always a teacher, and Hannah could no more resist wanting to help Ellie than she could stop breathing.

'Be practical,' he pleaded gently. 'There'd be years of study still ahead, and Ellie has a nine-month-old baby dependent on her. She made her choice before Daniel was born, but if she regrets it now, she's got parents who should help her.'

'They *don't* help,' Hannah pointed out. 'They're too busy disapproving of a daughter who hasn't lived up to their expectations.' She stared at Rufus for a moment. 'Go on – say it! I'm a stupid old fool who shouldn't try to interfere. True, but I hate waste, and the worst thing of all is to see a God-given talent lying idle.'

'I know,' Rufus agreed, 'but I doubt if there's anything you can do about it.' He hesitated for a moment, then went on. 'If you can take your mind off Ellie for a moment there's another problem to talk about. Wells Cathedral School is looking for new entrants in September. I let Tom go in for the competition more as a game than anything else, because he sings like a bird, but the outcome was extraordinary – they were impressed enough to offer him a place if he wants it. I have to let the choirmaster know quite soon.'

Hannah digested the news in silence for a moment. 'What will he say, do you think?' she asked finally.

'No, probably – if only because it would mean leaving Ben behind; boarders don't get to take their dogs along with them.'

There was another little pause before she spoke again. 'He'd get a good education there, Rufus, apart from wonderful music. What would you do with him otherwise when he leaves Cossenford School?''

'I hadn't made up my mind – Sexey's maybe, or Bruton. It was still eighteen months away, I reckoned.' Rufus stared down at his brown hands, locked together between his knees. 'The farm is his world, Hannah – he knows and loves every inch of it, and there he's as free as the wind.'

She nodded, knowing that it was true. Tom could spot a sedge warbler or a plover faster than his father could; he knew where to find the lovely blue damselflies, and the first marsh marigolds and wild irises. He belonged where his home was.

'He'd hate Wells to begin with – of course he would,' Hannah agreed slowly. 'But children are adaptable, Rufus. I think he'd make friends and settle down – he's a brave, self-reliant little boy.'

'Who, according to your niece, is suffering from an unnatural childhood! I was very short with her, I'm afraid, but the truth is that she's probably right.'

'Up to a point – but remember that Jane's own childhood was scarred by loneliness. Tom doesn't go short of love, which she probably did.'

Hannah stared at the man beside her for a moment, knowing the reason for the sadness in his face. Tom was Selina's son, all he had left of their life together. Going away to Wells would change him – couldn't help but do so – and Rufus didn't want him changed.

At last she broke the silence that had fallen; it took courage, because she knew she was trespassing on forbidden ground. 'You don't need me to tell you that Tom lacks a mother. It's also true that you lack a wife, but I expect you'll say you aren't inclined to do anything about that.'

'It's exactly what I'll say,' he agreed briefly, but his smile was sweet, forgiving her the intrusion. 'No matchmaking, please, Hannah! Trying to marry me off to poor Ellie isn't the answer to our problems.'

While Hannah tried to look as if the idea hadn't so much as crossed her mind, Rufus still pondered the future. Then he suddenly stood up, brushing his problems aside. 'I'd better do something useful since I'm here – like mow your lawn! Tom and I will disappear before Jane Westover gets back.'

'You won't; you'll stay to lunch,' Hannah snapped, glad to be able to sound definite again. 'The pair of you look thin – that feckless Annie Clark doesn't feed you properly.'

He was still smiling at the thought when Ben began to bark a welcome because someone was walking round the corner of the house.

'It's Jane, back already,' Hannah said, sounding very pleased. 'That's nice.'

Rufus watched her approach – a tall, slender figure in city clothes that reminded him of the first time he'd seen her, in this same garden. But she wasn't the wary, half-hostile girl she'd been then. Discovered happiness had made her beautiful. He knew that they could think what they liked of the man she'd gone to London to meet; it wouldn't matter to her. She was in love with Max Hasler, and contentment shone out of her. He didn't know why it should hurt so much – he didn't normally grudge other people their happiness. Perhaps it was because the joy Jane Westover was now feeling he had known with Selina, but that had been lost a long time ago.

He got up and walked away, without waiting to say hello, and Hannah was left to apologize. 'Rufus has got things on his mind,' she explained. 'He didn't mean to seem rude.'

Jane remembered their last exchange of words in the hall of the cottage and shook her head. 'I think he probably did, but it doesn't matter.'

'He and Tom are staying to lunch,' her aunt had to explain. 'I insisted.'

'Then I'd better go and see if there's anything to eat.' But first she smiled wryly at her aunt. 'In case anyone is interested, I had a lovely time in London!'

'I'm glad,' said Hannah. 'I expect you wished you didn't have to leave.'

Jane looked around her – at the sunlit garden scented now with wallflowers in bloom, the old stone house, and then the anxious, loving face of the woman who sat watching her.

'No, I didn't wish that,' she finally answered. 'I'm glad to be back.'

Fifteen

Absent-mindedly changing out of her London clothes, Jane thought about what she'd just said. It was true, not a well-intentioned fib for Hannah's benefit. She'd much rather be in Cossenford doing something useful than hang about in London, waiting for Max to find time to include her in his busy life. Instinctively she realized that she mustn't become dependent on him. He wasn't like other men she knew, afraid of what they saw as unfair competition; he'd come to despise any woman who simply handed over to him the tiring business of being responsible for her. She smiled at her image in the mirror, suitably countryfied again in jeans and a cotton shirt, and went downstairs in search of something to give Hannah's guests for lunch.

She put eggs on to boil, and assembled the rest of the ingredients for a colourful *salade niçoise*. With the meal ready and the table laid, she decorated it with forget-me-nots that now made a froth of heavenly blue beside every path. Did Hannah have to sow them every year or did they obligingly come up by themselves? she wondered. Like so much else, it was something she didn't know, but she promised herself that she would find out – then smiled at the memory of what Max had said: an English wife would want to carve up his beautiful lawns and make flower beds instead!

She went outside to call the workers indoors, only to find Tom already escorting Hannah back to the house. Rufus Venn was sweeping up lawn clippings, and the scent of the mown grass combined with the wallflowers' perfume was something else to store in her memory bank.

Five minutes later, washed and brushed up, the Venns were seated with Hannah at the kitchen table.

'Oh, pretty!' said Tom, looking not at the forget-me-nots but at the plate Jane had put in front of him. Then he grinned at his father. 'I don't know what some of these things are, do you? Annie Clark only gives us boring food.'

Aware that Jane waited for him to confess that he knew no more than Annie did, Rufus answered solemnly. 'It's called a *salade niçoise*, presumably because it was invented in a city in the south of France. The black things are called olives – delicious but beware of the stones they've probably got inside – and the pink strips aren't bits of Parrett eels but little fish called anchovies – delicious but very salty! Everything else I expect you know.' Then he smiled sweetly at Jane.

The challenge had been silly, she realized. Hadn't Hannah said that with their horse and caravan he and Selina had wandered the Continent for years? Rufus Venn wasn't the uncouth yokel of any crass Londoner's imagining. He was a much-travelled, widely experienced man who simply preferred the life he'd finally chosen. It would be as well to remember that before she crossed swords with him in future.

She was glad when Tom, carefully sampling the contents of his salad, beamed at her across the table. 'You were going to come and see the swans. They've got babies now, of course. The chicks are called cygnets, but I 'spect you already knew that.'

He waited so hopefully to be told that she knew nothing about swans at all that Jane felt obliged to be economical with the truth – she knew the name, but only because cygnets featured in a ballet she was very fond of, called *Swan Lake*.

Tom gave a little sigh – there was so much to learn. What, pray, was a ballet?

'A story told by people dancing to music,' Jane explained briefly. 'There are lots of different stories – this one is about a princess who gets turned into a swan.' She smiled at the expression on Tom's face but shook her head. 'All right – it sounds silly to you, but it's very beautiful and moving to watch. May I come and see your cygnets tomorrow after church?'

'Sure can,' said Tom, with an entrancing grin at his father, who would otherwise complain that he'd been watching too many American gangsters on television.

The salad was demolished, followed by the cheese and fruit that Jane brought to the table. Then Tom asked permission to leave on account of Ben's weakness for cheese. His keen nose told him that it was what they were eating, but if he wasn't to be allowed any, Tom thought it would be kinder to take him outside.

'One piece only,' Hannah said, trying to sound stern. 'To be eaten in the garden.'

When dog and smiling boy had disappeared, Rufus shook his head at Hannah. 'Emotional blackmail and you fell for it. That hound does not eat with us at home.'

'Quite right,' Hannah agreed calmly. 'Animals must be taught their proper place. Now, Rufus, tell me about Neil Gibson, please. The last time I asked Joshua he said the poor man was in a bad way.'

'Neil's being squeezed to death,' was the sombre answer. 'He's got the conservation people saying what he must do to safeguard the wetland ecology. But he has a close neighbour with the opposite idea – Luke Winters wants to lower the water table, dry out the meadows, and plough them up for arable crops. Neil's caught between the devil and the deep blue sea, because both sides are powerful, and he isn't.'

'What happens if he just ignores them all and pleases himself?' Jane asked.

'He goes bust,' Rufus answered bluntly, 'sooner rather than later.' It was tempting to ask whether a smart alec City lawyer had any more useful advice to offer, but he knew it would be unfair. He had no right to expect her to understand the conflicting pressures that some farmers were cracking under.

'So what *will* Neil do?' Hannah persisted.

'He'll have to sell up – either to Luke Winters, or to us, if Joshua has any hope of scraping enough capital together. On its own the Gibson farm is too small to survive; in today's conditions it makes sense to amalgamate, heartbreaking though it is for Neil.'

'But if Uncle Joshua can't meet the asking price, and this other neighbour buys Neil Gibson out, then you'll have him farming differently next door to *you*,' Jane risked another snub to point out.

'Our problem in a nutshell,' Rufus agreed, 'but we're bigger than Neil, with a little more clout.'

It was Hannah who decided to explain to Jane who Luke Winters was. 'I told you about James, the son of Horace and Jane Winters. His daughter, Emily, still lives at Talbot's, with her layabout husband. But James bought land on this side of the hills for his son to work – an insurance, I expect, against the day when the peat runs out.'

'So Luke Winters is . . . is Max's first cousin,' Jane said slowly. She smiled ruefully at her aunt. 'It's a tight little world in these parts – everyone you meet has a name that's familiar, and a connecting life story!'

'Of course,' Hannah agreed. 'That's how Levels people want to keep it, too. We aren't keen on incomers.'

'Well, you'll probably have to get used to them,' Jane pointed out, more sharply than she intended.

Rufus smiled at Hannah. 'Are we being warned that Max Hasler is likely to win his chapel bid? Perhaps Jane is kindly suggesting that we should back off while we've still got the chance!'

She could have sworn that genuine amusement lifted the corners of his mouth; but even malice would have been preferable to the suspicion that he found her faintly laughable. It might have been possible to admit to Hannah, but certainly not to him, that the disclosure about Luke Winters was also troubling. Matters were complicated enough already without another contentious strand being woven into the story. Jane Venn's desertion to the ranks of the Winters ought to have been accepted without bitterness long ago. But the two families were still bitterly at odds, and she could see why Max hadn't mentioned his cousin.

Pushing this new anxiety aside, she challenged Rufus with one last question. 'Does survival depend on size? Can Rushey hang on simply because it's bigger than Neil Gibson's farm?' She half expected another put-down, but after a moment he answered as gravely as she had spoken.

'Size helps in all sorts of ways, but Rushey has the added advantage of being a mixed farm. Thanks to Joshua's foresight we do all the things a good Somerset farm should be

able to do – dairying on the meadows, of course, but arable higher up, and sheep on the hills. We produce a lot of vegetables, even still grow cider apples. It doesn't add up to a fortune, but we get by.'

'That's what I wanted to know,' she answered, wondering why he then stared at her as if she'd taken him by surprise. But instead of continuing with the conversation he merely said it was time he collected up his hangers-on and took them home. He smiled at Jane on his way to the door. 'Thanks for the lunch. You'll catch me out next time – my culinary knowledge doesn't extend very far!'

She might have confessed that hers didn't either, but she wasn't inclined to yield any ground to Rufus Venn. Unable to place him, she felt at a disadvantage that ought to have been absurd. For a backwoods farm manager, if that was what he was, he was remarkably at ease with himself. She shrugged the thought aside, regretting that she'd promised Tom a visit the following day. Come to think of it, it had been another mistake to suggest that she'd be going to church. She wasn't part of this enclosed self-satisfied little world which, as she kept being told, refused to encourage outsiders to think they could break into its magic circle.

'You're looking cross!' Hannah's voice broke into her thoughts, reminding her that this forthright lady's eye missed very little of what went on. 'I'm afraid you don't take to Rufus. He doesn't usually look much, I grant you, but he cleans up surprisingly well.'

'I like his son,' Jane pointed out. 'I'm afraid that will have to do.' Then she smiled at her aunt. 'The trouble is that I don't quite know where I am at the moment – definitely out of my depth here, but not quite at home in London either until I get my job back.'

'Uncomfortable,' Hannah conceded. 'I can see that. I'm glad you enjoyed your party, though. If I didn't think to ask straight off, it was because my mind was fixed on something Rufus had been saying.'

She didn't seem inclined to report what that was and Jane didn't enquire. 'How did the choir practice go?' she asked instead. 'I'll be disappointed if Andrew Yeo doesn't think he's got a star in Ellie.'

'Oh, he thinks that all right, but the poor man's torn in two – he longs to keep a soprano who can actually sing; on the other hand, he reckons she should be encouraged to leave Cossenford as soon as possible and find a proper music teacher. Rufus insists that she'd still put Daniel first, so I don't see how it's to be done.'

It was another problem to consider, but Jane put it aside for a more immediate one. 'What about the public meeting – is there anything left to arrange?'

Hannah shook her head. 'All we need now is a good turnout next Friday, and the gift of tongues to descend on the vicar and our other committee members. I'd be obliged if you would help me get to the Town Hall, but you needn't do more than that. You don't even have to stay and listen.'

'I shall certainly stay,' Jane promised. 'I may not be committed to one side or the other, and I'm not entitled to vote, but I can't help being interested.'

Hannah nodded, and had the kindness not to drag the name of Max Hasler into the conversation. Instead, she veered off in a different direction. 'Wellies – you'll need them tomorrow because Tom doesn't do things by halves. His idea of a nature ramble probably means getting *in* the rhyne, not admiring the cygnets from dry land.'

'Delightful,' Jane managed to say. 'Will Ben want to frolic in the water with us, too? I'd think so, wouldn't you?' She asked the question solemnly, but it was too much for Hannah and the conversation ended in another gale of shared laughter.

The next morning in church she understood Andrew Yeo's dilemma. Galvanized by Ellie's presence among them, Cossenford's choir sounded as it had never sounded before. But the real revelation came during Communion, when she sang alone an 'Ave Maria' that Jane didn't recognize. Her voice soared up, pure and effortless as a bird's, so beautiful that even the carved angels on the roof-beams seemed to be smiling.

When the service was over the soloist had to accept a shower of compliments before she could retrieve Daniel from the vestry crèche and go outside. Jane was still there waiting for her.

124

'How was London?' Ellie wanted to know. 'Have you got time for coffee? There's a short cut through to Wash Row.'

'I'd love to come, but I must scoot home and change; I'm due at my uncle's farm. We'll get together soon though, Ellie. Thanks for looking after Aunt Hannah.'

Ellie's gap-toothed grin shone for a moment. 'I had the feeling she was looking after Daniel and me! Did the 'Ave Maria' sound all right, by the way? People here are very kind, but I know I'm rusty.'

'Then I just hope I'm around to hear you when you think you're in practice again – it sounded glorious to me.'

The colour rose under Ellie's fair skin, and Jane wagged a disapproving finger at her. 'You're supposed to learn how to behave like a diva. The idea is to spurn honest compliments, not blush with pleasure!'

Hearing his mother laugh, Daniel clapped his hands together and laughed too. Watching them, it seemed to Jane that Rufus Venn was probably right about Ellie Chant; tragic though the waste would be, she'd choose to remain fixed in the lonely little life she'd fashioned for herself out of heartbreak and betrayal.

Back at Maundy Cottage, Hannah was waiting to deliver a message. 'You've just missed Max Hasler, I'm afraid. He said not to ring back because he was going out, but he'll call this evening. He sent his love to you and his good wishes to me – very civil of him when we'll be fighting each other tooth and nail on Friday.'

For 'civil', Jane thought, read 'mocking' or 'insincere'. It was probably useless to try to make her aunt understand the mixture that was Max – business ruthlessness went with sensitivity, his indifference could be cruel, and then there was his tenderness, and always an abiding love of beauty.

'You won't believe it, I'm afraid,' she suggested, making one last attempt, 'but he'll have meant what he said. He'll argue his case on Friday as strongly as he can, but if he loses he'll applaud you as the winner and mean that as well.'

Hannah considered this for a moment, not for what it was intended to reveal about Max Hasler, but for what it explained about Jane's view of him. 'If you're right,' she answered at

last, 'he'll be a better Christian than I am. Applauding him if we lose is more than I could undertake to do.' Then she suddenly smiled at her niece. 'You'd best get off to Rushey – Tom will have been looking for you since breakfast-time.'

'Then I'll change and be on my way, but we must talk about Ellie when I get back.'

Ten minutes later, dressed in jeans, shirt and sweater, she pointed the car in the direction of Little Ham once more, concerned for the moment with the different problem Rufus Venn had raised over lunch the day before. The chances were that Joshua would choose to be hung, drawn and quartered before he'd discuss with a woman – and one called Westover at that – any financial problem that he had. If the farm *was* willed to Rufus, as Hannah had suggested, that would be an added reason for keeping Gideon's daughter in the dark.

She drove slowly, with the thought of the farm leading her mind back to Max. If she hadn't waited to talk to Ellie she would have been back in time to speak to him; any contact was precious, even a telephone conversation was something she hated to have missed. But that led her to something they *had* talked about on the night of the Clifford party. He required grand scenery, he'd said, and it was true that the landscape she was driving through wasn't grand – gentle green hills instead of harsh mountains, willow-lined streams, and little rivers that, in local parlance, 'riddled along' through the meadows on their rather unenthusiastic way to the sea. But she'd been right to insist that this quiet landscape was beautiful, with a beauty born of the unending care that had been taken of it. She understood now why men like her uncle would struggle all their lives to hand it on to the next generation at least as tended as they had found it.

There were no cattle in the yard this time when she drove in under the archway. Already, presumably, the animals were outside, feeding happily on the new grass that was speckled with wild flowers. Tom was there, clearly on the watch for her.

'I thought p'raps you weren't coming,' he said as she opened the car door and Ben bounded up to lick her nose. 'I 'spect

the vicar had a lot to talk about this morning. Dad says they never do know when to stop!'

'They never know whether we've been paying attention,' Jane pointed out, not disposed to agree with any of the sayings of Rufus Venn.

But she couldn't help smiling at his son. There was something about Tom's thin, freckled face under its thatch of fiery hair that would draw a smile from the Devil himself. Jane pitied the girl who hadn't stayed with him long enough to learn what she'd be missing by running away.

Tom was looking at her neat footwear regretfully. 'We don't *have* to wade, but . . .'

'It's more fun if we do,' she finished for him, squatting at the car door to change her shoes for the wellingtons Hannah had reminded her to buy.

Then, with Ben alternately dashing ahead and racing back to make sure he hadn't mislaid them, they walked and slid and sloshed their way through meadows criss-crossed with streams and rivulets to the deeper rhyne where the swans had made their nest. Sheltered by tall rushes and reeds, and now golden with water iris, it seemed the perfect spot to raise a family. First, though, Tom pulled a lead from his pocket and tied Ben to a willow branch.

'We mustn't go too near, either,' he said next, 'because the mother swan, she's called a pen, wouldn't like it. But look – there they are!' With the pride of a magician conjuring the required rabbits out of his top hat, he pointed to six tiny balls of brown fluff bobbing every which way on the surface of the stream. Behind them loomed the stately mother swan, pure white, beautiful and dangerous, who only relaxed her guard when they finally turned away.

With Ben freed again to chase birds that he had no expectation of catching, they walked slowly back to the farmhouse – slowly because Tom had so much to explain. He knew water-loving from meadow plants, and could name them all – things like butterbur, frogspit, duckweed and cotton grass. He could describe the life cycle of damselflies and water beetles; and point out where the godwits rested during their long migration flights. It came as a surprise to him when she had to

127

admit that she didn't know any of these indispensable facts of Levels life.

'But I 'spect you know about other things,' he suggested kindly. 'London things.'

She agreed that perhaps she did, then asked the question that was worrying her. 'You belong here, so of course you ought to know the plants and creatures that you share the countryside with. But what about the other things that boys usually think important – football, say, or pop music, computer games?'

His smile suggested that she was insane to even ask the question. 'Of course, I like them all right – Dad does, too. We watch football together. But it's only a game. The lapwings arriving, the eels and otters in the rhynes – they're *real*, Jane.'

He'd put it very succinctly, she thought; just the necessary distinction made between the games that grown men played and the important things that children like himself knew all about. Die now you self-styled experts and interpreters: out of the mouths of babes and sucklings still came the real truth!

Back at the car again she was about to thank Tom for a lovely visit and then drive away, but Joshua Venn chose that moment to walk towards them from the barn.

Tom offered Jane as a parting gift the news that they'd look for otters the next time she came, and then went off with Ben. Left alone with her uncle, without conscious thought she took the opportunity that presented itself.

'The name of Neil Gibson cropped up yesterday. Rufus seemed to think he would have to sell up.'

'He must, like plenty of others before him,' Joshua replied. 'Every season sees someone else go to the wall, thanks to the fools who govern us in Whitehall and the thieves in charge in Brussels.'

No mincing of words with Joshua, Jane reflected, any more than with his sister. 'It's a simplistic view,' she ventured.

'I'm a simple man,' said her uncle.

She was tempted to suggest that he was anything but, then decided against it in case he didn't also share Hannah's un-expected capacity for humour.

'I know that someone called Luke Winters might become

your neighbour if Neil Gibson goes,' she said instead.

'There's no "might" about it; he will. The man's got a father rich enough to buy half of Somerset if he wants it. It'll mean more pasture ploughed up for crops that were never meant to be grown here, and more pressure brought to bear on the river authorities to let the land dry out.'

Jane was silent for a moment – not astonished by the idea that had come into her head, only uncertain about how to offer it. 'If you *could* buy the farm, would you be able to work it – you and Rufus?'

The expected explosion came. 'We *can't* buy it, girl, not without ruining ourselves, so there's an end to it!' But as if he regretted shouting at her, he tried to speak more quietly. ''Tisn't your problem, Jane. I expect Rushey will go on as it is, even with half a dozen Winters next door.'

'Gideon Venn was my father,' she pointed out. 'Why shouldn't it be my problem as well as yours?' Before he could recover from this frontal attack she went firmly on. 'Uncle Joshua, listen, please. I earn a lot of money, much more than I need to live on. I'd like to put some of it into Neil Gibson's farm, so that it can be added to Rushey.'

From being flushed a moment before, his face had paled now and he suddenly looked a tired, elderly man. 'You don't know what you're saying . . . don't even understand how things are. Rushey will go to Rufus when I die. It's only fair – he's a Venn, and he's done more than his share of the work for years; after that it will be Tom's inheritance, not yours, even though you are Gideon's daughter.'

'I think it's fair, too – what do I know about running a farm in Somerset? That doesn't stop me wanting to help. Will you let me?'

Joshua's shake of the head answered before he did. 'No, I won't. Farming's a high-risk business now, and only fools like us who know no other way of living stick it out. Lose what you've earned however else you like, but not here. That's my last word, Jane.'

'I should have expected it,' she said with the calmness of despair. 'Aunt Hannah is kind enough to pretend that I sort of belong, but even she knows it isn't true, of course.'

She smiled faintly at the stubborn, set face of the man who stared at her. 'I shall simply hope that Neil Gibson gets to keep his land after all, by some miracle or other.'

She picked up her jacket and opened the car door, thinking that the conversation had ended, but she was halted by the sound of Joshua's voice, gruff and almost apologetic. 'I didn't thank you for the offer . . . I should have done.'

She simply waved it away and started the car. Her final visit to Rushey was over, and, the visit to the cygnets apart, it had been as much of a failure as the ones that had gone before.

Sixteen

She got back to Maundy Cottage to find Hannah, more wooden-faced than usual, entertaining unexpected visitors. Elizabeth Westover hastily explained the reason to Jane: they'd been in Wells that morning, and it had seemed a brilliant idea to drive the extra miles to Cossenford. It was hard to fathom what Hannah thought of the visitation, except that Jill's skintight jeans and shirt inadequately buttoned-up had been judged and found wanting for a Sabbath social call.

Aware that something was wrong, she was doing her best, and under the onslaught of so much vivacious charm even Hannah's defences were beginning to crack. Teasing sweetness was all very well but there was only so much of the display that Jane could bear to watch. She retired to the kitchen to make tea, and returned to the sitting room in time to hear that Cossenford's Manor House was being discussed.

'It's enchanting,' her mother said. 'I suppose it's belonged to the same Somerset family for generations.'

'It did,' Hannah agreed, 'but it was sold a year or two ago when Mildred Luscombe died. She was a spinster, with no heirs.'

'So who owns it now?' Jill wanted to know.

Hannah answered without looking at Jane. 'A man called Max Hasler. He's not here very much, but he has relatives across the hills in the Brue Valley.'

'Max . . . Max Hasler,' Jill said slowly. 'I've heard that name before.' They watched the actress at work being thoughtful, and Jane reckoned she could guess what would come next. 'Got it! He was the man who called at Hay's Mews one evening when I was there. He seemed very disappointed, Jane, when I said you were in Somerset.'

'I heard that you met,' Jane admitted. 'As Aunt Hannah says, he's not often in Cossenford, but we bumped into each other accidentally one day in church.' Jill wagged a teasing finger at her. 'You did more than that, methinks, if he calls on you in London! Can this be a conquest, sister dear?'

Jane reminded herself that it would be very wrong to hope for her sister to drop dead at her feet. But while she instead worked out what to say next, Hannah came to her rescue.

'Max Hasler is distantly related to the Venn family by marriage,' she announced in a voice from which every hint of feeling about the matter had been ironed out. 'Our concern with him at the moment is a local dispute: he would like to knock down a building we would prefer to keep. It has nothing to do with Jane – it's a Cossenford matter.'

Jill appeared to lose interest in the subject, and so it was Elizabeth's turn to come to the real point of their visit.

'We wanted to check up on Hannah, of course,' she said, smiling at her one-time sister-in-law, 'but also to ask a favour of Jane!' She turned to her elder daughter with the smile fading into a look of anxiety. 'Darling, if you're going to be here for a while still, could Jill go back to Hay's Mews for a week or two? She's had the most incredible luck – landed a part in one of Michael Rutherford's productions. Rehearsals start almost at once, and it would be *such* a help if she could be sure of somewhere comfortable to stay while she gets used to an actress's rather strange way of life!'

Jane didn't answer at once and again it was her aunt who filled the pause. 'What is the play?'

'Chekov's *Three Sisters*.' It was Jill who answered, dramatically, of course. 'I've got the smallest female part of all, but I shall make sure it counts!'

Jane asked a question of her own. 'What about your friend Charles – is his father giving his career a kick-start too?'

Jill now looked deeply regretful. 'Alas, no. Poor Charles is too dire for words, I'm afraid. He only lasted the course at Bristol because they couldn't bring themselves to sack the great Sir Michael's son.' She examined her fingernails for a moment, then looked directly at Jane. 'I left some things at your house – forgot them, actually. I wasn't trying to railroad

you into having me back. If you can't stand the idea, don't let Mummy twist your arm; theatrical digs are usually rather ghastly, but I'm sure I shall survive.'

It was cleverly done, Jane reflected – candid, brave, and a little wistful, with just the tiniest hint that her well-established sister would be an unfeeling, selfish bitch if she didn't help a girl who was still at the bottom of the ladder. Even Hannah, she could see, was wondering why Jill wasn't immediately being made welcome.

'Use the house, but not, please, as a long-term arrangement,' she finally answered over the lump of reluctance in her throat. 'I shall be back soon myself and I want, at some point, to be able to offer my spare room to a friend who doesn't have quite your advantages.'

'You see before you the perfect temporary house-guest,' Jill promised sweetly.

There seemed to be nothing left to say, except that Jill remembered to invite Hannah to the first night of the play. 'That horrid plaster will be off your leg by then. Mummy will be there, of course – you could come with her if Jane's too tied up with the handsome Max Hasler!'

Hannah was heard to say that a trip to London might be quite exciting and then, to Jane's enormous relief, her mother insisted firmly that it was time they started back to Bath.

With the front door closed again, Jane let out a long, thankful sigh, forgetting that her aunt was within earshot. As usual Hannah went straight to the heart of the matter. 'Why did I have the feeling that I was sitting on a barrel of gunpowder? Your mother and I never had a thought in common and probably don't even now, but we can at least tolerate each other.'

'And you think Jill and I can't? It's no credit to either of us, but that's pretty much how it is,' Jane agreed.

'Why?' Hannah asked. 'She's as pretty as a picture, engaging and very eager to please, but I refuse to believe you're jealous – and in any case there's no need.'

'How kind!' Jane said shortly. 'All I can tell you is that to share my house with her now requires as much effort as it cost her to share with me when we were younger.'

'Sad,' Hannah commented, for once inadequately. 'Do you really want your spare room for a friend, or was it an excuse?' 'Not an excuse, and it's what I want to talk to you about. I had Ellie in mind. If there's a chance that she can go on with her career, get a grant to return to studying in London, I'd like to help her. She'd need somewhere to stay, and she and Daniel could come to me. I know he'd still be a problem but we'd have to find a way of dealing with it.' Hannah didn't immediately reply and Jane stared at her for a moment. 'You don't like my idea. Why? Because it's bad, or because it won't work?'

'My dear, how could anything so generous be bad?' Hannah finally asked. 'But I really can't see that it would work. A singer has to *sing*, accept engagements, travel from one to another. How could Ellie do that, with Daniel to look after? If you're about to say that her parents could help, I can tell you that she'd refuse to ask them – they're people who think very small and she knows that already.'

There was silence in the room, and then Jane owned up to her other idea. 'I offered Uncle Joshua help in buying Neil Gibson's farm and got the refusal that I expected – expressed in no uncertain terms!' She smiled as she admitted it, but Hannah understood that the rejection had hurt.

'He's a stubborn man, Jane,' she said gently. 'In his philosophy we all have to rely on ourselves, not lean on other people, even when they offer help out of kindness.'

'The odd thing is that I came down here with no intention at all of getting involved,' Jane said, ruefully puzzling it out. 'I rather prided myself on not needing anyone else and secretly despised people who did – the Venn coming out in me obviously! But I see things differently here. Helping and being helped – that's what life ought to be about. I shall offer *that* idea to Uncle Joshua before I go back to London, and get another snub for my pains!'

Hannah thought of suggesting that Jill Westover, for all her seeming confidence, might also be someone to be helped, but abandoned the idea. She was a great admirer of *Don Quixote*, but she wasn't one to tilt at windmills herself.

Jane thought it time to change the subject; she was tired of

talking about ideas that nobody seemed to want. 'We saw the cygnets, Tom and I, and then I was given a natural history lesson. If I could have thought of a question to stump him, I'd have asked it, just to keep my end up. But everything that lives and grows here he seems to know about.'

'He's been well taught,' Hannah pointed out. 'Whenever the "experts" want to write a book about the Levels, it's Rufus they come and consult.' She hesitated for a moment, then decided to go on. '*He* has a problem, poor man. Tom's been offered a place at the choir school in Wells. He'll probably want to turn it down, in which case Rufus will have to decide – but decide now, instead of in eighteen months' time when Tom has to leave the school here in any case.'

'Are there any alternatives?' Jane asked.

'Several, provided Rufus can afford them, if he wants something better than the local comprehensive. Wells would provide a good general education as well as the best musical grounding there is – it's where Ellie began, incidentally. But being a chorister at the cathedral isn't easy; there'd be no running wild out of school hours; he'd have to board there.'

'Poor Tom . . . And poor Rufus,' Jane murmured, 'with no wife to help him make a choice.' She was familiar with Hannah's preferred novels by now, and added a comment that she knew would be understood. 'Jane Austen never imagined a man like him!'

'"All the privilege I claim for my own sex is that of loving longest, when existence or when hope is gone",' Hannah quoted sadly. 'No, she reckoned without Rufus Venn.'

'Did you know her . . . Selina, I mean?'

'Yes, I knew her. She could put spells on people – I think she was half-gypsy, half-witch.'

Jane studied her aunt's face, no longer seeing its plainness, but only the intelligence and character written there. 'What about you – did you never meet anyone who seemed worth loving?'

'Once, I did,' Hannah admitted slowly. 'He was a schoolmaster called Ian Hamilton – I only met farmers and schoolmasters! I'd have gladly married him, but it didn't work out; he was set on emigrating to Australia.'

'You didn't want to go?' Jane asked.

'When it came to the point, I couldn't. Elizabeth had already gone from Rushey, taking you with her, Gideon had just died, and Joshua would have been left to take care of Amos and run the farm alone.'

'I'm sorry – I never properly understood before,' Jane said quietly. 'You had good reason to hate my mother. Couldn't you have gone later, when Joshua had found a wife?'

'It was too late.' There was bleak humour in Hannah's face now. 'You see, I'd picked another stubborn man! Ian reckoned I'd have put him first if I'd loved him enough. In any case there wasn't time for waiting if we were going to start a family – I was already thirty-nine.'

'You never heard from him again?'

'Not directly, but a colleague bumped into him in Sydney a year or two later. Ian was married by then to an Australian girl.' She saw that Jane was looking sad, and shook her head. 'I got over it long ago, even though it hurt at the time. There was always too much to do to stop and remember that I was heartbroken. Looking back now, which I don't often do, I'm inclined to think God intended me for a spinster all along.'

But it hadn't been anything to do with Almighty God, Jane reflected. The cause of Hannah's abortive love affair had been the sterner moralities of those days; the codes of behaviour that had stood in the way of a woman who'd simply wanted happiness for herself. She was governed even now by the biblical instruction that the first shall be last – but suppose she was wrong in believing that Ellie would still turn down a chance to become what God had surely intended her to be?

She was pondering this question when the telephone rang in the hall, and she went to answer it knowing that it would be Max at the other end of the line. She could feel his presence as if he were actually there. Out of contact with him, it had been necessary to lock away the memory of their night together. But it only needed the sound of his voice to open her mind to him as freely as her body would have welcomed him if he'd walked in the door.

'Jane, my darling – you're there at last. I missed you this morning.'

'I was late back from church,' she tried to explain calmly. 'Then I went cygnet-hunting with Tom Venn, my new boyfriend!' There was a little silence at the end of the line. 'He's not quite ten, scarcely a serious rival, if that's what you're thinking.'

'I wasn't thinking at all – merely listening to the lovely, cool sound of your voice. It's what I first noticed about you and what I shall still enjoy when we're old and grey and full of sleep!'

She was silenced for a moment by this vision of them spending the rest of their lives together – it *was* a shared dream after all!

'*Liebling*, are you still there? Was the rendezvous with Tom the high excitement of the day?'

'Not quite – I got back to find my mother and Jill at Maundy Cottage – their first visit, and a new experience for Aunt Hannah, who hadn't encountered one of today's thoroughly modern actresses before! Still, she bore up very well, and rather enjoyed herself I think. Now, tell me about you, please.'

'What is there to tell? Only that I talk, eat and dream business, when I really want to be at Cossenford with you – playing the organ in church, and then going home together to the most splendid four-poster bed you've ever seen!'

Weak with the same longing herself, she managed to sound ridiculously prim. 'My mother admired your house very much.'

'And you confessed, of course, that you were deeply enamoured of its owner?'

'No, I was deeply deceitful instead – I said you were someone I'd just bumped into here! And to damage your *amour propre* still further, I have to tell you that Jill could only just remember meeting you that evening you called at Hay's Mews!' There was another pause, which again she quickly filled. 'Dear Max, I was teasing – like poor Madame Butterfly wanting to hide, so as not to die of joy at meeting Pinkerton again.'

'I'm answered . . . overcome, in fact,' he said in a husky voice, suddenly sounding unlike himself. 'Don't change, Jane, and don't ever disappear where I can't find you. Is that a promise?'

'Yes, it's a promise, Max.' It seemed odd to want to weep for happiness, but she had to swallow the lump in her throat before she could go on. 'I'm here till the middle of next week, when Aunt Hannah is to be taken to hospital to have the plaster removed from her leg. After that I can come back to London. But you'll be here before then, won't you? The public meeting is this coming Friday.'

'I shall certainly get to the Town Hall in time for that, and so as not to embarrass Hannah Venn we shall behave with the utmost formality. A polite nod is the very most we'll exchange, my dearest Jane. How shall we manage it, I wonder?'

'Max – I forgot something. My sister may lack experience but she has all the right connections! She's landed a part in a London production, and she'll be back in Hay's Mews before I shall.' He didn't answer at once, and she hastily apologized, sensing that it was an intrusion he didn't want. 'It was difficult to say no, but I did insist that she couldn't stay long – it's just until she finds digs or a flat of her own.'

'Then she must find it soon,' said Max definitely. 'Now, my dear one, you probably have some boring task to do for Hannah, and I have some even more boring figures to stare at. Take care of yourself, please, and limit your outings with other young men to the harmless Thomas Venn.'

'That's another promise,' she agreed, and then heard the line go dead.

She stayed where she was, though, still thinking about a conversation that she knew had been important. There wasn't any doubt now: she and Max were committed to each other. The future was going to be shared, which meant that for both of them their days of self-sufficiency were numbered. But instead of the regret she might once have felt there was only a deep contentment. She hoped it was the same for Max. He'd rung off too abruptly as usual; she'd wanted to ask him to work less hard, rest more, relax a little, because he'd sounded strained and, for once, almost unsure. Her instinct was that he even needed her in London, but she'd given an undertaking to Hannah, and common sense insisted that it was probably her own longing to see him that was getting out of hand.

Seventeen

The day of the public meeting hadn't quite arrived when the fine weather suddenly deserted them and Jane had her first experience of a true Levels soaking. Rain fell steadily, hour after hour, from a sky as grey as lias stone, and she could understand now how the little sluggish rivers – swollen by a thousand streams running off the surrounding hills – suddenly became torrents of 'thick' water.

In the past, when a deluge had coincided with a higher tide than usual surging up the Bristol Channel, the rivers had simply had to empty themselves over the 'excessively horizontal' landscape around them. Now a sophisticated system controlled all but the worst flooding. Now too, though, controversy raged as to how much water should be pumped into the man-made arteries of the Huntspill and the King's Sedgemoor Drain. It was the argument at the root of how the Levels should be managed, and Jane was beginning to realize the full seriousness of the divide between her uncle and men like Luke Winters.

She found herself wanting Rufus Venn to call; there were questions to be asked. Tom would have done almost as well but there was no sign of him either.

'They're neglecting you,' she complained to Hannah, half in earnest. 'Fair-weather friends!'

'They'll come when they can. You don't know how hard they must work in late spring.

Put firmly in her place, Jane made a face at her aunt and announced that she, at least, would brave the downpour and call on her friend in Wash Row. The lane was well named, she found, because Ellie's cottage could only be approached by a miniature bridge across the stream that now rushed past

each front door. But once inside, the little house offered visitors a warm welcome, thanks to Ellie's fondness for buttercup-yellow walls, bright cushions, and rag rugs strewn on the polished bare boards of the floor. Everything spoke of loving care that disguised a shortage of hard cash.

'Lovely – come on in,' said Ellie. 'You and Daniel can entertain each other while I make the coffee.'

Jane knelt down beside his playpen and inspected the tower of bricks that was being constructed, but she could make nothing of Daniel's efforts at conversation – he was an enchanting mystery as far as she was concerned. It was a relief when her hostess came back into the room.

'The coffee's delicious,' she said after the first sip, 'but I braved the rain today for a purpose – I wanted to talk about you, your career.'

Ellie pointed at her son. 'He's my career, but I don't suppose that's what you meant!'

'No, it isn't. Listen, please, and then I'll leave you in peace to think about it. You have, Ellie dear, an exceptional voice – we all know that now. Andrew Yeo is certain you'd get a grant to go on studying at the Royal College of Music, but for that you'd need to stay in London. It isn't a problem – you and Daniel could have my spare room. We'd need to find someone to look after him while you were attending lessons, but we'd make sure we got the right, kind person. That's my scheme.' She smiled tentatively at the fair-haired girl. 'I think Aunt Hannah's view is that I should have left well alone and not unsettled you, but I disagreed with her for once. Forgive me if I was the one who was wrong.'

Ellie spread her hands in a little gesture that expressed what she found hard to put into words. 'I'm not unsettled, Jane, just grateful for such kindness. If you'd made that offer a year ago I'd have leapt at it – I was full of grief and anger then. I resented the child I was carrying and made matters worse with my parents by quarrelling with them. But once Daniel was born I couldn't regret having him; I was suddenly content again.'

'I can see why,' Jane admitted, 'but it's still a terrible waste, you know.'

Ellie shook her fair head. 'Not such a waste as you think. Music colleges turn out people every year with voices better than mine, and even most of *them* won't manage to make themselves a career; only the luckiest and the most hard-working succeed. I love to sing, but if I can do that here and give pleasure to people, then nothing very much is being wasted.' She was silent for a moment, afraid of not having explained herself well enough. 'Don't be hurt if I say no, Jane – it's just that what I'm doing feels right.'

'Then who am I to go on arguing with you?' Jane said calmly. 'We'll forget the subject was ever mentioned.'

'But you look sad,' Ellie persisted. 'Not sad, perhaps – thoughtful.'

'And so I should be. Some time ago I made a painful choice of my own – put my career before the husband I was being offered. I'm thankful I did, because what I've found since is so much more wonderful. I still relish my job, but if I *have* to make another choice, I'll make it differently next time.'

'I'm glad,' said Ellie. 'Brilliant lawyers may not exactly grow on trees, but finding the right man to love is harder still – cling on to him like grim death is my advice!'

'Gratefully noted,' Jane agreed. 'Didn't I tell you I was on a steep learning curve?' Then she glanced out of the window. 'It's stopped raining, I do believe – time to make a dash for home before the next little squall arrives. Bring Daniel to lunch on Saturday, for a blow-by-blow account of Friday's public meeting.'

'Love to,' said Ellie. 'We're sending the one unencumbered inmate of Wash Row as our representative – she's being instructed to vote early and vote often on Hannah's behalf.'

'Excellent.' Jane blew Daniel a kiss, which he charmingly returned, and stepped out of Ellie's front door, still smiling.

For the first time since coming to Cossenford she could see signs of anxiety in her aunt. Perhaps infected by Max's attitude to the meeting – an amusing but essentially unnecessary waste of time – she'd missed some of Hannah's deep involvement in

141

what they hoped to do. The museum project wasn't a diversion dreamed up by well-meaning busybodies who hadn't enough to do. Behind their immediate struggle to keep the chapel lay a much more fundamental purpose. Hannah and her friends saw themselves as guardians of a town that was historic and beautiful, and there was nothing for Max to take lightly in that.

Jane longed for a chance to talk to him, to explain what he didn't understand, but since their conversation the previous Sunday there had been only one hurried call, confirming that he'd get to the Town Hall just before the start of the meeting.

They set out early from Maundy Cottage, Hannah looking pale but composed in her Sunday church-going suit. One worry faded as they drew up outside the hall – people were already beginning to arrive; Cossenford was taking the debate seriously. By the time the chairman of the proceedings began to consult his watch, the hall was full, with people even standing at the back.

'Who is the chairman?' Jane whispered to her aunt, from their vantage point in the front row.

'Planning officer at the District Council – not a man I like,' Hannah answered briefly. 'Too fat, too florid.'

Both objections were true, Jane conceded, but it remained to be seen how the planning officer would perform his impartial duties. Then she forgot about him in the shock of pleasure at seeing Max arrive, with three other men, to be shown also to the front row of chairs, but on the other side of the aisle. Before sitting down he looked towards Jane and Hannah, smiled, and offered them both a small, charming bow.

'Admit that he has nice manners,' Jane suggested to her aunt, mainly as an excuse for talking about him.

'Nice, yes,' Hannah agreed. *Nice* was something but it wasn't enough.

Then the doors were closed, the chairman rang a little bell, and the buzz of conversation obediently died away; the meeting had begun. Doing her best to remain an unbiased observer, Jane's first impression was that the planning officer was doing his job well. A pleasant greeting,

then he explained in a few words why they were all there
– this was the way democracy worked: a public debate, then
a majority decision.

'Does he think we don't know that?' Hannah muttered.

The planning officer went on. Both sides would accept the
decision without unpleasantness. In other words there would
be no appeal against it, because this was the sensible, adult
way that Cossenford worked.

'Very fulsome,' said Miss Venn, not quite *sotto voce*. 'I
don't like flattery, Jane.'

'Maybe not, but he knows that most people do,' she whispered back. 'Hush now, he's staring at us.'

Then the choice to be made was briskly laid out; they could
either accept the Preservation Society's scheme for a museum
and public park, or Mr Hasler's new residential development,
which would of course usefully include set-aside land not
covered by the Society's proposal. At this point a warning bell
rang in Jane's head. The planning officer wasn't an impartial
chairman after all, and the audience had just been given a
subtle hint as to where the District Council's sympathies lay.

The Society was asked to put its case first and Arthur
Cranston rose to his feet. Jane knew why the task had fallen
to him – he had a scholar's love of the Levels and their history,
and if the museum came into existence, *he* would be the one
to choose and label the exhibits. These things he could do –
become a dynamic public orator was something he couldn't
do.

'"Oh, for a Muse of Fire",' Hannah mumbled despairingly,
but there was only Arthur sitting down at last to respectful
applause.

Max's lawyer spoke next and at once the tempo changed.
He complimented the librarian, tongue in cheek Jane feared,
praised the Society for its devotion to Cossenford, and then
went on to demolish its proposal. In essence his argument was
the one she'd heard from Max himself: a town that lived in
the past died; a community that refused to welcome
newcomers ended up by driving out its own young, innova-
tive people. This received warm support – the lawyer had
struck a chord.

Then it was question time and, interpreting the comments as best she could, Jane sensed that the temper of the meeting was running slightly in Max's favour. The people with any kind of business interest were there in force, and they were more vocal than the citizens who preferred not to be marched towards a brave new world they didn't quite believe in. Finally, the chairman called for a brief summing-up from both sides before the votes were taken. This time, nudged by Hannah, the vicar stood up. He was no more fiery a speaker than Arthur Cranston, but at least he was eloquent in his own quiet way. No one in the hall could have doubted his sincerity, and his final plea was effective in its simplicity: he personally hoped that Cossenford could remain unchanged in a world too ready to tear down anything that had the label 'old' attached to it.

Max, given the advantage of speaking last, didn't make the mistake of mocking the vicar. Instead, he ignored the opposition's scheme altogether. It was the moment for Jane to discover how deeply she was torn, as she listened to him charming a partly hostile audience. He agreed that the Reverend Weston was right – his own plan *would* tear something down, but the chapel was merely late Victorian, not old as Cossenford understood the word. In its undistinguished place, and on land too long left neglected, would rise a development the town could be proud of – built in local stone and local style. Then, boldly, he drew their attention to himself. Only half a Cossenford man, and the other half not even English, he was well-qualified to speak for the incomers some people thought they didn't want. But the truth was that they could learn from and contribute to each other; all that was needed was the opportunity for collaboration.

Listening to the applause as he sat down, Jane knew that the museum's cause was lost. It had been a brilliant performance and she couldn't help feeling proud, but she also realized that she had wanted Hannah and her friends to win.

The vote was taken by a show of hands: 135 to 69 in favour of the new development. The vicar rose to concede defeat, and the chairman rounded off the proceedings with a patronizing

pat on the head for the Society; the museum had been a wonderful idea, but the practicalities of life had to come first.

Amid the buzz of conversation and the bustle of people making their way out, Hannah sat still, struggling against a very rare longing to burst into tears.

'Let's go home,' Jane said gently. 'You're worn out, and I could do with a stiff cup of cocoa myself.'

Hannah nodded and got to her feet just as Max crossed over from his side of the hall. He smiled at Jane, and seemed about to offer to escort them out, but Hannah forestalled him.

'Goodnight, Mr Hasler. Your case was weaker than ours, but you presented it better.' Then she turned away, dignified despite her crutches, leaving Jane free to talk with Max.

'You did well – very well,' she said at once. 'But the truth is that I'd have liked a win for Hannah.'

'Honest as always! Darling Jane, dare I suggest a shared celebration tonight? No – I think you'd turn me down. Am I right?'

His smile was hard to resist. She'd have given a great deal to put her hand in his and have him take her back to the Manor House. 'I'd come if I could,' she confessed. 'But, Max, I can't – especially tonight. If the vote had gone against you it would simply have been a business opportunity lost. It's much more than that for Hannah and her friends.'

He gave a little shrug; the tussle was over and one side had to lose – tough, perhaps, but that was how life was. She remembered it as exactly her own attitude in the past to any legal battle that she had won; it was a shock to discover that she now found it callous in him.

'I'll telephone tomorrow,' she said quickly. 'Goodnight, dear Max.' Then she left him and caught up with her aunt. There were people to be acknowledged on the way to the door, but Hannah was brief with them, for once using her injury as an excuse. Outside, Joshua and Rufus Venn were waiting by Jane's car.

'We didn't see you in the hall,' Hannah said. 'Perhaps you got the time wrong and you've just turned up!' She achieved a watery smile to ask pardon for her sharpness but Joshua was moved to give her shoulder a consoling pat.

'We were there,' he said gruffly. 'Not your fault you lost – money talks, and too many fools like the sound of it. There'll be something else for the Winters family to get their hands on soon – Gibson's farm is going to auction.'

There was a little pause that Rufus stepped in to fill. 'You're looking tired – we'll let Jane get you home.' Then he stooped to kiss his friend's cheek. 'Tom sends his love. We'll be along tomorrow to drink to the confusion of your enemies!'

She smiled more naturally this time. 'Ellie and Daniel are coming too – we'll spit in fate's eye and have a party!' But her voice changed as they drove away and she glanced at Jane's face. 'I'm sorry it's such a muddle. Don't let us spoil things for you and Max, Jane. You'll just have to accept the fact that Venns and Winters can't be soldered together; we're made of different kinds of metal.'

'As malleable as cast iron in the case of the Venns,' Jane agreed. 'I'll gladly get your lunch ready tomorrow, but then I shall be tactful and disappear. You can't let yourselves go about the Winters and Max if I'm there.'

'I'm sorry,' Hannah said again, and they exchanged a smile in which affection, wry humour and aching regret were all mixed up.

But the following morning, just as Jane came downstairs from taking up Hannah's breakfast tray, Max rang the cottage.

'I was going to call you,' she said, 'but I hesitated about waking an overworked, stressed-out businessman too early! May I please invite myself to lunch?'

'No, dear one, because I shan't be here – I've got to go back to London. Jane, come with me, please – come to Dolphin Square if your own house isn't free of lodgers. We need time together on our own.'

She knew that it was true, because the urgency in his voice echoed her own longing to forget any other claim and simply go where he went. But an even stronger compulsion finally dictated her reply.

'Max, I can't . . . I promised, you see . . . I told Hannah I'd be here until the plaster was removed from her leg.' There was no reassuring word at the other end of the line and she struggled on. 'It's only for a few more days. We're due at the

hospital on Tuesday, then she'll be able to move about freely again. Then I can go home, and you'll be the one always having to be somewhere else.' Silence still instead of the agreement she needed. 'You're not saying anything – are you very cross?' she asked simply.

'I'm puzzled; trying to remember why I need you so much,' he finally answered. 'I like compliant women as a rule, women who never tell me that I can't have what I want!'

'It sounds very bad for you,' she pointed out, reassured by the amusement she thought she could hear in his voice. 'And biddable women grow boring – I hope! Dear Max, where will you be five days from now?'

'I don't know, but I'll ring you then in London. Please be there, Jane.'

There was no time to promise that she would before the line went dead. She replaced the receiver, trying to shake off a feather-light touch of fear that the gods who sported with the lives of mortals were making merry at their expense. Were she and Max doomed to go on missing each other because other people, other problems, were fated to get in their way?

It was all nonsense, of course; she could just as well expect good fortune because she turned over the silver coins in her purse when she saw the crescent of a new moon. The problem of Hannah's lunch party, on the other hand, was real and imminent. She was still making up her mind whether to stay in for it or go out as promised when a series of clumps on the stairs announced that Hannah was on her way down. Safely at ground level, she confessed to a telephone conversation with Andrew Yeo in which she'd asked *him* to lunch as well. It was the moment, Jane decided, to suggest that since a waitress sound in mind and limb was going to be needed, she'd better be present herself. They could warn her when the subject of Max, the chapel, or Neil Gibson's farm was likely to crop up and she could retreat tactfully to the kitchen.

Hannah stared at her for a moment, thinking how little time had been needed to make her familiar and dear. 'You'll be glad to leave,' she said quietly. 'Divided loyalties are hurtful

things. We'll just enjoy ourselves today – no awkward subjects need crop up at all.'

Jane deposited a kiss on the top of her head by way of agreement and thought instead of the lunch now required for five adults, two children and one large dog. With the discovery of fish in Hannah's freezer, she decided on a large dish of kedgeree, something else that Annie Clark probably didn't prepare at Rushey. The first gooseberries, ready in the garden, would provide a pie, and when Tom providentially arrived early he was given the thorny privilege of picking them.

Hannah got what she wanted – a happy lunch party. Rufus turned out to be a useful man to have about the house, and Ellie kindly undertook the task of drawing Andrew Yeo out of his shell. Watching him laugh at something she said, Jane suddenly saw him as he was – a shy, lonely man embarking rather late on the novelty of enjoying life. Even the normally charitable Hannah had had to confess to giving thanks at his mother's funeral, because Maud Yeo had been one of those women whose frail looks had concealed an iron will and total selfishness. Even now Andrew hadn't quite stopped listening for what she required him to do next.

With music as a bond between them, he and Ellie were getting on like a house on fire, and Jane knew she wasn't the only one to observe this new friendship; Rufus Venn saw a great deal with those deep-set, rather beautiful eyes of his. He was quieter, more self-effacing than usual, and Jane wondered if – the memory of Selina notwithstanding – he would have preferred to monopolize Ellie himself.

With lunch over and the others sent out to enjoy the warm afternoon sunshine in the garden, Jane was busy clearing up indoors when Rufus reappeared in the kitchen.

'I know you can do it by yourself,' he said before she could protest. 'But I happen to like washing-up.'

She handed him a drying-up cloth without further argument, thinking that, although he smiled pleasantly, his face looked sad.

'Hannah told me about Tom's place at Wells,' she said impulsively. 'Have you decided what he should do?'

'He must go, of course; an opportunity like that can't be missed.' Rufus rubbed at an already dry willow-pattern plate, and then stared at the three little figures walking over their painted bridge. 'Odd, isn't it, that the right thing is usually the most painful!'

She suddenly wanted to touch his hand for comfort, but he moved away from her and the moment when it would have seemed natural was lost. Instead, an idea that she hadn't even known was in her mind was suddenly in her mouth, translated into words she couldn't take back.

'Hannah said not to talk about contentious things today, but this will be my only chance,' she said abruptly. 'Last night Uncle Joshua mentioned the auction of Neil Gibson's farm. Could that be stopped if an offer was made that he was ready to accept?'

'Auctions are the traditional way of selling land,' Rufus replied, 'but the farm's still his at the moment; he can do what he likes with it.'

'Then will you ask him what he'd consider a fair price?'

There was a little silence in the room before Rufus spoke again. 'Is this an enquiry on behalf of Max Hasler, or the Winters family? If so, I shall decline the task.'

'No, it's on my own behalf.' She was keyed up now, and acutely nervous, but she couldn't help smiling at the expression on his face. 'You're about to say that I scarcely know a heifer from a bullock! Quite true, but I'm not planning to leave London.'

'You've just got more money than you know what to do with, so why not throw some away on an unprofitable farm. Is that the general idea?'

He sounded angry now, and she didn't know why. 'The idea is to add it to Rushey,' she answered coolly. 'Then it won't be unprofitable.'

'Dear God, you're serious,' he said after a long pause. 'Though only He knows why.'

'I know why as well,' she insisted 'All I can offer is money, but if that will help to keep another small part of the Levels safe for a generation or two, then I shall reckon it money well spent.'

'Joshua refused your first offer – he'll refuse again, I'm almost sure,' Rufus pointed out.

Jane shook her head. 'I don't think even he could be stubborn enough to refuse an outright gift, and I'd say it was to safeguard Tom's inheritance in any case.'

Rufus didn't comment on this, being too busy thinking about the girl in front of him – slender, still elegant in her country clothes, entirely out of place in Hannah's kitchen, and yet somehow not out of place at all. 'Neil's acreage is quite small, but the land is good, and there are outbuildings and a farmhouse as well. Have you any idea what a fair price would be?'

'None at all. But I've been a highly paid lawyer for nearly ten years. I'd thought of buying myself a weekend home in an expensive part of Sussex. The money could be used much better here. Will you talk to Neil Gibson for me?'

'If that is what you want, yes, I will,' he agreed slowly, 'but you ought to consider one more thing: Luke Winters would have expected to get the farm at auction. He is Max Hasler's cousin, and they're a close-knit family, always looking out for each other's interests.'

Jane's smile was sweet but full of confidence. 'Max won last night. He'd be fair-minded enough to think that it's time the Venns had a victory, too!'

'Then I'll visit Neil this evening,' Rufus said. 'And now here's Ellie coming to see why we haven't finished the washing-up.'

'You can say we've been canoodling over the dishes,' Jane suggested cheerfully, but her smile faded as she saw him frown. 'It was a joke, not a statement of fact.'

'I think I realize that, Miss Westover,' said Rufus with a sudden retreat into formality. 'We hired hands still know our place, even in this day and age.'

Eighteen

There was no message from Rufus that evening, but she wasn't expecting one. Even if Neil Gibson had been at home, he would need time to think about her offer. Important matters weren't rushed down here; only city people had an insane obsession with speed.

She went to church the following morning – now something else that she didn't question – and was back in the cottage drinking coffee with Hannah when the telephone rang. It was Rufus with the news that Neil Gibson liked the idea of a private sale. A price was mentioned, but it could be negotiated, Neil had said.

'It doesn't even sound fair as it stands,' Jane protested. 'I was expecting a higher figure, not getting ready to beat the poor man down.'

'It's about right,' Rufus said brusquely. 'People aren't exactly queuing up to buy agricultural land, and Neil's is known to be unprofitable unless it can be added to an adjacent farm.'

Jane was silent for a moment. 'What about Luke Winters? Would *he* offer more in order to get it?'

'Oh, almost certainly, I think. But Neil won't gazump you if that's the question you're really asking.'

'It's not,' she nearly shouted, stung by some hostility in him that she felt but couldn't understand. 'I don't think you like my idea very much – is it because I'm interfering in matters best left to men, and dyed-in-the-wool Levels men at that?' She had a sudden image of him with a smile now lurking in his russet beard, because she'd sounded just like the troublesome, townee career woman he reckoned her to be.

'What I think doesn't count,' he said gently. 'It's Joshua

151

you have to worry about. If you can't talk him round, you'd do better to forget about Somerset and find your Sussex cottage after all.'

'I suppose you've had to talk to him about it, but please don't say that I'll be over this afternoon. If he knows that he'll disappear.'

'Yes, because he's frightened of you – but I expect you realize that already,' Rufus suggested, and then rang off before she could think of a suitable reply. She was left staring at the receiver in her hand, but seeing instead her uncle's wary, weather-beaten face. It was Rufus Venn having his little joke, of course; the woman hadn't been born that Joshua was afraid of.

Over lunch, sounding unconcerned, she mentioned that she was going to look in at Rushey to say goodbye to Tom.

'There's no need to tell me why you're really going,' Hannah agreed. 'I'd like it to be the chance to see Rufus, but I'm afraid you don't value him properly.'

Jane took a deep breath and managed to answer quietly. 'Let's say I don't value him any more than he values me; there's nothing wrong with that – we can't all love each other. But he's sounded Neil Gibson out for me about a private sale and now I've got to try to persuade Uncle Joshua to accept the farm as a gift.'

Hannah didn't look surprised, didn't seem to find it worth commenting on, so Jane went on herself. 'It should be an interesting conversation, don't you think? Only one of us may emerge alive.'

After careful thought her aunt finally replied. 'My money is on the female of the species – so much deadlier than the male!'

'Rufus said roughly the same thing,' it seemed necessary to admit, so that Hannah could have that pleasure as well.

She set out after lunch but turned off the now familiar road before she reached the farm. The National Trust had thoughtfully provided a lay-by from which to enjoy the panoramic view, but Jane stared out over the sunlit, river-threaded landscape, too deep in thought to notice it. Without Amanda Crichton's airy suggestion that she should meet Aunt Hannah, she probably wouldn't have come to Somerset at all. She'd

have been driven mad by boredom and loneliness in London or saddled herself with a country hideaway and been driven mad there instead. It would have meant missing more than she could bear to think about. But for the frightening little collapse that had begun it all, there'd have been no Cossenford, and no Max. Life was dangerously predicated on such accidental chances as these.

She got out of the car at last to stare at a landscape that stretched to the Quantocks on the horizon – not grand, Max had been right about that, but intimately planned and constantly changing with the season and the weather. Where she stood the road crested the Polden Hills, and eastward lay a different river valley. There was Avalon itself, burial place of the great King Arthur, the Island of the Blessed. Out of its flatness rose the mysterious conical hill of Glastonbury Tor, sacred both to Celtic mythology and to Christian legend, but pointing surely to heaven either way.

Back in the car, she drove the last few miles to the farm and arrived to find the yard deserted. But, as if he'd been expecting her, Joshua came out of the house before she'd opened the car door.

'The others are busy,' he said briefly, 'but I reckon it's me you've come to see. We'll take a walk if you don't mind; I've something to do.'

He led her past a row of empty loose boxes into a paddock where some horses were grazing. One of them, a big black mare, ambled over at once and snuffled in the pocket of Joshua's jacket as if this was something she was in the habit of doing.

'She's after her daily peppermint,' he said, gently stroking the mare's nose. 'We call her Blossom to make her feel more dainty.'

Jane stared at Blossom's carthorse proportions and decided that it was at least a nice idea. 'She has very large feet!' it seemed safe to say.

'Bred that way, to stop her sinking in our boggy ground; all the Levels workhorses used to be like that.'

The old horse was given a final pat, and then Joshua led the way back towards the house. The risk-free part of the

conversation was over, Jane realized, and he opened fire almost at once.

'I told you to leave Neil Gibson's farm alone, and I don't like Rufus talking to him behind my back.'

'I asked him to, so don't blame him, please,' Jane insisted. She could sense the mixture of stubbornness and resentment that filled the man beside her, but she wasn't prepared to give in without a struggle.

'Will you listen just for a moment? If you don't want the farm, can't cope with more land than you have already, then I shan't go on arguing. But if you simply can't bring yourself to accept a gift, then I shall think it's a very poor excuse for doing nothing.'

'You sound just like your aunt,' Joshua pointed out morosely. 'Bossy and much too opinionated.' But he stared at her face, and the concern he saw there made him speak in a more gentle voice. 'Maybe you want to help, Jane, but we prefer to manage on our own. Keep your money – you'll likely only lose it if you put it into farming.'

'I don't understand you,' she said with sudden fierceness. 'Don't you want to protect the Levels where you can? Or is it just empty talk when you argue for the right way of caring for this countryside?'

'Yes, that's what I've been doing,' Joshua agreed, seeming suddenly tired of the contest. 'Just talking. Rushey's looked after itself for the past fifty years.'

'I shouldn't have said that. Forgive me, please,' Jane asked simply, and then, without much hope, fired the only weapon she had left. 'You haven't asked why I wanted to help. Partly it's because I've learned the value of what's here – something lovely that will be irreplaceable if it's lost. But there's another reason as well. I know now the damage my mother did when she ran away from Rushey. I can't bring Gideon Venn back, any more than I can make it up to Aunt Hannah for the lover she sent away without her. All I can do is offer you Neil Gibson's land instead of letting it go to someone who will work it for profit instead of love.'

There was so long a silence that she feared he wasn't even going to reply. But he spoke at last, slowly, as if each word

was being dragged out of him against his will. 'I have to think about it, Jane . . . and talk to Rufus. He'll be in charge soon. We'll let you know.'

She nodded; even that was better than she'd expected. Now it was time to let the matter rest and talk of something else. 'I gather that Tom is going to Wells. He'll have a lovely time there when he gets used to it. But Rufus needn't be afraid that he won't want to come back – I doubt if anything could get in the way of that.'

'It's *his* future you want to keep safe,' Joshua suggested, neatly reading what was in her mind. But the sternness had gone from his mouth and it seemed to Jane that he shared her concern for Tom's inheritance.

'I won't wait for the others to come back,' she said, 'but say goodbye to them for me, please. The plaster's due to come off Aunt Hannah's leg on Tuesday; after that I'll be going back to London, but she knows where to get hold of me.'

They walked in silence to her car, neither of them quite sure what else there was to say. Then Jane turned to look at him. 'I don't mind sounding like my aunt.'

The first real smile he'd offered her creased his brown face. 'I didn't mean you to.' He opened the car door for her and this time waited for her to drive away. She could see him still standing there as she turned under the archway into the lane.

It was more than likely, even now, that he'd refuse her offer, but when she thought of him in the future she'd have to remember him with old Blossom – man and animal both bred to this small corner of the world and very content to live in it together.

Back at Maundy Cottage she reported to Hannah that they must wait to hear what Joshua decided.

'I doubt if he sounded grateful,' his sister suggested. 'More likely he was downright rude.'

'No, not rude; but certainly not grateful!' Jane smiled at her aunt, then abruptly spoke of something else. 'What about you? Assuming that the chapel will be pulled down, must you abandon the museum project altogether?'

'I was in a fair way to giving up last night,' Hannah

155

admitted. 'But I had an unexpected visitor while you were out. John Masterson called.'

Jane remembered the name. 'Husband of the dreaded Nan who terrorizes poor flower-arrangers in church?'

'The very same, but John is a nice man. I think he feels the Town Council should have given us more support, though he's too tactful to say so. He said something else though. The Council has been arguing for years about whether or not to pull down an empty warehouse on the edge of town. John says they'll give it to us if we provide the money to renovate it.'

'How do you feel about that?' Jane ventured.

'Pleased on the whole. I know it doesn't sound exciting, but it's got advantages. In any case, it's something positive – much better than just wringing our hands and thinking evil thoughts about Max Hasler!' Then she suddenly spoke in a different tone of voice. 'May I ask why you're staring at me like that?'

'I was saluting your lovely common sense,' Jane answered unexpectedly. 'It's a very underrated virtue,'

Speechless for a moment, and flummoxed by the compliment, Hannah finally found a reply. 'What nonsense you do talk. Still, I'll thank you for what you're offering Joshua – it's very generous, my dear.'

This was waved away, and Jane spoke of something else. 'Tom is going to Wells – I expect Rufus has told you that.'

Hannah nodded. 'He told me more than that. Imagine it: he knows where Selina is after all these years. They met all sorts of people in their wandering days, and some of them Rufus has stayed in touch with. He heard recently from someone who'd seen her.'

'Seen her where?'

'In Austria, where the circus she joined has its permanent home.'

Jane waited to be told the rest, but in the end had to ask for it. 'So what is he going to do – forget about her? Spend the rest of his life *not* forgetting about her . . .?'

'He'll go and find her when he can,' Hannah answered slowly. 'After Tom's gone off to school and the farm work gets a bit easier.'

After a little silence Jane put aside the image in her mind of Rufus on his lonely, and perhaps pointless journey. But Hannah was right – he would certainly make it. 'Hospital for you on Tuesday,' she said next. 'Will you be able to manage if I go back to London the following day?'

'I shall miss you, but I shall manage,' Hannah replied firmly. 'Of course you must go. I'll be a different woman when we leave the hospital.'

As far as her ankle was concerned that certainly turned out to be true. Now, with just an elastic stocking on her leg, Hannah could dispense with the crutches and even scorned to use a stick. But Jane went to pay a farewell call on Ellie when they got home, and asked her to keep an eye on an arthritic lady who liked to pretend that there was nothing wrong with her.

'Easily done,' Ellie agreed cheerfully. 'Daniel and I pass the door every day.' She stared at her visitor for a moment. 'You're anxious to get back to London – of course you are. Home's home, wherever it is.'

'Well, yes, but I promised someone I'd be there, and promises are important. By the way, Hannah isn't too disappointed about the chapel, though still deeply opposed to the new development. John Masterson is holding out a lifeline for the museum – an empty warehouse that Hannah is already converting in her mind's eye!'

Ellie was still looking thoughtful. 'You'll come back now and again, won't you?' There was no reply to this so she went on herself, more tentatively. 'Or am I wrong about that? Will you forget about Cossenford the moment you wave us goodbye?'

'No, I shan't,' Jane admitted rather ruefully, 'and I've being trying to work out why. My job involves me all the time with other people, but what they represent are problems that I have to solve as best I can. As human beings they scarcely register at all. That's not how life is here. There are important issues involving relations, and new friends like you, but a lot of other little strands woven into the material seem to matter as well – old William Bird next door who wants me to know every

morning how his auriculas are doing, or Mrs Mostyn further down the street who needs advice on which knitted squares to put with which, in case the donkeys at the sanctuary mind what sort of blankets they get.'

In his playpen in the middle of the floor Daniel laughed because his mother was laughing, but Ellie soon grew serious again. 'Cossenford hasn't changed; *you* have. She hesitated for a moment, then went on. 'I was going to ask a big favour, as a matter of fact. I haven't done anything about getting Daniel baptized. I still need to speak to the vicar, but when it's arranged will you be his godmother, please?'

'Not a privilege that would ever come my way in London,' Jane said huskily. 'You're making me a gift, not asking a favour.' Then a transforming smile lit her face. 'We have a communication problem at the moment, Daniel and I, but I shall be a doting godparent!'

Ellie gave her a hug and led the way to the door. 'Real words soon, I promise you. I thought of having the service just before Christmas. Wouldn't that be nice, Jane?'

She agreed that it would, and crossed the little bridge outside Ellie's front door thinking that 'nice' scarcely covered how lovely it would be to spend Christmas at the Manor House with Max. Every last one of the things she'd spurned before she discovered she wanted now – carols in a candlelit church, a tinsel-frosted Christmas tree, and even a fall of snow to transform the Levels into yet another new landscape.

'I'll need to learn my godmotherly duties,' she explained to Hannah at the cottage. 'For as long as Ellie's on her own, at least, I must help as much as I can.'

Hannah nodded and wished that she hadn't got a vivid image of Max Hasler in her mind as she'd seen him at the public meeting. He didn't look the sort of man to take much interest in a small child whose natural father had decided to abandon him.

Jane left the following morning, offering as a parting gift the idea that Hannah might like to bring Tom Venn to stay in London for a day or two during the summer holidays.

There was only one more thing to say and she found it very difficult. 'Nothing's certain, of course, but if I *am* here at

Christmas-time – with Max – will you let me bring him to see you, even if the Baptist chapel is no more, and his new houses are rising on the site?'

Hannah thought for a moment, then gave a little nod. 'Bring him by all means. I can't promise to like him, but I shall try my best. Will that do?'

'In the circumstances, it's handsome,' Jane agreed, then gave her aunt an affectionate hug, and quickly drove away.

Nineteen

She drove slowly along the Mews, aware of having to recover the habit of thinking of it as home. It was odd how little she'd missed it, and even more of a shock to realize that she hadn't given a thought to Clifford's since the night of Piers' birthday dinner. That would all change now, of course; soon it would be the small, grey country town that she couldn't recall, along with Somerset's green hills and lazy rivers.

She was unloading the boot of her car when she was halted by the unmistakeable voice of Mrs Drew-Brown.

'Back at last, I see, Jane – one doesn't like to be away too long, does one? Not that your house has been empty, of course; in fact there's been quite a lot of *va et vient*, as the French say! Your charming sister is very popular.'

'My charming half-sister,' Jane pointed out, knowing that her neighbour liked to be accurately informed. 'She's only here until she finds a place of her own.'

'An actress, I gather – so much more exciting than the rest of us. Still, we can't all be glamorous!'

With this parting shot she went back to her own front door, newly painted dark green and adorned with a gleaming brass knocker in the shape of a dolphin. There was this much to be said for Sonia Drew-Brown: her immaculately kept house set a standard the rest of them had to aspire to.

Indoors, although Jill wasn't there, signs of her occupation were scattered around – the sort of food she liked in the fridge, the latest magazines, and expensive florist's roses in a vase on the coffee table. Jane longed to have the house to herself, to share with Max. But for the moment his own flat in Dolphin Square would have to do. Even if *he* didn't mind

160

– and she thought he probably would – her own instinctive choice was not to sleep with him where Jill was in the bedroom next door.

She'd filled the window boxes with petunias and carnations brought from Cossenford, and was just setting out a scratch supper on the kitchen table when someone rang the doorbell downstairs. She took a moment to recognize the large, gangling figure of Charles Rutherford.

'We met in Bath – do you remember? At your mother's house,' he said quickly. 'I saw lights on and expected Jill to be here.'

'I came back from Somerset this afternoon,' Jane explained. 'Jill's still out, but won't you come in and wait for her?'

He hesitated, but then made up his mind. 'Thank you, if I won't be in your way.'

Jane led him upstairs and into the kitchen. 'I was about to eat when you arrived. Join me if you're not going on to dine somewhere else.'

He began by refusing, then absent-mindedly helped himself to pâté and toast, and soon got down to making short work of whatever she brought to the table. He was a charming guest, easy-mannered, interested in what she told him of Cossenford, and pleasantly diffident about himself. But finally Jane asked about his father's new production, in which she remembered Jill saying that he had no part.

Charlie's expression suddenly grew thoughtful. 'Lots of angst, I'm afraid, not that that's anything new; rehearsals are always nervy, nail-biting things. But it's why I especially wanted to see Jill. I'm with my parents in Chester Square at the moment, so I got to hear about today's goings-on.' He strengthened himself with another sip of wine and then smiled at Jane. 'My father's great in his own line – in fact it's what we call him: the Great Man! He knows exactly what he wants when it comes to shaping a performance. I don't mean that he doesn't trust his actors, but *he* says how they're to play together. Jill doesn't quite understand that yet.'

'You mean she tries to milk her part for everything she can get out of it,' Jane said frankly, 'even if it isn't what the play-wright or your father wants!'

161

'Something like that,' Charles Rutherford agreed. 'Even Jill can't turn what she's got into a large part, but it's important, and any other novice actress just out of drama school would give her eye teeth to get it at all. She'll go right to the top in the end – I'm sure of it – but not by arguing with experienced old hands like my father. I thought I might be able to explain that,' he finished hopefully. 'I'm very fond of her, you see, and I don't want her to muck things up.'

Jane gave a little inward sigh – he was so nice, so generous, and surely so unsuited to the bitchy, self-centred world of the theatre. But it seemed impossible to put that into words, and she asked a different question instead. 'What about you – how is your own career shaping?'

'Not at all, on the boards,' he admitted with a rueful grin. 'My pa doesn't hold out any hope of that! But he thinks I might be useful in other ways – I'm quite good at knowing what people who *can* act ought to do.'

'Another great director in the making,' Jane suggested, smiling at him, just as the street door was slammed down below and footsteps sounded on the stairs. The next moment Jill appeared in the doorway, checked at the sight of them, and for once couldn't decide which part to play.

Jane seized the advantage, knowing that she must take it at once or lose it. 'I'm back, as you can see, and Charles came expecting to find you here instead.'

'You didn't think to let me know you were coming?' Jill suggested with acid sweetness.

'No, I didn't – I live here,' she was reminded calmly. 'There's food left if you feel like joining us; otherwise I'll clear up and you and Charles can talk in the sitting room.'

Jill turned her attention now to the tall young man who'd politely got to his feet. She was flushed, a little tousled for once, and stunningly beautiful, but Jane also identified easily enough the signs of rage only just under control, and it seemed likely that, unusually, she'd been drinking.

'Charlie dear, I'm not sure I want to talk to you anywhere at the moment. Something tells me you've been sent by Papa – little Jill's got to behave . . . No more arguments like today's or she'll be out on her ear! Is that why you're here?'

'I wasn't *sent*,' he said stiffly. 'My father delivers his own instructions and you should have seen enough of him by now to know that. But I watched the rehearsal this morning, saw you upsetting the rhythm of the other players. It's something you'd have spotted yourself at once if you'd been watching another actress at work.'

Eyes glittering like jewels in a face that was now very pale, Jill smiled brilliantly at him. 'How kind, Charlie . . . How very sweet of you to give me the benefit of your expert advice!'

The jibe went home, of course, but Jane saw him shake his head like a boxer stung but not seriously damaged. 'You're going to be a great actress – I think my father believes that too. Just ease up a bit, Jill, that's all I'm asking.'

It hung in the balance for a second or two whether self-control would slip completely and she'd scream at him to go away. But she couldn't allow it to happen with Jane watching. She knew what she must do instead: breathe deeply, stay quiet and still, until she could remember that she was an actress.

'Sorry, Charlie . . . Forgive me, please. It's been a bad day, and I've made it worse by letting someone feed me whisky!' Voice husky with regret, she would have disarmed an arch misogynist, Jane thought. Poor Charles Rutherford didn't stand a chance.

He was smiling at her now, happy to think that he might have been able to help her after all. 'Bad day or not, you still look gorgeous, even though you're probably tired out. I'll go away now and leave you in peace.' Then he turned to Jane. 'Thank you for letting me wait – I really enjoyed my supper with you.'

'Come again,' she said cheerfully, as if the tension of the past few minutes didn't still linger in the air.

He nodded and walked out, composure remarkably intact, and infatuation, Jane feared, proof against almost any cruelty Jill might offer him.

The sound of the front door closing seemed too loud in the silence that was left behind, and Jane weighed up what would come next. A knock-down, drag-out fight was probably what her sister had in mind, but there was no way of knowing whether she could be deflected from this or not.

163

Jane finally risked a comment. 'Charles Rutherford is far-gone in love, but I expect you know that. He's also very nice.'

It was so unarguably a fact that even Jill couldn't quarrel with it. 'Yes, he's nice, but it doesn't make him a theatre critic, which is what the poor boy seems to think he is.'

'If you had a run-in with his father this morning, was that a good career move?'

She was offered a confident little smile. 'It won't have done any harm. Tomorrow I shall apologize very sweetly to the Great Man. He'll think he's won, but the point is that I shall have been noticed!'

'Which makes your world not much different from mine,' Jane suggested. 'We're all trying to get noticed.' Then before Jill could deliver her usual sneer on the subject of City lawyers, it was time to move the conversation on. 'What about some food if you haven't eaten all day?'

After a glance at the table, Jill shook her head. 'I don't think so, thanks – and by the way I don't bother with break-fast either.'

'Then don't go and stay with Aunt Hannah,' Jane advised. 'She'll make porridge for you and watch you eat it.'

'She's not my aunt, thank God. "Characters" are all very well onstage; I can do without them in real life.'

Jane bit back what she wanted to say. 'After the initial shock, she rather took to you at Cossenford,' she pointed out instead.

'I know – most people do! Now, if you don't object, I shall soak away the trials of the day in a long, hot bath.'

She drifted over to the little flight of stairs that led to her attic bedroom, and Jane let out a sigh of relief. Perhaps it would get easier; perhaps Jill would decide not to stay very long; perhaps they could avoid actual bloodshed before she left.

The next morning Jane was drinking coffee in the kitchen when her guest came downstairs.

'It's going to be a ghastly day,' Jill predicted, 'culminating in a dress rehearsal this evening. God knows when that will end, so don't wait up for me, sister dear!'

'I wasn't going to,' Jane said calmly. 'Let's get it estab-

lished here and now that we lead separate lives – that way we may not irritate each other too much.'

Jill offered a faint smile, agreeing, her sister supposed. Then she shrugged herself into a denim jacket, and slung over her shoulder a beautifully embroidered canvas bag. 'Mummy's handiwork, of course,' she said casually. 'I'm afraid she spoils me rotten.'

'I'm afraid you're right,' Jane agreed, and had the small, unworthy satisfaction of having scored for once.

Left alone, she tried not to anticipate when Max would ring, and even managed to pretend that she wouldn't mind too much if he wasn't able to ring at all. She knew what she *was* going to do – find someone who could give her German lessons – and she was hunting through the Yellow Pages for language teachers when the telephone rang.

'You *are* there,' said Max's voice. 'If you weren't, I'd already decided never to forgive you, even if Hannah Venn was on her deathbed.'

'I left her fully mobile again and probably not sorry to have the cottage to herself at last. Speaking of which, I'm afraid I'm not alone here – my half-sister still needs board and lodging. But if you'd like to dine here, she's out at the theatre all day and all evening as well.'

'It doesn't matter to us *where* she is,' said Max. 'We shall be at Glyndebourne, *Liebchen*. It's the opening night of the season there – *The Magic Flute*, almost my favourite opera. I trust you are free?'

'For Mozart, I am free,' she agreed solemnly. 'Dear Max, I won't ask how you got the tickets – they must be more precious than gold dust.'

He didn't say that they were, but simply insisted that she must be ready to be collected at half past two. Then just as she imagined that the conversation was over he added something more. 'Jane, do you mind if we come back here afterwards? It would be more convenient.'

She'd have agreed to a tent on Brighton beach if he'd suggested it, but sedately said instead that she could make do with Dolphin Square, and then replaced the receiver, still smiling.

With a note scribbled to Jill to say that she'd be away for the night, and a final check in her mirror, she was waiting for him when he arrived. He stared at her, slender and beautiful in a fitted jacket of silver-grey velvet and a taffeta skirt that mingled the same silver-grey with the colours of the sea.

'You always take me by surprise,' he said unevenly, 'even when I've imagined in advance just how lovely you'll look.'

'A compliment is always welcome,' she managed to say, aware that she had the same difficulty with him. They'd seen so little of each other that with each fresh meeting they had to begin again.

His car was at the door – not the Mercedes or the BMW she would have expected, but a sleek Jaguar, all style and quiet power. With her long skirt carefully tucked in, he smiled before starting the car.

'You and Mozart and an afternoon off – what more could a man ask for?'

Pure delight was clearly in store. Too cool for a picnic supper by the lake, the day was nevertheless fine, and the May countryside they drove into looked beautiful. The performance was riveting and, as was Glyndebourne's habit, a newly discovered young singer lit up the stage. In the long supper interval the thought of her prompted Jane to talk about Ellie Chant, whom Max at once refused to take seriously.

'My darling one, the rest of the Cossenford choir is so excruciating that you're delighted by anyone who can actually sing in tune!'

She smiled but stuck to her guns. 'Wait till you're next there, *then* tell me I'm wrong. It can't be managed, I'm afraid, because of Ellie's small son, but Andrew Yeo thinks she ought to go on.'

Max's glinting smile warned her what was likely to come next and she leaned across the table to lay her fingers over his mouth. 'I won't listen to a word against Andrew – he loves music, and he's a kind, gentle man.'

She saw Max's amusement change to thoughtfulness as he stared at her. 'Those qualities matter to you, don't they? Gentleness, kindness . . . I can't imagine how you've survived in the City!'

Jane considered this for a moment. 'It's true I grew up convinced that the fight was to the strong . . . and the clever! We were the shakers and the movers, the people who accomplished things. Then I was forced to stand back and take a more detached view, and now I'm not so sure that I like a world that takes no prisoners. I've also learned how much my father would have hated it.'

Max shrugged this aside. 'He could afford to, living the life of a farmer on the Somerset Levels. Back in harness again, my darling, you'll enjoy doing exactly what we all do – fight to win.'

She didn't persist, but she was momentarily disappointed. He hadn't understood that she was serious, or that she doubted how well she would fit back into the world she'd known. It had been a mistake to mention Cossenford at all and she was regretting it when he suddenly returned to the subject himself.

'I'm thinking of selling the Manor House, Jane. Will that please Hannah Venn and her friends?'

It felt like a sudden blow across her heart, and the lovely dream of Christmas there, with Max playing the piano for her in the fire-lit library, quietly shrivelled and died.

'Why? Why, when you love the house so much?' she managed to ask.

'The house is beautiful, but there are many others waiting to be found. It's the place that's wrong – so parochial and so smugly pleased with itself!' He copied the gesture she had made by laying a finger against her lips. 'I'm teasing, sweetheart, just to see you rush to Cossenford's defence. The truth is that my uncle can't live much longer, but his son probably won't want to take over the peat business. For reasons I cannot fathom he actually enjoys being a farmer. We shall put in a manager at Talbot's, and my interest in it will come to an end.'

Jane hesitated for a moment, wondering whether or not to mention her offer to Joshua, but he seemed so unlikely to accept it that she decided not to bring Neil Gibson's farm into the conversation. 'I'm sorry about James Winters,' she said slowly instead. 'I didn't realize that he was so very sick.'

'I shall miss him,' Max confessed. 'I know the Venns don't

like him, but I do.' Then he put the subject aside. 'Forget Somerset! I forbid you to look sad – we came here to be happy.'

At the same moment the warning bell sounded and it was time to return to the auditorium. There was more music still to come but some of the enchantment, even of this most magical of operas, had vanished, and afterwards on the long drive back to London neither of them could find much to say. Max's apartment, when they reached Dolphin Square, she found elegant but impersonal, and instead of being there she wanted very much to be in her own home.

As if he sensed the fact, he was especially tender to begin with but, even lying in his arms, she couldn't recapture the sheer joy of their first coming together. Pleasure was given and received, but she felt in him a kind of desperate, sad determination to blot out anything but themselves. It was a relief to hear his quiet breathing at last and know that, whatever demons drove him, for the moment he was no longer aware of them.

When she awoke herself, after finally falling into a troubled sleep, he was sitting beside her on the bed.

'My darling, I've got to go, I'm afraid. Breakfast awaits you – all you need do is ring the housekeeper when you're ready to leave.' He leaned over to kiss her goodbye, then framed her face gently in both hands. 'I've a feeling last night didn't live up to expectations, but it was my fault, not yours. Forgive me, please.'

She shook her head at the idea that any apology was needed, but she was troubled and he saw the unhappiness in her face.

'Tell me what's wrong – something is, I know.'

'Not wrong; uncertain perhaps,' she admitted, trying to smile at him. 'You'll have to forgive me if I sound like some . . . dreadful harpy intent on tying you down! If all you want is an occasional night together, I ought to be old enough by now to enjoy the pleasure it brings and in between times simply get on with my own life. But the truth is that I'd like to share more than that. You must tell me, please, if I'm being too greedy!'

168

Max lifted both her hands and carried them to his mouth. 'What I shall tell you first of all is that I love you, very much. I've known other women, Jane, but I haven't said that before to anyone. What I can't tell you now is how the future will be arranged, because I don't quite know myself. But somehow we will share it. Does that sound right?'

A smile transformed her face. 'It sounds perfect, Max, even if I'm never to have the pleasure of living at the Manor House!'

He shook his head, half laughing and half serious. 'You're hooked on Cossenford – I shall have to cure you of that. I've a boring dinner this evening that I can't get out of, but we'll do something tomorrow night. *Auf wiedersehen, Fräulein.*'

Then he was gone, and she was left alone. Dressed and breakfasted, she intended to leave at once, without admitting to herself that she didn't feel at home in Dolphin Square.

It would have been a relief to find her house empty, but Jill was there, obviously just emerged from the shower, with her hair wrapped in a towel. Jane was suddenly reminded that she and Max weren't the only human beings on the planet after all. There were other people to be thought about, and one of them was right here with a challenge of her own ahead.

'How did it go – the dress rehearsal?' she remembered to ask. 'I hope it was the disaster that's supposed to foretell a brilliant first night!'

Jill grimaced over the yoghurt she was spooning on to a mashed-up banana. 'It was bad, but not disastrous, so your guess is as good as mine about what it foretells.' She glanced at the suitcase Jane had put down. 'How was your evening – night, I should say – successful?'

Jane tried to sound calm. 'Lovely – *The Magic Flute* at Glyndebourne, so we were late back.'

'Rather you than me,' said Jill. 'I can manage Puccini now and then, and even Verdi if pushed, but that's my operatic limit. I refuse ever again to sit through anything written by a German.' She spooned up the rest of the banana and wandered over to the sink. 'Are you going to come to the first night tomorrow? I grabbed two tickets, as instructed by Mummy, but your dear Aunt Hannah has cried off. Charlie will be on

duty – he can look after you both. There'll be the usual party afterwards.'

Jane hesitated for a moment. 'I'd love to come, but may I let you know? I'm already sort of committed tomorrow, but Max is so clever about getting the things most people would find unobtainable that . . .' Aware that Jill was staring fixedly at her, she allowed the sentence to fade away.

'Max . . . is that what you said?'

'Yes – Max Hasler. He called one evening when I was down in Cossenford. Don't you remember?'

Jill's face was hidden for a moment by the curtain of golden hair she was now shaking out. Then, upright again, she smiled slightly. 'I remember very well. I chanced to meet him afterwards, as a matter of fact – he was at a party Charlie took me to, with a rather sensational blonde in tow, I have to say!'

'Why not? I'm sure he knows a great many women,' Jane agreed. 'And I know other men.'

'Were you with *him* last night?' It sounded like a serious question, not any kind of jibe, and Jane answered honestly.

'Yes, and it wasn't a meaningless one-night stand, if that's what you're thinking. Max and I know that it's important.' She smiled suddenly. 'If he *can* get a ticket for tomorrow, may I bring him?'

Jill seemed to be deep in thought, but at last she answered. 'Oh, by all means. He'll definitely add something to the evening.' Then she walked towards the door. 'I must get dressed. Charlie insists on driving me down to Marlow for lunch. I can't convince him that I'm not riven with first-night nerves.'

'Most actresses making their debut would be', Jane pointed out. 'As usual, you're a law unto yourself.'

'I rather think I am,' Jill agreed affably, and disappeared upstairs.

Twenty

Half an hour later she and a smiling Charlie drove away and Jane was free to ring Cossenford. Her aunt's gruff voice answered at once.

'How are you, and why aren't you coming to London tomorrow?' Jane asked.

'I didn't feel like it,' Hannah answered firmly, 'and I'm old enough to know whether I want to go jaunting off to London or not.'

'Tell me truly, please – are you really just not inclined to come?'

Hannah gave an audible sigh. 'You've only been gone two days – hardly time enough for me to have got myself into any mischief. And added to that, I've already had visits from Ellie Chant and Rufus. You can take it, Jane, that I'm extremely well.'

'All right – I believe you! But you can't cry off bringing Tom to London later on. I'm counting on you for that.'

'Of course we shall come,' Hannah confirmed huffily. 'In fact we've already discussed what we want to see.' Then her voice changed. 'What about you, my dear girl – is everything well with you?'

'Everything's just fine,' Jane agreed. She wondered whether to mention what Max had said about the Manor House and then decided against it. He must announce in his own good time what he intended to do. 'I haven't heard from Uncle Joshua,' she said instead, 'but I have to keep remembering that he works on Somerset time!'

'You'll hear when he's ready,' Hannah pointed out. 'I'd as soon try to hassle old Blossom as get Joshua to make up his mind in a hurry. Now, we've talked enough and this call is costing you money. Give your sister my good wishes for

tomorrow, please.' And with that the line went dead.

But before the end of the day more news came from Somerset, sooner than expected. Joshua rang to say that he and Rufus had reached a decision: if she still wanted to buy Neil Gibson's farm they would work it for her.

'That wasn't quite the plan,' Jane pointed out. 'You were intended to work it for yourselves, not me.'

'Well, that's something we're not prepared to do. It stays yours or we'll have nothing to do with it.'

In the slow, upward cadence of his voice, making any statement sound misleadingly like a question as it always did on the Levels, she heard the stubbornness ingrained over generations. As Hannah had said, there'd have been more hope of getting his old mare to reconsider the direction she meant to go in.

'We must arrange it in whatever way you'll agree to,' she said finally, omitting to mention that when the right time came she would simply transfer the ownership to Tom. With the name of Joshua's solicitor written down, so that she could get in touch with him at once, Jane said that she'd spoken to Hannah that morning. He agreed that all seemed to be well at Maundy Cottage, and then ended the call as abruptly as his sister had done.

In the course of the day she'd tried to reach Max at his apartment only to get the answerphone each time. But her conversation with Joshua was scarcely ended when he called back himself.

'You've been trying to call, my darling, but I've just got back from a thoroughly tedious evening. Speak low, speak love to me, please!'

'I was going to speak of something you may not want to hear – my sister's opening night tomorrow! Have you seen *The Three Sisters* so many times that even a new production by Michael Rutherford can't tempt you?' There was a little silence at the other end and she hurried on. 'I can't offer you a ticket – Jill's only got one to spare – but you're so clever at getting hold of things that I thought you might manage it.'

'Of course I should like to come,' Max agreed slowly. 'And I expect my "fixer" can come up with something. But there's a condition, my love – I *hate* first-night theatre parties, and the people who go to them.'

She would have enjoyed the glimpse of an unfamiliar world herself, but it was no hardship to forego something Max seemed to know and dislike. 'If you'll promise to arrive in time to meet my mother before curtain-up, we can leave afterwards whenever you like.'

'You're a pearl among women,' Max said seriously. 'Have I mentioned that?'

'Not in so many words!'

She could hear the smile in his voice now. 'I'll see you in the foyer, and if it will make you happy I'll even invite your mother to supper with us as well. Can self-sacrifice go further?'

'Wait till you see her – she's very beautiful! But in fact you're quite safe. She'll want to stay with Jill; she always has done. It used to hurt, now it doesn't. How does that sound?'

'Very satisfactory,' Max said, and then rang off.

She didn't see Jill and Charlie again that night, but in the morning it was all arranged: Jane's job would be to escort her mother from Paddington to the hotel, and then on to the theatre. Charlie was to be responsible for getting Jill there on time and in her right mind. He was very good for her, it seemed to Jane – gentle but firm, and impervious to the seesaw of gaiety and gloom on which she was now dizzily going up and down.

Left alone, Jane could spare a thought for her own future with Max. She was ready to admit now that he was right to sell the house in Cossenford. Better by far for the town that it should belong to people who could always be there, contributing something to the community. But where would they themselves live instead? Her house was too small, and his apartment was only a bachelor's convenient but unhomely pied-à-terre. Perhaps he intended their future to be ultimately in Germany. It wouldn't be what she would have chosen, but she'd learn to love it if she had to. But first Piers Clifford's kindness had to be repaid, and pride insisted that she end her career with the firm on a high note of achievement, not in the whimper of a long period of sick leave. Max would understand that; it was something he'd insist on himself.

At this point in her deliberations the telephone rang, and an unknown voice at the end of the line introduced itself as

Camilla Hastings. She sounded very self-assured, and coolly announced that Max wouldn't be able to make the theatre engagement after all.

'You mean he couldn't get a ticket?' Jane asked.

She was put firmly in her place at once. 'The ticket wouldn't have been a problem. But Max was called to Somerset early this morning – to someone who is dying there.'

'Then I'm very sorry,' Jane said at once. 'I didn't realize his uncle was quite so ill. Thank you for letting me know – I expect you've a lot of rescheduling of engagements to do.'

'Of course, but that's my job – to arrange Max's life for him.'

So she was the all-important 'fixer'. Jane had a vivid mental picture of her: exquisitely groomed down to the last hair, and probably possessing very elegant legs and long blonde hair. No motherly, middle-aged handmaiden for Max. The instinct to dislike her, sight unseen, was lamentably strong.

'Then I mustn't hold you up,' Jane said, nevertheless trying to sound cordial. 'Thank you again for letting me know.' She thought now only of Max setting off in the dawn on a long, sad drive that might not get him to James Winters in time. With his uncle's death, his connection with the Levels would almost certainly end, just as her own had begun. Fate was still amusing itself with getting their timings all wrong.

She had to leave for Paddington before the others returned, but she doubted whether Jill would care whether Max was in the audience that evening or not.

On the platform at Paddington Elizabeth was easily spotted, being looked after by a dazzled fellow passenger who seemed disappointed when Jane appeared.

'Boring but rather sweet,' said her mother, skilled by now at assessing any admirer she inevitably acquired. Then she forgot him and smiled at Jane. 'You look wonderful, but how is my other daughter bearing up? I know she thrives on excitement, but her first opening night is going to be an ordeal.'

'She's in the kind and sensible hands of Charles Rutherford,' Jane answered, steering her mother in the direction of the taxi queue. 'For as long as he's around, you don't have to worry about Jill.'

174

'He *is* a lamb,' Elizabeth agreed. 'But she's bound to get tired of him, I'm afraid – then he'll be hurt, and she will have to feel guilty.'

They had tea in the hotel, then Elizabeth got changed, and in good time they set off again for the theatre. Charlie was waiting for them in a foyer already abuzz with the excitement of an opening night. He was his usual charming self, but when he forgot to smile Jane thought his face looked strained.

'All well backstage?' she murmured.

'Well enough, I hope.' But he made the little warding-off-disaster gesture of crossing his fingers.

By the end of the first act there was no doubt about the audience's reaction. They knew they watched a masterpiece being magisterially directed and beautifully performed. When the curtain came down for the last time a roar of applause broke out, and Charlie in his seat next to Jane was finally able to relax and smile.

With Max not there, she was free to attend the party after all, and soon realized what she might have expected – that among the night's gathering of rich and famous she would bump into Piers Clifford. It was where he seemed to belong.

'My dear Jane – lovely to see you!' he said, trying not to look surprised. 'Are you anything to do with tonight's rising young star?'

'She's my half-sister, and that's my mother just over there, talking to Lady Rutherford.'

Piers raised an imaginary quizzing glass in Elizabeth's direction, and then at Jane. 'The three of you should definitely have sat for Gainsborough – I can see it now: *Mrs Westover and her daughters!*'

She thanked him for the fulsome compliment and said how much she looked forward to returning to work.

'Good – we miss you, Jane.' That sounded more sincere, but she was relieved when Charlie came to stand beside her.

'Help needed,' he muttered in her ear. 'Jill's drinking, and any moment now we're going to be in trouble. But there'll be even more of a scene if I try to take her away.'

Across the room Jane had a glimpse of her sister over-performing in the role of Hollywood vamp for an elderly

theatrical knight. She was certainly drinking, and would soon be out of control.

'I think you'd better let me try,' Jane suggested quietly. 'Look after Elizabeth, please, Charlie; just say we both decided we'd had enough partying for one night.'

She edged her way across the room to Jill. 'Forgive me for leaving early,' she said hoarsely, 'but I need to go home – I feel awful. I can't possibly expect you to come with me but ...' She closed her eyes for a moment, wondering what to do next if Jill decided to ignore an obvious plea for help. But after a glance at her pale face Jill smiled sweetly at the famous man now watching them both with interest.

'I'm afraid my sister needs putting to bed, and I'd better be the one to do it!' She led Jane towards the door, then stopped abruptly. 'Oh God – Mummy! Does she need rescuing too?'

'Charlie's looking after her,' Jane mumbled, but the thought of *Mrs Westover's daughters now departing from the party* made her give a half-hysterical little laugh that decided Jill to wait no longer, and a few minutes later they were in a taxi on their way to Hay's Mews. Nothing was said on the journey, and only when they were safely back indoors did Jane break the silence.

'I'm sorry, Jill dear – but apart from a thumping headache there isn't anything wrong with me – it's you we were worried about.'

Anything seemed possible – most probably that Jill would let fly with a guttersnipe tirade and then go straight back to the party. Instead, her pale face turned green, and she made a sudden anguished dive for the bathroom. Ten minutes later she came back into the room, white-faced and shivering, but relatively calm.

'Whisky on top of champagne is definitely not a good idea,' she confessed with a tremulous smile. 'What do you suggest next – the cup that cheers but does not inebriate?'

'I think so, but first you need warmth; wait while I get something to put round you.'

Wrapped in a cardigan she watched Jane make the tea, and then sat with her hands clasping the mug she'd been given. 'I was hating every minute of that party,' she admitted slowly, 'that's why I kept drinking.'

Jane stared at a girl it was hard to recognize – for once dishevelled, shaken and angry. 'What was wrong with tonight's party?' she asked gently.

'Tell me what was right with tonight at all – and you can start with the performance.' Jill's voice failed for a moment, and her eyes were bright with tears. 'I might as well not have been in the play for any chance I got to be noticed – our dear leading ladies saw to that! It was bad enough in rehearsal, but I accepted that the great Michael was boss – someone has to be. But tonight those bloody cows made sure I learnt my humble place in *their* scheme of things.'

It wasn't hurt pride, or spoiled-brat self-esteem trampled in the dust; Jane recognized heartbreak when she saw it. She leaned across the table and covered Jill's ice-cold hands with her own warm ones.

'Maybe it felt like that onstage. I promise you it's not how it looked to the audience. You *were* noticed, and you were very good. You know it's safe to believe me because I'm not in the habit of giving you undeserved praise.'

'Or any praise at all,' Jill pointed out resentfully.

'Well, maybe not – I reckoned you got enough of that from your parents.'

There was a little pause; then Jill suddenly spoke in a different tone of voice. 'Are you certain about tonight? Michael said nothing to me – he was too busy kissing the hands of the Great Dames.'

Jane smiled at her, suddenly wanting to offer not only reassurance but affection. 'Wait till your turn comes, and it will. Then you'll probably not mind when some new young threat is left to eat her heart out in the wings!'

Jill only acknowledged this with a little nod, but she smeared away her tears. They sipped their tea in silence but there was no discord in the room now; unlikely as it seemed, a sort of friendship had even come about between them, fragile but suddenly hopeful.

'Max Hasler wasn't at the party,' Jill suddenly remembered. 'Why was that?'

'He didn't even get to see the play. An uncle he seems more

fond of than his own father is dying down in Somerset – there was an emergency call early this morning.'

Jill stared at her sister across the table – someone known all her life, of course, but not really known at all. Had she ever looked properly at Jane's face before – probably not, or how could she have missed its quiet, understated beauty?

'This thing you have going with Max,' she said next. 'Is it serious?'

Finding no malice in the question, but only a serious need for the truth, Jane answered honestly. 'Yes, although I might have been afraid to admit that to you in the past. You would have seen it as a challenge!'

For once she saw uncertainty in her sister's face, as if she didn't know what to think or say. Then Jill recovered herself. 'He's probably twice my age,' she finally pointed out. 'What are you going to do – marry him, or "live in sin", as our grandparents used to say?'

'Marry him, I hope, but we haven't got the future worked out yet. For one reason or another we scarcely ever have any time together. It's a very unsatisfactory way to run a love affair!'

Jill hesitated, again strangely unsure of herself. 'You'll think it's none of my damn business, but I'll risk it anyway. From my very brief acquaintance with Max Hasler I'd say you'll be getting a difficult husband.'

'I'd say so, too,' Jane agreed. 'But I'm afraid an easy one now wouldn't do.'

Jill smiled at last, a warm, sweet smile her sister hadn't seen before. 'Thanks for salvaging me tonight – I'd have made a fool of myself otherwise.'

But Jane shook her head. 'Charlie would have thought of something – he's very resourceful. If he were ten years older, I'm not sure I wouldn't marry him instead of Max!'

'Much safer,' Jill agreed rather strangely, then hauled herself to her feet. 'I'm bushed, and you look tired as well. Let's call it a day and go to bed. In no time at all, my dear, resourceful friend will be here with the morning papers so that we can weep over the reviews!'

Twenty-One

It was tempting to try to get in touch with Max, but Jane knew she must resist it and leave him to ring when he could. What she had to do instead was to concentrate on her own affairs and talk to Joshua's solicitor again. She caught him just as he'd concluded matters with Neil Gibson. Pending some small legal formalities, she was now the owner of fifty acres of good Somerset pasture and the small farmhouse and outbuildings that went with them. It seemed a significant moment in her life. If only in a minor way, she was a landowner. She had responsibilities undreamt of a few months ago.

Her next call was to Joshua himself but he – according to Rufus Venn who answered instead – was on his way to a cattle market. She asked if they'd heard from the solicitor. Rufus agreed that they had.

'You don't sound nearly as excited about it as I am,' she couldn't help pointing out.

Rufus now agreed that he was not excited, only feeling sad on Neil Gibson's account. He had, she reflected, the unfailing knack of catching her off balance, and the worst of it was that the damned man was always right.

'I'm sorry,' she had to say. 'Of course it's a heartbreak for Neil Gibson. But at least he knows that his land will be loved and looked after – doesn't that help?'

'I expect it does.' Then Rufus relented a little. 'He's also very grateful for a private sale – it's saved him quite a lot of money. He'll be taking his livestock, but everything else is yours.'

'That's really why I rang,' Jane said. 'What are we to do about the house? Would you and Tom like to live in it, by any chance?'

179

'And leave Joshua here on his own? I don't think so, thank you.'

The disclaimer was polite, but irritatingly unhelpful as well. 'You couldn't,' she asked with a suggestion of gritted teeth, 'be a little more constructive, I suppose? Tell me, please, what to do with a perfectly good house that neither of you wants.'

She imagined him, deeply blue-eyed like his son, sighing a little and wondering how soon he could escape to the work that waited for him outdoors.

'There's Charlie Clark's brother, Ted,' he suggested at last. 'The poor chap rents a room in Little Ham at the moment. With a house to live in, he could marry his girl and settle down. He's a good cowman; we don't want to lose him.'

'There, you see?' said Jane, trying to sound like Miss Hannah Venn, schoolmistress. 'You know the answer when you try.'

'And I might also just wring your neck one of these days,' Rufus said pleasantly. 'Meanwhile, I suppose you expect me to sort things out here?'

'Yes, please,' she agreed. 'And, Rufus, I am very grateful.'

'"The soft answer that turneth away wrath"! *Au revoir*, Miss Westover.' And with that the line went dead.

She was still wondering why wrath needed to be turned away, when Jill sauntered downstairs, still in dressing gown and slippers, in search of coffee. At the same moment Charlie rang the doorbell and was let in with an armful of newspapers and flowers.

A few minutes later there was no doubt about it – the play had been very warmly received. The *Times* reviewer even went so far as to claim it as the only production he'd seen of a great play that had gone to its true heart. Each critic singled out different members of the cast for praise, but all made a mention of the beautiful young newcomer; The *Daily Telegraph* even kindly suggested that Jill Westover was an actress to watch.

'Damned with faint praise, wouldn't you say?' Jill suggested woefully.

Charlie was the first to answer. 'Don't be daft, love! You were in starry company, don't forget; most beginners wouldn't

have been noticed at all.' He leant across the paper-strewn table to plant a kiss on her mouth. 'Cheer up – I promised Elizabeth I'd give you lunch, but she wants you to go shopping with her first.'

Revived by the prospect of a morning's happy trawl through Harvey Nichols, Jill rushed upstairs to dress, leaving Jane alone with Charlie.

'It's going to be all right, isn't it?' she asked.

'No doubt about it,' he confirmed. 'My father is a happy man today, and he isn't always after a play opens!' Then his smile faded. 'Jill will leave me behind one of these days – I know that. But it won't matter; we'll always be friends.'

'I think so, too,' Jane agreed. 'But I hope she realizes how fortunate she is.'

He looked shyly pleased but didn't answer; then she went to answer the telephone and it was the call she wanted. The sombre note in Max's voice was enough to warn her of what was coming.

'Tell me the bad news,' she said gently.

'James died last night, so at least I was able to say goodbye to him. Luke's away, unfortunately, but he'll get here tomorrow. My aunt and cousin are here, but they weep a lot and don't seem capable of doing anything else.'

'Poor Max – I'm so sorry; you've lost a friend and that hurts. Is there anything I can do to help?'

'Just having you around would help,' Max said unexpectedly. 'I know you're only just back in London, but could you bear to keep me company at the Manor House for a day or two? I wasn't prepared for death to be quite as unsettling as it is!'

'I'd set off now, except for one thing. My mother is still here and I invited her to dinner this evening while Jill is at the theatre. But I know what I could do – drive her home to Bath tomorrow and then go on to Cossenford. Would that be all right?'

'Perfect, sweetheart; I must be here tomorrow morning in any case. I can be at the house by mid-afternoon. Now, tell me about things at your end. I hope Camilla got in touch?'

'Of course – very efficiently – and the play went well; you

181

must see it when you get back to London. This morning's reviews are very good, and even Jill got mentioned.'

'So she's not giving you a hard time – that's something! Now, I must go. Until tomorrow, *Liebchen*.'

She went back to Charlie in the kitchen, to report the change of plan. 'I've got to go back to Somerset tomorrow. It means that I can drive my mother home, and then go on to Cossenford. Could you warn her about that? We can settle the details when she comes this evening.'

'Will do,' said Charlie. 'She'd much rather travel back with you.' He paused for a moment, then went on more thoughtfully. 'I know she wants Jill's success more than anything, but it will mean that she loses her. Then she'll need *you*, Jane.'

The idea was so strange that it took a moment to realize that it might be true.

She smiled at him with warm affection. 'Were you born aware of other people, or have you learned to observe them very carefully?'

'My father's doing, I think,' he confessed. 'His view is that a good director needs to watch human nature in action, with patience and humility – his words, not mine. I think he's right, and in any case people are endlessly interesting. Don't you find that, Jane?'

'I didn't,' she said slowly, 'and I realize now that I was neither patient nor humble. But I'm learning!'

It was as far as they got before Jill reappeared, dressed to kill in case by chance someone recognized her. Jane realized that the harmless vanity would have irritated her a little while ago; now she found it touching. She *was* learning, it seemed.

There was some tidying up to do when Jill and Charlie had gone, and then shopping for the dinner she must give Elizabeth. On the way back she caught up with Amanda Crichton, also walking home for once when usually she was inseparable from her battered scarlet Mini.

'Long time no see,' said Amanda with a faint air of reserve and a brief smile.

'I should have called,' Jane admitted quickly. 'Shall we do some catching up over a cup of coffee?'

She thought her neighbour was about to refuse, but Amanda nodded, and gave her usual friendly grin.

They were settled in the kitchen with mugs of coffee in front of them when Amanda raised the subject of Jill. 'Is she going to stay much longer? I seem to remember you weren't keen to have her at all.'

'I wasn't, but we're learning to tolerate each other quite well. She'll be here on her own for a day or two, because I'm wanted back in Somerset.'

'Aunt Hannah in trouble again?'

'No, she's fine. It's my dear Max – Max Hasler – who needs help.'

Amanda was silent for a moment. 'He sounds important in your life,' she suggested.

'He is – in fact he's my future!' There was another little pause, and Jane could see her friend considering what to say next.

'Mrs D-B, nosey cow that she is, saw you going off with a fair-haired man in an expensive green Jaguar. She surmised a visit to Glyndebourne because you were both in evening dress in the middle of the day. Was that Max?'

Jane nodded. 'Opera's one of our shared passions, I'm glad to say.'

Amanda fiddled unnecessarily with a shoelace, then straightened up with her usually vivid face wiped clean of expression. 'Nice to be enamoured of someone who's also an old family friend,' she suggested, and saw with despair that Jane's smile was rueful.

'He isn't that, I'm afraid – my father's relations think they have reason to dislike him, and my mother hasn't even met him yet. Jill has, but only very briefly.'

There was another pause, but it wasn't the easy silence liable to occur in a conversation between friends. Amanda's strained expression confirmed, in any case, that something was wrong. She shook her head when Jane quickly asked if she was feeling unwell, but the hands wrapped round her coffee mug were suddenly trembling.

'I'm all right, thanks, but . . . Oh God, Julian wanted me to promise not to interfere, and now I can't be sure whether he was right or not.'

'Nor can I if you don't tell me what's the matter,' Jane said anxiously.

Amanda looked inclined to bolt down the stairs, but she took a deep breath to steady herself and managed to speak calmly.

'It was that damned car – so immediately recognizable when Sonia Drew-Brown talked about it! You see, I'd noticed it twice before, parked outside your house all night after you'd gone back to Somerset. In fact, I almost rammed it accidentally when I was trying to back the Mini out early one morning. A man – Max, I assume – rushed out to make sure I didn't scratch his beautiful piece of machinery.'

The silence in the room was now so thick and heavy that Amanda had the sensation of trying to breathe through a wad of cotton wool. She made herself look at Jane, and saw a white, still face that might have belonged to a dead woman except for the suffering in the dark eyes. 'I'm sorry . . . so sorry,' she whispered. 'Julian was right – I shouldn't have said anything at all.'

'He was wrong,' Jane answered quietly. 'I don't know how Max came to be there, but there'll have been a good reason. He'll tell me when I see him, and then we shan't have to think about it any more.'

Her mouth twitched into something that was meant to be a reassuring smile, but once started it seemed unable to stop smiling, and she had to put up her hand to straighten it again. 'I'm not sure how long I'll be away,' she went on. 'Max has a family funeral to arrange and a lot of things to see to; I don't want to get in the way while all that's going on.' It registered in some dim, still functioning corner of her mind that she sounded rational and unconcerned. Acting seemed to come naturally to the Westovers. 'I can save my mother a tedious train journey home tomorrow, drive her to Bath and then go on to meet Max.'

She stood up as if the conversation had ended, and Amanda felt dismissed.

'Drive carefully,' was all she could find to offer. 'Julian hates me to say that, but I say it all the same.' Her hand sketched a wave, futile in its cheerfulness, and then she went

away to weep for Jane in the safety of her own home.

It seemed very quiet when she'd gone, and the room felt cold despite the sunny day outside. But Jane didn't move, or even consciously consider the meaning of what Amanda had said. Her mind seemed absorbed instead in a single vivid image of her friend's little red car bumper to bumper with Max's lordly Jaguar. Had Mrs Drew-Brown missed that confrontation? Surely not; she missed nothing that went on in Hay's Mews.

The long-case clock in the sitting room chimed noon, breaking into her trance-like concentration on the picture in her mind. Reality came flooding in – she had packing to do, dinner to prepare, people to smile at and talk to when they came back. Taken one by one, she could manage all these things and the day would somehow become normal again; soon she'd be able to believe that nothing catastrophic had happened after all.

She was in the kitchen stuffing chicken breasts with ham and cheese and trying not to feel sick at the thought of eating them when Charlie rang. They'd bumped into old friends from Bristol and were going to eat with them before Jill went to the theatre.

'Tell her, please, that I'll be leaving early in the morning before she gets up,' Jane said.

'Will do . . . Are you all right? Your voice sounds funny.'

'Cold coming, I think. Thanks for all your help, Charlie. Don't devote your entire life to my little sister.' Then, because her voice refused to function any more, she replaced the receiver.

There was still the evening to get through, but Elizabeth needed very little help in keeping the conversation going. There was the previous night's success to analyse in detail, and Jill's glittering future to predict.

'I had quite a long chat with Michael Rutherford last night,' she said happily. 'He thinks she's earned a place in his repertory company, and she couldn't have a better start to her career than that.'

'Sad for you, though,' Jane was able to point out. 'You won't see much of her in future.'

'I know that, but it doesn't matter, I want her to be happy.' Elizabeth hesitated a moment and then went on. 'Must you go back to Somerset tomorrow? You look tired. Surely Hannah doesn't still need nursemaiding?'

'It's not Hannah I'm going for.' The truth couldn't be admitted to now, but she remembered something that would do instead. 'I'm going to look at my new property! A small farm adjoining Rushey came on the market and I decided to buy it.' The consternation on her mother's face allowed her to smile almost naturally.

'My darling girl, you're mad – quite mad!' Elizabeth pronounced seriously. 'Have you forgotten that you live and work in London, and know nothing about farming in any case?'

'I didn't buy it for myself. Uncle Joshua and Rufus Venn are going to work it for me. Between us we're keeping a little bit more of the Levels as they should be kept – not altered, or exploited, or ruined by businessmen instead of cared for by farmers.'

Elizabeth saw the sudden flush of colour in her daughter's pale face and knew that more had happened than she was being told. But they weren't in the habit of exchanging confidences, and she realized that the most she could do to help was claim that she herself was tired, and pretend that she hadn't noticed the effort Jane had made all evening,

'It's the effect London has on me,' she said ruefully. 'I must be getting old! But there's no need to escort me back to the hotel – let me manage on my own.'

'I'll escort you to a taxi, at least, and I'll collect you tomorrow – about nine thirty if that suits.'

The following morning she was up and out of the house far too early in her desperate need to avoid meeting Jill. Time enough for that when she'd seen Max and the sick uncertainty in her heart had been wiped away. With an hour to kill she parked the car and rambled through Kensington Gardens, trying to concentrate on what she must still believe was going to be her future. Germany was an old and civilized country – except for recurring bouts of national madness, at least.

She'd learn to be happy there. But London on a fine morning in late May . . . Could that be beaten, or even matched? She doubted it.

With the hands of her watch creeping round at last, she threaded her way through the heavy morning traffic in Knightsbridge and found Elizabeth waiting for her in the hotel lobby. She was a good passenger – untalkative while her chauffeuse needed to concentrate on the busy road, and not inclined to fidget distractingly.

When they pulled up outside the house in Royal Crescent Jane gave a little sigh of relief before she turned to smile at her mother. 'Mission accomplished!'

'Very smoothly, I have to say. Now, darling, some lunch before you go on?'

'Thanks, but no – I've got an appointment to keep. I'll come and see you soon, though.' She got out of the car to retrieve her mother's suitcase and carry it to the front door.

'Wait a moment – there's something I want you to have,' Elizabeth said.

She disappeared inside the house and returned a moment later with a bulky package carefully wrapped in brown paper. 'It's what Hannah sent me after your father died. I think she intended it for you, but I never imagined that you'd want it, until now.'

Jane kissed her mother goodbye and drove away with the parcel on the seat beside her. At any other time she would have been very curious about it; now she could only think of her meeting with Max. She was going to be too early for that as well, unless she stopped and ate some lunch. But the sandwich she ordered at a wayside pub couldn't be swallowed, so she drank coffee instead and waited for the dragging minutes to pass.

At half past three she drove into Cossenford and the little grey town seemed to receive her kindly, as if welcoming her home. She parked the car in the square and, repeating the pattern of her first visit, walked up the path to the church. But this time, though still peaceful and serene, it *was* empty; there was no Max unrolling Bach's great harmonies beneath his fingers. She walked back through the churchyard and turned towards the Manor House.

Twenty-Two

The *senhor* was at home, his smiling Portuguese maid confirmed, but speaking on the telephone. If the *senhorita* would have the goodness to wait in the library, he would, *sem duvida*, come soon. She was shown into a room that was still welcoming with its French windows now open to the terrace and sunlit lawns. But she preferred it fire-lit and lamp-lit as she'd seen it once before.

She was looking out at the garden when the sound of the door closing behind her announced that Max was in the room. But when she turned he didn't come towards her, and he didn't smile. For a moment she was unable to register that strangeness; even with her heart racing and her throat dry, she felt the remembered surge of joy at seeing him. Then he spoke, but with the voice of someone she didn't know.

'Punctual as always,' he said, and she understood that, while she was desperately troubled, he was simply angry.

'You could say hello,' she pointed out unevenly. 'Wouldn't that be nice?'

'My dear Jane, *hello*! Is that nice enough?'

She was confronting a cold-eyed stranger, not the man it had been so easy to laugh with and love, but the hostility they now seemed to be caught up in was inexplicable as well as hurtful. She'd come prepared for a quite different ordeal.

'I know you're deeply upset about your uncle,' she said quietly, 'but I don't understand why it's making you angry with me.'

Max lessened the physical distance between them by propping himself up against one side of the great stone fireplace.

'I saw my cousin Luke this morning,' Max explained smoothly. 'He'd just got back from France. On top of having

lost his father, he discovered that the neighbouring farm that he expected to buy had already been sold. He didn't know the new owner, but I did.'

'Myself,' Jane confirmed, now understanding what the battle was about. 'I wanted it for Joshua Venn, but he and Rufus would only agree to work it for me, not accept it outright.'

'It didn't occur to you to tell me what you had in mind? Were you afraid I'd talk you out of such a piece of folly? Is the score between the Venns and my family now settled, or does the vendetta still go on?'

The questions rained on her like blows, sparking her own anger. 'Don't try to intimidate me, Max. What I did had nothing to do with the past, and I didn't tell you because Uncle Joshua seemed so unlikely to accept what I was suggesting.'

'I see – it was a whim that suddenly occurred to you. Today I think I'll go out and buy a farm!'

'Not a whim,' she answered steadily. 'I bought Neil Gibson's farm to stop your cousin working it his way, because it's the wrong way for the Levels. I might as well also say that I still think your family's relentless extraction of the peat is wrong, but there's nothing I can do about that.'

She stood in front of him, slender and delicate, but stubborn as hell, he thought. His mind might want a more malleable woman, but his heart couldn't help saluting her. He'd been right to pick her as the one to partner him.

'You're very opinionated for someone who's come rather late to the place,' he commented almost mildly. It was time to retreat to safer ground, but he could only allow himself to do it gradually.

She registered the change of tone, and knew what would come next. Having registered his disapproval, Max would set himself to charm her back to laughter and ease again; some damage had been done, he would think, but it could be repaired and soon forgotten.

But the damage wasn't done with yet. 'Now I need to ask *you* something,' she said suddenly. 'While I was away you spent some time – some nights – in Hay's Mews. Would you mind telling me why?'

189

There was a long pause before he answered. 'So your charming sister couldn't resist letting you know. I suppose she wanted to hurt you. I'm sorry I teased you about disliking her.'

'I don't dislike her, and she told me nothing except that she'd met you at a party. You forget that I live in a small, enclosed mews and your car is too beautiful not to be noticed and talked about.'

Watching him, she knew that there was only one answer to the question she'd asked; she'd known it all along, of course. He wouldn't even try to deny it – not Max's way. He would simply repeat what he'd said once before – that she mustn't be surprised at the frailty of human nature. He came to stand beside her – elegant, handsome, and with all his old, easy confidence intact beneath an air of pleading.

'Listen, please, Jane. I met Jill accidentally at a tedious party given by the Rutherfords. She was beautiful and bored, and I was angry with you for going back to Somerset. But I also had something to prove to myself: I was still a free man, despite the memorable night that you and I had spent together. Habit dies hard, and I wasn't ready to admit that only one particular woman would do from then on. Jill was available and perhaps thought I'd be a more exciting companion than the youth she was with. But she wasn't upset when our brief fling ended; we'd both known it would. She didn't know that you and I had been lovers.'

Jane accepted this as true, but realized that Jill knew now. It explained the recent change in their relationship.

'My little sister is growing up,' she commented. 'She used to like to make it clear that she'd taken something I thought was mine. It was my mistake, of course, to imagine that you *were* mine.' Hurt and self-derision combined made her voice shake, but she retreated when Max took a step towards her, and he could see now how close he was to losing her.

'The mistake was all mine,' he insisted. 'My futile attempt to prove that I could do without you produced exactly the opposite result. I wanted to tell you that night we came back from Glyndebourne, but I was suddenly afraid.'

190

'There was always the risk that Jill might tell me,' Jane pointed out.

'I know, but life is full of risks, and I gambled on my assessment of her – that something that hadn't been very successful would be forgotten. Dear one, please don't look at me so gravely. I know I've hurt you, but it was through stupidity alone, not through intention – never that, Jane. I promise you that we can have a lovely life together.'

She could see clearly enough the moments of pleasure and shared delight, but they wouldn't be enough to fill the long years ahead.

Finally, she shook her head. 'I don't think so.' The quiet statement could have referred to people other than themselves; with all the detachment in the world she seemed to be discussing a couple they both happened to be acquainted with.

Max took time to answer – no surprise there; she knew that, gambler or not, he wasn't an impulsive man. 'I love you very much,' he said at last. 'And I need you in my life. You promised to share it with me. Can't you see that what happened with Jill was completely unimportant?'

'Taking it in turns to sleep with us doesn't seem entirely unimportant to me,' she insisted, 'and even one night with her wasn't enough to prove that you were still a free man. But that isn't what really troubles me. We have much deeper differences than that.'

A flick of the head showed that she'd irritated him again. 'Family feuds that shouldn't concern us; or is it that you can't forget the Venns on the war memorial and dread that I might be going to ask you to live in Germany?'

She thought of the lonely soldier in the square, head bent over the butt of his downturned rifle, guarding so movingly the names inscribed on the stone. 'I thought I was prepared for that, but perhaps our past history does matter. It was another of my mistakes to pretend that it wouldn't.'

He suddenly closed the gap between them and took her shoulders in a hard grip. 'Don't go, please. Stay and let me love you. I can make you forget all the past history there ever was and all our own mistakes as well.' He would have pulled her into his arms but she braced herself with her hands against

his chest. She was exhausted now, and couldn't bear the confrontation to last much longer.

'Physical need is a very powerful argument,' she agreed hoarsely. 'But it isn't enough to get us through all the years ahead together, with the things we see differently dividing us more and more all the time. I'm going to say goodbye now, Max, while I still can.' She looked round the room as if saying goodbye to it too, and then offered him a faint little smile. 'Find nice new owners for this lovely house – it deserves them, and so does Cossenford!'

'I don't much care what Cossenford deserves,' he said harshly.

'I know – that's one of the differences between us,' she agreed. Then she walked past him out of the room, and he made no attempt to stop her.

Back in the square, she managed to remember that she'd left her car there. She got in, and closed her eyes. Soon she might be able to decide what to do next, but for the moment there was only the empty space in which she floated. Pain would have been preferable, because it would have seemed real, but she could feel nothing at all.

A sudden tap on the car window finally roused her. It was Andrew Yeo, peering at her so anxiously that she had to wind down the window and try to smile at him.

'Jane . . . Hannah didn't mention that you were coming back. Are you all right – not unwell?"

She started to explain that her aunt didn't know about this visit, but talking was a mistake – her throat closed up and the tears that she hadn't shed in front of Max suddenly began to trickle down her face. Fumbling for a tissue, she scrubbed them away, trying to regain control of herself, trying not to laugh hysterically at his appalled expression.

'It was a sudden arrangement – to come and visit someone else,' she managed to say. 'I'm sorry about the tears, Andrew! Take no notice; I'm perfectly all right.'

He knew it wasn't true, but instinct told him that his experience was too limited to know what to do. He needed his dear friend who, thank God, was due to meet him in the church.

'Come and listen to our rehearsal,' he begged. 'Ellie's singing something for us tomorrow.'

It seemed easier to agree than argue. Jane obediently got out of the car, and he took her by the hand as if she were a distraught child who might run away. His blessed Ellie was already there, waiting with Daniel.

'Look who I found outside,' he said, trying to sound cheerful. 'Hannah doesn't know she's here yet.'

Ellie saw but tactfully ignored the traces of Jane's tears and simply gave her a loving hug instead. 'Now we can feel complete again – we've missed you.' She lifted Daniel out of his pushchair and handed him to Jane. 'You can cuddle each other and listen to the mess we're about to make of something that ought to sound beautiful!'

But it wasn't a mess. Ellie's rendering of 'I know that my Redeemer liveth' was pure and true, lifting even the most despairing soul a little nearer heaven. With Daniel's warm arms clasped round her neck, Jane listened and felt her numbed body coming to life again. It was painful – like recovering from severe frostbite – but it was preferable to feeling nothing at all. She could even register things that didn't involve herself: Ellie's smile when she looked at Andrew for instance, and the visible change in him. Taking care of Ellie and Daniel – clearly his firm intention from now on – was going to be the making of him.

With the rehearsal over, the soloist retrieved her son, kissed his smiling face, and tucked him back in the pushchair. 'Now, what about tea at home?'

Jane shook her head. 'Not today, Ellie dear. I must go and see Hannah, but there's something else I want to do first.' She blew them a collective kiss and walked away down the aisle.

Andrew waited until she was out of earshot. 'She was weeping outside. Should we have persuaded her to come with us?'

'I don't think so – she wanted us to let her go alone.'

He accepted what Ellie said, knowing that although she was only half his age she'd learned more about life than he had. From now on he wanted her to teach him while he looked after her and Daniel, and soon he was going to pluck up the courage to tell her so.

With a wave to them as she drove past, Jane turned out of the town towards Little Ham. It wasn't a conscious decision to go to Rushey or to Neil Gibson's farm – *her* farm now – the car just seemed to be heading that way. But up on the Polden ridge she suddenly turned into the lay-by where she'd stopped once before. The landscape she saw was differently coloured now – greener than anything she could ever have imagined, not defined by hedges as other counties were, but by the willow and alder-fringed ribbons of water that enclosed the lush meadows. She needed Tom Venn there to tell her what she was looking at – he could have identified every plant and living creature that shared this wetland heart of Somerset.

The little wind coming through the open window was gentle on her face. She'd rest here for a while, and then go back to Maundy Cottage. But her hand touched the package that her mother had hurried indoors to find only an hour or two ago. She undid the wrapping and found a book inside, the size of a small, old-fashioned ledger, with covers of marbled board reinforced at the corners with faded crimson leather. There was an inscription on the title page, written in a schoolboy's clear hand:

A Common-place Book
Belonging to Gideon William Venn,
Aged fourteen, at Rushey Farm in Somersetshire

She didn't turn the page at once, too occupied at first with trying to remember what a commonplace book was – a kind of scrapbook, she thought, compiled over a long span of years. Then the realization of what she held swept over her – this was the only legacy she'd ever had from her father. Whatever else he'd left behind had been disposed of while she was still a child, and even her memory of him had now faded.

The schoolboy Gideon had begun his book by recording daily life at Rushey. Domestic events within the farmhouse seemed not to have interested him very much, but sightings of a Bewick's swan, the arrival of a swarm of lapwings, or the first glimpse of a wild iris coming into bloom were a different matter. These things were noted with a naturalist's

precision, and Gideon's text was scattered with small, enchanting pen drawings as well – the be-whiskered face of an otter suddenly leapt out from the page, or a wild goose in flight.

Not stopping to read carefully, she turned on to later entries that spoke of her father's growing devotion to other things – the magical Arthurian legends, poetry, and the beautiful girl who briefly became his wife. Dead at forty-three, Gideon had left only this entrancing and revealing memorial, and Jane realized now that she might never have received it at all if she hadn't told her mother about buying Neil Gibson's farm.

Gideon had died before all the pages were filled, but she promised herself that when she made over the farm to Tom Venn she would give him her father's book as well. About to wrap it up again, she turned to the last entry that Gideon had written: a couple of lines from a poem by Robert Frost. 'I have miles to go, and promises to keep, before I sleep.' She knew that she only read the words, but for a moment it seemed that she was a small child again, listening to her father speak them. There was something else that she thought she now knew for certain: he hadn't committed suicide. Unhappy though he had been, when he died he was a man with promises still to keep.

At last, she turned the car and drove back to Cossenford. Hannah's cottage was now draped in an early climbing rose, a veil of pure white against the grey stone.

There was no reply when she rang the bell. Feeling sharply disappointed, Jane was on the point of turning away when the door opened and she saw her aunt standing there.

'I was afraid you were out,' Jane said unsteadily, aware that she was close to tears again.

'I was in the garden,' Hannah pointed out. 'If I'd known you were going to turn up, I'd have been watching for you.'

'It's been a long day. Could I have my room back just for . . .' It was as far as she got before her voice failed.

'For as long as you want, of course. Come in child,' said Hannah, holding out her arms.

Twenty-Three

'It will be cold ham and salad for supper,' her aunt announced as she came downstairs. 'Nothing fancy, I'm afraid.'

'The first time I came it was shepherd's pie,' Jane remembered. 'Nothing fancy about that either, but it was very good.' She looked at Hannah's green apron and remembered their conversation on the doorstep. 'I interrupted what you were doing. Lend me some old boots and I'll help you. It would be nice to be out of doors.'

Hannah registered the fact that whatever had prompted this sudden visit wasn't for discussing, at least not yet. Her niece had come with luggage, expecting to stay somewhere, but not at Maundy Cottage. Rushey seemed unlikely, so that only left her friend Max at the Manor House. It was tempting to fish by mentioning that she knew, via Rufus and old Walter Chedzoy, of James Winters' death, but Jane's white face prevented her from prying. Instead, she spoke briskly of what needed doing in the garden.

'Take your choice: plant out annuals or prune the forsythia and early clematis.'

'The annuals, it had better be – they sound as if they need less skill.'

Given instructions as to where to work, Jane trowelled the small plants into the earth and felt her jangled nerves gradually relax. There were real and lasting pleasures still to be had, like Ellie's lovely singing, or the moist, rich soil under her fingers, and Hannah's smile when they caught each other's eye. The heady, fevered rapture she'd known with Max had been an ephemeral thing and the memory of it would fade in time.

Her trug of plants was empty when Hannah finally called

a halt. 'Sherry time,' she said with a firm but slightly shame-faced air. 'Don't stare – it's your fault for starting me on the habit. If I ever come face to face with my father again, I shall have to explain that an evening glass of Croft's Original is *not* the first step on the road to everlasting hell.'

'Quite right,' Jane agreed with her first real smile of the day.

They went indoors, removed the traces of their labours, and Jane poured the sherry, which they decided to take out into the garden again. It was a warm, still evening, and Hannah's resident blackbird – surely perched intentionally where they could see him on the topmost branch of an old Beauty of Bath apple tree – sang his song just for them.

'"They shall be accounted poet Kings, who simply tell the most heart-easing things",' Jane quoted softly. 'I think Keats might have added our blackbird to the poet kings, don't you?'

'Some heart-easing is needed, I'm afraid,' Hannah commented, not looking at the girl beside her. 'Tell me if it helps, but not otherwise.'

'There isn't much to tell.' Jane took a sip of sherry, and crumbled a small cheese biscuit for the expectant robin that waited three feet away. 'Max's uncle died the night before last and now it seems to be his job to hold the Winters family together. I was going to keep him company at the Manor House but we had a blazing row instead – first about Neil Gibson's farm, which Luke Winters had wanted to buy, and then about other things as well.' She smiled almost apologetically at her aunt. 'It seemed as if we were going to bury the Venn versus Winters hatchet once and for all, but all I've done is make things worse.'

Hannah skirted round the subject of Max Hasler. 'You don't regret buying Neil's farm, I hope,' she said instead.

'No, I don't regret that – all the more so now, because when we got back to Bath this morning Elizabeth gave me my father's commonplace book. She'd kept it all these years thinking that I wouldn't want it. It's hard to believe that until a few months ago she would have been quite right.'

Hannah made her own contribution to the robin, and then asked another question. 'What are you going to do now – stay here? I'd like you to.'

Jane touched her hand for a moment by way of a silent thank you, but said that she had things to do in London. 'I'd like to go to Rushey first, though, and talk to Uncle Joshua. Rufus mentioned that one of the men might like to live in a farmhouse I certainly don't need myself. I'll drive over in the morning and go home from there.'

'You won't even come to church?'

'No, but I can tell you what Ellie is going to sing! She was rehearsing it with Andrew Yeo this afternoon. Am I right to think she might end up marrying him one of these days?'

'Of course,' Hannah said firmly. 'But if Andrew takes too long about it, I shall have to give him a little push. Where's the sense in wasting happiness?'

Jane didn't reply to this, but simply told the robin he'd eaten enough biscuits for one day. Then she gathered up their empty glasses and led the way indoors.

She set out for Rushey after breakfast the next morning, having waved Hannah off to church. Someone was working in the farm's now-familiar yard but it was a burly, youngish man she didn't know.

'Mornin',' he said in a soft Somerset voice. 'And 'tes a good'un, I reckon.' As usual, it came out as a question, to which Jane agreed.

'I'm looking for my uncle, Joshua Venn,' she went on to explain, 'but may I ask who you are – Charlie or Ted?'

'I'm Charlie – Ted's my little brother. I reckon you'll be the London lady what's bought Neil's place.'

She agreed again; then it was her turn in this game of questions and answers. 'Has Ted been told he can live in the farmhouse if he wants to?'

Charlie nodded vigorously and a smile spread over his brown face. ''Tes lovely job,' he pronounced in the well-worn local phrase for anything especially pleasing. 'Ted's happy as a lark, and so's his Jenny.'

'I'm very glad,' Jane answered, smiling in turn, just as Joshua walked into the yard from the direction of the paddock.

198

'Blossom's peppermint time?' she asked by way of greeting, and saw him nod.

'Don't London people ever say when they're coming?' It wasn't much of a welcome but she was beginning to know him now. This was Joshua not at all displeased to see her there.

'I wondered if you'd have time to take me to the farm,' she suggested. 'There are things we probably need to talk about.'

'Rufus and Tom are just going there – best ride over with them, I reckon.'

He had Hannah's sense of humour after all, she realized – there had been no sign of it until now. But before she could explain that she'd never climbed on a horse in her life, Ben came bounding out of the kitchen followed by his owner, with Rufus bringing up the rear. The Labrador at least seemed delighted to see her, and Tom looked pleased.

'It's Jane,' Joshua told them unnecessarily. 'She'd like to go to the farm with you, but not on a horse, I reckon.'

'Why not? You couldn't fall off Blossom,' Tom promised, sizing up the situation. 'She won't even trot any more.'

'Dear Tom, I don't even know how to get on,' she had to admit. 'You ride over and I'll meet you there.'

But Rufus finally entered and ended the discussion. 'We'll all go in the jeep, if Jane can manage to climb on that.' His voice sounded pleasantly amused, but once again she was made aware that Rufus Venn was not her friend. It was a mere pinprick of hurt and didn't matter, but she would have liked to know the reason.

They bumped their way over the old drove roads that the cattle used when they were being moved, but the journey was mercifully brief. At the end of it Tom and the dog went off on some urgent inspection of their own, while Jane stared at a small, compact house tucked into the same hills that sheltered Rushey so protectively from the north winds.

'It's nice,' she decided. 'Little Ted and his Jenny ought to be happy here.' Then an enquiring glance from Rufus made her go on. 'I met Charlie when I arrived this morning.'

Rufus seemed prepared to smile at last. 'Perhaps he didn't

explain that "little Ted" is six inches taller than he is and weighs something over fifteen stone!'

Jane shook her head. 'No, he didn't say that. Now, may I see the inside? It's empty, I assume.'

'Yes, but it's been well looked after. Neil wasn't a man to neglect his property or his land.'

Jane turned to stare at her companion. 'You liked him, didn't you – felt that he shouldn't have had to leave?'

'Yes, but I'm not blaming you for that.' Then he unlocked the front door and ushered her inside. The arrangement of the house was simple enough – a large, all-purpose kitchen, and a parlour on the ground floor; two bedrooms upstairs, and a third room that had been turned into a bathroom long after the house was built.

'It may not look much to you,' Rufus said, leaning against the doorframe of the larger bedroom, 'but it will seem like paradise to Ted and Jenny.'

'It's no smaller than my house in London,' Jane pointed out coolly. 'It looks all right to me, too.' She walked over to the window and stared out. 'What will you do with the land?'

'Raise a new pedigree herd on it, mostly, that will need to be separate from our other livestock; there's just the right space for it here.'

'Will that involve Rushey in expenditure you hadn't bargained for?'

'It will, but we shall manage,' Rufus confirmed in a voice she knew better than to argue with. 'You won't see any return on your investment for a while, I'm afraid; it will take a year or two to build up the herd.'

'If I'd been anxious about a return on capital investment, I wouldn't have bought a farm,' Jane pointed out.

'Quite so,' Rufus agreed. 'Shall we go back now?'

'If Tom and Ben are retrievable.'

'We have our methods for that,' he said solemnly. These methods turned out to be two fingers against his teeth, producing a piercing whistle. If not musical, it certainly had the desired result because child and hound reappeared, and they made the brief journey back to Rushey in the jeep with Ben lovingly licking the back of her neck.

Joshua unexpectedly asked her to stay and eat with them but she refused, making an excuse that wouldn't leave him feeling snubbed. She reminded Tom about his London visit when the summer holidays began and then, because it seemed necessary, put out her hand to Rufus.

'Thanks for all your help – to me as well as to Aunt Hannah,' she said. Her hand was held in his warm one, but only for a second or two. He was quick to release her and answer formally.

'Think nothing of it, Miss Westover.'

'Why do you call her that – she's Jane,' Tom pointed out.

'Think nothing of it, Jane,' he corrected himself. 'I think my son would like you to stay longer next time.'

She smiled at Tom but got back into her own car without saying anything more. She would not tell this strangely hostile man that, unless Hannah ever needed her again, she would have no reason to return to Somerset.

The Sunday traffic going back to London was light at midday. Her surface concentration was on the road but at a deeper level her mind looked at a future without Max. It wouldn't be long before pain faded and thankfulness kicked in. That was the thing to cling to: the knowledge that she'd come close to foregoing everything familiar and treasured for a man she'd known so little as not to know at all.

Not long from now, she'd be back at Clifford's – that was where she belonged. She'd got muddled during the past month or two, even begun to imagine that she'd lost the taste for the cut and thrust of City life, but that had simply been born of fear. She could admit it now: she *had* been afraid after leaving St Martha's. Now there was the sting of failure, and the old ache of loneliness to contend with, but she'd manage – rise above the bad moments along the way, as Jill liked to say with her brilliant smile.

But the thought of Jill brought her face to face with her most immediate problem: they couldn't share the same house and never meet, and it wouldn't be long before Jill discovered that her sister's brief love affair was over. Then she would inevitably guess the reason. Other sisters could probably deal

with it – they'd weep and laugh together and jointly swear about the iniquities of men – but their own relationship was too new for that. They were only just learning to like each other.

She pulled up outside her house and frowned at the wilting petunias in the window boxes. When she opened the front door, mail was still lying on the mat, as if Jill hadn't been there yesterday to pick it up. The puzzle was solved a moment later: Jill had moved out. A note lying on the kitchen table explained that her Bristol friends had recommended a land-lady familiar with the strange working hours of theatricals because she had been one herself once. She had an empty top-floor flat in her house in Onslow Square, and the rent, though ruinous, could be managed with a little help from James Westover's legacy to his daughter. Jill reckoned that she'd sponged on her sister quite enough, that Jane must be sick of sharing her house by now – in fact, she'd been an angel to put up with it for so long. The revealing part of the note came in its long postscript. Elizabeth's explanation for Jane's sudden return to Somerset – something about property needing to be inspected – sounded rather wild; Jill's own reading was that the self-sufficient Max Hasler had decided he couldn't live without her – bully for Jane!

For Jill it seemed unexpectedly discreet and kind. She clearly believed that Max himself wouldn't refer to what had happened, and so she could assume that her sister need never know. All that *was* essential was her own immediate depar-ture from the house, since even Max's considerable sangfroid might be shaken at having to meet them both there at once.

Jane folded the note, aware of a jumble of emotions that she was too tired to sort out. Relief came into it – she was thankful that the problem she couldn't solve had been solved for her – but the house felt strangely empty now without Jill. Wounds had to heal, but one day she hoped they'd be able to talk about Max. There was, according to the book of Ecclesiastes, 'a time to weep and a time to laugh', because to everything there was a season. With the weeping finally over, they might even get to laughing about Max, however unlikely it seemed at the moment.

Jane looked at Jill's note again, to confirm that, whether by accident or design, it didn't include her new address. But the Rutherfords were listed in the directory and when Jane rang the number it was Charlie who answered her call.

'Jane – back already, what a nice surprise!' He sounded his pleasant, friendly self, but she sensed that an effort was required.

'I didn't have to stay long this time,' she explained briefly. 'Charlie, do you know where Jill is now? She left a note but it doesn't mention her new address.'

'Flat three, fourteen Onslow Square' he said at once. 'No telephone number yet, though. She couldn't wait to move in before it was reconnected. You know how it is with Jill. Tomorrow won't do if she wants something; it has to be today.'

Jane did know, but she asked something else. 'How is the play going?'

'Sell-out. It could run and run, but my father still believes in repertory theatre, so they're already rehearsing for what comes next.'

'What does come next?'

'*The Tempest*! The Great Man's taking a risk, I happen to think – he's giving the plum part of Prospero's daughter to Jill. She'll make the most beautiful Miranda that ever was, but she's a bit above herself at the moment.'

Jane worked out what this statement meant. 'You told her so, I expect, and have now fallen out of favour.'

'Well, yes,' Charlie admitted. 'A temporary coolness, let's say.' But he sounded sad, as if he feared the falling-out this time might be permanent. Then he spoke again in a different tone of voice. 'Lucky me – I'm off to New York, going to work in a theatre there that happens to belong to a family friend.'

'But you're unhappy about leaving Jill?'

'Well, yes,' he said again. 'She doesn't realize it, but she still needs looking after.'

'Charlie dear – stop worrying! Try to cultivate a grain of selfishness, please, and give a thought to your own career!' At least it made him laugh as he said goodbye.

That evening, watering her thirsty window boxes, she saw

Amanda Crichton drive along the mews. 'Don't disappear,' she called down. 'I want to talk to you.'

'All well with you and . . . and Max?' Amanda ventured bravely when they were face to face, trying to ignore the memory of their last conversation.

'He's got work to do in Somerset,' Jane said briefly, 'and Jill's found a flat of her own, so the house is all mine again! Her play's doing very well, but if I can get tickets, will you come? I'd like to see it again.'

'Love to – it would be good for Julian to be the one who stays at home for a change!'

With a tactful mention of her sister's name at the box office Jane got them in the following evening. The performance, well into its stride now, was producing ensemble playing of the highest order.

'The big names are wonderful,' Amanda said when the final curtain came down, 'but Jill's right up there with them. Don't you agree?'

'Yes, I do,' Jane admitted, smiling at her. 'Let's go and tell her so.'

They found her dressing room and went in to find Jill alone for once, removing her stage make-up. She saw them in the mirror and smiled, but she looked tired, and Jane remembered what Charlie had said. His father was taking a risk on a young, inexperienced member of his company, and perhaps Jill was under too much strain.

'It was even better tonight,' Jane said simply. 'Well done, little sister.'

Jill's cheeks flushed with sudden colour. 'Thanks . . . thank you both for coming.' She wiped cold cream off her face and managed a casual question. 'How did things go in Somerset? Has Max come back with you?'

'No – he has a lot to do down there. I wasn't being any help, so I left.' She steadied her voice and went on. 'Elizabeth did have the story right. I've bought a farm that adjoins my uncle's, and we had a spectacular row about it.'

'Did that matter?' Amanda asked, seeing that Jill seemed disinclined to say anything.

'It mattered very much – he wanted it for his cousin!' Jane

smiled at them convincingly. 'There's more to it than who owns the land – the way it's worked is fundamental to preserving the Levels. Unless you know the place I can't make you understand how vital it is, but Max is on one side, and I'm on the other.'

'That's what the row was about?' Jill asked anxiously. 'That's really what it was about?'

'Yes,' Jane confirmed, certain now of being able to manage this conversation. 'But there'd have been other problems in future, even if we could have settled this one. I have a career in London that I couldn't have given up to go and live in Germany.' She looked at her sister. 'What now? Shall we feed you some supper, or do you just want to get to bed?'

'Bed, I think,' Jill confessed ruefully. 'Doing one play and rehearsing another is going to kill my social life!'

'Charlie told me – I rang him to find out where you were. His father's got great faith in you.'

'Which is more than Charlie has,' Jill said resentfully. 'The pig is off to New York without me! Well, down with men, I say! I'm afraid Amanda's stuck with her nice Julian, but we Westovers can do without them.'

'"The play's the thing",' her sister quoted gravely, and Jill's entrancing grin reappeared. She could relax now, certain that she hadn't taken the one thing Jane had really wanted.

Twenty-Four

Jane clung to her survival plan as the weeks of early summer passed. A long walk through one of the parks before the morning rush began, and some overdue redecoration inside her house.

July brought Mediterranean summer weather and she took to eating meals out of doors, trying not to compare her stark designer plot with Hannah's glorious muddle of foliage and flowers. Filling the unforgiving minutes of each day wasn't too difficult, but the nights were something else. Then loneliness walked in, and the knowledge that she could still have been with Max, caught up in loving until sleep came.

There were friendly chats on the phone with Jill, and brief conversations with Hannah, who couldn't bear a call to last more than three minutes. Charlie sent an occasional postcard, enjoying himself but clearly homesick for London. The only surprise was an invitation to dinner at Piers Clifford's beautiful Hampstead house. She suspected that, between them, Max and the Rutherfords had notched up her social value in Piers' observant eye. But it was reassuring to be told that a legal battle was brewing that he reckoned would get her nicely back into the swing of things.

Opening night of *The Tempest* came with Charlie still in New York. She thought Jill had expected him to be back to see, as he'd predicted, a Miranda so beautiful that every red-blooded male in the audience had no option but to fall in love with her.

Jane forwent the first-night party, tired after a day of preparation for her Somerset guests the following morning. She'd even filled terracotta pots with geraniums and sweetly scented lilies in the desperate hope of convincing Hannah that what

206

she looked out on was a garden. The original plan for her aunt and Tom to come by train had recently been changed. Rufus would now drive them up on his way to Gatwick Airport. Hannah had been more than usually terse about this alteration, merely saying that he was on his way to Austria. They would leave very early so as to arrive in time for breakfast – Tom saw no reason not to get the most out of his first day in London.

She half expected the jeep to come bucking along the Mews, destroying its Sunday morning peace, but instead a perfectly respectable Rover pulled up outside her front door. What, she wondered, would Sonia Drew-Brown make of the little group that now emerged? An excited red-headed schoolboy, a digni-fied maiden aunt perhaps, and a large, bearded man who looked around as if wondering how any sane mortal could live in the enclosed and suffocating space he found himself confined in.

'Not too early for you, I hope,' he said politely, when Hannah had been shown to her bedroom and Tom was inves-tigating the bathroom upstairs. 'We thought it would be nice to go to Kew.'

'Aunt Hannah mentioned Austria,' she ventured.

'Tomorrow morning – I'll stay at Gatwick tonight.'

Getting information out of him was like getting blood out of a stone. 'Just so that I don't say the wrong thing, Tom knows why you're going?'

'Of course – it's his mother that I'm going to see.'

Not for the first time she'd been quietly snubbed by Rufus Venn, but she made allowances for him now. That smiling composure was all very well, but the man wouldn't have been human without the turmoil that she sensed being held under tight control.

They hadn't got far with breakfast when the doorbell rang again. Tom offered to answer it and reappeared a moment later with Jill in tow – making, to her sister's astonishment, a rare Sunday entrance before midday.

'Jane told me you were coming,' she said, smiling bril-liantly. 'I didn't see why I should be left out of the fun. Dear Aunt Hannah, you wouldn't come to see the play, but I forgive you!'

She was introduced to Rufus and Tom, accepted some coffee, and then asked to be allowed to join in whatever they were going to do.

'We're going to Kew,' Jane pointed out. 'Are you sure you want to come?' She waited to be told, against all the evidence to the contrary, that her sister was just a country girl at heart, but Jill simply looked at Rufus. 'I shan't know the name of a single thing, but if you can put up with that, I'd love to tag along.'

'Anything that stumps me, Tom will probably know,' Rufus suggested, but he didn't get an answering smile from his son, and Jane suspected that, to one of them at least, Jill's inclusion in the party wasn't welcome.

It was an enjoyable day nevertheless, made more so by the perfect summer weather. Jane kept an eye on Hannah, to make sure that she didn't walk too far, and after lunch suggested that they find a shady seat and leave the others to go exploring.

'I checked with Rufus that Tom knows why he's going to Austria,' Jane said when her aunt was settled. 'Do you suppose they think that Selina might agree to come back to England?'

'They haven't told me what they think and I haven't asked them.' Hannah paused, considering what to say next. 'Rufus could be forgiven for thinking that your sister is very taken with him. I can't blame her, of course – he's a very taking man – but I'm afraid she's wasting her time.'

Jane considered this for a moment and finally admitted that Jill probably *would* see him as a challenge. It was true that, deeply tanned, and with his russet hair and beard well trimmed, he looked attractively different from the men she was accustomed to meeting in the theatre.

When the three of them came back Jill seemed to have made some progress – measured, for Jane, by Tom's unsmiling face. Not wanting him to be hurt, she made an excuse to dawdle behind the others, and tried to explain.

'I expect you've gathered that my sister is an actress. You won't have met theatre people before, so you don't know that they tend to behave differently from the rest of us.'

'You mean they wave their hands about and talk a lot?' Tom asked disapprovingly.

'Well, yes – that's part of what they do, but it's hard for

them to stop when they aren't actually working. It makes them tiring to be with sometimes!'

He considered this for a moment. 'You aren't tiring, Jane.'

'It's kind of you to say so,' she answered solemnly, and was rewarded with his shy grin. 'How did you escape this morning without Ben?'

'I explained to him that we were coming back soon, and Uncle Josh had his favourite breakfast ready, but he still looked sad. Dad says we must have another puppy for when I go to school – it'll be company for him.'

'So it will,' Jane agreed.

They walked in silence for a moment, then Tom suddenly launched a question she hadn't expected. 'Dad's going to Austria – do you know why?'

'Yes,' she admitted, but could think of nothing else that seemed safe to say.

'My mother might want to come home,' Tom suggested after a small pause. 'But . . . she may be very busy, so perhaps I'll just go with Dad to see her another time.'

The note of hope in his voice was painful, and Jane knew a sudden, fierce urge to be able to face the woman who'd abandoned them and shout what a fool she was – a cruel, monstrously selfish fool. But there was only Tom beside her, his red head down, studying the ground.

At Hay's Mews again Jill accepted her sister's small hint that it was time she went home, and did it in her own fashion by regretfully informing Rufus that Jane reckoned she'd gate-crashed their party long enough.

'Enhanced our party,' he corrected her with a smile. 'Tom and I enjoyed showing off with all the names you didn't know!'

Watching the little scene, Jane realized again how seriously she'd once underrated him. He wouldn't for a moment consider living a city life, but he wasn't disconcerted by it; he could take her beautiful, tantalizing sister in his even stride, and somehow harmlessly defuse the charge she couldn't resist offering.

With supper over, he said goodbye to Hannah, and then looked at Tom. 'Two lovely days with Aunt Hannah and Jane, then I'll be back to collect you. Take care of them, please.'

Tom nodded but couldn't speak, and simply hugged his father instead. Jane made an excuse of locking the front door to follow Rufus downstairs.

'Bon voyage,' she said. 'Travel safely.'

'Thanks, and thank you for giving Tom this treat. It's good for him not to have me around for a day or two. But you were too kind this afternoon. By neglecting him a little for Jill I hoped to make him cross enough not to mind when I left.'

'Then you must keep the junior officers informed next time,' she suggested. 'Not knowing the strategy, we're liable to make mistakes.'

Rufus nodded, then abruptly changed the subject. 'You aren't like your sister.'

'Very true.' She was tired of explaining their true relationship; and it was self-evident that she didn't possess Jill's stunning beauty. Perhaps she was expected to apologize for that.

But then came another switch. 'I'm sorry about Max Hasler. Jill mentioned that it was buying Neil's farm that spoilt things.'

'Well, you did warn me that it might,' she pointed out.

He stared at her for a moment, noting her thinness. She might manage to sound unconcerned, but the cost of losing Max Hasler was written on her face. He'd been down that road himself and knew the pain of it.

'I'm sorry,' he said again, and this time she believed him. She considered asking him to bring Selina back, gagged and bound if necessary, if only for the sake of his son, but before she could make up her mind he made a move of his own that left her speechless. He leant forward and gave her mouth a brief, sweet kiss.

'That's for Tom,' he murmured. 'Say goodnight to him for me.'

Then, before she could recover her breath, he'd let himself out into the street.

The following afternoon, on the outskirts of a small Austrian town, Rufus edged his way through the ordered chaos of Hans Meier's circus encampment. Directed to a gleaming home on wheels, he stared at it, remembering the gaily painted gypsy caravan in which he and Selina had once roamed the Continent. He forced himself to knock on the door and a moment later

she was there in front of him – familiar and yet a stranger.

She was the first to speak, and her husky voice, at least, was unchanged. 'So . . . you found me, I never thought you would. Come in, Rufus.'

Inside the caravan, looking at her unsmiling face, he knew that his journey, like the years of waiting, had been pointless. 'I thought you might be ready to come home,' he finally suggested.

'This *is* my home,' she said. 'It has been ever since Hans took me in.' Now it was her turn to stare, trying to rediscover in this large, quiet man the reckless young adventurer she'd run away with. 'You're different . . . not just older. But I suppose I am, too.'

He nodded, unable to say that his coltish, half-wild girl had become a woman he didn't know. 'What do you do here?' he asked instead.

She half-smiled now. 'Am I Hans's wife or mistress, do you mean? Neither – I've become the daughter he never had. When he's too tired to run the circus himself, I shall do it for him.'

That explained it all, of course. She wasn't just involved in this strange little world; she was at the heart of it. There'd never been the slightest chance of her needing what she'd left behind.

'Tom is nearly ten now,' he decided to remind her. 'He knows I'm here . . . still hopes you'll come back and meet him.'

Selina shrugged, half-irritated, half-regretful. 'You must tell him that I can't ever go back to England. He was our mistake. You chose to settle down. My life is here, travelling with the circus; it always will be.'

Rufus nodded, accepting what she said. He felt immensely tired, like a man recovering from an illness, but light-headed with relief as well; something left painfully incomplete had at last been settled.

'Tom wasn't a mistake,' he insisted gently, 'he's the best treasure I have; so now I'll go back to him.'

Selina smiled suddenly, not wanting to see him leave. 'You could stay and watch tonight's performance.'

'I could, but I dislike circuses almost as much as I dislike zoos! Goodbye, my dear. Stay happy in your wanderings.' His upraised hand sketched a salute, and then he let himself out of the caravan.

Twenty-Five

The day's programme of sightseeing had taken them eastward to the City: the Tower of London at Tom's request, and St Paul's because Hannah especially asked to see it, but she declined while they were there to make the long climb up to the Whispering Gallery. They could leave her down below, listening to an unseen organist practising for evensong.

She wasn't usually much impressed by size – small was beautiful in her view – but she had to admit to herself that Wren's great cathedral offered the serenity and glorious sense of space that he had surely set out to create. A jingle from an old nursery rhyme came back to her: 'London's burning, London's burning . . . fire, fire . . .' She had the unforgettable image in her mind, as did most people, of the golden cross on St Paul's dome shining above a city engulfed in smoke and flames. What dreadful, dreadful times they had been.

'Wake up, Aunt Hannah,' said Tom's voice in her ear. 'The Whispering Gallery *does* work – we've tried it. But Jane didn't seem to like the idea of the walk round the outside of the dome.'

'More truthfully, wild horses wouldn't have dragged her out there,' Jane admitted, smiling at her aunt. 'You look tired, and it's time we went home. The rest of London will have to wait for another visit.' But they went back via a bookshop in Piccadilly, where she invited Tom to choose three books to take home with him.

'Dad would say I ought only to take one,' he said, agonizing over whether to choose *Wetland Life in the Somerset Levels* or a beautifully illustrated edition of *The Birds of Somerset*.

'He'd be sensible enough to realize that you need them both,' she said firmly, then added to the little pile her own

choice for him: Kenneth Graham's *The Wind in the Willows*. A little fantasy was surely needed to help the facts go down.

With the evening fine and warm, they rounded off the day by eating supper in the garden, and the cold curried chicken in mayonnaise was another new experience for Tom – the best food he'd eaten in his life so far, he reckoned. Hannah, suspecting its richness, was a little more cautious, but even she was tempted to a second helping.

Jane was indoors fetching some lemon sorbet for pudding when the telephone rang. It was Rufus, announcing that he was back at Gatwick. 'I could come to breakfast again tomorrow,' he suggested wistfully. 'I hate hotels, and especially this one.'

'Breakfast by all means,' she agreed. 'I'd say come now, but you'd have to sleep on the floor. The hotel might be preferable.'

He decided that it would, and then asked to speak to his son. She called to Tom to come indoors, put the sorbet back in the fridge, and went to join Hannah outside.

'Rufus is back at Gatwick; he'll be here early tomorrow,' she reported briefly.

'How did he sound – happy? Depressed?'

Jane considered the question thoughtfully. 'Mostly tired, I think. Not gay as a lark, and obviously alone.'

'I'm not sure whether I wanted Selina to come or not,' Hannah admitted. 'I can't see her changing, apart from growing older, and the girl she was could never have settled down at Rushey. Even your mother couldn't manage it, and she wasn't a half-wild creature with wandering in her blood.'

She relapsed into silence, and Jane tried not to think about the conversation going on between Rufus and his son. At least it was brief, because Tom soon came out and sat down at the table again. He fidgeted with his pudding spoon, and spoke without looking at them.

'Mum couldn't come. She's very busy, with lots of horses to look after . . . people, too. Dad says they need her there.' Then he did speak to Jane. 'He said I mustn't forget to thank you for looking after me.'

'Consider it said,' she suggested unevenly. 'I don't know

what I shall do with myself when you and Aunt Hannah go home tomorrow.' It made him smile at her with heartbreaking sweetness, and she went to retrieve the melting sorbet, trying to remember that at least part of what had gone into the making of Tom Venn must have come from his absent mother. And there was more than that to give her reluctant credit for: Rufus had found in her something to love that no other woman had been able to make up for since.

With supper cleared away and darkness falling, they abandoned the garden and went back indoors. It was the moment, Jane thought, to produce her father's commonplace book for Tom to browse through until it was time for bed. He lingered, of course, over the photographs and drawings, happy to recognize them faster than Hannah did. Looking at his absorbed face, Jane hoped that Selina had been at least temporarily forgotten. Children were supposed to live in the present moment, so for now perhaps Gideon's book would be comfort enough. But her heart ached for Rufus Venn as well, still lonely and likely to remain so.

Tom was looking at the book again when she went into the sitting room the following morning.

'Jane, it's lovely but it isn't finished,' he said, having discovered the blank pages at the end of it.

'I know,' she agreed, smiling at him. 'I haven't had it long enough to read properly yet, but when you're fourteen – which is how old my father was when he began putting it together – I'd like you to have it, Tom, so that maybe you can finish it.'

He gave a little nod by way of answer, but only, she knew, because words had failed him. Instead of speaking, he carried the book to the shelf he'd seen Jane take it from, and gave it a little pat. She thought she wouldn't be surprised to see him at the door on his fourteenth birthday, having come to claim his property.

Then he announced that he'd just walk to the end of the Mews to try and meet his father driving in.

Ten minutes later he and Rufus were at the door, one of them so clearly a small edition of the other that Selina appeared

to have contributed very little, after all, at least to the exterior of her son.

'Breakfast isn't ready,' Jane said by way of greeting, 'and nor is Aunt Hannah – you've got time for a stroll. Walk up Sloane Street, cross Knightsbridge, and you'll come to Hyde Park. If you get lost, just ask a policeman.'

Rufus glanced at his watch. 'We'll be back at half-past eight, with or without the help of the constabulary.'

She waved them off, went to report to Hannah that the traveller was back, and then set about laying the table in the kitchen. Above the clatter of grinding coffee beans she heard the doorbell ring and went downstairs to find Jill on the doorstep, clutching a bulky, wrapped parcel.

'I wanted to say goodbye to Aunt Hannah and give Tom a little present. Don't tell me I've missed them; I've never been up so early in my life!' She caught the faint hesitation in Jane's face and tried to pretend it didn't matter. 'If they're still here and I'm gatecrashing again I can just leave the parcel and go away.'

'Don't be silly; of course you're coming in. Rufus and Tom are out walking, but they'll be back any minute, then we can all have breakfast together before they take Aunt Hannah back to Cossenford.'

She led the way upstairs, hoping that this time Tom wouldn't resent Jill's presence.

'I want Rufus to see the play,' she said. 'I want him to stay and see it tonight. Couldn't Aunt Hannah and Tom go home by train?' She blushed faintly at the astonishment in her sister's face. 'Don't look so surprised – you must have known that day we went to Kew that something wonderful was happening! It's as if he's been with me ever since.'

It was tempting to pretend that she was acting again, enjoying a new role all the more because her sister would find it hard to know whether to believe it or not. But the throb in her voice wasn't faked, and nor was the wonder in her face. The giving of unwanted advice was a thankless task at any time, and Jane foresaw that it would be more than usually pointless now, but she felt obliged to try.

'Jill dear, you've spent less than a day in Rufus Venn's

215

company; that does not entitle you to think you've fallen in love with him.'

'No one "thinks" about falling in love,' Jill pointed out. 'They just do it; it happens. It's happened to me, so gloriously that I can't believe it hasn't happened to Rufus too.'

She was inside a spun-glass bubble of delight, entirely sealed off from reality. It wasn't something new – Jane had had ample opportunity in the past to watch something Jill *wanted* become, in her imagination, the thing she actually *had*.

'Will you listen to me for a moment?' she suggested quietly. 'Fact number one: you live and work unsociable hours in London, while Rufus is a dedicated farmer in rural Somerset. Fact number two: he is still bound heart and mind to someone else – Tom's mother, to be precise. One of those facts would be enough to scupper your love affair; both of them mean that you're on a hiding to nothing if you make up your mind you want Rufus Venn.'

Jill simply smiled her bewitching smile, not at all upset by an assessment that could scarcely be contradicted. 'Now it's your turn to listen to me. Dear Jane, I know the score as well as you do. I can't *not* be an actress; it's what I am, and a farmer's wife is one role I don't intend to play. I don't even want Rufus as a lover, though I can't help feeling he'd be an exciting one. The truth is that a world well lost for love, or sex, is nonsense; I've tried it and I know.'

Jane stared at her sister, wondering whether she knew or understood her at all. 'So if you don't see Rufus Venn as a husband or a lover, what's left?'

'Everything that matters,' Jill said simply. 'Knowing that he loves me means I'll be safe in future. Knowing where he is, I'll always be able to find him when I need him – he'll be the lovely ballast that keeps my rickety little ship from sinking!'

It had, Jane realized, the simple ring of truth about it. 'What about Rufus?' she asked after a pause. 'What does he get out of it?'

Jill smiled sweetly. 'The happiness of knowing how much I need him. A different man, more selfish, less generous than

he is, wouldn't find that enough. But Rufus will – and looking after me he'll be able to forget that stupid woman in Austria at last.'

Unable to reply, Jane was thankful to hear the doorbell ring again. 'Go and let them in,' she said, 'and remember if you can that you came to give Tom a present, not to lure his father into a breathtakingly one-sided love affair.'

Ten minutes later she went back to the sitting room to find that Hannah was now there as well, and the four of them were clustered round what Jill had brought: the stage designer's original small model of Prospero's enchanted island, complete with wave-fringed shores, woodland glades, and the magician's cell. Realized in the theatre, it had been ravishingly beautiful; even in its model form it made a gift to kindle a child's imagination.

'I scarcely like to break the spell,' Jane said matter-of-factly, 'but if anyone's interested, breakfast is finally being served.'

With the excuse of playing hostess, she needed to take little part in the conversation. She could consider instead the 'taking' man – Hannah's apt phrase, she remembered – who seemed to have become so necessary to her sister. Jill wouldn't have missed the outward signs of grace – eyes that, like Tom's, were deeply blue, or the firm-lipped mouth framed in its russet beard. But she'd found more important things in Rufus Venn: the strength that went with physical size allied, in his case, to unfailing gentleness – at least to everyone but her sister, Jane. Jill would probably have been pleased about that.

Breakfast over at last, she found herself wanting them all to leave. She'd listened to them talking long enough, and she wanted, for no reason she could fathom, to sit in a dark corner by herself and weep. That wasn't true, of course; she knew what ailed her. She still ached for Max, and only the relief of getting back to work would now save her from raging melancholia.

She heard Rufus say that it was time to leave, and managed to smile at him for the sheer relief of it. The luggage was taken downstairs, goodbyes and thank yous said. Jane need only wave them on their way, with Jill installed in the car as

well so that she could be dropped off at her flat on the way. Then, instead of driving off, Rufus suddenly came back to where she stood at the door.

'Are you all right?' he asked quietly. 'You weren't joining in the general chatter. Jill thinks you're unhappy because of being without Max Hasler. If she's right, we should never have let you buy the farm.'

'You didn't "let" me – I thrust it on Uncle Joshua,' she reminded him. 'I miss Max, of course, but I miss my job much more. Otherwise I'm as right as rain, thank you all very much, and nobody's concern is needed. I hope I can say the same for you.' Having started to 'chatter', she now couldn't seem to stop. 'Did you settle your affairs in Austria?'

'To the extent that I know Tom's mother won't ever be coming back, yes, I suppose I did.'

'If you haven't told *him* that, I think it's time you did; it's cruel to let him just keep hoping. But you're about to tell me again that you don't need my advice on how to deal with your son.'

'Something to that effect,' he agreed, 'but at least I have to thank you for giving him a visit he won't forget.' He hesitated as if about to say something else, then changed his mind and walked back to the car.

She stood there, watching Tom wave through the rear window until the car turned out into Sloane Street, and then she went inside and closed the door.

Twenty-Six

The August days dragged past so slowly that at times they seemed to have resisted all natural laws and stopped moving altogether. It was tempting to do what thousands of other people were obviously doing and escape from the hot, dusty streets. She could fly to Sydney, perhaps, to see whether the opera house really did look like the wind-filled sails of a ship. She could learn to fly a hot-air balloon, or go sand dune surfing in the Namibian desert. But in the end she stayed where she was, held by some instinctive belief that she must work out her salvation in London where she belonged.

Her return to Clifford's was a mere three days away when Hannah broke her normal rule and made a long-distance telephone call herself. She was careful not to enquire about her niece's health or state of mind, although it took great resolution not to. Instead, she announced that she had two items of news concerning Max Hasler. The first was that an estate agent had been seen introducing the Manor House to prospective buyers.

'It's what I expected,' Jane said calmly. 'Max told me weeks ago that he was thinking of selling.'

Her attempt at delivering one surprise thwarted, Hannah offered her second one. 'Did he also happen to mention that the Baptist chapel site won't be his for much longer?'

A silence at the other end of the line was more promising. 'No, he didn't,' Jane finally admitted. 'Are you sure about that?'

'Of course I'm sure! As if I'd ring London to pass on mere gossip. Arthur Cranston spoke to the new people yesterday – developers from London. The sale of the land is as good as settled. It remains to be seen what they intend to do with it,

but I very much doubt that Mr Hasler's assurances to us will be honoured.'

Jane saw no way of avoiding what she was expected to say next. 'I suppose you think he's behaved very badly towards Cossenford?'

'Yes, I do. I'm sorry to say this if it hurts you, but Max Hasler's fine words at the public meeting meant nothing. If the opportunity ever presents itself, I shall tell him so.'

She would, Jane knew. The truth as Hannah saw it would be what Max got unsparingly.

'Did Arthur say why there'd been a change of plan? There must be a reason.'

'My dear Jane, rich men don't need reasons like other people; they have whims instead.'

'Miss Venn's First Law!' Jane observed wryly, but this wasn't something to be laughed away. She knew how deeply Hannah would feel that they'd been cheated and betrayed. 'I expect it's already been thought of,' she suggested after a little pause, 'but, if not, the Town Council must get in touch with the new owners of the site at once, and insist that the original proposals are adhered to. If they hedge, they must be threatened with an immediate appeal against what they propose instead.'

'Of course! I'll go and see John Masterson now,' Hannah said more cheerfully. 'He's a nice man, but if he's done anything so far but wring his hands I shall be very surprised. I'll keep in touch, Jane.' And with that she rang off.

It wasn't hard to visualize her, frail but indomitable, setting out for the Town Hall. She'd at least been given the comfort of doing something; it was more painful, Jane reflected, to have to sit and think about Max. She couldn't believe that pique or wounded pride or even the whim Hannah had suggested was cause enough for the sudden change of plan. But it left the worse alternative that a shrewd and unscrupulous businessman had simply seen an opportunity to turn a handsome profit on a deal.

Whatever it was, she needed to know, and the only way to find out was to ask Max himself. Her telephone call to his number produced the result she might have expected – the

cool voice of Camilla Hastings, happy to explain that at that moment he was on his way to Paris.

'Then my call is pointless,' Jane said. 'There's no message, thank you.'

'I'll mention that you rang – it *is* Jane Westover, isn't it?'

She had to confirm that it was, imagining Camilla's pleased smile at a little display of one-upmanship. The mention probably wouldn't be made, and would be useless even if it was. But it turned out that she was wrong twice over, because Max telephoned two days later.

'Jane, I'm returning the call Camilla said you made. Since you're in London instead of some godforsaken part of Somerset, why not meet me for a drink? Shall we say the Connaught in an hour's time? Then you can decide whether you'd like to dine with me as well.'

It was Max at his most charmingly autocratic, but she agreed to the suggestion. 'The Connaught at seven.' She evened the score by hanging up first for once.

Thanks to the usual evening traffic snarl-up she was ten minutes late in arriving. Max was already there, reading through some papers, but he pushed them aside and stood up as she walked into the bar. She managed to smile at him but didn't offer to shake hands because her own were trembling.

'I'm glad you came prepared to be kept waiting – I could have walked along Knightsbridge faster than the taxi crawled.'

'I cheated – had an earlier appointment here,' he admitted fairly. He ordered chilled white wine from a hovering waiter, then leaned back in his chair to look at her. She was thinner than he remembered. Beneath the cap of short, dark hair the lovely planes of her face were more clearly visible, but her full, sweet mouth hadn't changed, and nor had the impression of style that was her own particular hallmark. He'd missed her very much, but he was still angry. She should have understood how right they were together.

Disconcerted by his inspection, she found something to say first. 'You're supposed to ask why I rang!'

'Dear Jane, why did you ring?'

The acid smoothness didn't help but she soldiered on. 'Because Aunt Hannah likes to keep me informed of what

goes on in Cossenford. All the news at the moment concerns you – the sale of the Manor House, of course, but also the change of ownership of the chapel site. Is that true as well?'

He took a little sip of wine before answering. 'It's true,' he said at last. 'I found I'd lost interest in Cossenford.'

Unaware that she'd been holding her breath, she let out a long sigh. 'So Aunt Hannah was right. Your performance at the public meeting was simply to get you the vote. Cossenford's future didn't come into it. With the site in your pocket, you could sell it on at a profit whenever the right buyer turned up.'

He made no attempt to deny it. 'I should have said I'd lost interest in Somerset. My cousin has, too, in case you're interested in buying any more farms!'

She ignored the barb; scarcely noticed it in fact. 'Luke Winters was supposed to be a dedicated farmer – wasn't that genuine either?'

The scorn in her voice seemed to sting now more than the accusation against himself. 'Of course it was genuine,' he said fiercely. 'But Luke won't continue to farm on the Levels. He knows how he wants to work his land, knows what crops he wants to grow. He does *not* want to be told – by his neighbours or by the petty bureaucrats at the Nature Conservancy Council, that he must use methods that will keep him poor however hard he works. That strikes him, and me, as unfair.'

'The "petty bureaucrats" are scientists,' she pointed out. 'Men trying to preserve the wetlands because they're unique and irreplaceable. Why destroy them just to grow crops that could be more naturally grown elsewhere?'

'To prove a point, of course . . . And for the fun of the challenge. There's no pleasure in doing what is easy.'

She held up her hands in a gesture of despair. 'It's our usual problem, Max. We shall never be able to agree about what is important, so there's no point in arguing any more.' She hesitated for a moment, then went on. 'Perhaps this is useless too, but I'll ask anyway. If you're still negotiating with the new owners of the chapel site, could you try to insist that they follow your original proposals? You won the vote at the public meeting because of them.'

'I can't insist, but I will ask,' he said quietly. 'Do you believe me?' She nodded, and saw him smile. 'Good! Now are you going to have dinner with me?'

Every nerve in her body wanted to say yes, but Max setting out to convince her that they must be together would be more than she could bear.

'You'll have to excuse me,' she managed to say. 'I start back at Clifford's tomorrow after a break of six months. A frugal supper and an early night are needed, because I'm sure I shall be under close inspection.'

She stood up to leave, but he caught hold of her hands. 'Listen, please. If you go now, I shan't ask again. No one is allowed to reject me more than twice, it's very bad for morale! But I do still want you very much . . . I need you, Jane; can't you admit that you need me?'

'I admit to missing you,' she agreed quietly, 'but I know that we can't make each other happy.'

She turned and fled, leaving a curious waiter who had been watching them to wonder why the tall, fair-haired man still stood there after she'd gone.

Her first day back at Clifford's was always going to be an ordeal – she was prepared for that – but it turned out to be even harder than she'd expected. Her new boss was a senior partner she was scarcely acquainted with, and she sensed his suspicion that the chairman had foisted on him a key player who might prove to be too frail, too rusty, or simply not competent enough. The friendliest welcome came from Piers Clifford himself, but even this created its own problem: she seemed to be marked down now as the chairman's pet protégée. Office gossip being what it was, in no time at all there would probably be a rumour going the rounds that she was sleeping with him as well.

At the end of her first week she was sharply aware of life's unfortunate habit of dealing in ironies; her longed-for return to work had so far left her feeling only tired and depressed. But at home on Saturday morning, it was a happy surprise to receive a telephone call from Charles Rutherford, back in London, asking if he could come round.

'You're a sight for sore eyes,' she said when he arrived later in the afternoon. 'But you aren't the same Charlie – New York has made a difference to you.' She smiled at him, trying to put her finger on the change. 'You're more . . . *seasoned* is the word I'm looking for.'

'A compliment?' he asked doubtfully.

'Of course, and it's lovely to have you back. Have you seen Jill?'

'Only from the back row of the stalls – I just managed to catch almost the last performance of *The Tempest*; they start the Rattigan play on Monday, the final production of the season. When I rang her she seemed to have difficulty remembering who I was!'

'Jill's way of pointing out that you'd left her alone for too long.'

'More than that,' Charlie said thoughtfully. 'I clearly wasn't needed any more, from which I deduce that she's found someone else to rely on. True, or not true, Jane?'

'True, I'm afraid,' she had to answer, 'but perhaps only temporarily – he's a farmer in Somerset; it isn't exactly a convenient infatuation.' Not anxious to talk about Rufus Venn, she quickly changed tack. 'What did you think of the play – and of Miranda?'

'Magical, wonderful production – the Great Man's best shot at it yet, I think. Jill looks beautiful – she can't help that – and she's been skilfully coached, but after watching her again I'm sure now that my new American friend is right. She's movie star material, not a true thesp.'

Even more winded by his conviction than by what he'd just said, Jane stared at him open-mouthed. 'Did I hear right? Not a theatre actress?' she managed to ask. 'And if not, why not?'

'Sheer lack of size, for one thing – she's too small to dominate the stage; she has to try too hard. And lack of stamina's another problem – she won't stand up to a long run, physically or mentally. My father's aware of that now, I think.'

'Then let *him* tell her, please – not you, Charlie,' Jane pleaded. 'At least, not if you still care about her.'

'My job is to deliver the good news first,' he replied with a smile. 'The American friend I mentioned is the film director,

Martin Raban. He's seen both of Jill's performances and reckons she's entirely the girl he wants, provided she isn't camera-shy, but I'd bet good money that she won't be.'

'Then what?' Jane asked incredulously. 'Hollywood?'

'Not straight off; his next film is being shot here. I'm going to be his English adviser, and learn a lot about film directing at the same time!'

'Because that's what you want to do? Is that your future?'

Charlie nodded. 'It's what I'm hoping to do,' he said, with the new-found certainty he'd brought home with him. 'Now, enough of me and Jill – what about you? It's September already, so you're back at work. Is that why you sounded tired when I rang?'

She'd forgotten his habit of closely observing and listening to other people. 'I hope the first week will later seem to have been the most difficult,' she admitted ruefully. 'I didn't enjoy it at all.' The question in his face made her go on. 'It used to be an article of faith – the City was where everything that mattered was happening, but the mantra doesn't work any more, however fervently I say it! Helping one greedy business-man to outwit another equally greedy businessman no longer seems what I believed to be the real world. Aunt Hannah fighting to keep Cossenford unspoilt, my uncle farming in the old ways that protect instead of destroying the land, my friend Ellie Chant bringing up a small son single-handed . . . These are the real people that I now know.'

'Difficult,' Charlie agreed, 'but why can't they both be real, Jane – the City and Cossenford? They're all people, wherever you know them. Your little town probably has its share of sinners, and not all businessmen are trying to grind their competitors' faces in the dust!' He grinned at her with warm affection. 'I'm afraid that's the end of Dr Rutherford's diag-nosis for the moment – I need to catch Jill at the theatre between performances. But we'll go to the Rattigan play together next week, shall we?'

'Lovely,' Jane agreed. 'I'll look forward to it, Charlie.'

After he'd gone she tried to imagine the reception he'd get from Jill. A career in Hollywood doesn't come the way of many young actresses just out of drama school, and she'd be

well aware of that. But on the other hand, Jane was sure she'd be very reluctant to admit that the theatre wasn't the best choice she could have made.

When the doorbell rang again a few minutes later, she anticipated finding Charlie back to say that he'd forgotten something. But she opened the door to another visitor altogether – a large, red-bearded man whose usual disreputable working clothes had been exchanged for a blazer and grey flannels. She found nothing to say for a moment, so Rufus spoke first.

'I hoped you'd be here – I've got some messages to deliver. If you aren't going to ask me in I can do it on the doorstep, but I missed lunch and a crust of something to eat would be very welcome before I catch the train home.' She distrusted the note of wistfulness in his voice, but he looked genuinely tired and she led him upstairs into the kitchen.

'If you're in a hurry it will have to be bread and cheese, plus coffee – or a glass of red wine?'

'Wine, please – I believe it's good for me,' he said solemnly.

She handed him a bottle to open while she set out the food and sliced chicory, tomatoes and avocados to go with the cheese. 'You didn't travel to London just to bring messages,' she said when they were seated at the table.

'No. I promised Jill I'd see the play before it finished, so it had to be this afternoon's matinee. I waited long enough afterwards to tell her how good it had been and then came away – she still had the evening performance to face.'

Jane thought of Charlie, probably arriving as Rufus left. It was turning into a French farce, except that this farce wasn't funny enough. Charlie couldn't help but adore her wayward sister, and Rufus had been made to feel that it was him she now totally relied on.

'Tell me about Tom first,' Jane suggested. 'How is he getting on at Wells?'

'Coping, at least. In fact he's probably doing a little better without us than we are doing without him. Ben mopes, and shadows every move I make in case I suddenly disappear as well. Joshua fortunately has the new animals to think about, but he misses Tom.' Rufus sipped his wine and helped himself to cheese and salad. 'One of the messages comes from Tom.

He wishes you to know that he's started to keep a diary – this is in case he should forget something he wants to put into your father's commonplace book. Should you really give it to him, by the way?'

'I think so,' Jane said calmly. 'He'll value it properly. Next message, please.'

'This one's from Ellie Chant. Daniel is going to be baptized just before Christmas, and his godmother is required to be at the ceremony – we mention it in case she's thinking of spending the holiday in some exotic spot.'

'She's thinking of Cossenford, if Aunt Hannah will have her.'

'That's all right then,' said Rufus. 'As it happens, the next message comes from Hannah. The Baptist chapel is in the process of being demolished, but Max Hasler has given the ground it was on, and the surrounding churchyard, to the town; the new developers only get the fields beyond. Hannah has been given the task of designing a public garden for Cossenford. The message to you from Max Hasler, via Hannah, is that this is payback time. She hopes you understand it, because she doesn't.'

Rufus glanced at Jane's face, and then stared at his wine glass instead, waiting for her to answer.

'Yes, I understand it,' she said at last. In case Rufus waited for an explanation she couldn't give, she went on speaking. 'Max didn't mention that when I saw him recently, but he did say that Luke Winters was giving up his farm. Have you and Uncle Joshua heard about that?'

Rufus nodded. 'The Nature Conservancy Council want to turn it into what they call a Site of Special Scientific Interest. In layman's language that means making it a protected wetland area.'

'So it's good news,' Jane suggested, wondering why his face was so expressionless.

'Well, yes, it is. But it brings the scientists to our doorstep and, like all officials, they can be heavy-handed at times; not the easiest people to deal with.'

Rufus glanced at his watch, reminding her that he had a train to catch. Watching him, she realized how little she knew about him. She wasn't even sure of his age, although the over-

227

head light in the kitchen showed her the glint of silver in his hair and beard. Perhaps ten years older than herself and stronger than most, but seeming for the moment as if too much was being asked of him. With Selina gone, Jill had simply moved into the vacuum in his life – someone else who might need looking after. But suppose he didn't understand how volatile, how self-motivated she was . . .

'It was good of you to come to see the play,' Jane said suddenly. 'I hope my little sister was properly grateful.'

'She was herself,' he answered. 'Sweet and captivating!'

She would be, of course, but was she even now considering a future that held no place for Rufus Venn?

'She's what you say,' Jane agreed gravely. 'Sweet and captivating; but she's also seriously concerned with herself. She doesn't *intend* for other people to get hurt – the plan is simply for them to want what she wants for herself – but it doesn't always work out like that.'

A smile, half-hidden in the russet beard, touched his mouth for a moment. 'You mean she's one of those siren maidens sitting on a rock, singing to any passing sailors rash enough to listen!'

'Something like that,' Jane agreed with difficulty.

'Well, of course you're right, and the passing sailor deserves his eventual fate if he's foolish enough to stop; but remember the pleasure the maiden gives him. It's not just a one-way thing! Now, I must go if I'm to catch the train. Thank you for the supper, Jane – I can let myself out.'

A moment later she was left alone to consider the hopeless jumble that was now her mind – screen tests for Jill, Daniel's christening, the eventual fate of Rufus Venn – but none of them were quite able to blot out the memory of her last meeting with Max. She knew now that Hannah had been right. He'd bought the site purely as a speculation, with no thought of Cossenford. There had never been a change of plan at all – only, very recently, a change of heart that had acknowledged payback time with his gift of the land for Hannah's garden. It was all that was left of their brief love affair, but at least it was something.

Twenty-Seven

It was the middle of October – St Luke's day and also Hannah's birthday. She would normally have expected a visit from Tom and Rufus, but not today. Tom would be in Wells, and his father's visits to Maundy Cottage had become scarce of late. Though the affection between her and Rufus was deep, she knew it didn't entitle her to pry into his affairs. Nor could she allow herself to feel hurt if, preoccupied with problems of his own, he overlooked her birthday for once.

At least the day itself was beautiful, serene and golden as an October day should be. She went out into the garden, noting how many of the clumps in the borders needed splitting up. But the work was too heavy for her now; she must find a jobbing gardener so that Rufus needn't feel obliged to find time to come and help.

She was sweeping up a carpet of fallen leaves when the garden gate clicked behind her. He had come after all, familiar and dear.

'Happy birthday,' he said, bending down to kiss her cheek. 'No Tom today, so I've brought Boswell instead – meet Ben's new playmate!' He held out for her inspection the squirming bundle of black fur tucked inside his jacket. 'Not quite house-trained yet, so I'm glad you're out here!'

He set the puppy on the ground, and they watched the small, enchanting creature set about demolishing Hannah's neat pile of leaves.

'Tom will love him,' she said, 'but what about Ben?'

'He will, too; the poor chap's lonely at the moment.' Rufus looked round the garden's dying blaze of crimson and gold, seeing, as Hannah had, the work that waited to be done. 'I'll be over soon to tidy up. You're not to tackle it yourself.'

'I was going to find someone else,' she admitted. 'You work too hard as it is.'

Instead of replying, he delved into his pocket and handed her a small package. 'Sit down and open this while I fetch us some coffee.'

What she unwrapped was a photograph in a simple silver frame. Tom's face looked out at her, smiling above the ruffed collar of his chorister's gown. She was still staring at it when Rufus came back.

'He looks happy,' she said unsteadily. 'If you are still worrying about him, I don't think there's any need.'

'I know. He'd rather be at Rushey, but he understands that he has to go to school, and he does love the music.'

Hannah suddenly asked a question she'd shirked until now. 'Have you told him that Selina won't be coming back?'

She saw Rufus nod, and thought it might be all the answer she would get, but then he continued. 'I think he'd already guessed when I first came back from Austria. He's still only a small boy but he seems to understand – perhaps because he's enough like his mother. It lessens the hurt, I think.'

It was Hannah's turn to nod, but she thought it time to ask an easier question. 'How are things at Rushey? I haven't seen Joshua for weeks.'

Her companion's tired face broke into a grin. 'He's got a new lease of life. Our pedigree herd is going to sweep the board, he reckons, at next year's Bath and West show!' Then, serious again, Rufus asked a question of his own. 'Do you hear from Jane?'

'She sent lovely flowers this morning – must have seen the date in one of my books, I suppose.' But Hannah frowned over what she was going to say next. 'Perhaps it's just my fancy, but I have the feeling when she telephones that she isn't settled any more . . . She's trying to make up her mind about something – about someone, is what I expect I mean.'

'About Max Hasler, surely?' Rufus suggested quietly. 'When I called on her in London she mentioned having seen him again.'

'Strange man,' Hannah commented rather sadly. 'Ruthless most of the time, then generous when you least expect it. I

did hope he wouldn't be the one Jane wanted – selfish of me, of course – because I knew he wouldn't stay long in Cossenford.'

Rufus didn't reply, too busy, it seemed, watching the puppy's antics.

'Bring Boswell into the kitchen,' she suggested. 'He can't do much harm there, and I want to show you my plan for the new garden.'

A few moments later she had spread out her sketch on the table. There was a central pool and fountain, surrounded by lawns with ornamental trees. A wide herbaceous border curved round two sides of the plot – Hannah didn't like straight lines in a garden. 'It leaves this bit here,' she said, pointing to a blank space in the sketch, 'where the gravestones were – long ago, I know, but I still feel the ground shouldn't be disturbed.'

'Why not a little wilderness, then – a wild-flower place that the birds and butterflies can share?'

The suggestion made her smile at once. 'Of course, Rufus, it's exactly what we should have. Thank you for that, and for my birthday present. I shall write and tell Tom how well he looks. I want to hear him sing before long.'

'We'll go to the cathedral together on Christmas morning,' Rufus promised. 'He's allowed time off after that, so we'll be able to bring him home.'

'Jane will be here – she'll want to go to the cathedral too.'

'Perhaps not if she's made up her mind about things by then,' he pointed out. 'Don't bank on seeing her, Hannah love – you might be disappointed. Now, I must be off, but I'll be back soon to put the garden to bed for the winter.'

With the puppy scooped up and tucked back inside his jacket, he let himself out of the cottage and she was left to think about what he'd just said. It confirmed something she already knew: Rufus, normally the most tolerant of men, had no generosity to spare for Max Hasler, and very little for Jane because of her connection with him. It was saddening, and a puzzle too, when she could now see nothing to be wary of in her niece and so much to love. She gave a little sigh, wishing that life could be less complicated than it so often was. But at least her garden plan was now complete and she could

deliver it to the Town Hall. There would, of course, be some opposition to the little wilderness. Already she could hear Nan Masterson's voice – '*Weeds*, my dear Hannah?' – but an occasional tussle with Nan was something they both enjoyed, and she'd get the garden she wanted in the end.

The wet autumn had gone unnoticed in London as far as Jane was concerned; all her concentration was on the stress and stimulation of the job, and for relaxation there were the pleasures that she thought she'd missed in Cossenford – theatres, cinemas, and even the retail therapy of shopping for clothes she didn't need.

These things that she struggled to enjoy again were a remembered part of London life, but there was something unexpected as well: her growing friendship with Piers Clifford. It had begun accidentally when Charlie had taken her to the last of his father's season of plays – Rattigan's *The Winslow Boy*, with Jill doing well enough in the lovely part of the boy's suffragette elder sister. Piers Clifford had been in the audience and they had shared an interval drink with him and the glamorous socialite he was escorting.

Piers had invited her, a day or two later, to help entertain a visiting American couple, both of them notable lawyers in New York. That, at least, was explainable – they all spoke the same language, could enjoy each other's company. Then came Piers' next suggestion: dinner at his house in Hampstead. It was time to refuse, as tactfully as possible. Clifford's bush telegraph system was mysterious but effective, and ever since her return to work there had been innuendos too elusive to be smiled away.

She was at home that evening, comfortable in old slacks and a sweater, when the doorbell rang. It was a shock to hear Piers announcing himself on the entryphone. A convincing lie was hard to produce on the spur of the moment, and she was too conscious of his generosity towards her to rudely send him away.

She brought sherry to the sitting room and found him examining her pictures – some good original watercolours, and the best reproductions she'd been able to find of two of

232

her favourite paintings – Vermeer's serene *Young Woman Reading a Letter* and a hauntingly misty view of Venice by Guardi.

'I like looking at other people's pictures,' Piers Clifford admitted, 'but that isn't why I came. You're free to refuse my invitations if you don't like the sound of them, but I wanted to make sure you didn't refuse because you were unwell.'

'That's very kind,' she said, a little unevenly. 'I refused because I was tired, but I'm certainly not unwell. I hope Duncan Grant doesn't have that impression of me!'

'His impression is that you're the best junior partner we've had. He says you're handling a difficult case all the more beautifully because you're doing it as a purely intellectual exercise. But your mind and heart used to be engaged . . . In fact you probably got too involved. Are you afraid that emotional strain will make you ill again?'

She considered the question for a moment, knowing that he would want an honest answer. 'It isn't fear of illness, but something harder to deal with and more unexpected. I don't quite seem to belong in my job any more.'

'Because you haven't been made welcome?'

Jane shook her head. 'No, it isn't that. During the six months I was away I found a different world. I was the clever, experienced whizz-kid from the big city, with all the answers at my fingertips. But in Somerset I found that *I* was the one who knew nothing at all – at least, not about anything that's important there.'

'Important *there*,' Piers Clifford pointed out, 'but irrelevant, surely, to a girl who does the job you do.'

'I'm afraid so! What do we know up here about acts of disinterested kindness, and loving one's neighbour? Who cares in London whether our land and the wildlife that depends on it are protected or not? Who will fight to preserve whatever seems valuable?' She suddenly came to a halt, embarrassed to have sounded too intense, and anything but the urban sophisticate she was supposed to be.

Piers Clifford was staring at her, but she had no idea why. It didn't occur to her that he was shaken out of his habitual

dislike of being made to feel emotion – his own or anyone else's.

'I accept that we and your Somerset friends inhabit different worlds,' he finally agreed. 'The question is – which are you going to choose? It'll have to be that, won't it – a choice?'

She smiled faintly, despite her agitation at the conversation becoming unexpectedly serious. Trust the man who ran Clifford's so brilliantly to go straight to the heart of the matter. His sharpness was no surprise, but her own certainty was. No conscious thought was needed; the decision was clear in her mind.

'The choice is to leave Clifford's – for good this time – as soon as I've wound up the present case.' The words were out and couldn't be unsaid, but she didn't regret them; for the first time in weeks she felt sure of something again. 'It must seem like the worst kind of ingratitude when you've treated me so generously, but mind and heart are both needed, and heart is lacking now.'

He framed his next question carefully. 'Does Max Hasler have something to do with that? It wouldn't be surprising – he's an impressive man.'

'He is,' she confirmed quietly. 'It might once have had a great deal to do with him, but not now. I don't know what I shall do in future, but I'll find something.'

Piers nodded, remembering sadly the day he'd sent her away on her long spell of sick leave. She'd been unsure that she could survive it then, but now there was no such uncertainty in her, and the ache of loss this time was going to be his own.

'We shall miss you,' he said quietly. '*I* shall miss you very much, but I know better than to try to make you change your mind.'

He drained his glass and got up to leave, but stood looking at her gravely for a moment. 'Listen to the voice of experience Jane – life's lonely on your own, so fix the problem with Max Hasler if you can.'

Close to sudden tears she could only nod and watch him leave. Capable of speaking at all, she could have explained that loneliness was something she knew about. It wasn't a

234

problem that could be 'fixed', but somehow she'd learn, as Ellie Chant had done, to build a different life for herself.

A month later, with the case she'd been fighting convincingly won – an unethical takeover bid from an American company that she believed needed defeating – her career at Clifford's came to an end. At her own request it wasn't public knowledge that she wouldn't return after the Christmas break – this, at least, she'd managed to keep off the bush telegraph. Amid the usual pre-Christmas excitement and gaiety she said a quiet goodbye to Duncan Grant, and then faced the more painful duty of knocking on the chairman's door.

He looked tired, she thought, and sad – it made him harder to cope with than Duncan, who'd been merely angry with her for refusing to stay.

'What now, Jane?' he asked gently. 'What next, I suppose I mean?'

'Christmas in Somerset,' she explained, 'and that includes the baptism of my godson, Daniel, and a visit to Wells Cathedral to hear an honorary nephew make his chorister's debut – he's got the tricky part of page to good King Wenceslas!'

'Important things,' Piers agreed, reminding her of an earlier conversation. 'What comes after Christmas?'

Fearful of weeping, she hastened on. 'I've got an ambition to teach small children, but my dear Aunt Hannah will tell me whether I'm suitable material or not!' She stopped suddenly, because her eyes were prickling with tears. 'I'm talking too much and what I should be saying is simply thank you . . . for all your kindness and . . . and affection.' Her voice failed her altogether, and she simply held out her hands instead.

Piers caught them in a painful grip, then kissed them in a gesture that was heart-stopping because it was so untypical.

'Lucky small children, I think – how could Aunt Hannah possibly turn you down? We'll stay in touch, Jane – is that a promise?'

She nodded blindly, then released herself and made for the door. It was more than time to go, and she thanked God that she could leave while everyone else was enjoying the office

party in the boardroom. Walking part of the way home until the tears dried on her cheeks and she could face the Underground, she knew that it had been a final goodbye from her job, and from Piers Clifford. They wouldn't stay in touch, and she doubted whether he'd believed it any more than she had. But, leaving this time, she needn't feel unhinged by loneliness and isolation; she was a landowner with responsibilities and she was going home to Cossenford for Christmas.

Twenty-Eight

With Daniel's baptismal service timed for the day before Christmas Eve, it meant driving out of London early the following morning. The worst of the holiday exodus hadn't begun, but two lots of roadworks inconveniently sited where the A303 was narrowest reduced progress to an agonizing crawl. Stonehenge emerged out of the morning mist and slowly disappeared again, and then, almost in sight of her turn-off that was still as unreachable as the moon, the traffic finally came to a halt altogether. Soon word travelled down the line that there had been an accident up ahead. Now, at least, she could safely use her mobile phone to warn Hannah that she might have to set off for the church alone.

Two hours later, with the blockage cleared, progress was resumed, and she stopped the car in Cossenford's market square just as the church clock chimed two. There was nothing for it but to go in as she was. The hero of the occasion wouldn't mind how she was dressed, but she doubted if the vicar expected a godmother to turn up in slacks and a sweater, with her hands still trembling from the nervous frustrations of the journey.

Inside the lovely peaceful place her nerves quietened, and she could offer up a little prayer of gratitude before the service began. Hannah turned round to smile, and then whispered to Ellie beside her that Jane was there after all, so everything was as it should be.

A small surprise was to register the russet head and broad back of Rufus Venn in the pew in front, but then she realized that he was there for the same reason as she was. Gathered round the font at the culmination of the service, he nodded a greeting to his fellow godparent, but he didn't smile at her.

His face was illuminated by the baptismal candle being lit for Daniel, and it suddenly hurt her to see him looking grave and sad. Who was he missing? she wondered. Tom, Selina, or even the wayward Jill who, already convinced that she was on the threshold of a dazzling film career, had very little thought for her rural love affair . . .

She had to put the thought aside because it was time to join Rufus in making their promises on Daniel's behalf, to renounce evil and turn to Christ. Apart from being sacred, it also seemed the most intimate moment she had ever shared with a man. She would do her best with the promises, but she suspected that Rufus might make a better job of them than she would herself. Then he turned and smiled at her while she still held Daniel in her arms, and she suddenly knew that it was their own child they should have been baptising.

It wasn't the moment she'd have chosen for her own Damascus-road revelation. It scarcely seemed possible that between one heartbeat and the next she should know beyond the slightest doubt what had kept her from staying with Max. This new knowledge left her light-headed. She needed to escape, needed time to be sure that, tired and disorientated as she was, this wasn't just another mistake. But then Ellie was hugging her and explaining that tea would be waiting for them in Wash Row.

The only mercy was to hear Rufus say that he must get back to Rushey to finish the day's interrupted work. Without him there she could slowly pull herself together, and smile, and blame the horrendous journey for the fact that she was overwrought. But, safely back at Maundy Cottage at last, she struggled not to weep with relief at the sight of its holly-wreathed front door. Here was the refuge she sorely needed.

It was a strange Christmas after that – surface joy intensified rather than destroyed by an undercurrent of pain. She wouldn't forget any of it: Midnight Mass at Cossenford with Ellie leading the choir up the aisle of the candle-lit church; the drive to Wells the following morning through a frosty, sun-bright landscape; Rufus' face as he listened to his son's voice, sweet and joyous as birdsong, soaring up in the best children's carol of all. She was standing next to Joshua Venn,

also proudly present, and he turned to smile at her when she slipped her hand into his.

They took Tom home to Rushey at the end of the service, and, after his emotional reunion with Ben and the overdue introduction to Boswell, sat down to roast goose and Christmas pudding with Charlie, Ted, and their wives. It wasn't until the following evening, in Hannah's fire-lit parlour, that the right time for talking arrived.

'I've resigned from Clifford's,' Jane suddenly began. 'Almost from the moment I went back I knew that I didn't belong there any more, but I pretended that it was simply a matter of getting used to the job again.'

'I thought something was troubling you whenever you rang,' said Hannah. 'It isn't a surprise. But even living in Germany, you'll still come and visit, won't you? I hope that's a promise, Jane.'

It took a moment for her aunt's meaning to sink in, so long ago did it already seem that her life had centred around Max Hasler.

'I'm not going to live in Germany,' she finally got round to answering. 'I'm not going to live anywhere at all with Max, if that's what you're imagining.'

Trying not to look relieved, Hannah poked the fire instead, producing a sudden flame that lit up her face. 'Do we get told what you *are* going to do?' she asked.

'When I know myself!' Jane's smile acknowledged that it was an irritating answer, while she thought about what to say next. 'I know what I'm not going to do any more: practise company law. I thought I'd learn how to teach small children, be another Hannah Venn – or try to be at least! But first I'm going to make a trip to Italy. Come with me, Aunt Hannah – why not?'

'Thank you, my dear, but not just now,' she was told firmly. 'I must help Arthur Cranston with the plans for the museum – they're coming along well, by the way – and there's Cossenford's garden to be thought about as well.' She hesitated for a moment before going on. 'It was generous of Max Hasler to give us not only the land, but also money towards the cost of making the garden. I thought you might have had something to do with that.'

'Only very indirectly, perhaps,' Jane admitted. 'I didn't know about the gift until Rufus gave me your message.' It was a mistake to mention his name but, now that she had, she wanted to go on talking about him. 'He looked tired yesterday – Rufus, I mean.'

'What do you expect?' Hannah asked sharply. 'He works hard enough for two men, he misses Tom, and he lives an unnatural life with my dear, but self-contained brother, who's long got beyond wanting a woman in his home. On top of that, Rufus even has to care for tiresome old women like me!'

'And tiresome young ones like my sister,' Jane added. 'Jill's convinced that it gives Rufus pleasure to help whenever she needs propping up. From something he said once, I think she may even be right.'

'I think so too. He told me how captivating she is – his adjective, of course; I don't use fancy words like that.'

Jane turned her head away, like a boxer trying to avoid a blow, but she forced herself to accept the truth. 'Even in her own exotic world my sister stands out. How must she appear to a hard-driven, lonely farmer on the Somerset Levels? Like some lovely will-o'–the- wisp, I should think – here one minute, gone the next.'

Hannah nodded, sadly agreeing with this conclusion. 'I was rather hoping that Rufus would see Ellie for the splendid girl she is, but the poor dear man does seem to get drawn to the exotic – first Selina, and now Jill. Such a pity, I can't help thinking.'

Transfixed by pain, and also terrified that she might burst out laughing at the sheer inadequacy of the word Hannah had chosen, she managed to agree that, yes, it was a pity. Then she escaped from the room, offering to scramble eggs for their supper as a reprieve from the rich food they had recently been eating.

She left the cottage two days later, promising to let Hannah know where she would be in Italy. Just as the new year dawned she was on a flight to Bari, almost at the foot of the penin-sula. With Norman Douglas and H. V. Morton as her literary travelling companions, she was grimly determined to enjoy

her own pilgrimage round the enchanted coast. Glorious Norman churches facing a sunlit Ionian Sea would drive out of her mind, if anything could, the memory of the russet-bearded man smiling at her in a Gothic cathedral across the mountains far to the north.

It was a marvellous journey and aching loneliness only crept in at night when she faced a solitary supper. But Messrs Morton and Douglas were good company, and she sometimes met lone travellers like herself, happy to share the day's discoveries over a meal and the rough local wine.

Three weeks after leaving England she was tired of continually driving on not very easy roads, and she decided it was time to halt for longer than usual. She chose the island city of Taranto guarding its landlocked lagoon. Settled into a hotel whose modern comforts would have astounded earlier travellers to a once-poor and malaria-ridden region, she telephoned Cossenford.

'I suppose you're going to tell me you're bathed in warm sunshine,' Hannah said tartly.

'Yes, *and* I've got the blue gulf of Taranto practically outside my window!'

'Very nice, I'm sure. There's a lot of water here, too, but most of it's frozen right now.'

'I did ask you to come with me,' Jane pointed out. 'Apart from the English climate in January, is everything else all right?'

Hannah agreed that it was, wrote down the number she was given, admitted that it was nice to have a chat, and then said goodbye. Smiling at the typical end to a conversation with her aunt, Jane replaced the receiver and went out to explore the treasures of the city's national museum.

Two evenings later she sat studying her map over dinner. It was time to move on, and she needed to pick her next port of call. She'd just selected Sibari at the western end of the gulf when a waiter appeared to call her to the telephone.

'Jane, it's Rufus here,' a voice said, unnecessarily when every nerve in her body told her who it was.

Her heart faltered for a moment, then raced to make up for it. 'Is something wrong with Hannah?' Why else would he

ring? Had she had a stroke, been knocked down in the street? Her mind was listing other dreadful possibilities, but she had to listen instead because he was speaking again.

'Hannah's all right. It's Joshua, I'm afraid. He had a very serious heart attack two days ago. There seemed a chance that he could survive it, but he died last night.'

She now realized that the pain in her hand was due to gripping the receiver too tightly. She unclenched her fingers and collapsed into the chair in the cubicle. 'I'm so sorry, Rufus,' she managed to say. 'He wouldn't have wanted to be left an invalid but . . . but . . .' She swallowed the lump in her throat and tried a question instead. 'You said Hannah's all right, but are you sure? This must be terribly hard for her.'

'She's managing,' Rufus said briefly. 'It would help if you could get back, though, at least in time for the funeral. It's not fixed yet, but it will be early next week.'

'I'll leave tomorrow.' Jane tried and failed to visualize the map she'd been studying. 'If I'm not near an international airport I'll have to go up to Naples and get a flight from there. Somehow or other I'll be in Cossenford by the day after tomorrow. Will you tell Hannah that, please? I'll need to get on with making arrangements here.'

He agreed that he would, said he was sorry that her holiday was spoilt, and rang off – a true Venn, she told herself tearfully. There had been no time to say how much she felt for his own shock and sadness. And there was Tom to think about, too. Joshua had been his undemonstrative but true friend. She remembered the pride in her uncle's face as he listened to the Christmas service in the cathedral. Somerset seemed too far away – she wanted to be there now, with Hannah and Rufus. The thought pricked her out of the paralysis that had held her sitting by the telephone, and she went to the reception desk to ask for help with the quickest way of getting home.

By mid-afternoon the following day she was at Naples airport just in time to board a flight for London. She spent that night in her own house, and set out again early the next morning.

Exhausted by the perpetual motion of the past few days,

she stopped the car outside Maundy Cottage reluctant for the moment to make the next effort. But Hannah had seen her arrive, and came hurrying out to meet and hug her on the pavement.

'Stupid one! It's freezing, and you came out without a coat.' Jane scolded, trying not to weep. 'You'll be ill next.'

'No, I won't.' Hannah was herself to that extent, but her mouth trembled when she smiled. 'Jane dear, I'm sorry we've ruined your travels, but it's so lovely to have you back. Rufus said you'd be here today, but I didn't believe him – you had such a long way to come.'

Jane blinked away her tears. 'I didn't walk – there are things called aeroplanes! Now, go indoors, please, while I see to the luggage.'

With Hannah settled again by the fire, holding out her cold hands to the blaze, Jane heard what had happened at Rushey.

'It was harder weather than we usually get here,' Hannah explained sadly. 'We'd had a week of frost day and night, so it was heavy work keeping the animals fed. Joshua was in the barn, forking out hay – getting overheated doing that, of course, and then walking into the freezing air outside. Rufus went back into the yard to find him on the ground. It took the ambulance a little while to arrive, but the poor men did their best. For a while we thought Joshua would hang on, but he couldn't . . . couldn't keep on fighting . . .' Her voice broke and she simply watched the flames dancing on the hearth – seeing there, Jane thought, pictures of her brother's long life at Rushey.

'Where is Uncle Joshua's funeral to be?' she finally asked. 'At the Friends' meeting house?'

Hannah shook her head. 'There was no point – he'd not attended a Quaker service for twenty years, nor the church at Little Ham at all. We asked Clive Weston and he suggested a service here, so that's what we shall have, next Monday. Between them, Clive, Andrew and Ellie will make it beautiful.'

Jane hesitated a moment. 'I rang my mother before I left London. She would like to attend – if you don't mind, that is.'

'Dear child, why should I mind? I'll be glad to see her.'

Unable to ask about Rufus, Jane asked about his son instead, and her aunt's sad face smiled at the thought of Tom.

'The choirmaster said he could come home for a few days. He wanted to be at the funeral, of course, but he's a comfort to Rufus as well.' It was Hannah's turn to hesitate. 'Rushey goes to Rufus now – that doesn't upset you, Jane?'

'Of course not – what else would have been right or fair or even common sense?'

Hannah smiled. 'I just thought I'd ask,' she said. 'He's left the choice of readings and hymns to me – Clive Weston's coming round to help.'

'Not being qualified to help, I'll take a little walk instead,' Jane suggested. 'I've been sitting too much in cars and aeroplanes.' She heeded her aunt's instruction to wrap up, then let herself out of the cottage. With no particular purpose in mind, she went in the direction of what had been the chapel. The building had been demolished now, and already she could see the ground plan of Hannah's design laid out, in readiness for planting in the spring. She stood there for a moment visualizing how it would look – Max's gift to Cossenford. But the freezing air wasn't for lingering in and she walked on, unaware of her route until she recognized the ornamental gate in front of her. She stared through the wrought-iron at the wide lawns, still whitened by the frost that had clung all day. Then a pleasant voice spoke behind her.

'Are you looking for something?'

She turned to see a young woman smiling rather warily at her. 'I think I was laying a ghost! The last owner was someone I knew very well. It's a lovely house – I hope you'll be happy living here,' Jane said.

'We love it already; the house is perfect. But I have got plans for the garden – so boring, all this grass, don't you think?'

Jane nodded, but didn't explain why she was smiling. She said instead that she must return to her aunt's house and walked away, visualizing the lawns carved up by all the flower beds the new owner obviously had in mind.

Twenty-Nine

While Hannah was out the following morning an un-expected visitor arrived: Tom on his own, for once not shepherded by Ben.

'They don't like me taking him on the bus,' he explained to Jane. 'Silly really 'cause he's as gentle as a lamb.'

'But a bit big with it,' she suggested gravely, and saw Tom's pale face break into a grin. 'How's Boswell getting on?'

'He's a great help. Ben loves him, of course, but he makes Dad laugh as well. We'd be sad without him just now.' His mouth quivered, but he remembered that he'd been entrusted with the task of seeing that Aunt Hannah and his dear Jane were all right. 'I can stay to lunch, Dad says – he'll come for me this afternoon.'

Jane realized then why he was there – Rufus had wanted to let him escape from the empty house. But Tom was already talking again.

'We got the atlas out to see where you were – it looked a long way away, and I wanted you here. I knew Dad did too, because his face looked so very sad. Couldn't you stay now? Must you go away again?' She heard the note of anxiety in his voice and knew why it was there – in his brief but chequered acquaintance with life only his father could be relied upon not to disappear.

A moment or two ago she'd have said that she didn't yet know what she was going to do, but it was no longer true. Tom had just shown her what the future might be – it was there in front of her, perilously uncertain but she knew she had to try it. 'I think perhaps I can stay . . . I'd like to, anyway.'

245

'That's all right then,' said Tom, with his lovely sweet smile, just as Hannah arrived back with her shopping.

It was mid-afternoon when Rufus arrived. Looking tired and strained, he refused to come in as there was work waiting to be done at Rushey. Tom kissed Hannah and Jane goodbye, then made a dash for the jeep where Ben and Boswell were waiting for him. Jane followed Rufus down the path.

'Could you wait, please, I need to ask you something.' He turned to look at her and saw in her face what she was about to say. 'Was Uncle Joshua's death my fault for giving him the extra work and worry of Neil Gibson's farm?'

Rufus took a step towards her, then stopped, as if the instinct to take hold of her hands had had to be resisted. 'Don't think that – not for a moment, Jane,' he said as firmly as he could. 'Joshua hadn't been so happy in years. What happened could just as easily have happened at any time.'

'But it was too soon. He was going to win at the Bath and West . . .'

Rufus smiled the heart-stopping smile that his son had inherited. 'He already had – the rosettes were there on the dresser in his mind's eye!'

Ben barked from the jeep, interrupting whatever else they might have said, and Rufus lifted his hand and walked away.

It was a good funeral, everyone agreed, with lovely music, and a touching tribute from another Levels farmer who had known Joshua all his life. Rufus read the lesson, and Tom held Jane's hand while they listened. Afterwards, dispensing tea at Maundy Cottage, she discovered not only that her mother was there, but also Jill, dressed to flattering effect in black, and hovering always close to Rufus.

Elizabeth Westover had to go to the kitchen to find her elder daughter. 'Jane, darling, here you are! Why couldn't Hannah have organized some help? There's no chance to talk to you.'

'Talk now,' Jane said, smiling at her.

'I want to know what you're going to do. Jill says you've left Clifford's, but I can scarcely believe it – I thought you loved being there.'

'I did, but now I've decided to do something else, that's all.'

'Another City firm, I suppose; James always said you had to keep moving to make progress up the ladder!'

'I'm sure he was right.' Jane agreed cheerfully. 'Nothing's fixed yet, but I promise to let you know when it is.' Then she smiled again and asked her mother to carry a tray of tea into the sitting room.

That evening, when the guests had gone and the house was quiet, she told Hannah that she'd be leaving in the morning.

'Back to London, I suppose,' her aunt remarked rather sadly.

Jane took a deep breath before answering. 'No, I thought of going to Rushey. I'm hoping Rufus will let me share the farm with him and Tom.'

Silenced for once, Hannah took time to work out the implications of what had just been said. She opened her mouth to ask if she'd understood them aright, then closed it again. Her instinct – correct as it happened – was that she'd been given all the information she was going to get. 'Well, why not?' she agreed cautiously at last. 'But what happens if Rufus doesn't like the idea?'

'Then I shall have to come back here.' Jane smiled at her aunt, then said goodnight and went to bed.

She set off for Little Ham the following morning, timing her arrival for when Rufus would have left to return Tom to Wells. The door into the back porch was unlocked, and she let herself into a house that felt cold and very empty.

It was unknown territory to her, except for the kitchen, and her brief view of the sitting room. A tour of inspection revealed a bigger house than she'd expected, full of nooks and crannies that could have been charming if anyone had bothered with them, but it was clear that no one had. She went back downstairs to the cheerless sitting room, trying to consider its possibilities while she waited to see Rufus drive past and turn in under the archway. When he walked into the kitchen a few minutes later she was putting out coffee mugs and seeming heroically unconcerned. But the room was very quiet and she feared that he could hear the erratic beating of her heart. For

247

something to do she made coffee that probably neither of them would drink. At last he found his voice.

'Jane . . . you're always welcome, of course, but I thought Jill said you were going back to London.'

His expressionless face suggested so little interest in whether she went or stayed that she realized how difficult this interview was going to be. But she was there and must go through with it.

'Not London . . . I had the idea that you might let me stay here – share Rushey with you and Tom.' She had to wait an unnervingly long time while he considered, as Hannah had done, the meaning of what she'd said.

'Because you think Joshua should have left Rushey to you?' he finally asked. 'It's true you have more right to it than I do.'

'It's yours, then Tom's,' she insisted. 'I only want to be allowed to help.'

In a face now drained of colour his eyes looked intensely blue – but made so by anger, she feared, not affection or delight. 'Be serious, please. Your life's in London, where your home also is. Jill said you couldn't make up your mind whether to marry Max Hasler, but passing the time here while you decide doesn't strike me as much of an idea.'

'Rufus, tell me once more something that "Jill said" about me and I shall run screaming from the house! I am *not* going to marry Max, or any other man my sister can name. I've given up my job because I no longer want to live and work in London. I hoped I could stay here.'

She watched his face, desperate for some small sign that the mask of indifference or disbelief would crack. But he still spoke with the voice of a man whose emotions – whatever they might be – were under iron control. 'Oh, now I see what it is. You still feel responsible for your uncle's death, and you think we can't cope here without some help. I'm sure your offer is kindly meant, Jane, but we don't need it. We miss Joshua, but we shall manage very well.'

'Manage?' She flung the word back at him, suddenly goaded into forgetting both caution for herself and the fear of hurting him. 'Perhaps you can make do with the half-life you lead

here, but what about Tom? Doesn't he deserve more than a desolate house and his dependence on you and a couple of dogs for all the loving he gets?'

There was no doubt about his anger now. 'What do you suggest instead – that he should grow to depend on you, and then find himself much worse off than he is now, as soon as you get tired of the harsh realities of life here and go tripping back to London?'

The mask of indifference had cracked now, but she could see nothing reassuring in his face. Tom had unintentionally, but cruelly misled her. Far from needing her there, his father wanted only to see the back of a woman he preferred to despise.

'I don't know whether you believe that or not,' she said steadily. 'I see the truth differently. You feel threatened by my suggestion. Instead of living normally like other men do, you've settled for lifelong worship at Selina's shrine. A little platonic love affair with Jill doesn't interfere with that because you know she's no more ready to take it seriously than you are.'

This time she thought she had probably poked the lion once too often and that his wrath would surely break about her head, but when he spoke again he sounded only immeasurably tired and sad.

'You're right to this extent: I've deliberately kept the memory of Selina alive – for Tom, not for myself. I believed that she'd need us one day and come back, and when that happened I couldn't let him find his mother a stranger. Now I know that she'll never leave Hans Meier. I also know the truth about Jill. It pleases her to pretend that she needs me, and she thinks it pleases me. It's a little fantasy that does no one any harm.'

'It does your son no good,' she pointed out quietly. 'Will you let me stay for him?'

'Not even for him, Jane. I saw you once come back from being in London with Max Hasler. I'd have needed to be blind not to see how much you loved him.'

'You loved Selina, I loved Max – mistakenly as it happens. Life's going to be a long, lonely business if we're never allowed to love anyone else.'

'Back where you belong, you won't go unloved; I'm sure of that,' he insisted. 'For me it doesn't matter – I'm content with life as it is.' He even smiled as he said it, to make it more convincing. Soon, he prayed, she would think that this dreadful interview had lasted long enough and would go away before he had to shout the truth – that unless he was allowed to love her, heart and mind and body, it would be intolerable to have her in the house, even for Tom's sake.

She saw the smile and accepted defeat. Like Omar Khayyam, she'd come out by the same door wherein she went. Unlike him, she had learnt something: one-way love might be the saddest, most futile thing in the world, but Rufus himself had survived it, and so could she.

'Then I must leave you to get on with your life,' she said, 'and start work on mine.'

She began by picking up the untouched mugs of coffee, intending to take them to the sink, but they slipped out of her trembling fingers and crashed to the stone floor. Staring at a mess of spilt coffee and broken pottery that echoed her own disintegrating state too painfully, she could do nothing to check the tears that now began to trickle down her face.

'Jane . . . don't cry – the mugs don't matter,' Rufus said hoarsely.

In a voice choked with sobs she couldn't quite manage to shout at him, but she tried. 'Of course they matter – can't you even understand that?'

He closed the gap between them in a couple of strides and gripped her shoulders. 'What else don't I understand? Tell me, please.'

'You understand nothing at all,' she said with sad despair. 'I didn't come here out of pity, or because I was trying to decide what to do with my life. I *knew* I wanted to be here, taking care of . . . Tom . . . and Ben . . . and . . .' It was becoming ridiculous – in a moment she'd be listing Boswell as well.

But Rufus understood now; he could see the truth in her face, its sad longing. 'You'd be a sort of . . . housekeeper?' he suggested gravely. 'Is that the idea?'

She nodded, prepared to accept something so preposterous, but incapable of putting it into words. Then he went on

himself. 'Now it's your turn not to understand. I put up with my life here because I've no time or chance to change it. What would make it intolerable would be your presence in the house as anything but my wife ... my *wife*, Jane.'

'Don't shout – I heard you,' she said resentfully. But suddenly her face changed, radiance shining through the tear stains. 'Rufus, did you say *wife*? Are you sure?'

He smiled in spite of himself at the earnest questions, but answered seriously. 'I'm sure, my love, but very nervous. You have nothing to be afraid of – just the faint memory of a girl I loved a long time ago, a girl who no longer exists. I must get the better of a man you've scarcely stopped loving, and all I can offer in place of the life you're giving up is what you see here. There's nothing picturesque about Rushey in the cold, wet months of winter.'

She could smile herself now, knowing that his battle was already won, but she knew that she wouldn't tell him so quite yet – history insisted that they must approach happiness gradually this time. That way he would believe in it, and so would she.

'"To everything there is a season",' she quoted softly, '"and a time to every purpose under heaven ... A time to weep and a time to laugh; a time to mourn, and a time to dance" ... Oh, Rufus, after so much heartache, shall *we* learn to dance?'

He smiled at her. 'We shall go on mourning Joshua, but let us by all means dance as well!' He held out his arms to her just as the kitchen door was pushed open behind them. With a joyous bark the Labrador knocked her off her feet and both she and Rufus collapsed in a helpless, laughing heap in the Windsor armchair while Ben, very pleased with himself, tried to climb in as well. With order finally restored, Rufus shook his head. 'We'd better forego the dancing, I think,' he said unsteadily. 'Ben will . . . will insist on joining in!'

But Jane was looking at the now-empty Windsor chair. 'He's gone,' she said with a note of wonder in her voice. 'At last, Grandfather Amos' shade isn't still sitting there, frowning at me.'

'I expect he knows that you're going to revert to being Jane Venn – no more of this Westover nonsense!' Then he suddenly grew serious again. 'It's going to be all right, isn't it, Jane? Our arrangement *is* going to work?'

'It's going to work beautifully,' she said with gentle conviction. 'I think Hannah's always known it would!'

This first world edition published in Great Britain 2004 by
SEVERN HOUSE PUBLISHERS LTD of
9–15 High Street, Sutton, Surrey SM1 1DF.
This first world edition published in the USA 2004 by
SEVERN HOUSE PUBLISHERS INC of
595 Madison Avenue, New York, N.Y. 10022.

British Library Cataloguing in Publication Data

Stewart, Sally
   A time to dance
   1.   Environmental protection - England - Somerset - Fiction
   2.   Somerset Levels (England) - Fiction
   3.   Love stories
   I.   Title
   823.9'14 [F]

   ISBN 0-7278-6094-1

Typeset by Palimpsest Book Production Ltd.,
Polmont, Stirlingshire, Scotland.
Printed and bound in Great Britain by
MPG Books Ltd., Bodmin, Cornwall.

A TIME TO DANCE

Sally Stewart

severn
House

Recent Titles by Sally Stewart from Severn House

APPOINTMENT IN VENICE
CASTLES IN SPAIN
CURLEW ISLAND
THE DAISY CHAIN
FLOODTIDE
LOST AND FOUND
MOOD INDIGO
POSTCARDS FROM A STRANGER
A RARE BEAUTY
TRAVELLING GIRL

A TIME TO DANCE

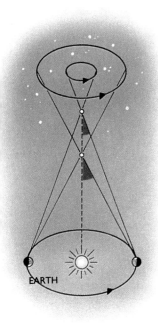

Measuring distances

As the Earth moves around the Sun, the position of a nearby star on the sky changes in a regular way. The position of a more distant star changes by a smaller amount. This apparent shift is called parallax. If astronomers can measure the parallax angles, knowing the distance between the Earth and the Sun, they can then work out the distance from the Sun to the star.

EARTH

The truth about Orion

THE seven brightest stars in Orion are in the same area of sky and seem to be the same distance away. In fact, they lie at very different distances. Brilliant blue-white Rigel is at a distance of 900 light-years, nearly three times farther away than the bright red star Betelgeuse. Mintaka actually gives out more light than Betelgeuse but appears fainter because, at a distance of 2,300 light-years, it is farther away than any of the others.

MINTAKA
SAIPH
ALNILAM
ALNITAK
RIGEL
BELLATRIX
BETELGEUSE

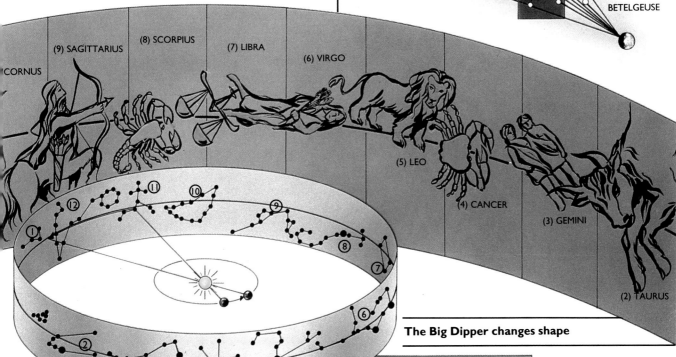

(9) SAGITTARIUS   (8) SCORPIUS   (7) LIBRA   (6) VIRGO

CORNUS

(5) LEO

(4) CANCER

(3) GEMINI

(2) TAURUS

The Big Dipper changes shape

PRESENT

FUTURE

EVERY star moves through space, but stars are so far away that their positions on the sky change only very slowly, too slowly to be noticed by the naked eye during a human lifetime. The upper illustration here shows the Big Dipper as it is now, and the lower view shows what it will look like 100,000 years from now. This motion of a star on the sky is called its proper motion. Barnard's star, a faint red star six light-years away, has the largest known proper motion. It will move through an angle equal to the size of the Moon in the sky in just 180 years.

A path through the zodiac

If we could see the stars in daylight we would be able to see the position of the Sun against the background stars.

The apparent path that the Sun traces against these stars in the course of a year is called the ecliptic, and the band of sky extending to about 9 degrees on either side of the ecliptic is called the Zodiac. The Moon and planets also move within this band.

The twelve principal constellations of the zodiac are: Aries (the Ram), Taurus (the Bull), Gemini (the Twins), Cancer (the Crab), Leo (the Lion), Virgo (the Virgin), Libra (the Scales), Scorpius (the Scorpion), Sagittarius (the Archer), Capricornus (the Sea-Goat), Aquarius (the Water-Bearer), and Pisces (the Fishes). A slow change in the direction of the Earth's axis means that the ancient 'signs of the zodiac' do not now coincide with these constellations.

THE UNIVERSE

TIME, space, and matter all began, so astronomers believe, in one truly momentous event: a hot, dense explosion, called the Big Bang, which took place between 10 and 20 thousand million years ago.

In the first few millionths of a second, as the universe expanded incredibly quickly, many complicated events

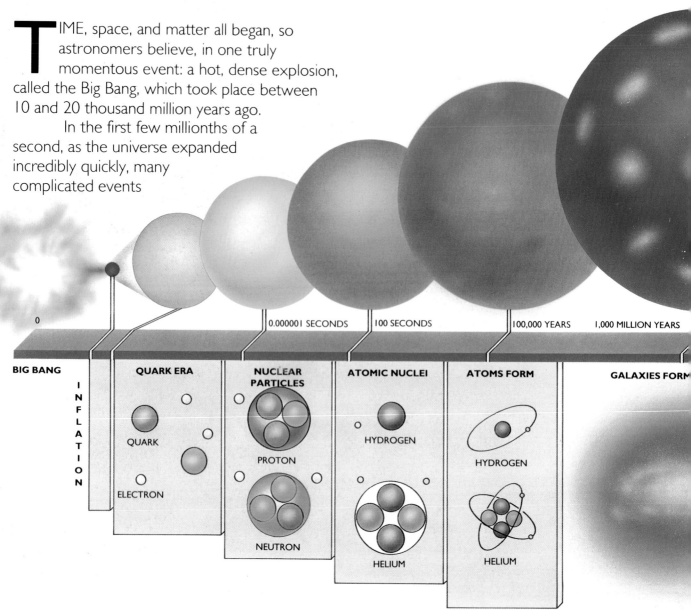

| 0 | | 0.000001 SECONDS | 100 SECONDS | 100,000 YEARS | 1,000 MILLION YEARS |

BIG BANG

INFLATION

QUARK ERA
QUARK
ELECTRON

NUCLEAR PARTICLES
PROTON
NEUTRON

ATOMIC NUCLEI
HYDROGEN
HELIUM

ATOMS FORM
HYDROGEN
HELIUM

GALAXIES FORM

happened. The first steps in the creation of matter itself are of immense interest to scientists everywhere. Many important experiments are conducted in order to study these events – a field of science known as particle physics.

Atoms are the building blocks of all kinds of matter, from grains of sand to people, from planets to stars. Although atoms are very tiny, they are composed of even smaller particles. It is these particles that were made in the Big Bang, eventually forming galaxies billions of years later. Such was the violence of that event that galaxies, or clusters of galaxies, are still rushing apart today in an ever-expanding universe.

The birth of atoms
Immediately after the start of the Big Bang, space expanded incredibly quickly for a very short time. This process, which lasted for the minutest fraction of a second, is called inflation. After that, expansion began to slow down and different kinds of particles including quarks and electrons made their appearance. Just one millionth of a second after the birth of the universe, the quarks had clumped together to form new particles called protons and neutrons.

After a hundred seconds or so some of the protons and nearly all of the neutrons gathered into bunches consisting of two protons and two neutrons. Eventually, each bunch, or atomic nucleus, captured two electrons to form a helium atom, and each remaining proton captured a single electron to form a hydrogen atom. The first building blocks of matter had been born.

14

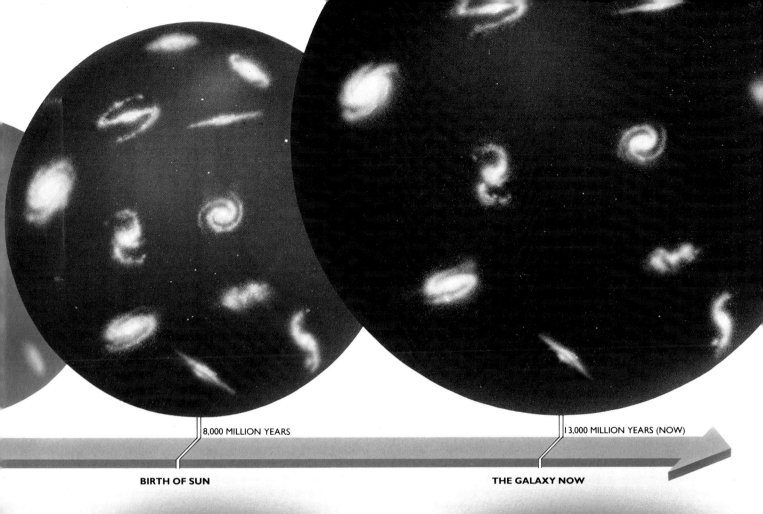

8,000 MILLION YEARS

13,000 MILLION YEARS (NOW)

BIRTH OF SUN

THE GALAXY NOW

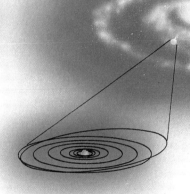

THE SOLAR SYSTEM

Big Crunch?

THE expansion of the universe is gradually slowing down. Galaxies may continue to move apart forever. However, gravity – a force of attraction between bodies in the universe – may eventually halt the expansion. Then, the galaxies will start to fall together until everything collides in a 'Big Crunch'. No one yet can tell whether the universe is 'open' (expanding forever) or 'closed' (destined eventually to collapse in upon itself).

DISTANCE

OPEN (EVER-EXPANDING)

CLOSED

BIG BANG   **TIME**   BIG CRUNCH

The birth of galaxies

By the time atoms of hydrogen and helium had formed, the searing heat of the Big Bang had cooled down and the dense gas of earlier times was becoming more thinly spread out as space continued to expand.

Gradually, though, perhaps 1,000 million years after the Big Bang, huge clouds of gas, held together by gravity, began to collapse to form galaxies and clusters of galaxies. As time went on, stars began to form inside galaxies and galaxies began to develop their familiar elliptical and spiral shapes.

About 5,000 million years ago, in our own Milky Way galaxy, the Sun was born. Planets began to form around the Sun, and one of those planets was the Earth, our home.

MODERN ASTRONOMY

On the island of Hawaii, the peak of Mauna Kea, a dormant volcano (height 4,160 metres) is the highest and one of the best observing sites in the world. Many large telescopes have been set up there to get above the denser, cloudier layers of the atmosphere.

THE telescope, an instrument for seeing magnified images of distant objects, has always been the astronomer's basic tool. Without it, very little could be learned about the mysteries of the universe.

There are two basic types of telescope. A refractor uses a lens, called the objective, to collect light; a reflector uses a concave, or primary, mirror instead. The diameter of the objective or primary mirror is called the aperture, and a telescope is usually described by the size of its aperture.

Modern astronomers work almost entirely with big reflectors. In the last twenty years, ten giant reflectors have been built, with apertures ranging from 3 to 6 metres. The largest single-mirror telescopes are the 5.1-metre on Mt. Palomer, California (completed in 1948) and the 6-metre installed in 1976 on Mt. Semirodriki in the Caucasus Mountains, Russia. It is very difficult and expensive to make huge single mirrors. Astronomers are beginning to use multiple-mirror telescopes (where several mirrors bring light to the same point) and mirrors made up of many small pieces that give the same effect as a single large mirror. The first really large instrument of this kind is the 10-metre Keck telescope.

Telescopes are housed in large buildings called observatories. Observatories located at or near sea level sit beneath the dense blanket of our atmosphere. Even when the Earth's atmosphere is clear of cloud, dust, and pollution, it is so unsteady that light is distorted as it passes through. Stars twinkle, and their images seen through high-powered telescopes wobble and become blurred.

Most large modern observatories are on high

The Keck telescope
The Keck telescope on Mauna Kea uses 36 computer-controlled hexagonal (six-sided) mirrors to give the same effect as a single mirror 10 metres in diameter. This giant telescope weighs over 270 tonnes.

SECONDARY MIRROR

CONCAVE MIRROR

RADIO ANTENNA

SOLAR PANEL

The HST: a reflecting telescope.

A telescope in space
The Hubble space telescope (HST) has a 2.4-metre diameter main mirror. It orbits at a height of 650 kilometres, where it is clear of the obscuring effects of the atmosphere. An error in the shape of its primary mirror, discovered after its launch in 1990, was put right after an optical correction package was inserted into the telescope by Shuttle astronauts in 1993. Its sensitive instruments are now able to detect details ten times finer and fainter than any ground-based telescopes can reveal.

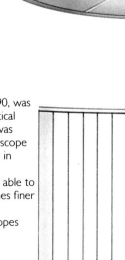

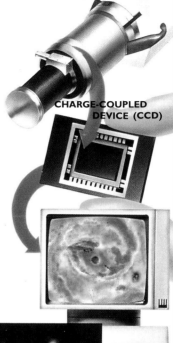

William Herschel telescope

The William Herschel telescope has a concave mirror, 4.2 metres in diameter, that reflects light to a second mirror near the top of the telescope frame. Light then travels back down the telescope to a third mirror that reflects it to a point at the side of the tube. Light is then detected and analysed electronically. Like most large modern telescopes, this one is computer-controlled.

mountain locations above the densest, cloudiest parts of the atmosphere, but even there, conditions are far from perfect. The ideal place for a big telescope would be in space, or on the surface of the airless Moon. The largest telescope so far launched into orbit is the Hubble space telescope, launched in 1990.

Photography plays a very important part in astronomy. A photographic emulsion (the light-sensitive material on a film or plate) collects light, so the longer the exposure, the fainter the objects that can be detected. Although there are limits to this, photography allows us to 'see' stars much fainter than the human eye can make out. A photograph can record thousands or even millions of star images at one time.

Even photographic emulsions are not as efficient as astronomers would like! They record only a fraction of the light that falls on them. There are now electronic devices that can detect and record up to 70 per cent of the incoming light: for example, the charge-coupled device (CCD). This consists of a silicon chip a centimetre or so across, divided up into a hundred thousand little squares called pixels. If the image of a faint galaxy is focused onto a CCD, electric charges build up that depend on how much light has fallen on each pixel. By recording these charges, pictures of faint galaxies can be built up in a fraction of the time that would be needed for photography. Electronic cameras with CCDs also reveal much fainter objects than photographs can show.

Professional astronomers spend little if any time actually looking through telescopes. Complex instruments have replaced human eyes. Astronomers watch what the telescope is viewing on television screens, and use computers to control their telescopes and analyse the incoming information.

CHARGE-COUPLED DEVICE (CCD)

Image-processing can make fuzzy images sharper.

Amateur astronomy

Many thousands of people enjoy astronomy as a hobby. Equipped with a star map, a red flashlight (to avoid dazzling eyes at night), warm clothing, and using the naked eye, binoculars, or a telescope, anyone can carry out useful observations. You can keep watch on the changing appearance of the planets and the brightnesses of variable stars. One day you may even be lucky enough to discover a new comet or a nova!

All stars are hot globes of gas, but they can have very different properties.

In the night sky some stars appear brighter than others. A star can appear bright simply because it is very close to us, or faint because it is very far away. The brightest star in the sky is Sirius. Although it gives out 26 times as much light as the Sun, it appears bright mainly because it is one of the nearest stars. There are far more powerful stars which emit more than 100,000 times as much light

Hertzsprung-Russell star diagram

THIS diagram is named for its inventors, Ejnar Hertzsprung and Henry Russell. The scale on the left shows light

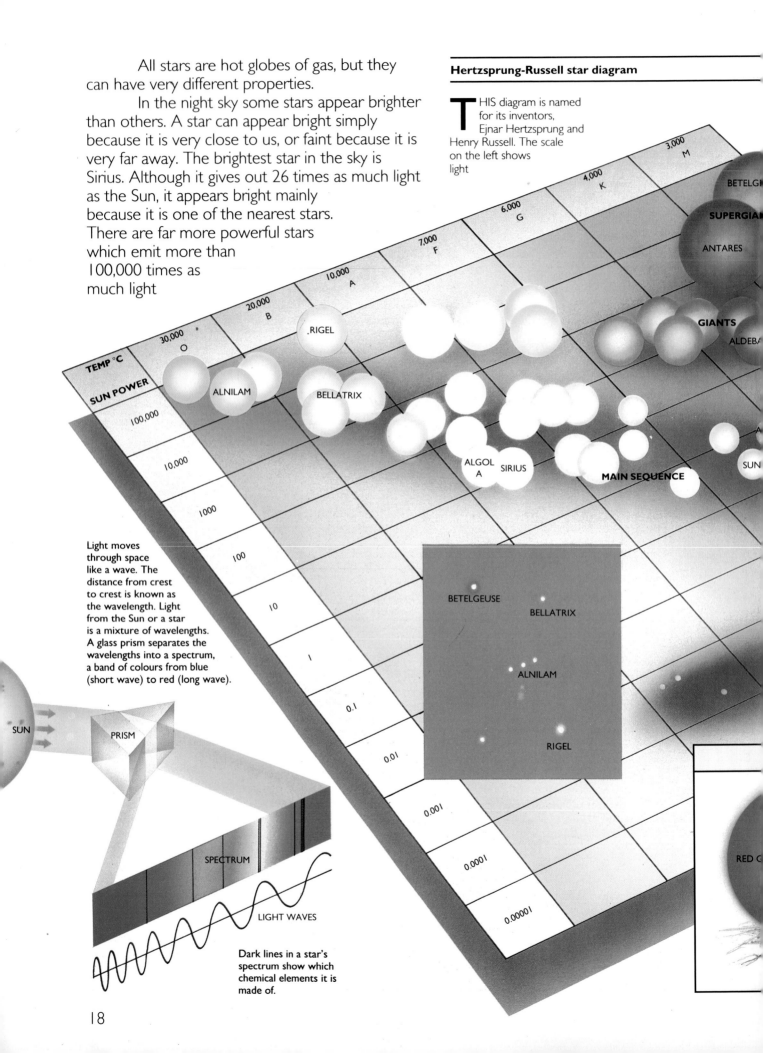

TEMP °C

SUN POWER

MAIN SEQUENCE

SUPERGIANTS

GIANTS

BETELGEUSE

ANTARES

ALDEBARAN

RIGEL

ALNILAM

BELLATRIX

ALGOL A

SIRIUS

SUN

RED G

Light moves through space like a wave. The distance from crest to crest is known as the wavelength. Light from the Sun or a star is a mixture of wavelengths. A glass prism separates the wavelengths into a spectrum, a band of colours from blue (short wave) to red (long wave).

SUN

PRISM

SPECTRUM

LIGHT WAVES

Dark lines in a star's spectrum show which chemical elements it is made of.

18

output, or brightness, compared to the Sun. The scale along the top shows surface temperature in degrees Celsius. It also shows spectral classes (O, B, A, F, G, K, M). The appearance of a star's spectrum (see diagram, *bottom left*) decides its spectral class. Most stars lie on the main sequence, a band that stretches from top left (hot, bright) to bottom right (cool, faint). The named stars include four of the bright stars in Orion – Betelgeuse, Rigel, Bellatrix, and Alnilam. Above and to the right of the main sequence are the giants; below and to the left are the dwarfs.

The star that winks
Once every 2.9 days, the star Algol, in the constellation of Perseus, fades to a third of its normal brightness. In fact, it consists of two stars which revolve around each other (a binary), so close together, that they look like a single star. When one star passes in front of the other it blocks out some of the light, and Algol fades. Algol is the best known eclipsing binary.

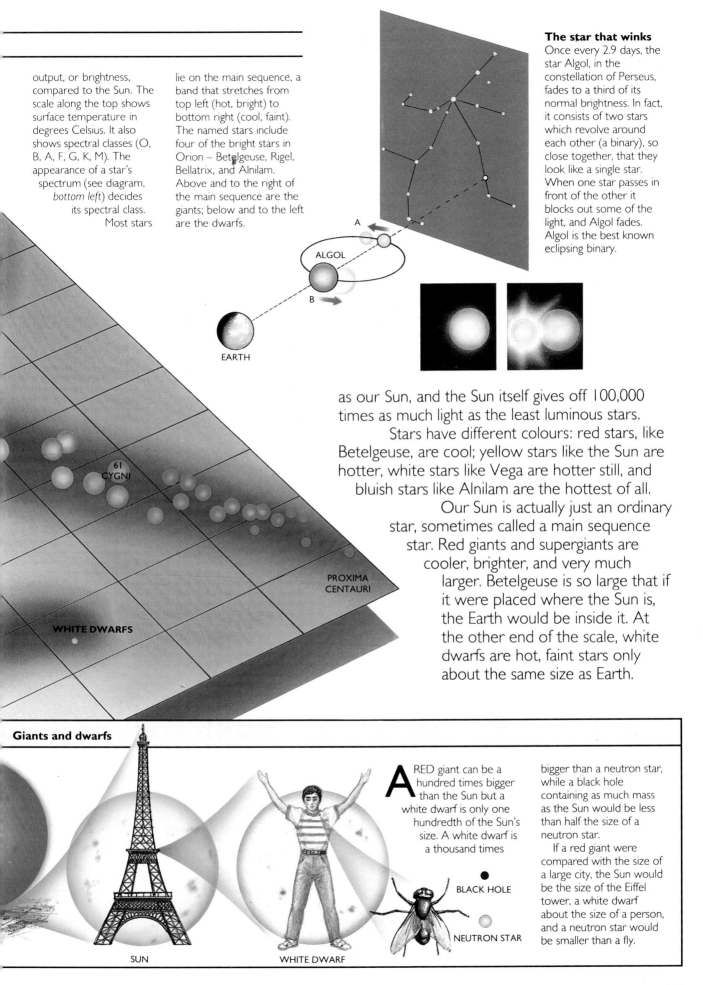

A

ALGOL

B

EARTH

61 CYGNI

PROXIMA CENTAURI

WHITE DWARFS

as our Sun, and the Sun itself gives off 100,000 times as much light as the least luminous stars. Stars have different colours: red stars, like Betelgeuse, are cool; yellow stars like the Sun are hotter, white stars like Vega are hotter still, and bluish stars like Alnilam are the hottest of all. Our Sun is actually just an ordinary star, sometimes called a main sequence star. Red giants and supergiants are cooler, brighter, and very much larger. Betelgeuse is so large that if it were placed where the Sun is, the Earth would be inside it. At the other end of the scale, white dwarfs are hot, faint stars only about the same size as Earth.

Giants and dwarfs

A RED giant can be a hundred times bigger than the Sun but a white dwarf is only one hundredth of the Sun's size. A white dwarf is a thousand times bigger than a neutron star, while a black hole containing as much mass as the Sun would be less than half the size of a neutron star.

If a red giant were compared with the size of a large city, the Sun would be the size of the Eiffel tower, a white dwarf about the size of a person, and a neutron star would be smaller than a fly.

BLACK HOLE

NEUTRON STAR

SUN

WHITE DWARF

The life and death of a star

PROTOSTAR

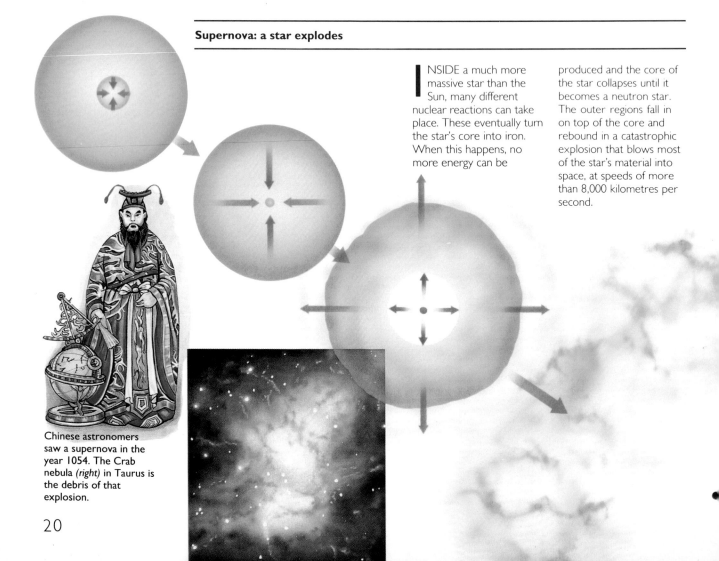

ORION NEBULA

This glowing cloud of gas lies 1,600 light-years away, below the three stars of Orion's belt. It shines because it contains some very hot young stars. Infrared observations show that this cloud also contains many newly-forming stars.

A STAR like the Sun forms when a cloud of gas begins to shrink because of the pull of its own gravity. The cloud becomes hotter as it shrinks and begins to glow a dull red colour. When the temp-

Hydrogen fuel begins to burn outside the core, and the star swells up to become a red giant. As a red giant it quickly eats up its remaining reserves of fuel. The star throws off its outer layers to form an expanding shell called a planetary nebula, like the Helix nebula *(right)*. Its

MAIN SEQUENCE

erature in its central core reaches about 10 million degrees, nuclear reactions begin to generate large amounts of energy. The star then becomes a main sequence star and changes only very slowly for the next 10,000 million years. Eventually the star's core runs out of fuel and begins to shrink, and becomes hotter.

core then becomes a shrunken white dwarf. Over many billions of years, the white dwarf cools and fades, to end up as a cold black dwarf.

Supernova: a star explodes

INSIDE a much more massive star than the Sun, many different nuclear reactions can take place. These eventually turn the star's core into iron. When this happens, no more energy can be

produced and the core of the star collapses until it becomes a neutron star. The outer regions fall in on top of the core and rebound in a catastrophic explosion that blows most of the star's material into space, at speeds of more than 8,000 kilometres per second.

Chinese astronomers saw a supernova in the year 1054. The Crab nebula *(right)* in Taurus is the debris of that explosion.

20

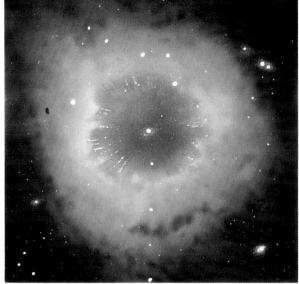

HELIX NEBULA

Stars are born when regions inside giant gas clouds collapse on themselves. They become fully-fledged stars when their interiors become hot enough for nuclear reactions to take place. These reactions convert part of the star's mass into energy.

Stars that are more massive than the Sun become much more bright and they burn up their reserves of fuel very rapidly. Whereas stars like the Sun should live for at least 10,000 million years, a star of twenty times the Sun's mass will last for only about 10 million years. Stars like the Sun end their days as white dwarfs, which slowly cool down as time goes by. Stars ten or more times the Sun's mass will probably explode as supernovas, scattering debris far into space and leaving behind dense neutron stars. The most massive stars of all will probably collapse until they become black holes.

RED GIANT

PLANETARY NEBULA

WHITE DWARF

BLACK DWARF

A nova is a star that suddenly flares up because of an explosion on its surface. It then fades back to normal.

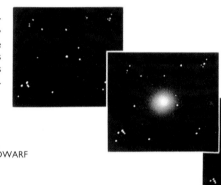

DID YOU KNOW?

Twelve of the least massive stars (brown dwarfs) would balance the Sun on a pair of scales. About 100 Suns would be needed to balance the most massive star.

Neutron stars spin very quickly and emit narrow beams of radio waves. Each time the beam points towards the Earth we observe a flash just as we do whenever the beam of a lighthouse points our way.

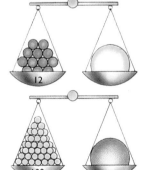

12

100

A piece of white dwarf material the size of a sugar cube would weigh the same as a small car. A cube of neutron star would weigh as much as a small mountain.

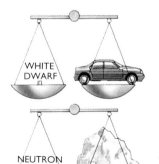

WHITE DWARF

NEUTRON STAR

BRIGHTNESS

0   2   4   6   8
DAYS

Many stars vary in brightness. Cepheid variables are stars that are approaching old age. They expand and contract in a regular way, and their brightness and temperature changes as they do so. Bigger, brighter Cepheids take longer to vary than smaller, fainter ones.

21

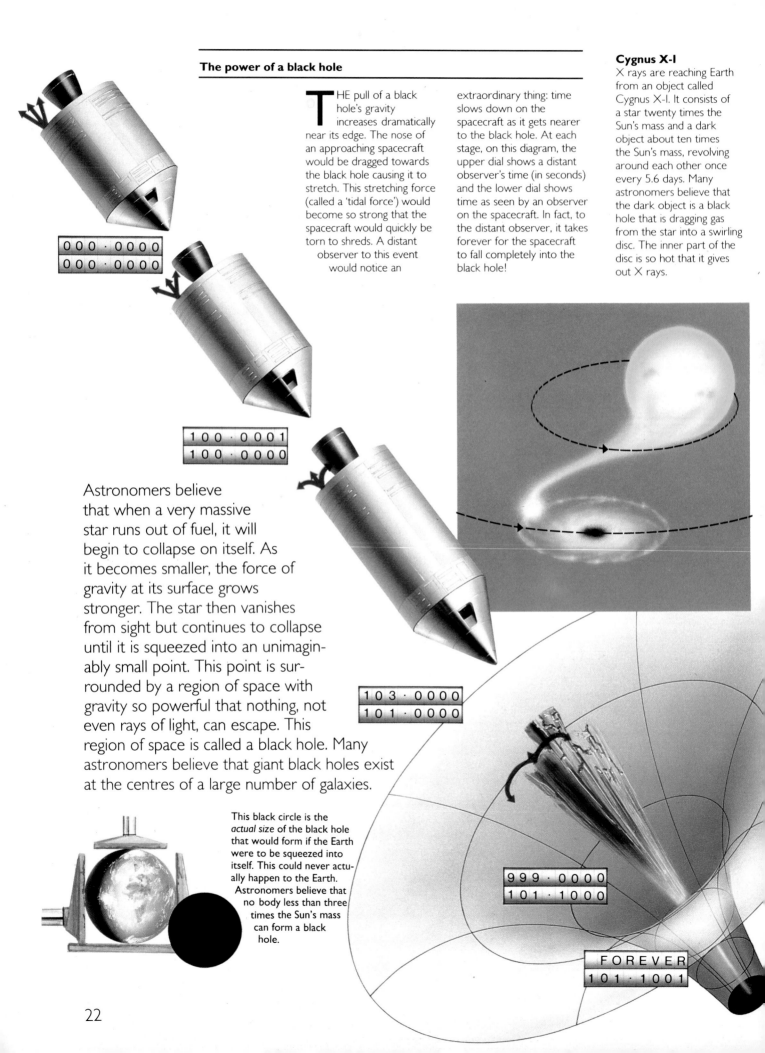

The power of a black hole

THE pull of a black hole's gravity increases dramatically near its edge. The nose of an approaching spacecraft would be dragged towards the black hole causing it to stretch. This stretching force (called a 'tidal force') would become so strong that the spacecraft would quickly be torn to shreds. A distant observer to this event would notice an extraordinary thing: time slows down on the spacecraft as it gets nearer to the black hole. At each stage, on this diagram, the upper dial shows a distant observer's time (in seconds) and the lower dial shows time as seen by an observer on the spacecraft. In fact, to the distant observer, it takes forever for the spacecraft to fall completely into the black hole!

Cygnus X-I

X rays are reaching Earth from an object called Cygnus X-I. It consists of a star twenty times the Sun's mass and a dark object about ten times the Sun's mass, revolving around each other once every 5.6 days. Many astronomers believe that the dark object is a black hole that is dragging gas from the star into a swirling disc. The inner part of the disc is so hot that it gives out X rays.

Astronomers believe that when a very massive star runs out of fuel, it will begin to collapse on itself. As it becomes smaller, the force of gravity at its surface grows stronger. The star then vanishes from sight but continues to collapse until it is squeezed into an unimaginably small point. This point is surrounded by a region of space with gravity so powerful that nothing, not even rays of light, can escape. This region of space is called a black hole. Many astronomers believe that giant black holes exist at the centres of a large number of galaxies.

This black circle is the *actual size* of the black hole that would form if the Earth were to be squeezed into itself. This could never actually happen to the Earth. Astronomers believe that no body less than three times the Sun's mass can form a black hole.

000 · 0000
000 · 0000

100 · 0001
100 · 0000

103 · 0000
101 · 0000

999 · 0000
101 · 1000

FOREVER
101 · 1001

INVISIBLE ASTRONOMY

Rosat

Launched in 1990, Rosat is the most sensitive X-ray satellite so far put into space. It carries a 0.8-metre X-ray telescope and an ultraviolet camera.

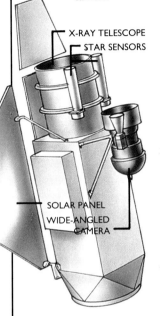

X-RAY TELESCOPE
STAR SENSORS
SOLAR PANEL
WIDE-ANGLED CAMERA

THE different colours of visible light form a tiny part of a huge range of wavelengths called the electromagnetic spectrum. Waves that are shorter than visible light include ultraviolet light, X rays, and gamma rays. Waves longer than visible light include infrared, microwave, and radio. Many objects in space give out invisible rays as well as, or instead of, visible light. It is possible, however, with the help of computers, to produce visible images of these invisible rays.

Visible light and wavelengths between about a sixth of a centimetre and 20 metres reach the ground and are studied by optical and radio astronomers. A small amount of infrared reaches mountain-top observatories, but all other wavelengths are blocked out by the atmosphere. In order to study gamma rays, X rays, ultraviolet, and much of the infrared, astronomers have to use specialized instruments that are above the atmosphere on orbiting satellites. Invisible radiations allow astronomers to study distant events and objects in space, such as pulsars, supernova remnants, gas clouds, newly-forming stars, and quasars.

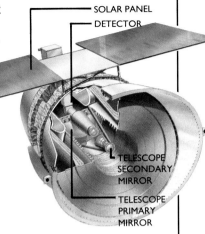

SOLAR PANEL
DETECTOR
TELESCOPE SECONDARY MIRROR
TELESCOPE PRIMARY MIRROR

IRAS

The Infrared Astronomical Satellite (IRAS) was launched in 1983. Its 0.6-metre telescope was cooled down to −270°C to improve its performance. In its nine-month lifetime, it identified over 200,000 infrared sources.

| GAMMA RAYS | X RAYS | ULTRAVIOLET | INFRARED | MICROWAVES | RADIO WAVES |

VISIBLE

An X-ray image of the Sun (*bottom*) looks very different from an ordinary view.

Radio telescope

The Effelsberg radio telescope near Bonn in Germany has a dish measuring 100 metres in diameter. It can be aimed at any point in the sky and is the largest steerable radio dish in the world. Radio waves from space are collected by the dish and focused onto a receiving system mounted on a tripod.

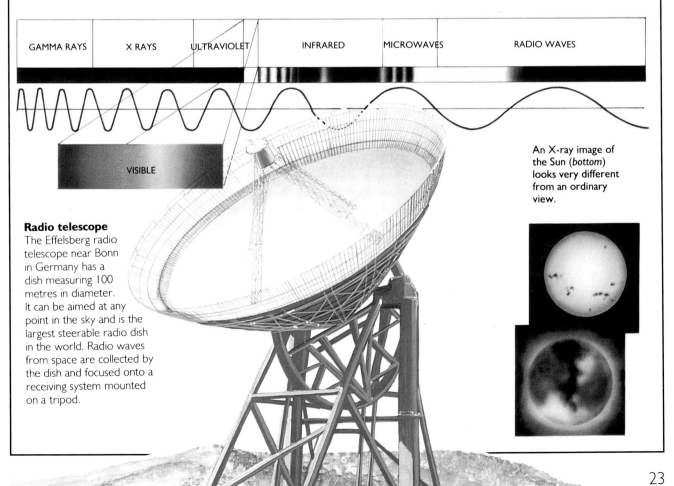

On a clear, dark night when there is no Moon, you can see a faint band of cloudy light stretching right across the sky. This is the Milky Way, a side view of the huge concentration of stars, dust, and gas to which our own Solar System belongs. The Milky Way galaxy, as it is called, contains about 100 billion stars. It is shaped like a flattened disc with a bulge at the centre, or nucleus. Great arms containing the brightest stars and the gas clouds in which new stars are born spiral out from this nucleus. On one of these spiral arms, about three fifths of the way from the centre to the edge, is our own parent star, the Sun, just an ordinary star in a family of billions.

All the matter in the Galaxy rotates around its centre. The Sun travels at a speed of 250 kilometres per second, but the Galaxy is so vast that it still takes 230 million years to complete a single revolution!

Nearly everything you can see with the naked eye in the night sky belongs to the Milky Way galaxy – but there are three exceptions. Visible in the southern hemisphere are two

The Milky Way Galaxy

VIEWED from the Earth, our galaxy is a cloudy trail of stars across the night sky. If we were to see the Milky Way from far out in space it would look like a gigantic spiral of stars with a bulge in the centre. Seen farther away and from the side, the disc looks like two fried eggs back to back.

ELLIPTICALS

SO

Classification of galaxies
Once astronomers had discovered the existence of galaxies beyond our own Milky Way, they set to work trying to find patterns in the different

types of galaxies they saw. The American astronomer Edwin Hubble (1889-1953) drew up the first classification scheme, still used by observers today. He recognized three forms of galaxies: elliptical (E)

(shaped like an egg), spiral, and irregular. He also found that there were two different types of spiral galaxies – ones where the spiral arms emerge from the central bulge (S) and ones where the arms are

linked to the ends of a bar of stars lying across the galactic centre (SB). SO galaxies are midway between ellipticals and spirals.

SUN

100,000 LIGHT-YEARS

Massive energy machines
Some galaxies, called active galaxies, give out far more energy than do ordinary galaxies. All of these seem to have very powerful energy sources in their centres, or nuclei. A quasar may be a hyperactive galactic nucleus that contains a super-massive black hole.

BLACK HOLE

ACTIVE GALAXY

SPIRALS

DIRECTION OF ROTATION

Galaxies seem to occur in groups or clusters *(see above)*. The largest clusters can contain up to several thousand members. The Milky Way belongs to a group of about 30 galaxies known as the Local Group. The Local Group is part of the Virgo supercluster, a huge system of galaxies 100 million light-years across.

BARRED SPIRALS

cloudy patches known as the Large and Small Magellanic Clouds, after the Portuguese explorer Ferdinand Magellan. In the northern hemisphere, there is a faint blip of light in the constellation of Andromeda. These three objects are other galaxies, far distant from our own. The light from the Andromeda spiral, which is similar in shape to the Milky Way galaxy, has taken more than 2 million years to reach us.

25

THE SOLAR SYSTEM

METEOROIDS

COMET

JUPITER

MARS

VENUS

EARTH

SUN

ASTEROIDS

MERCURY

IO

EUROPA

GANYMEDE

CALLISTO

MOON

SUN

MERCURY VENUS EARTH MARS

JUPITER

RHEA

TITAN

SATURN

0.39 1.00 1.52   ASTEROIDS   5.20   9.54
0.72   DISTANCE FROM SUN (AU)

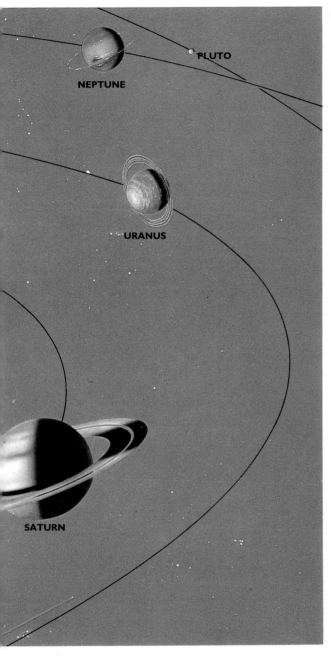

PLUTO

NEPTUNE

URANUS

SATURN

T HE SOLAR SYSTEM consists of the Sun, nine planets, a host of smaller bodies and some thinly-spread gas and dust. In order of distance from the Sun, the planets are: Mercury, Venus, Earth, Mars, Jupiter, Saturn, Uranus, Neptune, and Pluto. The first four are called the terrestrial planets because, like the Earth, they are small, dense bodies with solid surfaces. The next four are the giant, or Jovian, planets, which are much larger but less dense than the Earth. Like the Sun, they mainly consist of the elements hydrogen and helium and do not have solid surfaces. Pluto, the most distant planet, is a tiny, icy world.

Minor members of the Solar System include asteroids, which are small rocky bodies up to 920 kilometres in size, and comets, whose icy bodies give off gas and dust each time they approach the Sun.

A map of the Solar System
All of the planets travel around the Sun in the same direction. Apart from Mercury and Pluto, their orbits are almost exact circles; Pluto's extends from well beyond to just inside Neptune's. Many thousands of small rocky bodies (asteroids) lie between Mars and Jupiter. Comets have elongated orbits that are often tilted at large angles to the planets' orbits. Streams of tiny particles (meteoroids) follow similar paths.

Scale of the planets
The Sun and planets are shown to their correct comparative sizes, as are moons larger than 1,450 kilometres in diameter. The bar along the bottom gives the distance of each planet from the Sun.

Seen from Pluto, the Sun, which bathes our own planet in light, is no more than an extremely brilliant star in a perpetual night sky.

EARTH

PLUTO

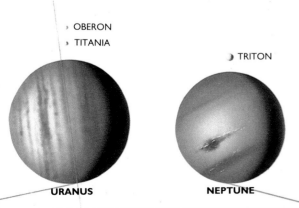

› OBERON
› TITANIA

› TRITON

URANUS   NEPTUNE   PLUTO

30.06   39.53

27

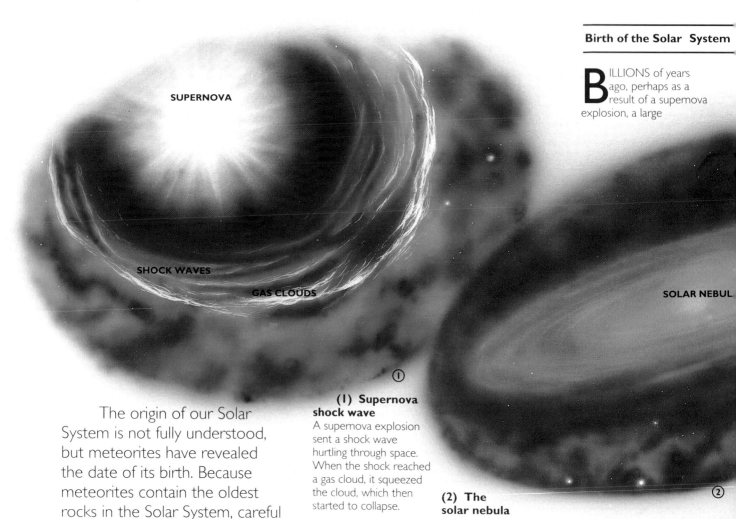

SUPERNOVA

SHOCK WAVES

GAS CLOUDS

SOLAR NEBUL

①

②

BILLIONS of years ago, perhaps as a result of a supernova explosion, a large

The origin of our Solar System is not fully understood, but meteorites have revealed the date of its birth. Because meteorites contain the oldest rocks in the Solar System, careful analysis of them tells us that they, and the planets, were formed about 4.6 thousand million years ago. Most astronomers believe that the Sun and Solar System were born when a huge cloud of gas and dust collapsed under the pull of its own gravity. While no one knows for certain how the collapse began, it has been suggested that a nearby supernova explosion was the cause.

(1) Supernova shock wave
A supernova explosion sent a shock wave hurtling through space. When the shock reached a gas cloud, it squeezed the cloud, which then started to collapse.

(2) The solar nebula
As the cloud collapsed, it began to spin, and formed a swirling disc of gas and dust called the solar nebula. The centre of the solar nebula grew hotter and denser than the surrounding disc, which was hot near the centre but cool at the edge.

(3) Building the planets
Small particles began to stick together to form larger clumps, which grew eventually to kilometres across in size. Collisions between these bodies built up the terrestrial planets and the cores of the giant planets.

Fate of the Earth

IN 5 or 6 thousand million years from now, the Sun will swell up to become a red giant – a hundred times larger and several hundred times brighter than it is at present. The Earth will lose its atmosphere and oceans, and its surface will begin to melt as the temperature rises to 1,400°C. As the Sun continues to expand and the Earth melts, Venus would appear as a black dot against the swollen Sun.

cloud of gas and dust began to fall together. The central part became the Sun and the remainder settled into a spinning disc. Rocky particles formed in the hotter inner parts of the disc, and rocky and icy particles formed in its cooler outer zones. The inner planets, including the Earth, formed from rocky particles and the giant planets from rocky and icy particles. The giant planets also pulled in a lot of gas.

③

As the centre of the cloud continued to shrink, it also heated up, eventually becoming a star – the Sun. Within the rest of the cloud, over a period of about 100 million years, more and more particles gradually stuck together until the planets were formed. The giant planets, which formed in the outer part of the cloud, contained icy materials as well as rocky materials. Uranus and Neptune, especially, contained a lot of ice. Each of the giants attracted huge envelopes of gas. Jupiter and Saturn ended up with deep oceans of liquid hydrogen and helium around their cores. Comets probably contain original icy and dusty material that dates back to the birth of the Solar System.

④

GIANT PLANET

⑤

GAS

(5) The Solar System today
The Solar System is now 4.6 thousand million years old. The Sun is a middle-aged star, and the planets have their familiar features.

(4) The nebula disperses
As the young Sun became hotter and brighter it blew away the remaining gas and dust. It also blew away the original atmospheres that had formed around the terrestrial planets. Farther from the Sun, the giant planets were able to hold on to deep envelopes of gas.

29

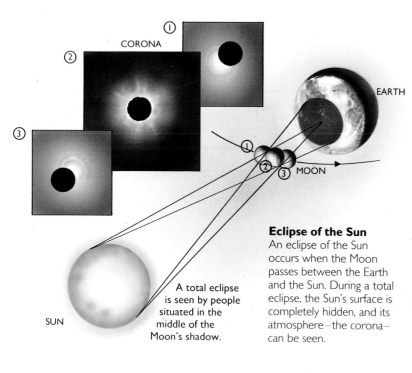

CORONA

① ② ③

SUN

EARTH

MOON

① ② ③

A total eclipse is seen by people situated in the middle of the Moon's shadow.

Eclipse of the Sun
An eclipse of the Sun occurs when the Moon passes between the Earth and the Sun. During a total eclipse, the Sun's surface is completely hidden, and its atmosphere—the corona—can be seen.

Structure of the Sun

THERE is constant activity inside and on the surface of the Sun. Energy generated in the Sun's core flows out through the radiative zone and into the convective zone. Here, hot gas rises to the surface, gives out energy, then sinks down to be heated again.

Dark patches on the photosphere (visible surface) are called sunspots. They are areas of intense magnetic activity and look dark because they are cooler than their surroundings. Above the photosphere is the chromosphere and beyond that, the corona—the Sun's faint outer atmosphere. Huge plumes of gas, called prominences, shoot up into the corona. Violent explosions called flares erupt above sunspot groups.

The Sun is a huge, dynamic globe of gas. It has a diameter of 1.4 million kilometres – big enough to contain nearly 1,400,000 bodies the size of the Earth! Less dense than the Earth, it is made up almost entirely of the lightest elements, hydrogen (73 per cent) and helium (25 per cent).

The Sun's visible surface, called the photosphere, has a temperature of just under 5,500°. The temperature rises to a maximum of about 15,000,000°C at the centre of the Sun. The Sun shines because it is generating energy in its core by means of nuclear reactions that convert hydrogen into helium. So many reactions take place that the Sun converts more than 4 million tonnes of matter into energy every second. The Sun has enough fuel to keep it shining for at least another 5,000 million years.

CHROMOSPHERE

SUNSPOTS

PROMINENCE

PHOTOSPHERE

FLARE

CORONA

PROMINENCE

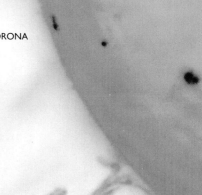

Daytime darkness
During a total eclipse, the sky becomes darker, the brighter stars become visible, and the temperature drops noticeably. The effect is rather like twilight. Birds, insects, and animals sometimes behave as if night has fallen and prepare to go to sleep.

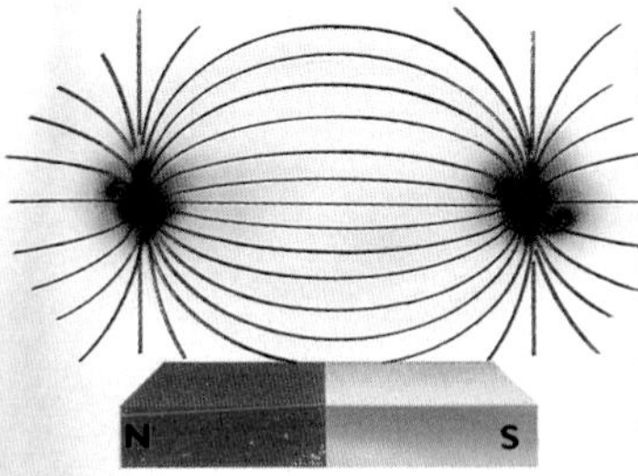

Sunspots

Sunspots have strong magnetic fields and usually occur in pairs or groups. In a sunspot pair, one spot has a north magnetic pole and the other a south pole, just as if there were a bar magnet lying underneath the surface between the spots.

N   S

CONVECTIVE ZONE

RADIATIVE ZONE

CORE

DID YOU KNOW?

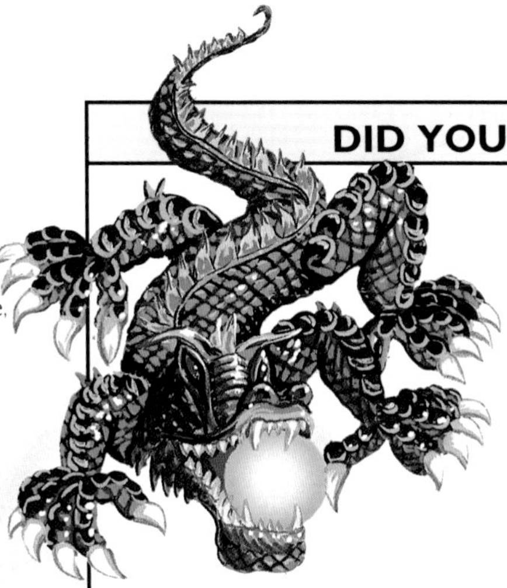

People in ancient times were afraid of eclipses. The Chinese used to think that an eclipse was caused by a dragon trying to swallow the Sun. Whenever an eclipse began they would make as much noise as possible to frighten the dragon away. They were always successful!

The largest eruptive prominences can shoot up to heights of 480,000 kilometres above the Sun's surface. They can erupt into space at speeds of more than 3 million kilometres per hour. Sometimes material is thrown up so fast that it escapes from the Sun altogether.

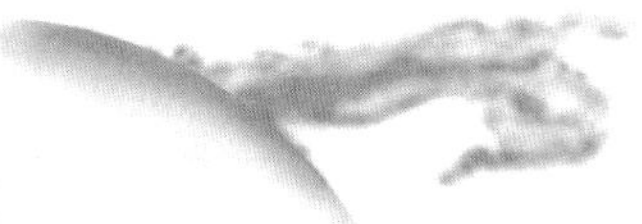

WARNING! NEVER LOOK AT THE SUN THROUGH A TELESCOPE OR BINOCULARS. The concentrated heat and light would blind you. It is harmful to your eyes to stare directly at the Sun even without a telescope or binoculars.

A photon (a tiny bit of light energy) suffers so many collisions on its way from the core that it can easily take a million years to reach the surface. Once it leaves the surface, it takes only 8.3 minutes to reach the Earth.

PATH OF PHOTON

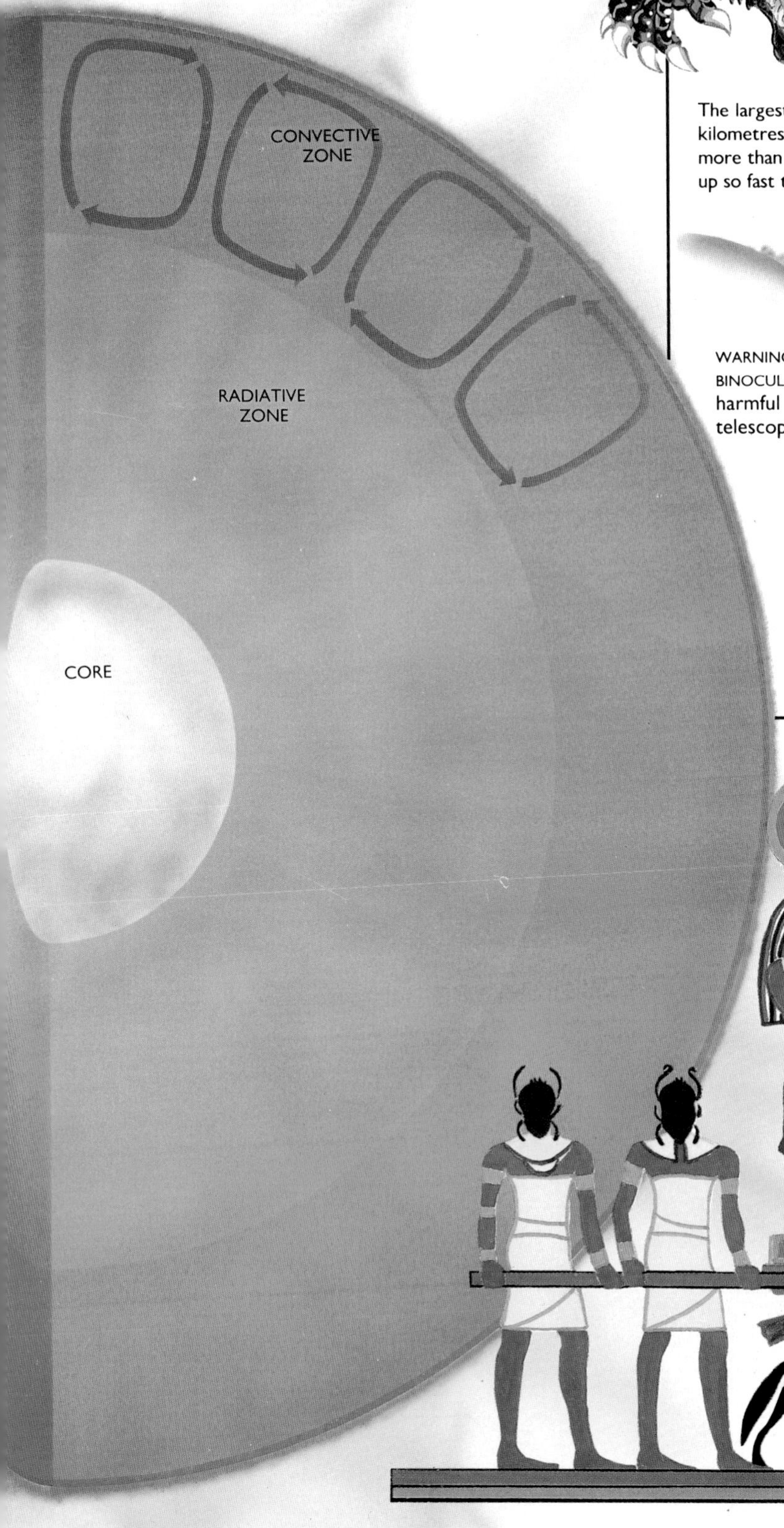

Egyptian Sun god

The ancient Egyptians believed that the Sun was a god called Ra who travelled across the sky each day. Here Ra is carried by four minor gods. His head is like a falcon with the Sun on top.

31

A COMET usually follows a very elongated orbit. As it approaches the Sun, its nucleus heats up and gas and dust spread out from the centre to form the comet's head, or coma.

A comet often develops both a gas tail and a dust tail. The solar wind—a stream of atomic particles flowing out from the Sun—drives the gas tail away at high speeds. Meanwhile,

sunlight pushes dust particles out of the comet's head. Because the dust particles move more slowly than the gas, they lag behind the comet's head and form a curved tail.

A comet approaches the Sun head first, but after its closest approach it moves away tail first. As it gets farther from the Sun, the comet fades and both its tails shrink.

GAS TAIL
DUST TAIL
SUN

A bright comet can be a spectacular sight. Moving slowly against the background stars, it seems to hang in the sky like a ghostly sword for days or even weeks. In the past, comets were regarded as evil omens, and it was said that the appearance of a comet foretold the death of a famous person. Less of a mystery or source of super-stition now, we know that comets are large lumps of ice that revolve around the Sun in elongated orbits. Comets seem to appear suddenly because they brighten only when they come close to the Sun.

Asteroids are rocky or rocky metallic bodies that range in size from a few hundred kilometres to less than one kilometre. Most asteroids have orbits that lie between those of Mars and Jupiter, but a small number, called the Apollo asteroids, have paths that cross the Earth's orbit.

The Solar System contains vast numbers of meteoroids, particles ranging in size from less than a hundred thousandth of a centimetre to tens or even hundreds of metres. When a tiny meteoroid plunges

Nucleus of a comet

A typical comet has a nucleus that is irregular in shape, a few kilometres in diameter, and made up of a mixture of ice and dust. In 1986 the *Giotto* spacecraft flew within 600 kilometres of the nucleus of Halley's comet and showed that its irregular nucleus has a black dusty crust. As sunlight heats the nucleus, gas and dust escape through cracks and craters in the crust.

Encounter with an asteroid

SO far, detailed images of two asteroids, Gaspra and Ida, have been taken at close range by the *Galileo* spacecraft, which made two flights through the asteroid belt (in 1991 and 1993) while on its way from Earth to Jupiter. Future spacecraft missions may be launched specifically to investigate asteroids or to follow the orbit of a comet, studying how it changes as it approaches and moves away from the Sun. The main features of these spacecraft include the instruments that are mounted well away from the body of the craft – the communications dish and the propulsion module.

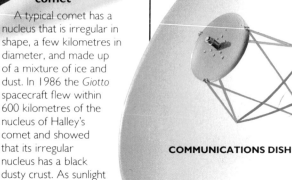

COMMUNICATIONS DISH

INSTRUMENTS

ASTEROID

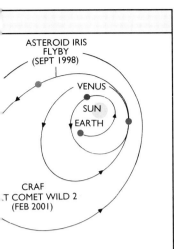

ASTEROID IRIS
FLYBY
(SEPT 1998)

VENUS

SUN

EARTH

CRAF
.T COMET WILD 2
(FEB 2001)

The route for the planned Comet Rendezvous-Asteroid Flyby mission (CRAF) passes the asteroid Iris and then meets up with comet Wild 2 and follows it along its orbit.

Meteorite impact

When a meteorite enters the Earth's atmosphere, it is heated by friction and its surface begins to melt and stream away. Most meteorites are stony bodies that tend to break up into fragments. Iron meteorites are more likely to reach the ground in one piece, and bodies larger than about 100 tonnes hit the ground so hard that they blast out craters. The Barringer crater in Arizona is 1200 metres wide and nearly 180 metres deep. It was probably produced

into the atmosphere at high speed, it is vaporised in a brief streak of light that we call a meteor (or shooting star). Most small meteoroids are dusty debris from old comets. Larger rocky, rocky metallic, or metallic meteoroids are probably fragments left over from collisions between asteroids. Bodies of this kind, which survive plummeting through the atmosphere to reach ground level, are known as meteorites.

by a 50,000-tonne meteorite about 40,000 years ago.

METEORITE

BARRINGER CRATER

Meteor shower

A shower of meteors is seen when the Earth crosses a meteoroid stream. Because these meteoroids are all travelling in the same direction, their tracks seem to spread out from a single point in the sky called the radiant.

EARTH

METEOROID
STREAM

PROPULSION
MODULE

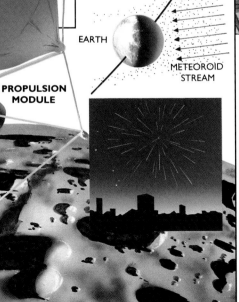

DID YOU KNOW?

Halley's comet was seen in 1066 and is shown in the famous Bayeux tapestry that commemorates the Norman conquest of England. The comet was thought to be a bad omen for King Harold, who was killed at the Battle of Hastings. His courtiers (left) point the comet out.

Edmond Halley was the first person to prove that comets travel around the Sun. He realized that comets seen in 1531, 1607, and 1682 were the same comet and correctly said that the comet would return in 1758. The comet was then named in his honour.

The dinosaurs may have been wiped out 65 million years ago by changes in the climate after an asteroid or comet struck the Earth.

Ceres, the largest asteroid, is about a quarter of the size of the Moon. The smallest known asteroid is not much bigger than the Empire State Building in New York City.

MOON

SMALLEST
ASTEROID

CERES

EMPIRE STATE BUILDING

THE INNER PLANETS

EARTH

OUR own planet, the Earth, is the third from the Sun and the largest of the four terrestrial planets. Its main surface features, which are visible from space, are the continental landmasses, the oceans, and the polar ice caps. The Earth is unique in being the only planet in the Solar System with liquid water on its surface.

Beneath the Earth's solid surface, the temperature increases rapidly, reaching a maximum of over 5,000°C in the dense metallic core. The atmosphere is composed mainly of the gases nitrogen (78 per cent) and oxygen (21 per cent), with varying amounts of water vapour. Oxygen would disappear from the atmosphere if it were not replaced by the oxygen given out from plant life. The Earth is the only planet known to support life.

MOUNTAIN CHAIN

CRUST

INNER COR

OUTER CORE

OCEAN

LOWER MANTL

UPPER MANTLE

Structure of the Earth

The Earth's core consists mainly of iron and nickel. The inner core is solid and the outer core is liquid. The core is surrounded by a dense rocky mantle and a thin outer crust. The surface layer consists of sections called plates. Slow circulation in the upper mantle carries the plates around at speeds of 2 centimetres or so per year. Collisons between plates on land or under the sea give rise to chains of mountains and volcanoes and cause earthquakes. Molten matter flows out from the mantle where plates move apart.

250 MILLION YEARS AGO

TODAY

About 250 million years ago, most of the continents were joined. South America was linked to Africa; North America and Greenland to Europe. Gradually they moved apart to make the continents we know today.

View from space

The main landmass in this view from space is the continent of Africa and the Arabian peninsula. The image also shows the Indian and Atlantic oceans, together with swirling cloud patterns over the stormy Antarctic Ocean, north of the Antarctic ice cap.

Origin of life on Earth

THE Earth was formed about 4,500 million years ago. For the first 500 million years a rain of rocky, metallic, and icy bodies pounded the surface. Gas leaking from its hot interior provided an atmosphere, and oceans formed as the surface cooled down. Complicated molecules (groups of atoms) soon began to form in seas and pools, and the first primitive life forms (single cells) appeared 3,500 million years ago. Advanced living creatures evolved first in the oceans and then moved onto the land.

From 4.5 to 4 billion years ago, the Earth was heavily bombarded by meteorites and larger bodies.

CONTINENT

Oceans began to form about 3.8 billion years ago.

MIDOCEANIC RIDGE

The Earth's atmosphere was formed by gases escaping from its hot interior and by comets striking the surface.

By 350 million years ago, fish had evolved in the seas.

Land creatures first appeared about 300 million years ago. Dinosaurs began to evolve about 200 million years ago, but died out some 65 million years ago.

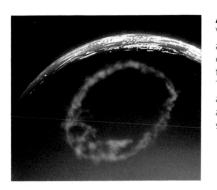

Aurora from space
Viewed from above, auroral displays usually occur in a band centred on the north magnetic pole. This band is where charged atomic particles enter the atmosphere, the result of a solar magnetic storm.

The Sun is vital to us. It provides light, heat, and energy, without which life on Earth would be impossible.

X rays and short-wave ultraviolet radiation from the Sun are absorbed high in the Earth's atmosphere and heat the thin gas to very high temperatures. Lower down, in the stratosphere, ultraviolet light is absorbed by the gas called ozone. This warms the stratosphere and protects us from these otherwise harmful rays from the Sun.

In the northern hemisphere the polar area is light in summer (2) and is dark in winter (4). For the southern hemisphere, (4) is summer and (2) is winter.

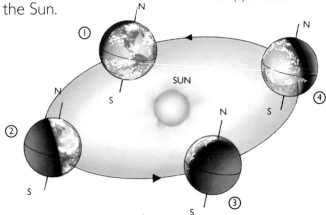

Warmed by sunlight the Earth's surface gives out heat in the form of infrared radiation. The lowest layer—the troposphere—is heated mainly by this radiation and so is colder at higher altitudes.

Besides heating our atmosphere, the Sun also drives the Earth's winds and weather systems. Because more solar energy reaches the equator than the poles, warm air near the equator rises and flows toward the poles. Meanwhile, the cold polar air sinks and flows toward the equator. Rain is also a result of

Auroral display

THE aurora is a varying display of light often seen in the polar skies as brilliant bands of colour. Auroral displays are often called the northern lights (aurora borealis) or southern lights (aurora australis).

An aurora occurs when electrons and protons from space smash into atoms and molecules in the upper atmosphere. This causes them to give out light—

Effect of the solar wind

AROUND the Earth is the magnetosphere, where the Earth's magnetic field exerts considerable power. The solar wind blows around the magnetosphere, squeezing it on the sunward side and drawing it out into a long tail on the far side. As the solar wind blows in gusts, its strength varies, and the shape of the magnetosphere also changes.

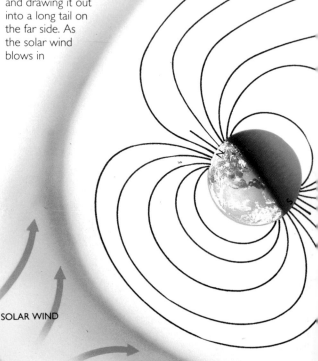

SOLAR WIND

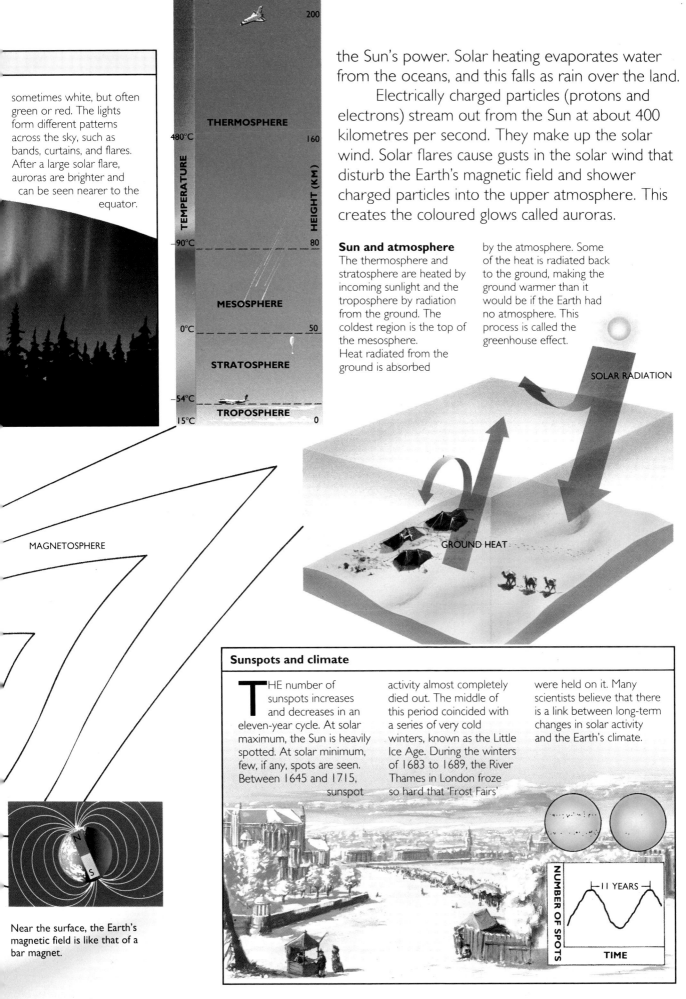

sometimes white, but often green or red. The lights form different patterns across the sky, such as bands, curtains, and flares. After a large solar flare, auroras are brighter and can be seen nearer to the equator.

the Sun's power. Solar heating evaporates water from the oceans, and this falls as rain over the land.

Electrically charged particles (protons and electrons) stream out from the Sun at about 400 kilometres per second. They make up the solar wind. Solar flares cause gusts in the solar wind that disturb the Earth's magnetic field and shower charged particles into the upper atmosphere. This creates the coloured glows called auroras.

Sun and atmosphere

The thermosphere and stratosphere are heated by incoming sunlight and the troposphere by radiation from the ground. The coldest region is the top of the mesosphere. Heat radiated from the ground is absorbed by the atmosphere. Some of the heat is radiated back to the ground, making the ground warmer than it would be if the Earth had no atmosphere. This process is called the greenhouse effect.

THERMOSPHERE

480°C

MESOSPHERE

-90°C

0°C

STRATOSPHERE

-54°C

TROPOSPHERE

15°C

TEMPERATURE

HEIGHT (KM)

200

160

80

50

0

SOLAR RADIATION

GROUND HEAT

MAGNETOSPHERE

Near the surface, the Earth's magnetic field is like that of a bar magnet.

N

S

Sunspots and climate

THE number of sunspots increases and decreases in an eleven-year cycle. At solar maximum, the Sun is heavily spotted. At solar minimum, few, if any, spots are seen. Between 1645 and 1715, sunspot activity almost completely died out. The middle of this period coincided with a series of very cold winters, known as the Little Ice Age. During the winters of 1683 to 1689, the River Thames in London froze so hard that 'Frost Fairs' were held on it. Many scientists believe that there is a link between long-term changes in solar activity and the Earth's climate.

NUMBER OF SPOTS

├── 11 YEARS ──┤

TIME

The Moon is the Earth's natural satellite and our nearest neighbour in space. It travels around the Earth in 27.3 days. It spins once on its axis in the same period of time, so it always keeps the same face turned towards the Earth. The far side of the Moon, therefore, can only be seen from a spacecraft.

Because the Moon is a globe, only half of it is lit by the Sun at a time. When the Moon is close to the Sun in the sky, the Sun illuminates the far side, while the side facing the Earth is in shadow. This is called the 'New Moon' phase. As the Moon moves farther around its orbit, more of its Earth-facing side is lit until, at 'Full Moon', it is on the opposite side of the Earth from the Sun and appears fully illuminated. Half of the Moon's disc is lit midway between New and Full, which is called the 'First Quarter' and midway between Full and New, which is called the 'Last Quarter'.

With a diameter of 3,475 kilometres, the Moon is just over a

Map of the Moon

MAIN features of the Moon have Latin names. The dark plains are called *mare*, which is Latin for 'sea', for that is what early telescopic observers thought they might be. The southern hemisphere contains lighter-coloured highlands peppered with craters. The largest craters are Bailly, 293 kilometres in diameter, and Clavius (232 kilometres). The 95-kilometre-wide crater Copernicus is surrounded by a huge splash of debris that can be seen with the naked eye. Between July 1969 and December 1972, six crewed Apollo missions landed on the Moon. The Apollo landing sites are marked by circled numbers on the map.

A view from lunar orbit
This is a typical view of the Moon as seen from an orbiting spacecraft. The main crater is Langrenus, which lies to the east of *Mare Foecunditatis*, the Sea of Fertility. It is 135 kilometres across and its walls rise to heights of about 2.4 kilometres above the crater floor. Like many other large craters, Langrenus has terraced walls and central mountain peaks. East of Langrenus is a heavily cratered area.

Inside the Moon

The Moon may have an iron-rich core with a radius of about 305 kilometres. This may be surrounded by a partly molten zone. The rocky mantle is about 998 kilometres thick. The crust varies in thickness from about 32 kilometres beneath the *mare* to over 97 kilometres in parts of the highlands.

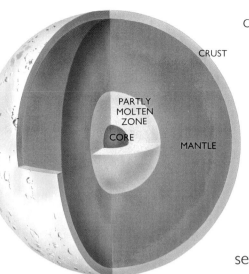

CRUST

PARTLY MOLTEN ZONE

CORE

MANTLE

quarter of the Earth's size. It is a barren world, with no atmosphere and no water. Its pitted surface is covered with craters blasted out by the impact of giant meteorites and asteroid-sized bodies. Most of the impacts took place during the first billion years after the formation of the Moon. The dark plains are regions of volcanic rock called basalt, which flowed out from beneath the surface to fill huge basins previously formed by several colossal impacts.

Apollo landing site

This image shows the Apollo 15 landing site near Mount Hadley. The sky is completely black because the Moon has no air to scatter light and make a blue sky. The landing craft, or Lunar Module, stands in the background. Apollo 15 was the first mission to use the Lunar Rover to explore the region around the spacecraft.

CLEOMEDES

⑰

MARE CRISIUM

MARE TRANQUILLITATIS

⑪

MARE FOECUNDITATIS

LANGRENUS

MARE NECTARIS

PETAVIUS

Phases and tides

FULL MOON

SPRING HIGH

NEAP HIGH

NEAP HIGH

THIRD QUARTER

SPRING HIGH

FIRST QUARTER

NEW MOON

SUNLIGHT

The Moon's proximity affects the Earth's oceans. The pull of the Moon raises tidal bulges on the side of the Earth below the Moon and on the opposite side.

THE shape of the Moon seems to change as it orbits Earth. At the New Moon, the side facing Earth is dark. As the Moon moves around the Earth, more of the Earth-facing side is lit. At the Full Moon phase it appears fully illuminated.

As the Earth spins around, any position on its surface passes two tidal bulges a day, causing a daily rise and fall of the tide.

The Sun also pulls at the Earth, and extreme tidal changes occur when the Sun and Moon are in line (spring tides). The smallest-ranging tides (neap tides) occur when the Sun and Moon pull from different directions – at the first or third quarter.

High spring tide and low spring tide *(below)*.

MERCURY AND VENUS

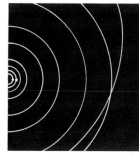

MERCURY and Venus are nearer to the Sun than we are and overtake the Earth at regular intervals during their orbits. Each planet can sometimes be seen in the eastern sky shortly before sunrise or in the western sky soon after sunset. Mercury is difficult to see, but Venus, when it appears, is the brightest object in the sky apart from the Sun and the Moon.

Mercury is a small, barren world that rushes around the Sun once every 88 days. With a diameter of 4,877 kilometres, it is only slightly larger than the Moon. Like the Moon it is covered with craters and has no atmosphere.

Craters of Mercury
In 1974, the *Mariner 10* spacecraft showed that Mercury is peppered with craters, ranging in size from a hundred metres to several hundred kilometres across. The largest feature is the Caloris Basin, which is 1,300 kilometres in diameter and surrounded by rings of mountains. It was probably formed by the impact of a massive meteorite billions of years ago.

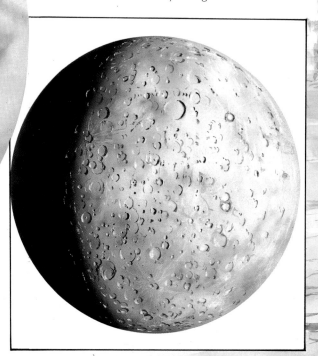

Clouds of Venus
Venus is permanently covered by clouds. They revolve around the planet in about four days and also circulate from the equator toward the poles. This causes the V-shaped formations seen here.

Venusian landscape

THE main features of the planet's surface are rolling uplands (70 per cent of the surface area), lowland plains (20 per cent), and highlands (10 per cent).

The two main highland regions are *Ishtar Terra* in the northern hemisphere and *Aphrodite Terra* near the equator. The Maxwell Mountains in *Ishtar* rise to heights of over 11 kilometres above the average surface level. Other features include valleys, ridges, and cliffs. There are also shallow craters up to 280 kilometres across, large volcanoes, and lava plains. Some of the volcanoes may be active.

The cloud layer is so thick that the Sun cannot be seen directly. Daylight brightness is subdued, like that on Earth during a daytime thunderstorm.

The artist's impression below shows what the Venusian landscape may look like.

Inside Mercury

Mercury probably has a large metallic core, with a radius of about 1,770 kilometres, about 75 per cent of the planet's radius. Above this, there is probably a rocky mantle and a lighter crust.

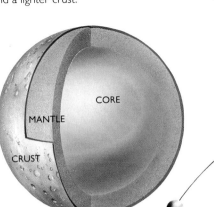

Another Earth?

Many people used to think that conditions on Venus might be similar to those on Earth. Some even suggested that Venus might be able to support thick vegetation, with forests, seas, and a range of wildlife.

Orbits and phases

WHEN Venus passes between the Earth and the Sun, its dark side faces us. Gradually, we begin to see part of its sunlit side. The phase of Venus then grows from a thin crescent to the half-moon stage when the angle between Venus and the Sun is greatest. The phase continues to grow and reaches the full-moon stage when Venus passes behind the Sun. It shrinks back to a thin crescent as Venus begins to catch up with the Earth again. Mercury follows a similar cycle.

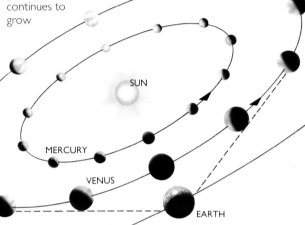

SUN

MERCURY

VENUS

EARTH

Inside Venus

Venus is slightly less dense than the Earth, and its metallic core may be slightly smaller than that of the Earth. Whether the core is liquid or solid is not known. Beyond the core there is probably a rocky mantle. The Venusian crust may be twice as thick as the Earth's crust. Shrouding the whole planet, the main cloud layers in the atmosphere are at heights of between 45 and 65 kilometres.

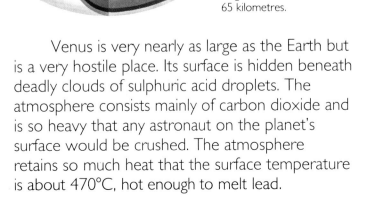

CRUST

MANTLE

CORE

CLOUD LAYER

Venus is very nearly as large as the Earth but is a very hostile place. Its surface is hidden beneath deadly clouds of sulphuric acid droplets. The atmosphere consists mainly of carbon dioxide and is so heavy that any astronaut on the planet's surface would be crushed. The atmosphere retains so much heat that the surface temperature is about 470°C, hot enough to melt lead.

41

TRAVELLING INTO SPACE

WITHOUT the rocket, neither astronaut nor machine could have journeyed into space. The principle of the rocket is simple. If gas is contained in a closed chamber (such as an inflated balloon), the pressure will be the same on every part of the chamber. If gas is allowed to escape through an opening, the balance will be upset. As gas escapes in one direction, the chamber (rocket) will accelerate in the opposite direction. Try releasing the neck of an inflated balloon, and see how it shoots away! By a similar means of propulsion, astronauts and their craft are launched into space.

Yuri Gagarin, the first man to go into orbit, was launched by a Soviet A-series vehicle on April 12, 1961. The Soyuz launch vehicle currently used to take astronauts and materials to and from the orbiting space station, *Mir*, is larger, but it was developed from the same launcher. The Apollo missions to the Moon were launched by the

Space Shuttle flight

The Shuttle orbiter can carry a crew of up to eight people.

At launch, the orbiter is attached to an external tank (ET) that supplies the orbiter's main engines. Two solid-fuel boosters (SRBs) are attached to the ET. The SRBs and main engines fire together. The SRBs drop off after 2 minutes, followed shortly

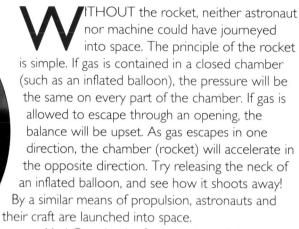

EXTERNAL TANK (ET)

SOLID-FUEL BOOSTERS (SRBs)

CREWED MANOEVRING UNIT (CMU)

United States

NASA

LAUNCH PAD

Future travel

New designs in space technology include the space station, *Freedom (1)*, and Hotol *(2)*, a space plane that will take off and land like an ordinary aircraft. Future spacecraft face the danger of crashing into some of the many pieces of old satellites and rockets now in orbit *(3)*.

① ② ③

Space firsts

The first artificial satellite was *Sputnik 1*, launched into orbit by the Soviet Union on October 4, 1957.

The Soviet cosmonaut Yuri Gagarin made the first crewed spaceflight on April 12, 1961. He completed one orbit of the Earth, reaching a maximum height of 327 kilometres, and landed 108 minutes after lift-off.

The first woman to go into orbit was the Soviet cosmonaut Valentina Tereshkova, launched on June 16, 1963.

by the ET.

Strapped to their backs, rocket-powered manned maneuvering units help astronauts to move outside the orbiter. After work is completed and any cargo released, the orbiter is braked by the firing of small rocket motors. It drops into the atmosphere and is slowed and heated by friction. Finally, it lands on a runway.

Saturn V vehicle. Standing 110 metres tall and weighing about 3,240 tonnes, it was by far the most powerful rocket of its time. Because space flights are very expensive, the American Space Shuttle was a breakthrough. As the world's first reusable spacecraft it was designed to cut the cost of launches by up to 90 per cent. The first orbital flight of a shuttle was made in 1981.

The United States intends to build a crewed space station, called *Freedom*, starting in the late 1990s. It will include contributions from Europe, Japan, and Canada. First, a frame 155 metres long will be built, onto which living and experimental areas will be attached. Solar panels at each end will supply electrical power. Besides being a research centre, *Freedom* will become a new base for robotic and crewed space expeditions – a stepping-stone to the Moon, Mars, and beyond.

④

⑤

RE-ENTRY

SATELLITE

AUTOMATIC LANDING

TOUCHDOWN

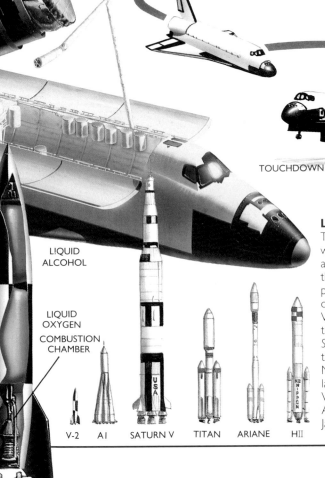

LIQUID ALCOHOL

LIQUID OXYGEN

COMBUSTION CHAMBER

V-2   A1   SATURN V   TITAN   ARIANE   HII

Launch vehicles
⑥

The German V-2 *(far left)* was propelled by liquid alcohol and liquid oxygen that mixed and burned to produce hot gases in the combustion chamber. The V-2 is compared here with the Soviet A1 that launched *Sputnik 1*, the giant Saturn V that launched men to the Moon, and the Titan that launched the Voyagers and Vikings, the European Ariane, and the Japanese HII.

Mining on the Moon
In the 21st century, a permanent lunar base (4) may be used for mining lunar materials. These could be transported from the Moon by cargo craft (5) and into orbit around the Earth. They could then be used to build large structures such as space stations (6).

MARS

MANY people used to believe that Mars was inhabited by intelligent beings, and even as recently as 1960, many astronomers thought that some form of vegetation might exist there. Many believers in Martian life were disappointed, however, when two Viking spacecraft landed on Mars in 1976 and analysed the soil. They found no evidence of life of any kind.

Mars is a small world, about half the Earth's diameter and a tenth of its mass. Often called the red planet, its colour is caused by the iron oxide, or rust, in its soil.

Martian globe

This view shows one side of Mars. The main features include the giant extinct volcano *Olympus Mons* and three large volcanoes near the equator. As shown by the Latin names that describe them, many landforms on Mars are similar to those found on Earth: *planum* (plateau), *planitia* (plain), *tholus* (domed hill), *mons* (mountain or volcano), *montes* (mountains).

A layer of dust coats the surface of Deimos.

Stickney Crater on the surface of Phobos.

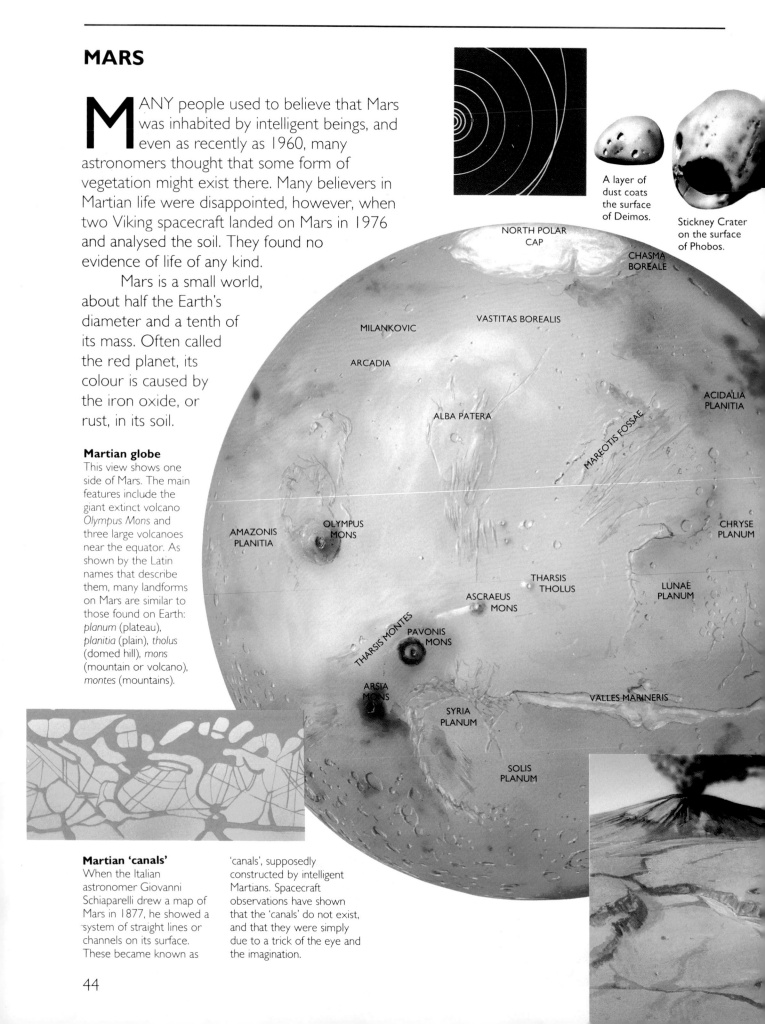

NORTH POLAR CAP

CHASMA BOREALE

VASTITAS BOREALIS

MILANKOVIC

ARCADIA

ACIDALIA PLANITIA

ALBA PATERA

MAREOTIS FOSSAE

AMAZONIS PLANITIA

OLYMPUS MONS

CHRYSE PLANUM

THARSIS THOLUS

LUNAE PLANUM

ASCRAEUS MONS

THARSIS MONTES

PAVONIS MONS

ARSIA MONS

VALLES MARINERIS

SYRIA PLANUM

SOLIS PLANUM

Martian 'canals'

When the Italian astronomer Giovanni Schiaparelli drew a map of Mars in 1877, he showed a system of straight lines or channels on its surface. These became known as 'canals', supposedly constructed by intelligent Martians. Spacecraft observations have shown that the 'canals' do not exist, and that they were simply due to a trick of the eye and the imagination.

Inside Mars

Because we know that Mars is less dense than the Earth, we can also tell that it does not have the large iron core that our planet possesses. Evidence from orbiting spacecraft suggests that it has a core of some kind, possibly made up of a compound such as iron sulphide that is less dense than pure iron. It is likely to be about 2,400 kilometres in diameter and surrounded by a rocky mantle. The Martian crust is about 95 kilometres thick.

CORE

CRUST

MANTLE

On the dusty, boulder-strewn surface there are huge but apparently extinct volcanoes, giant canyons, and features that look like dried-up riverbeds. A vast canyon system called *Valles Marineris* runs for about 4,000 kilometres and has a maximum depth of 6.5 kilometres. It is four times deeper than the Grand Canyon in Arizona!

The thin Martian atmosphere consists mainly of carbon dioxide. Although the surface temperature sometimes creeps above 0°C at the equator, the average is about −50°C, and it drops to −135°C at the winter pole.

Martian satellites

Phobos, the inner moon, travels around Mars in just 7.6 hours, less than one third of a Martian day. Deimos revolves around Mars in 30.2 hours. Both are rocky bodies of irregular shape.

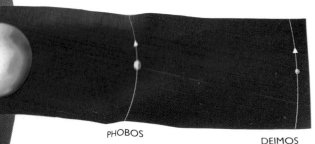

PHOBOS

DEIMOS

DID YOU KNOW?

OLYMPUS MONS   MOUNT EVEREST

The summit of *Olympus Mons* stands over 25 kilometres above the mean Martian surface. By comparison, Earth's Mount Everest seems tiny.

People used to believe that scenes like this might be possible on Mars!

N

S

The north polar cap reaches its maximum size during the northern hemisphere winter. The cap begins to shrink in the spring. During the summer, the northern cap shrinks to its smallest and the southern cap grows to its largest.

Long ago, when Martian volcanoes were pouring out gas, dust, and lava, the atmosphere would have been thicker than it is now. Heavy rains may have fallen, and rivers would have flowed across the planet's surface.

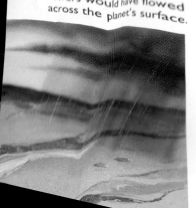

Mission to Mars

CREWED missions to Mars may begin early in the 21st century. One NASA mission plan is illustrated here.

After leaving Earth orbit, the spacecraft splits into two parts that spin around each other on the ends of a long tether. This is intended to produce a sensation similar to gravity in the crew quarters. After the spacecraft has entered orbit around Mars, a lander vehicle will take the crew to the surface. The round trip may take as long as three years, with the crew spending over a year on the Martian surface.

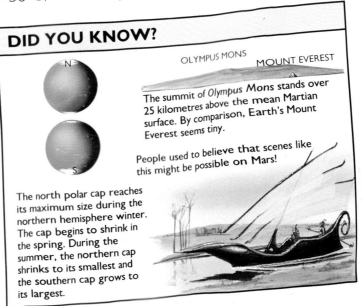

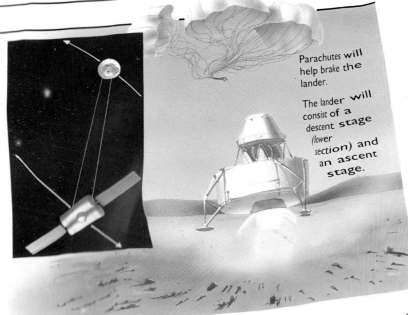

Parachutes will help brake the lander.

The lander will consist of a descent stage (lower section) and an ascent stage.

THE OUTER PLANETS

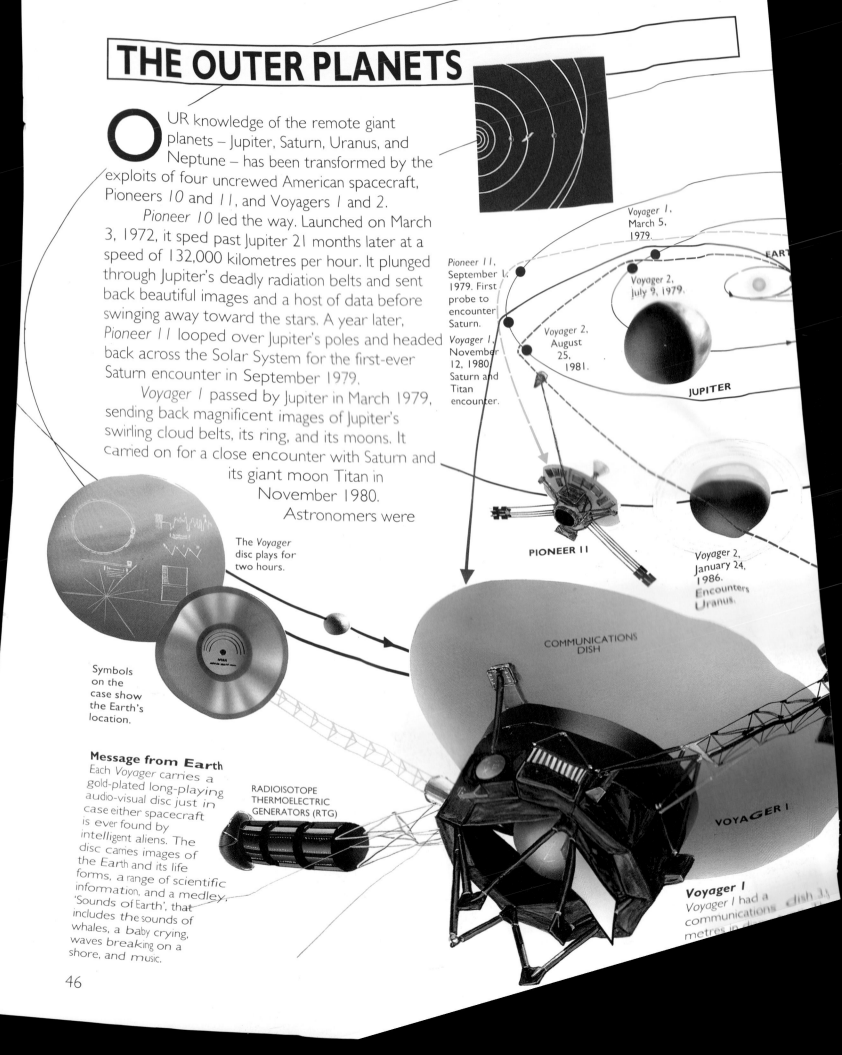

OUR knowledge of the remote giant planets – Jupiter, Saturn, Uranus, and Neptune – has been transformed by the exploits of four uncrewed American spacecraft, Pioneers 10 and 11, and Voyagers 1 and 2.

Pioneer 10 led the way. Launched on March 3, 1972, it sped past Jupiter 21 months later at a speed of 132,000 kilometres per hour. It plunged through Jupiter's deadly radiation belts and sent back beautiful images and a host of data before swinging away toward the stars. A year later, *Pioneer 11* looped over Jupiter's poles and headed back across the Solar System for the first-ever Saturn encounter in September 1979.

Voyager 1 passed by Jupiter in March 1979, sending back magnificent images of Jupiter's swirling cloud belts, its ring, and its moons. It carried on for a close encounter with Saturn and its giant moon Titan in November 1980.

Astronomers were

Voyager 1,
March 5,
1979.

Pioneer 11,
September 1,
1979. First
probe to
encounter
Saturn.

Voyager 1,
November
12, 1980,
Saturn and
Titan
encounter.

Voyager 2,
July 9, 1979.

Voyager 2,
August
25,
1981.

EART

JUPITER

PIONEER 11

Voyager 2,
January 24,
1986.
Encounters
Uranus.

The *Voyager* disc plays for two hours.

Symbols on the case show the Earth's location.

COMMUNICATIONS DISH

Message from Earth
Each *Voyager* carries a gold-plated long-playing audio-visual disc just in case either spacecraft is ever found by intelligent aliens. The disc carries images of the Earth and its life forms, a range of scientific information, and a medley, 'Sounds of Earth', that includes the sounds of whales, a baby crying, waves breaking on a shore, and music.

RADIOISOTOPE THERMOELECTRIC GENERATORS (RTG)

VOYAGER 1

Voyager 1
Voyager 1 had a communications dish 3.5 metres in di

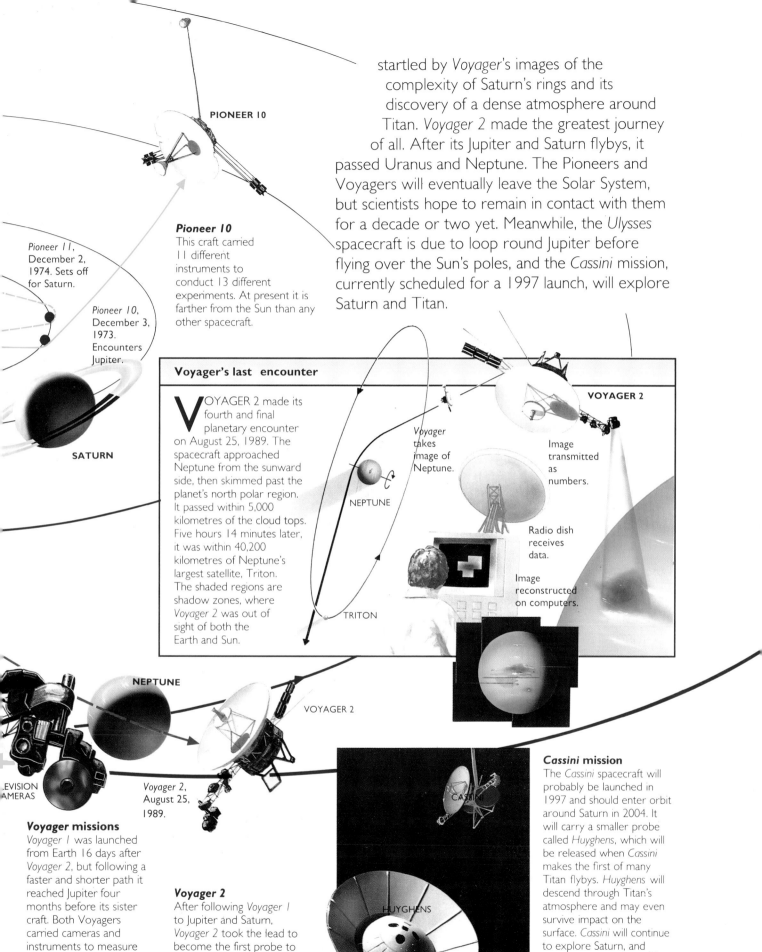

PIONEER 10

Pioneer 10
This craft carried 11 different instruments to conduct 13 different experiments. At present it is farther from the Sun than any other spacecraft.

Pioneer 11, December 2, 1974. Sets off for Saturn.

Pioneer 10, December 3, 1973. Encounters Jupiter.

SATURN

startled by *Voyager*'s images of the complexity of Saturn's rings and its discovery of a dense atmosphere around Titan. *Voyager 2* made the greatest journey of all. After its Jupiter and Saturn flybys, it passed Uranus and Neptune. The Pioneers and Voyagers will eventually leave the Solar System, but scientists hope to remain in contact with them for a decade or two yet. Meanwhile, the *Ulysses* spacecraft is due to loop round Jupiter before flying over the Sun's poles, and the *Cassini* mission, currently scheduled for a 1997 launch, will explore Saturn and Titan.

Voyager's last encounter

VOYAGER 2 made its fourth and final planetary encounter on August 25, 1989. The spacecraft approached Neptune from the sunward side, then skimmed past the planet's north polar region. It passed within 5,000 kilometres of the cloud tops. Five hours 14 minutes later, it was within 40,200 kilometres of Neptune's largest satellite, Triton. The shaded regions are shadow zones, where *Voyager 2* was out of sight of both the Earth and Sun.

Voyager takes image of Neptune.

NEPTUNE

TRITON

VOYAGER 2

Image transmitted as numbers.

Radio dish receives data.

Image reconstructed on computers.

NEPTUNE

VOYAGER 2

Voyager 2, August 25, 1989.

EVISION AMERAS

Voyager missions
Voyager 1 was launched from Earth 16 days after *Voyager 2,* but following a faster and shorter path it reached Jupiter four months before its sister craft. Both Voyagers carried cameras and instruments to measure temperature and magnetic fields. RTG provided electrical power.

Voyager 2
After following *Voyager 1* to Jupiter and Saturn, *Voyager 2* took the lead to become the first probe to reach Uranus in January 1986 and Neptune in August 1989.

CASSI

HUYGHENS

TITAN

Cassini mission
The *Cassini* spacecraft will probably be launched in 1997 and should enter orbit around Saturn in 2004. It will carry a smaller probe called *Huyghens*, which will be released when *Cassini* makes the first of many Titan flybys. *Huyghens* will descend through Titan's atmosphere and may even survive impact on the surface. *Cassini* will continue to explore Saturn, and its rings and moons, for several years.

JUPITER

GIANT Jupiter is the largest of the planets. With a diameter eleven times that of the Earth, its globe could contain over a thousand planets the same size as ours! It is more than twice as massive as all the other planets in the Solar System put together.

Despite its huge size, Jupiter rotates on its axis in just 9 hours 55 minutes. Because it spins so quickly, it bulges at the equator and is slightly flattened at the poles. Covered in light and dark bands of turbulent cloud, Jupiter can easily be seen in some detail through a fairly small telescope. Like the Sun, Jupiter is composed

Jupiter's moons
The outer satellites were probably once asteroids, now captured and imprisoned in their orbits by Jupiter. The innermost eight may have been born in the same cloud of matter as Jupiter itself.

Jupiter and its ring
Jupiter's swirling clouds form bright zones and darker belts which lie parallel to its equator. The zones are higher and colder than the belts. Constantly moving, the waves, eddies, and plumes in the belts change shape rapidly. Jupiter also has a ring system, first discovered by *Voyager 1* in 1979. Unlike Saturn's, the ring is faint, dark, and dusty, and probably only a few kilometres thick.

1 2 3 4	5 6 7 8	CALLISTO	GANYMEDE	EUROPA	IO	9 10 11 12
1. SINOPE	5. ELARA					9. THEBE
2. PASIPHAE	6. LYSITHEA					10. AMALTHEA
3. CARME	7. HIMALIA					11. ADRASTEA
4. ANANKE	8. LEDA					12. METIS

Inside Jupiter

JUPITER's poisonous atmosphere extends below the visible clouds to a depth of about 965 kilometres. There it meets a deep ocean of liquid hydrogen. About 19,300 kilometres down, liquid hydrogen behaves like a metal. This liquid metallic hydrogen zone is more than 40,220 kilometres deep. Right at the centre is an extremely hot, rocky core.

LIQUID HYDROGEN

LIQUID METALLIC HYDROGEN

CORE

ATMOSPHERE

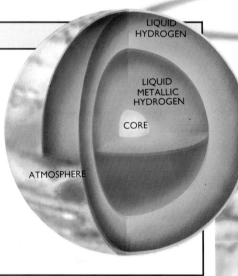

The Great Red Spot
The Great Red Spot is a stormy region of high pressure. The sequence of images (*right*) shows that it rotates in a counter-clockwise direction, taking about six days to do so. Turbulent air currents flow past the Spot in opposite directions on its north and south sides. Waves and eddies are whipped up wherever these currents collide with the Spot. Smaller white spots either revolve around it, or merge with it.

IO EUROPA

GANYMEDE CALLISTO

Galilean satellites

The four 'Galileans' – Io, Europa, Ganymede, and Callisto – were the first satellites, apart of course from our Moon, to be discovered. Io and Europa are similar in size to the Earth's Moon and are rocky bodies. Europa is coated with a layer of ice. Ganymede and Callisto, both made from a mixture of rock and ice, are about the same size as the planet Mercury.

Galileo mission

BECAUSE its booster was not powerful enough to reach Jupiter directly, the *Galileo* spacecraft was sent to fly by Venus once and the Earth twice. Each time it swings past a planet, *Galileo* can pick up more energy, until it is moving fast enough to travel the distance to Jupiter.

Galileo should reach Jupiter in December 1995. It will study Jupiter and its moons from orbit and release a small probe that will plunge into the depths of Jupiter's atmosphere.

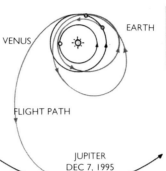

VENUS EARTH

FLIGHT PATH

JUPITER
DEC 7, 1995

mainly of the elements hydrogen and helium. Beneath the cloud there is no solid surface, and apart from a central rocky core, Jupiter is a spinning globe of liquid. Although the cloud tops are cold (about −138°C), the interior of Jupiter has a central temperature of over 20,000°C, and the planet gives out twice as much heat as it receives from the Sun. Jupiter has a family of sixteen satellites and a thin dusty ring, but its most famous feature is the Great Red Spot, now known to be a huge rotating weather system.

Volcanoes on Io

In 1979 the two *Voyager* spacecraft discovered nine active volcanoes on the satellite Io. Shown here is an eruption in progress, with a 290-kilometre-high plume of material ejected into space. Io has no impact craters on its surface. The mountains and *calderas* (volcanic craters) are due to past and present volcanic activity. The yellowish colour of the surface is caused by the presence of sulphur.

SATURN

SATURN is the sixth farthest planet from the Sun, the most distant known in ancient times. To many people, Saturn is also the most fascinating planet because of its system of beautiful rings.

Saturn is one of the four giant planets, and, like the other three, is composed mainly of hydrogen and helium. It is the second largest planet in the Solar System after Jupiter, with a diameter at its equator 9 times larger than the Earth's. It spins very quickly, taking only 10 hours 39 minutes to complete a rotation, and so shows a definite bulge at its equator.

Close-up pictures of Saturn's globe show it as striped. What we see is the upper part of the planet's deep atmosphere. The darker and lighter bands are long, narrow layers of cloud circling the planet. Very strong winds blow in Saturn's atmosphere, sometimes with speeds of more than 1,600 kilometres per hour.

The rings of Saturn have

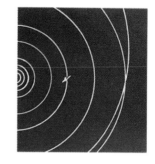

Inside Saturn
Saturn's globe may consist of a central rocky icy core surrounded by a layer of liquid metallic hydrogen and a deep envelope of liquid hydrogen. The thick atmosphere is composed mainly of hydrogen and helium gases.

ATMOSPHER

The jewel of the skies
Saturn's rings would be a marvellous sight from one of its moons. But only a small telescope is needed to view the main part of the ring system from Earth. A small telescope will also show Saturn's giant moon Titan and its changing position as it revolves around Saturn.

MIMAS

DIONE

The rings of Saturn

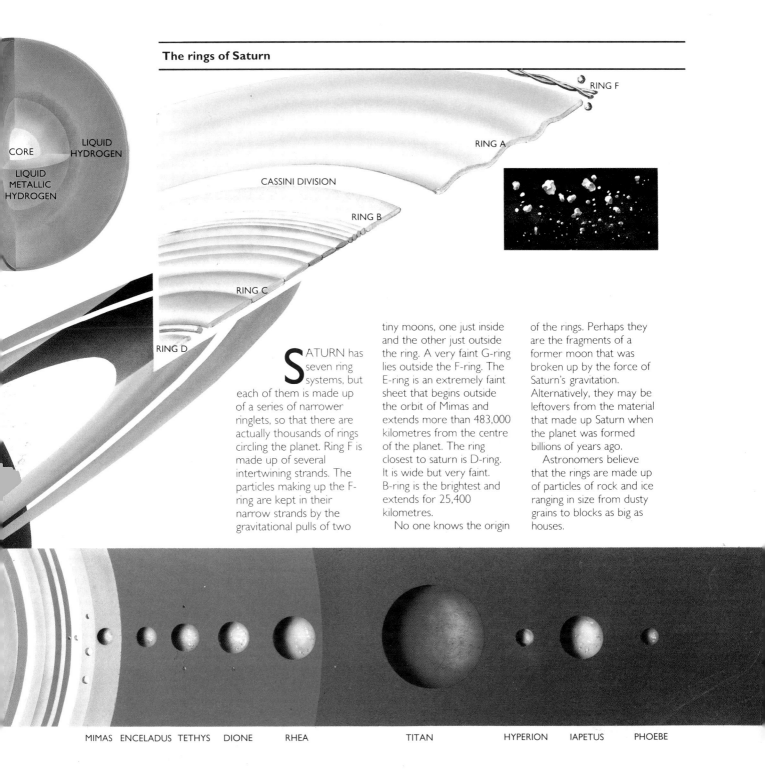

CORE

LIQUID HYDROGEN

LIQUID METALLIC HYDROGEN

RING F

RING A

CASSINI DIVISION

RING B

RING C

RING D

MIMAS ENCELADUS TETHYS DIONE RHEA TITAN HYPERION IAPETUS PHOEBE

SATURN has seven ring systems, but each of them is made up of a series of narrower ringlets, so that there are actually thousands of rings circling the planet. Ring F is made up of several intertwining strands. The particles making up the F-ring are kept in their narrow strands by the gravitational pulls of two tiny moons, one just inside and the other just outside the ring. A very faint G-ring lies outside the F-ring. The E-ring is an extremely faint sheet that begins outside the orbit of Mimas and extends more than 483,000 kilometres from the centre of the planet. The ring closest to saturn is D-ring. It is wide but very faint. B-ring is the brightest and extends for 25,400 kilometres.

No one knows the origin of the rings. Perhaps they are the fragments of a former moon that was broken up by the force of Saturn's gravitation. Alternatively, they may be leftovers from the material that made up Saturn when the planet was formed billions of years ago.

Astronomers believe that the rings are made up of particles of rock and ice ranging in size from dusty grains to blocks as big as houses.

Saturn's moons

The *Voyager* spacecrafts' flybys discovered much new information about Saturn and its family of moons. Nine were previously known from observation by telescope,

HYPERION

but Voyagers *1* and *2* found a total of about 18. Some are very small, and it is still uncertain exactly how many there are. Titan is the largest moon and has a dense atmosphere composed mainly of nitrogen. The middle-sized moons have icy crusts with rocky cores. Their surfaces are peppered with craters probably caused by meteorite bombardment.

been visible through telescopes for more than 300 years and have intrigued astronomers ever since they were discovered. They circle the planet exactly at its equator and cast a clear shadow. Close inspection by the *Voyager* space probes revealed the existence of several separate rings and a much more complicated structure of the ring system than previously thought. Saturn rotates on a tilted axis, so our view of the rings from Earth changes as Saturn moves around the Sun.

URANUS

URANUS was the first planet to be discovered through a telescope. Mercury, Venus, Mars, Jupiter, and Saturn all can be seen with the naked eye, and since ancient times they have been known as planets. But it was not until March 13, 1781, that the historic discovery of another planet was made. Uranus, the seventh planet from the Sun, was found by William Herschel through a telescope he had made himself.

Smaller and denser than Jupiter or Saturn, Uranus is the third largest planet in the Solar System. With a diameter of 51,200 kilometres, it is nearly four times the size of the Earth. The deep Uranian atmosphere of hydrogen and helium also contains methane gas, which gives the planet its blue-green colour. Cloud belts around Uranus are very cold, with temperatures of below −185°C. The axis of Uranus is tilted in an unusual way. No planet has its axis exactly perpendicular to the plane of its orbit, but most

1965
1985
SUN
1923
1945

Seasons of Uranus
Because of the way its axis is tilted, the north and south poles of Uranus point alternately towards and away from the Sun as the planet travels around its orbit. At each pole a 42-year 'day' or season of continual sunlight is followed by 42 years of darkness.

1. BELINDA
2. CRESSIDA
3. PORTIA
4. ROSALIND

OBERON   TITANIA   UMBRIEL   ARIEL   MIRANDA   PUCK   1 2 3 4 5 6 7 8   9

5. DESDEMONA
6. JULIET
7. BIANCA
8. OPHELIA
9. CORDELIA

The moons of Uranus
Uranus has fifteen satellites, the ten smallest of which were discovered by the spacecraft *Voyager 2*. With a few exceptions, such as Titania, the moons follow a well-ordered pattern in their positioning. Generally, the closer they are to Uranus, the smaller their size. Titania, the largest, is 1,580 kilometres across.

The largest moons consist of a mixture of ice and rock. Various features of their rugged landscapes, including the dramatic canyons and craters of Umbriel, have been revealed by *Voyager*'s close-up photography. The smaller satellites are tiny worlds ranging from 160 kilometres to under 26 kilometres in diameter.

Miranda is about seven times smaller than the Earth's Moon. *Voyager 2* provided some spectacular photographs of its surface. Strange dark grooves, light chevron-shaped markings, mountains, valleys, and cliffs up to 14 kilometres high have been recorded. Long ago, Miranda may have broken up and re-formed in a jumbled way to create the unusual markings.

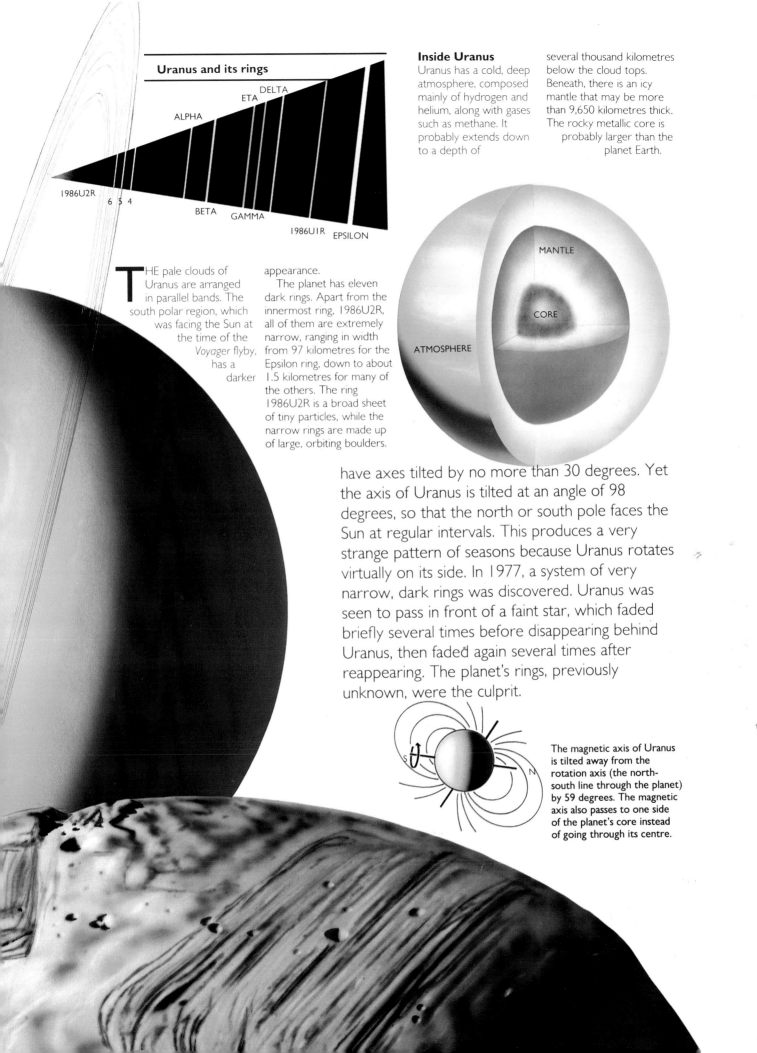

Uranus and its rings

1986U2R
6 5 4
ALPHA
ETA
DELTA
BETA
GAMMA
1986U1R
EPSILON

Inside Uranus

Uranus has a cold, deep atmosphere, composed mainly of hydrogen and helium, along with gases such as methane. It probably extends down to a depth of several thousand kilometres below the cloud tops. Beneath, there is an icy mantle that may be more than 9,650 kilometres thick. The rocky metallic core is probably larger than the planet Earth.

MANTLE

CORE

ATMOSPHERE

THE pale clouds of Uranus are arranged in parallel bands. The south polar region, which was facing the Sun at the time of the *Voyager* flyby, has a darker appearance.

The planet has eleven dark rings. Apart from the innermost ring, 1986U2R, all of them are extremely narrow, ranging in width from 97 kilometres for the Epsilon ring, down to about 1.5 kilometres for many of the others. The ring 1986U2R is a broad sheet of tiny particles, while the narrow rings are made up of large, orbiting boulders.

have axes tilted by no more than 30 degrees. Yet the axis of Uranus is tilted at an angle of 98 degrees, so that the north or south pole faces the Sun at regular intervals. This produces a very strange pattern of seasons because Uranus rotates virtually on its side. In 1977, a system of very narrow, dark rings was discovered. Uranus was seen to pass in front of a faint star, which faded briefly several times before disappearing behind Uranus, then faded again several times after reappearing. The planet's rings, previously unknown, were the culprit.

The magnetic axis of Uranus is tilted away from the rotation axis (the north-south line through the planet) by 59 degrees. The magnetic axis also passes to one side of the planet's core instead of going through its centre.

NEPTUNE

NEPTUNE was the first planet to be discovered as the result of prediction. Astronomers had noticed that Uranus was not moving quite as they expected, and so they began to think that another, more distant planet might be disturbing its orbit. John Adams in England and Urbain Le Verrier in France independently calculated where the missing planet should be, and it was duly found in September 1846, by Johann Galle and Heinrich D'Arrest of the Berlin Observatory.

With a diameter of 50,000 kilometres, it is slightly smaller than Uranus. It is thirty times further from the Sun than the Earth is and takes nearly 165 years to complete each orbit. *Voyager 2*'s magnificent pictures showed that Neptune is a bluish planet with parallel cloud belts and bright high-altitude methane

Great Dark Spot
About the same size as the Earth, the Great Dark Spot is a stormy weather system. The bright wispy clouds occur 50 to 100 kilometres above the planet's main layer of cloud.

Neptune seen from Triton
From a spacecraft hovering above the southern hemisphere of Triton, this is what you would see. South is at the top of the image, and from this angle the Great Dark Spot, a smaller dark spot, and the faint ring system are visible on Neptune. The area around Triton's south pole, seen here, is covered in nitrogen ice.

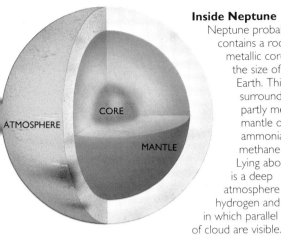

Inside Neptune

Neptune probably contains a rocky metallic core about the size of the Earth. This is surrounded by a partly melted mantle of water, ammonia, and methane ices. Lying above this is a deep atmosphere of hydrogen and helium in which parallel bands of cloud are visible.

ATMOSPHERE

CORE

MANTLE

1989N3R

1989N4R

1989N2R

1989N1R

Neptune's satellites

The innermost moons (1989N1 to 1989N6) are small irregular worlds with darkish surfaces and diameters ranging from 50 to 400 kilometres. Nereid, the outermost moon, has a highly elliptical orbit. Its mean distance from Neptune is 5,512,000 kilometres. Triton, with a diameter of 2,700 kilometres, is by far the largest of Neptune's moons. Triton's exposed icy surface has ridges, cracks, craters, and plains, and a pink polar cap of frozen nitrogen and methane.

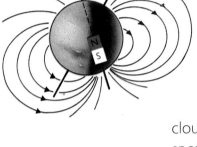

N

S

Neptune's magnetic axis is tilted toward its rotation axis by an angle of 47 degrees. The magnetic field behaves as if there were a bar magnet located off-centre, away from the rotation axis, and about halfway to the surface.

NEPTUNE has two very narrow rings and two faint broader ones.

The innermost ring, 1989N3R, is a faint dusty ring that may be up to 1,690 kilometres wide. The next ring, 1989N2R, is only about 14 kilometres wide. Ring 1989N4R is a broad dusty sheet 5,800 kilometres wide. The outermost, 1989N1R, is only about 50 kilometres wide. Photographs taken by *Voyager* show that there are three brighter regions on the outermost ring where its material is more concentrated.

clouds. The most striking feature is a huge dark spot, known as the Great Dark Spot, which seems similar to the Great Red Spot on Jupiter. Like Jupiter and Saturn, Neptune gives out more energy than it receives from the Sun and so must be very hot inside. (Strangely, Uranus is an exception and does not seem to emit energy in this way.)

Neptune has a ring system and eight moons. Triton, the largest moon, is a fascinating world. It has a very thin atmosphere made up mainly of nitrogen with a small amount of methane. It has volcanoes or geysers on its surface, and at −235°C, it is the coldest known place in the Solar System.

N6 N5 N3   N4   N2   1989N1   TRITON   NEREID

A visit to Triton

IF you could stand on the icy surface of Triton, the scene might well look like this. An erupting geyser is ejecting nitrogen that is laden with darker material brought from beneath the surface. The geyser's plume drifts slowly downwind, and as the darker material falls to the ground, it paints a shadowy streak on the underlying ice.

PLUTO

PLUTO is, for most of the time, the farthest planet from the Sun. However, Pluto reached perihelion (its closest approach to the Sun) in 1989, and so Neptune takes the place as most distant planet until 1999.

Pluto is a tiny world, composed of a mixture of rock and ice. With a diameter of 2,300 kilometres, it is by far the smallest of the planets and is even smaller than seven of the moons in the Solar System. It rotates in 6.4 days, and variations in its brightness suggest there are darker and lighter patches on its surface. The surface is probably covered with methane ice and may be pitted with craters. Pluto is a very cold world (below −210°C), but when it is near perihelion, some of its ice evaporates to give it an exceedingly thin atmosphere.

Pluto's strange orbit
At perihelion, Pluto is closer to the Sun than Neptune is, but because its orbit is tilted at an angle of 17 degrees, it passes above Neptune's orbit each time the orbits cross. The diagram on the left shows the position of Pluto and Neptune as they were late in 1990.

NEPTUNE PLUTO
SUN
29.7 AU
49.4 AU
CHARON

Inside Pluto
Pluto probably contains a core about 1,770 kilometres in diameter, made of a rock-ice mixture. This is surrounded by a 240-kilometre water-ice mantle and a thin crust of methane ice.

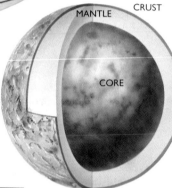

MANTLE CRUST
CORE

Discovery of Pluto
Pluto's slow motion, in relation to background stars, shows up in photographs taken at twenty-four-hour intervals. Clyde Tombaugh discovered Pluto by noting how its tiny image had changed position between photographs taken on January 23 and 29, 1930.

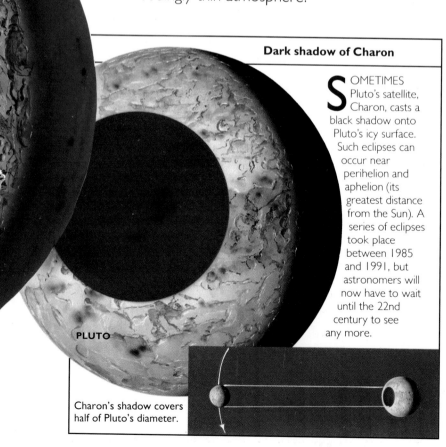

CHARON

PLUTO

Dark shadow of Charon

SOMETIMES Pluto's satellite, Charon, casts a black shadow onto Pluto's icy surface. Such eclipses can occur near perihelion and aphelion (its greatest distance from the Sun). A series of eclipses took place between 1985 and 1991, but astronomers will now have to wait until the 22nd century to see any more.

Charon's shadow covers half of Pluto's diameter.

Planet X

SINCE the late 19th century, astronomers have believed that there is another planet – Planet X – that is affecting the orbit of Uranus. Pluto was found to be far too small to have an effect and some astronomers believe that there is a tenth planet yet to be discovered.

Clyde Tombaugh used a new 33-centimetre refractor at the Flagstaff Observatory in Arizona to find Pluto in 1930.

IS THERE LIFE BEYOND EARTH?

N the universe, the only life we know exists on a planet, our Earth, which revolves around a star, our Sun. There are 100 billion stars in our galaxy alone, and astronomers believe that many of them have planets. Modern technology has not yet breached the vast distances to give us a direct view of planets beyond our Solar System. We do know, however, that some stars are surrounded by discs of dust similar to the one from which our Solar System was born. A good example is the star Beta Pictoris (*below left*), perhaps itself a newly forming system of planets.

Many scientists think that suitable conditions exist on many planets and that life, perhaps even intelligent life, must be common in the universe. Others feel the complex chain of events that led to life on Earth was unique.

We cannot travel to the stars yet, but we can search for messages that alien civilizations may be broadcasting, and we can try sending out our own messages into space. The first attempt to broadcast our own existence was made on November 16, 1974, when a coded message was sent from the 300-metre Arecibo radio dish (*below*) towards the star cluster M13 (*below right*) in the constellation Hercules (*bottom right*). M13 contains several hundred thousand stars, but because it is 25,000 light-years away, if we ever receive a reply, it will be 50,000 years from now!

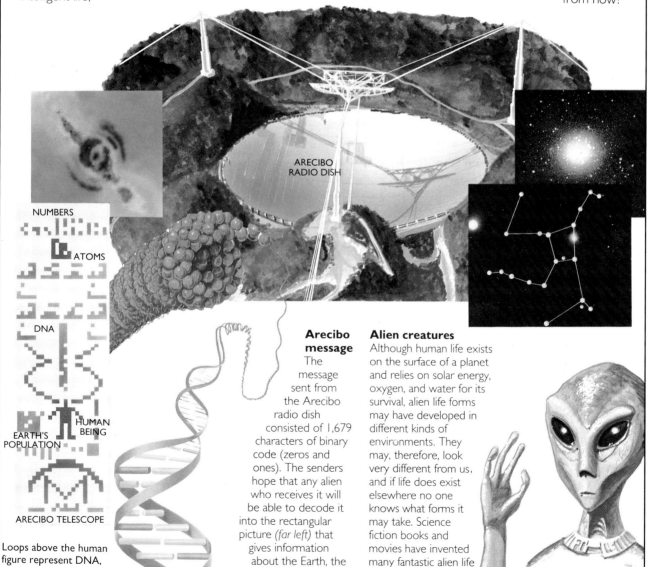

NUMBERS

ATOMS

DNA

EARTH'S POPULATION

HUMAN BEING

ARECIBO TELESCOPE

ARECIBO RADIO DISH

Loops above the human figure represent DNA, the twisted string of molecules that carries the information needed to reproduce life.

Arecibo message
The message sent from the Arecibo radio dish consisted of 1,679 characters of binary code (zeros and ones). The senders hope that any alien who receives it will be able to decode it into the rectangular picture (*far left*) that gives information about the Earth, the Solar System, human beings, and the way the message was sent.

Alien creatures
Although human life exists on the surface of a planet and relies on solar energy, oxygen, and water for its survival, alien life forms may have developed in different kinds of environments. They may, therefore, look very different from us, and if life does exist elsewhere no one knows what forms it may take. Science fiction books and movies have invented many fantastic alien life forms, but no one knows for sure how close or far from the truth any of them are!

SPACE FACTS

THE PLANETS

Mean distance from Sun	Mercury	Venus	Earth	Mars	Jupiter	Saturn	Uranus	Neptune	Pluto
Astronomical units (AU)	0.39	0.72	1.00	1.52	5.20	9.54	19.18	30.06	39.44
Millions of kilometres	58	108	150	228	779	1,427	2,869	4,496	5,899
Time taken to orbit Sun									
Earth years	0.24	0.62	1.00	1.88	11.86	29.46	84.01	164.79	247.7
Diameter (at planet's equator)									
Kilometres	4,877	12,100	12,753	6,785	142,879	120,514	51,166	49,557	2,300
Mass (times Earth's)	0.055	0.815	1.000	0.107	317.9	95.2	14.5	17.1	0.002
Density (water = 1)	5.43	5.25	5.52	3.95	1.33	0.69	1.29	1.64	2.03

PLANETARY SATELLITES

Planet	Satellites	Mean distance from planet (kilometres)	Maximum diameter (kilometres)
Earth	Moon	384,390	3,480
Mars	Phobos	9,380	27
	Deimos	23,460	16
Jupiter	Metis	127,930	40
	Adrastea	128,950	25
	Amalthea	181,330	275
	Thebe	221,880	95
	Io	421,560	3,640
	Europa	670,790	3,140
	Ganymede	106,980	5,260
	Callisto	1,882,530	4,790
	Leda	11,090,840	16
	Himalia	11,477,000	175
	Lysithea	11,716,740	40
	Elara	11,734,440	80
	Ananke	21,190,530	30
	Carme	22,526,000	40
	Pasiphae	23,491,400	70
	Sinope	23,652,300	40
Saturn	1981S13	133,550	19
	Atlas	137,620	40
	Prometheus	139,320	135
	Pandora	141,670	110
	Epimetheus	151,390	135
	Janus	151,440	225
	Mimas	185,520	385
	Enceladus	237,970	500
	Tethys	294,610	1,050
	Telesto	294,610	25
	Calypso	294,610	30
	Dione	377,310	1,120
	Helene	377,310	35
	Rhea	526,950	1,530
	Titan	1,221,550	5,150
	Hyperion	1,480,680	345
	Iapetus	3,560,720	1,440
	Phoebe	12,949,230	215

Planet	Satellites	Mean distance from planet (kilometres)	Maximum diameter (kilometres)
Uranus	Cordelia	49,730	30
	Ophelia	53,740	30
	Bianca	59,150	40
	Cressida	61,750	70
	Desdemona	62,650	55
	Juliet	64,360	80
	Portia	66,080	110
	Rosalind	69,910	55
	Belinda	75,240	70
	Puck	85,980	150
	Miranda	129,750	465
	Ariel	191,150	1,160
	Umbriel	265,970	1,165
	Titania	435,720	1,575
	Oberon	582,460	1,520
Neptune	1989N6	47,950	50
	1989N5	50,040	80
	1989N3	52,450	175
	1989N4	61,950	150
	1989N2	73,530	190
	1989N1	117,620	400
	Triton	354,780	2,700
	Nereid	5,512,430	340
Pluto	Charon	19,630	1,190

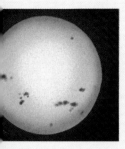

PROFILE OF THE SUN

Diameter (times Earth's)	109
Kilometres	1,390,000
Mass (times Earth's)	332,800
Mean density (water = 1)	1.410
Rotation period (at equator)	24.9 days
Composition	73% hydrogen
	25% helium
	2% heavier elements
Surface temperature	5,500°C
Central temperature	15,000,000°C
Age	4,600 million years

THE BRIGHTEST STARS IN THE SKY

Name	Constellation to which star belongs	Apparent magnitude
Sirius	Canis Major	−1.46
Canopus	Carina	−0.72
Rigil Kent (Alpha Centauri)	Centaurus	−0.27
Arcturus	Bootes	−0.04
Vega	Lyra	+0.03
Capella	Auriga	+0.08
Rigel	Orion	+0.12
Procyon	Canis Minor	+0.38
Achernar	Eridanus	+0.46
Betelgeuse	Orion	+0.50 (var)

Note: (var) means that the star varies in brightness.
Apparent magnitude: brightness, as seen from Earth; the lower the magnitude, the brighter the star.

THE NEAREST STARS

Star	Distance (light-years)	Apparent magnitude
Proxima Centauri	4.2	+11.0
Alpha Centauri	4.3	−0.3
Barnard's star	6.0	+9.5
Wolf 359	7.7	+13.5
Lalande 21185	8.2	+7.5
UV Ceti	8.4	+12.5
Sirius	8.6	−1.46
Ross 154	9.4	+10.5
Ross 248	10.4	+12.3
Epsilon Eridani	10.8	+3.7
Ross 128	10.9	+11.1

Note: Proxima Centauri is part of the Alpha Centauri system.
Apparent magnitude: brightness, as seen from Earth; the lower the magnitude, the brighter the star.

SOLAR ECLIPSES 1995-2005

Date	Type of eclipse	Area from which eclipses can best be seen
1995 Apr 29	annular	South Pacific Ocean, Peru, Brazil, South Atlantic Ocean
1995 Oct 24	total	Iran, India, East Indies, Pacific Ocean
1996 Apr 17	partial	Antarctic
1996 Oct 12	partial	Arctic
1997 Mar 9	total	Russia, Arctic Ocean
1997 Sep 2	partial	Antarctic
1998 Feb 26	total	Pacific Ocean, S. of Panama, Atlantic Ocean
1998 Aug 22	annular	Indian Ocean, East Indies, Pacific Ocean
1999 Feb 16	annular	Indian Ocean, Australia, Pacific Ocean
1999 Aug 11	total	Atlantic Ocean, England, France, Central Europe, Turkey, India
2000 Feb 5	partial	Antarctic
2000 Jul 1	partial	South America, South Pacific
2000 Jul 31	partial	Northern Russia, Arctic, Northwestern USA and Canada
2000 Dec 25	partial	USA, West Atlantic
2001 Jun 21	total	Atlantic, South Africa
2001 Dec 14	annular	Central America, Pacific
2002 Jun 10	annular	Pacific
2002 Dec 4	total	South Africa, Indian Ocean Australia
2003 May 31	annular	Iceland
2003 Nov 23	total	Antarctic
2004 Apr 19	partial	Antarctic
2004 Oct 14	partial	Arctic
2005 Apr 8	total	Pacific, America, north of South America
2005 Oct 3	annular	Atlantic, Spain, Africa, Indian Ocean

Note: Total or partial solar eclipses can only be seen from a narrow band on the Earth's surface.

LUNAR ECLIPSES 2000-2005

Date	Extent of eclipse	Date	Extent of eclipse
1995 Apr 15	partial (11%)	2000 Jul 16	total
1996 Apr 4	total	2001 Jan 9	total
1996 Sep 27	total	2001 Jul 5	partial (49%)
1997 Mar 24	partial (82%)	2003 May 16	total
1997 Sep 16	total	2003 Nov 9	total
1999 Jul 28	partial (40%)	2004 May 4	total
2000 Jan 21	total	2004 Oct 28	total

Note: Each eclipse of the Moon can be seen from about half of the Earth's surface.

GLOSSARY

Aperture   The clear diameter of the lens or mirror that collects light in a telescope.

Aphelion   The point in its orbit where a planet is at its greatest distance from the Sun.

Asteroid   A small rocky body that revolves around the Sun. Most asteroids follow orbits that lie between the orbits of Mars and Jupiter.

Astronomical unit (AU)   The mean distance between the Sun and the Earth: 150 million kilometres.

Atmosphere   The envelope of gas that surrounds a planet, satellite, or star.

Atom   A basic unit of matter consisting of a heavy nucleus, made up of protons and neutrons, surrounded by a number of electrons. Atoms of different chemical elements contain different numbers of protons; for example, a hydrogen nucleus consists of one proton, a helium nucleus of two protons and two neutrons, and so on. A neutral atom has the same number of electrons as protons.

Binary star   A pair of stars that revolve around each other.

Black hole   A region of space surrounding a collapsed object, within which gravity is so powerful that nothing, not even light, can escape.

Comet   A body made of ice and dust that develops a head (the coma) and one or more tails each time it makes a close approach to the Sun.

Constellation   A grouping of stars and the area of sky in which those stars are located. The entire sky, or celestial sphere, is divided into 88 constellations.

Density   How compact a substance is; the amount of mass per unit volume.

Eclipse   The passage of one body through the shadow of another. An eclipse of the Moon occurs when the Moon passes into the Earth's shadow. An eclipse of the Sun occurs when the Moon passes in front of the Sun, blocking out all or part of its light.

Electromagnetic radiation   An electric and magnetic disturbance that travels like a wave through space at the speed of light – 299,000 kilometres per second. Examples are light, radio waves, and X rays.

Electromagnetic spectrum   The complete range of electromagnetic radiation from the shortest to the longest wavelengths.

Electron   An elementary particle of low mass and negative electrical charge.

Galaxy   A huge system of stars, gas, and dust. The galaxy to which the Sun belongs (see *Milky Way*) is 100,000 light-years in diameter.

Gravitation (gravity)   The force by which each body is attracted toward every other one; for example, the force that keeps satellites in orbit around planets and planets in orbit around stars.

Light-year   The distance travelled by light in one year: 9.3 billion kilometres.

Luminosity   The total amount of light and other kinds of radiation emitted per second by a star or other celestial body.

Mass   The amount of matter in an object.

Meteor   The brief streak of light seen in the sky when a tiny particle called a meteoroid plunges into the Earth's atmosphere and is destroyed by friction.

Meteorite   A lump of matter that survives falling from space through the atmosphere and reaches the Earth's surface.

Milky Way   A faint band of starlight that runs across the sky. It is made up of the combined light of millions of stars lying in the disc of our galaxy.

Milky Way galaxy	The galaxy that contains the Sun. It is a spiral galaxy about 100,000 light-years in diameter encompassing about 100,000 million stars.
Moon	The Earth's natural satellite and our nearest neighbour in space. The term *moon* is often used to describe a satellite of another planet.
Nebula	A huge cloud of gas and dust in space. A luminous (or 'emission') nebula shines because it contains very hot stars. A dark nebula is a dust cloud that blots out background stars.
Neutron	A subatomic particle with zero electrical charge and a mass similar to a proton.
Neutron star	A highly compressed star made up mainly of neutrons; the remnant core of a massive star that exploded as a supernova.
Nova	A star that suddenly flares up to a hundred, a thousand, or even a million times its original brightness, then fades back to its original brightness.
Orbit	The path followed by one celestial body around another; for example, the path of the Moon around the Earth, or the path of the Earth around the Sun.
Perihelion	The point in its orbit where a planet is at its nearest to the Sun.
Phases	The apparent change in shape of the Moon (or other body) as the angle between Sun, Moon, and Earth changes and we see differing amounts of its illuminated hemisphere.
Photon	A tiny bit of light energy. A beam of light can be thought of as a stream of photons, travelling at the speed of light.
Planet	A smaller body that revolves around a star. Nine planets revolve around the Sun. They shine by reflecting sunlight; they do not emit visible light of their own.
Proton	A heavy subatomic particle with a positive electrical charge that is a building block of atomic nuclei. The nucleus of a hydrogen atom, for example, consists of one proton.
Pulsar	A source in the sky that emits short, regularly spaced pulses of radio radiation. Pulsars are believed to be rapidly spinning neutron stars that emit narrow beams of radiation.
Quasar	An object that looks rather like a star but is very distant and extremely luminous. A quasar is believed to be the tiny brilliant nucleus of a remote galaxy.
Reflector	A telescope that uses a mirror (the primary mirror) to collect light.
Refractor	A telescope that uses a lens (the objective) to collect light.
Satellite	A smaller body that travels around a planet. The Moon is the Earth's natural satellite. An artificial satellite is a manufactured device in orbit around a planet.
Solar System	The system consisting of the Sun, the planets and their satellites, the asteroids, the comets, and any other matter that revolves around the Sun.
Solar wind	The stream of atomic particles, mainly protons and electrons, that flows away from the Sun.
Spectrum	The rainbow band of colours produced when white light (a mixture of wavelengths) is separated into its different wavelengths by passing through a prism. The spectrum extends beyond the visible range to shorter and longer wavelengths.
Star	A globe of gases that emits light because its surface is very hot; for example, the Sun.
Sun	The star around which the Earth revolves. It is a globe of gas — mainly hydrogen and helium — that is generating energy by means of nuclear reactions in its core.
Sunspot	A cooler patch on the Sun's surface that looks dark compared to its brilliant, hotter surroundings.
Supernova	A catastrophic explosion in which a star is blown apart.
Universe	Everything that exists; the whole of space and all the matter it contains.

INDEX